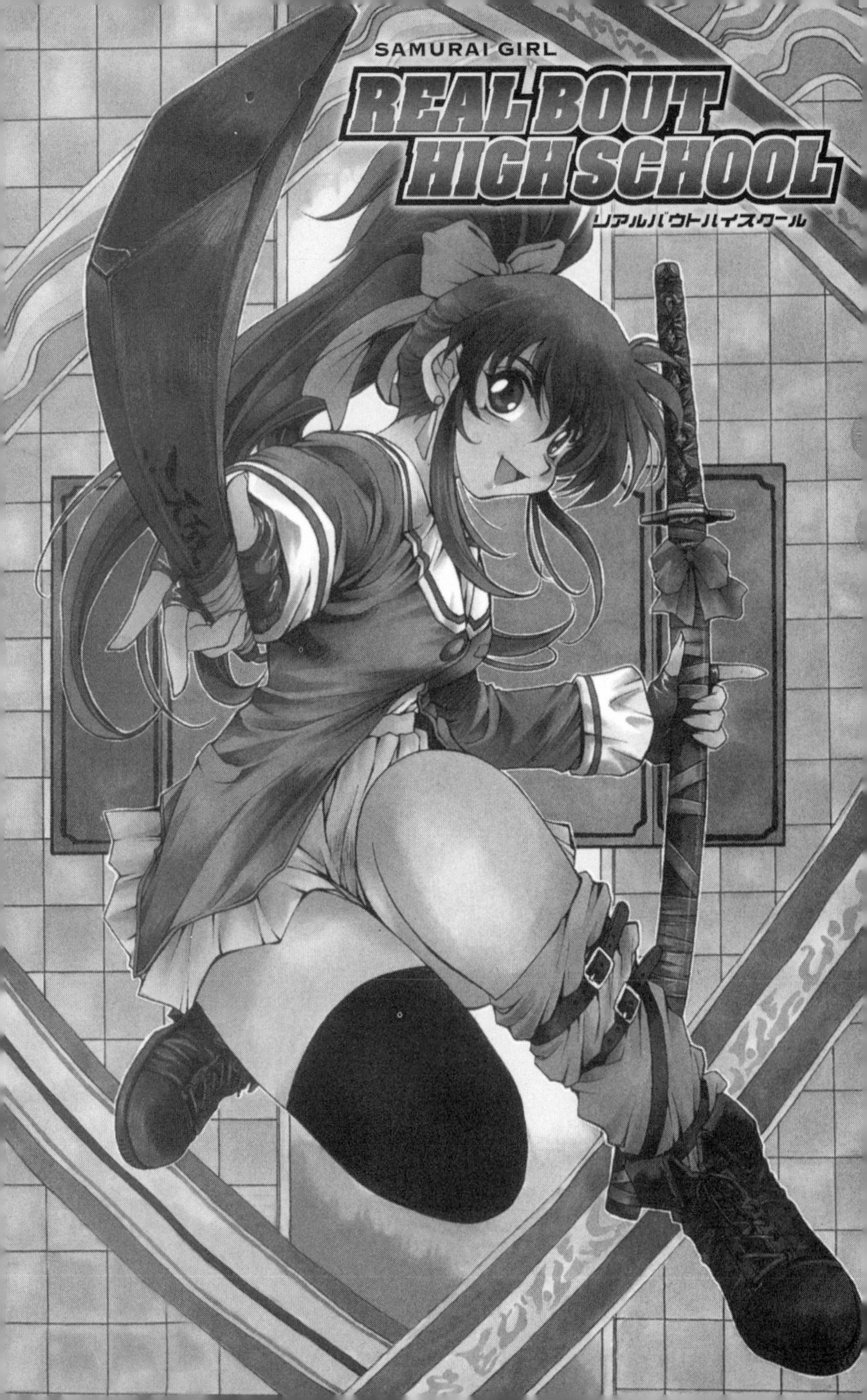
SAMURAI GIRL
REAL BOUT HIGH SCHOOL
リアルバウトハイスクール

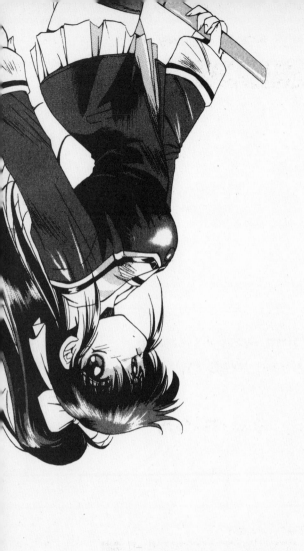

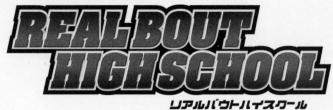

SAMURAI GIRL
REAL BOUT HIGH SCHOOL
リアルバウトハイスクール

Volume 1

Art by Sora Inoue
Story by Reiji Saiga

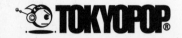

Los Angeles • Tokyo • London

Translator – Lucan Duran
Production Specialist – Colin Mahan
Graphic Designer – Thea Willis
Cover Designer – Rod Sampson
Editors – Stephanie Donnelly and Robert Coyner
Associate Editors – Paul Morrissey, Trisha Kunimoto
and Eric Althoff

Editor - Jake Forbes
Managing Editor - Jill Freshney
Production Coordinator - Antonio DePietro
Production Manager - Jennifer Miller
Art Director - Matt Alford
Editorial Director - Jeremy Ross
VP of Production - Ron Klamert
President & C.O.O. - John Parker
Publisher & C.E.O. - Stuart Levy

Email: editor@TOKYOPOP.com
Come visit us online at www.TOKYOPOP.com

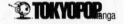 TOKYOPOP manga

TOKYOPOP Inc.
5900 Wilshire Blvd. Suite 2000
Los Angeles, CA 90036

ISBN: 1-931514-95-X
First TOKYOPOP printing: March 2002

13 12 11 10 9 8 7 6 5 4

Printed in the USA

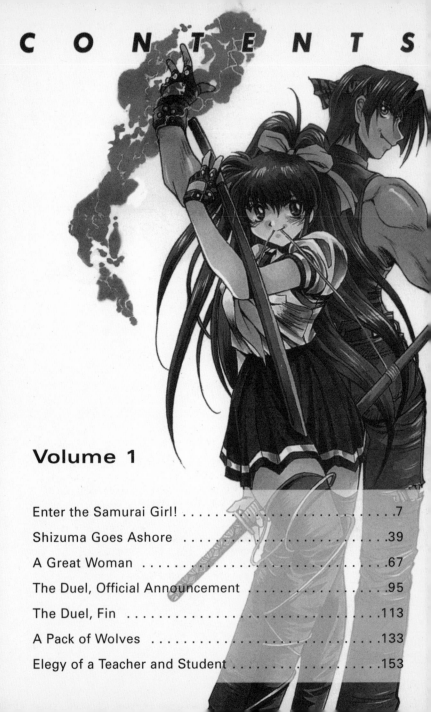

CONTENTS

Volume 1

Enter the Samurai Girl! 7

Shizuma Goes Ashore 39

A Great Woman 67

The Duel, Official Announcement 95

The Duel, Fin 113

A Pack of Wolves 133

Elegy of a Teacher and Student 153

Daimon High Directory

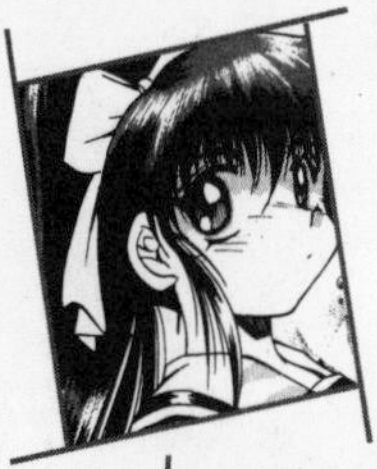

Ryoko - Though she's the undefeated martial arts champion of Daimon High School, she still has many of the same insecurities that befall most teenage girls - she feels awkward about her maturing body, she has a crush on the most popular boy in school, she longs to become a dynamic woman... and the call of the warrior sounds in her ears like a perpetual siren.

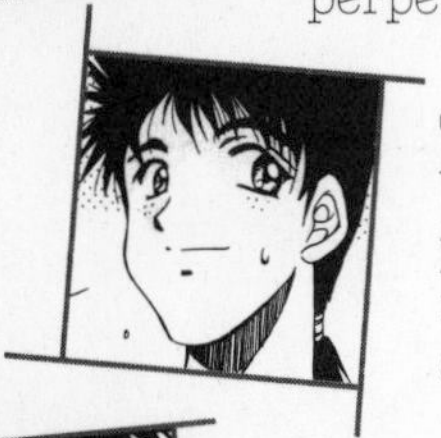

Tatsuya - Perhaps oblivious to the bevy of beauties fawning over him, this Kendo Club president just wants space to practice in the increasingly crowded landscape of Daimon's after school clubs.

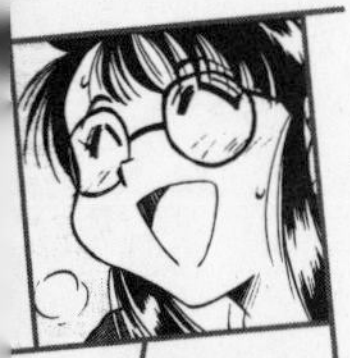

Hitomi - Longs for true friendship with Ryoko, perhaps to save the champion from her own passions.

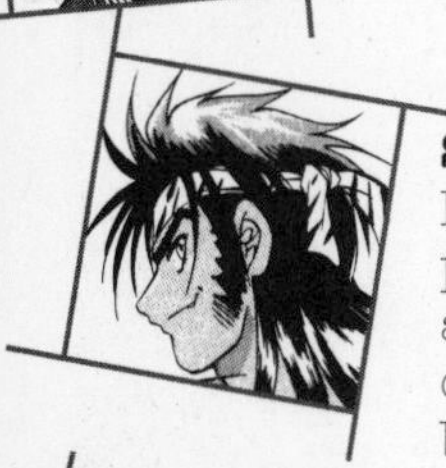

Shizuma - A recent transfer to Daimon, he's an ass-kicking, ball-busting, knuckle-grinding, bare-fisted, pec-flexing, uni-browed fighting machine that is attracted to the school's propensity for brawls. Of course, he's as much about glory and honor as bashing heads and kicking ass.

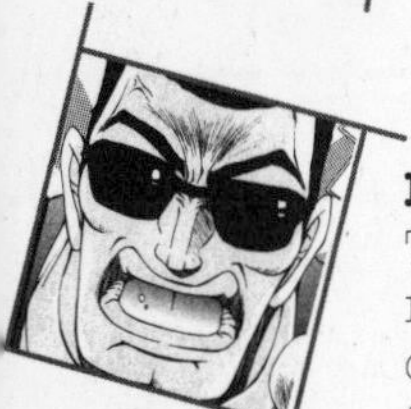

Principal Todo - Hardly the quintessential educator, Todo believes that the best way to develop youthful minds is by having them beaten in. He uses the abundance of martial arts clubs on campus as a pretence to stage elaborate fights.

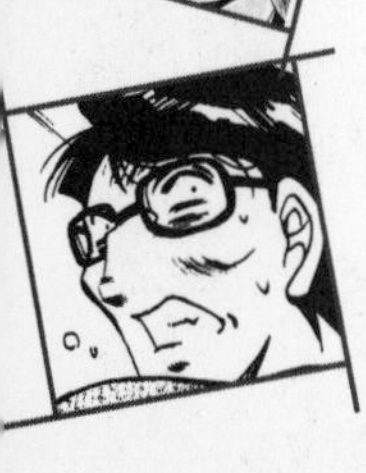

Saotome Sensei - Believes in hard love and strict discipline. He wants his kids to learn, but he's not going to take their lip. However, as he gets older, and the students get bigger, he might have to come up with other ways to get his point across.

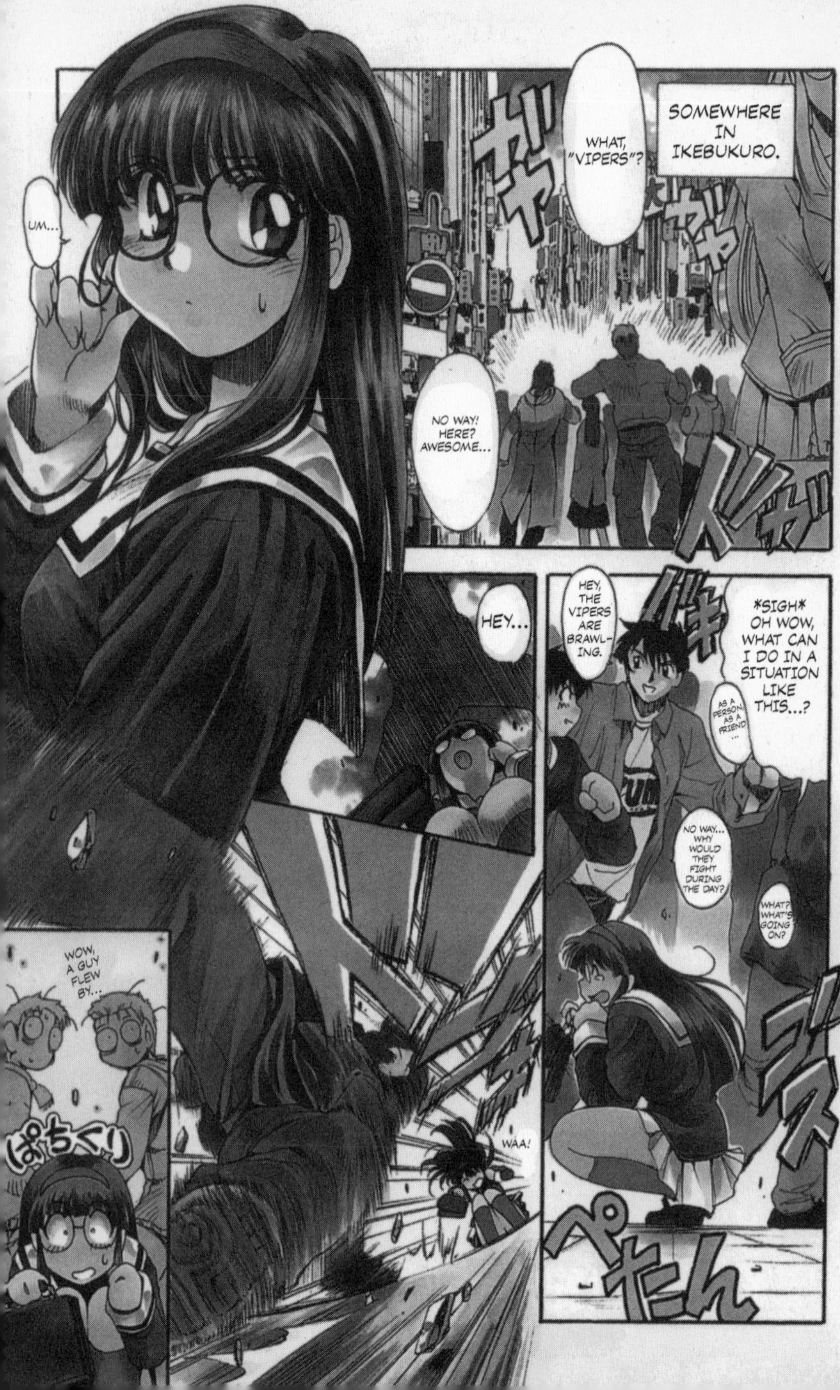
SOMEWHERE IN IKEBUKURO.
WHAT, "VIPERS"?
NO WAY! HERE? AWESOME...
SIGH OH WOW, WHAT CAN I DO IN A SITUATION LIKE THIS...?
AS A PERSON, AS A FRIEND...
HEY, THE VIPERS ARE BRAWL-ING.
NO WAY... WHY WOULD THEY FIGHT DURING THE DAY?
WHAT? WHAT'S GOING ON?
ぺたん
HEY...
UM...
WAA!
WOW, A GUY FLEW BY...
ぱちくり

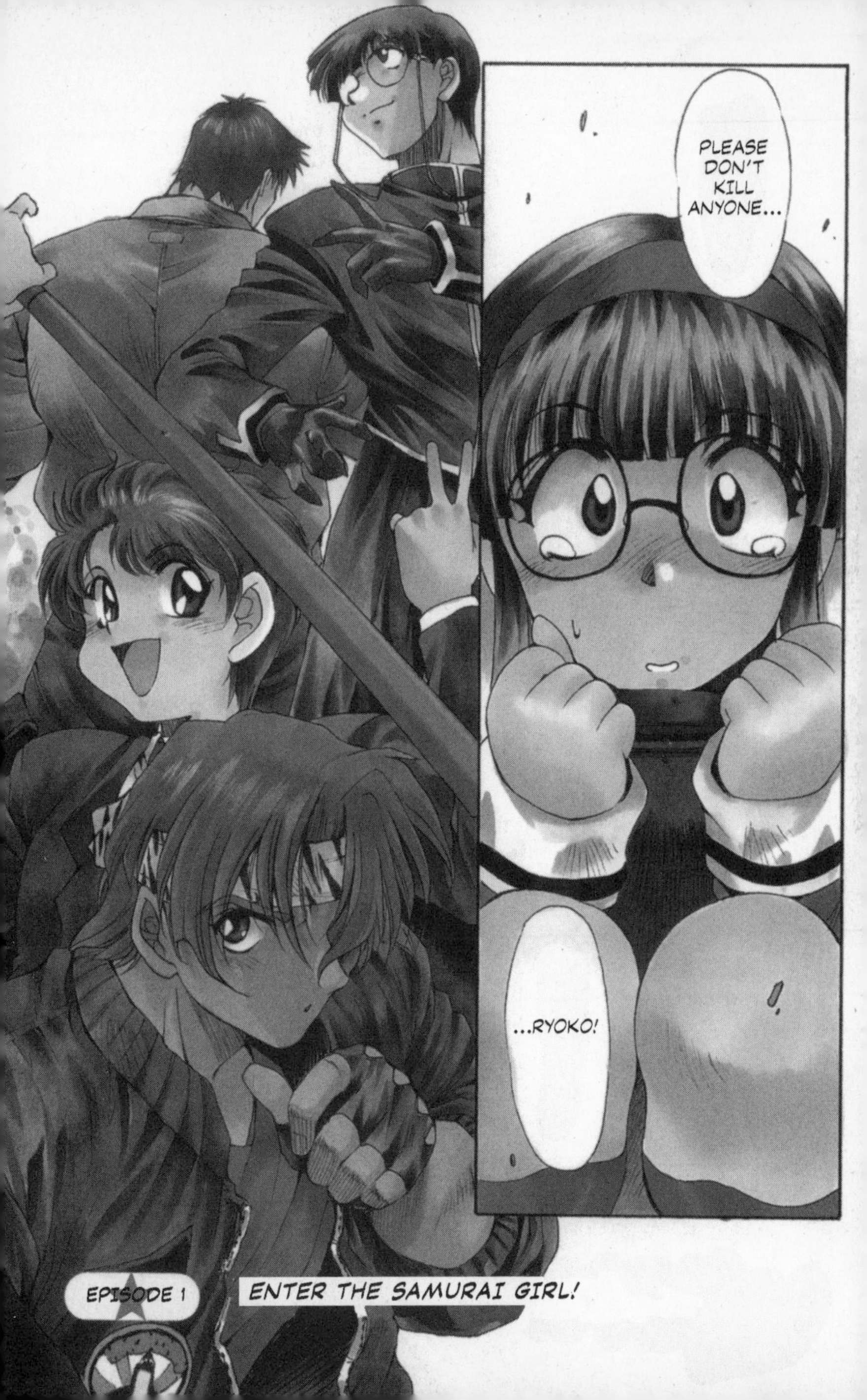
PLEASE DON'T KILL ANYONE...
...RYOKO!
EPISODE 1
ENTER THE SAMURAI GIRL!

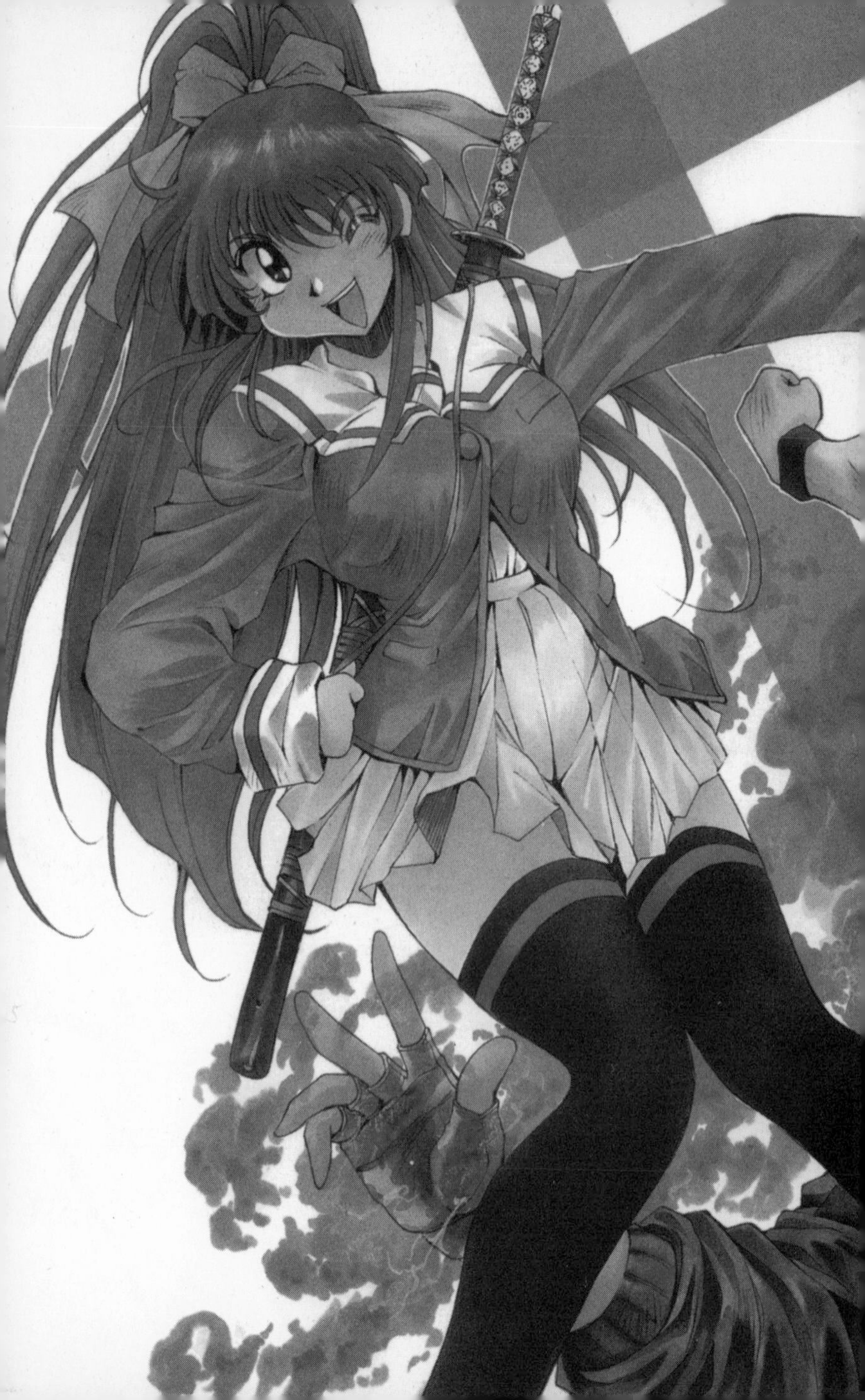

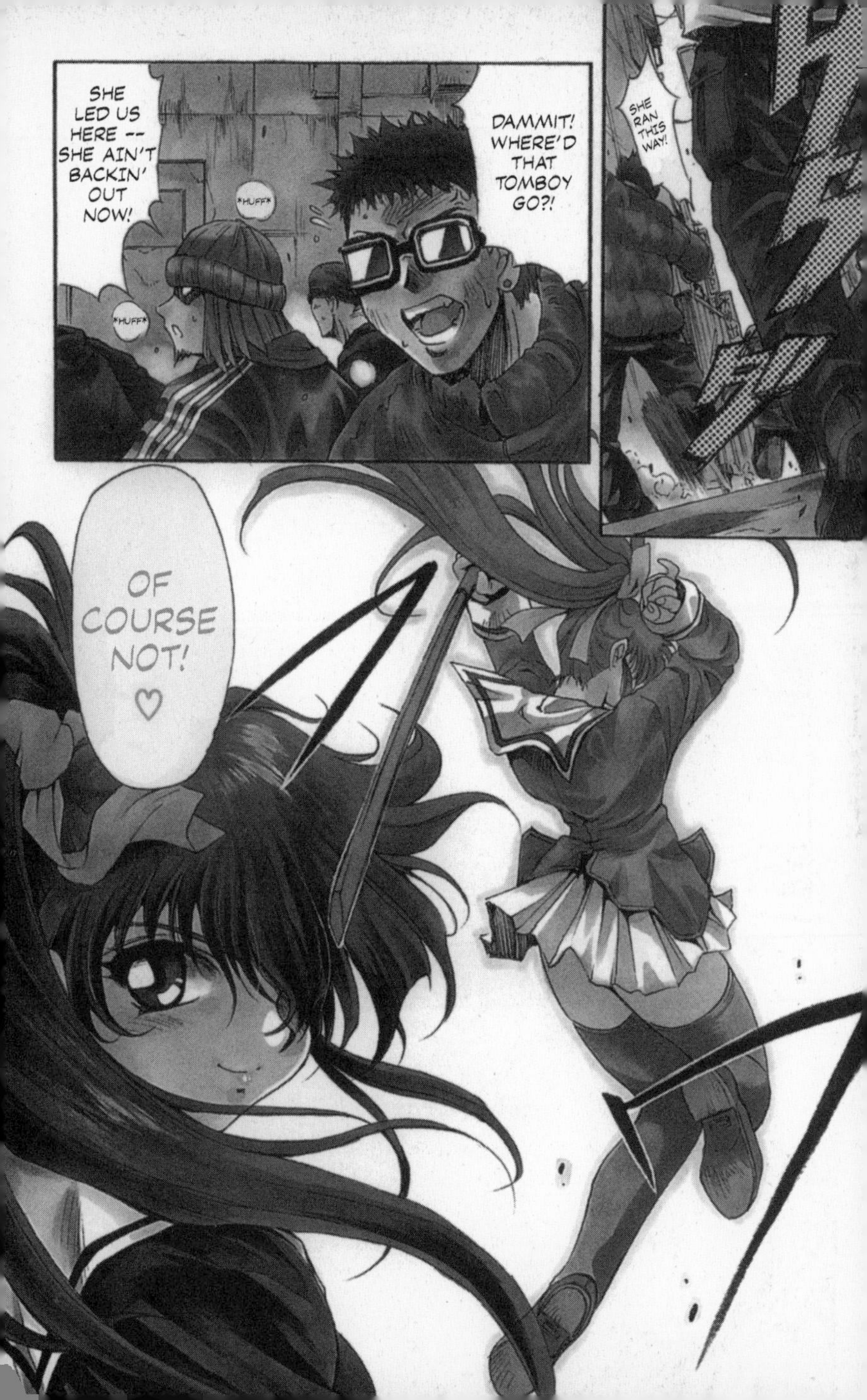
SHE RAN THIS WAY!
DAMMIT! WHERE'D THAT TOMBOY GO?!
HUFF
SHE LED US HERE -- SHE AIN'T BACKIN' OUT NOW!
HUFF
OF COURSE NOT! ♡

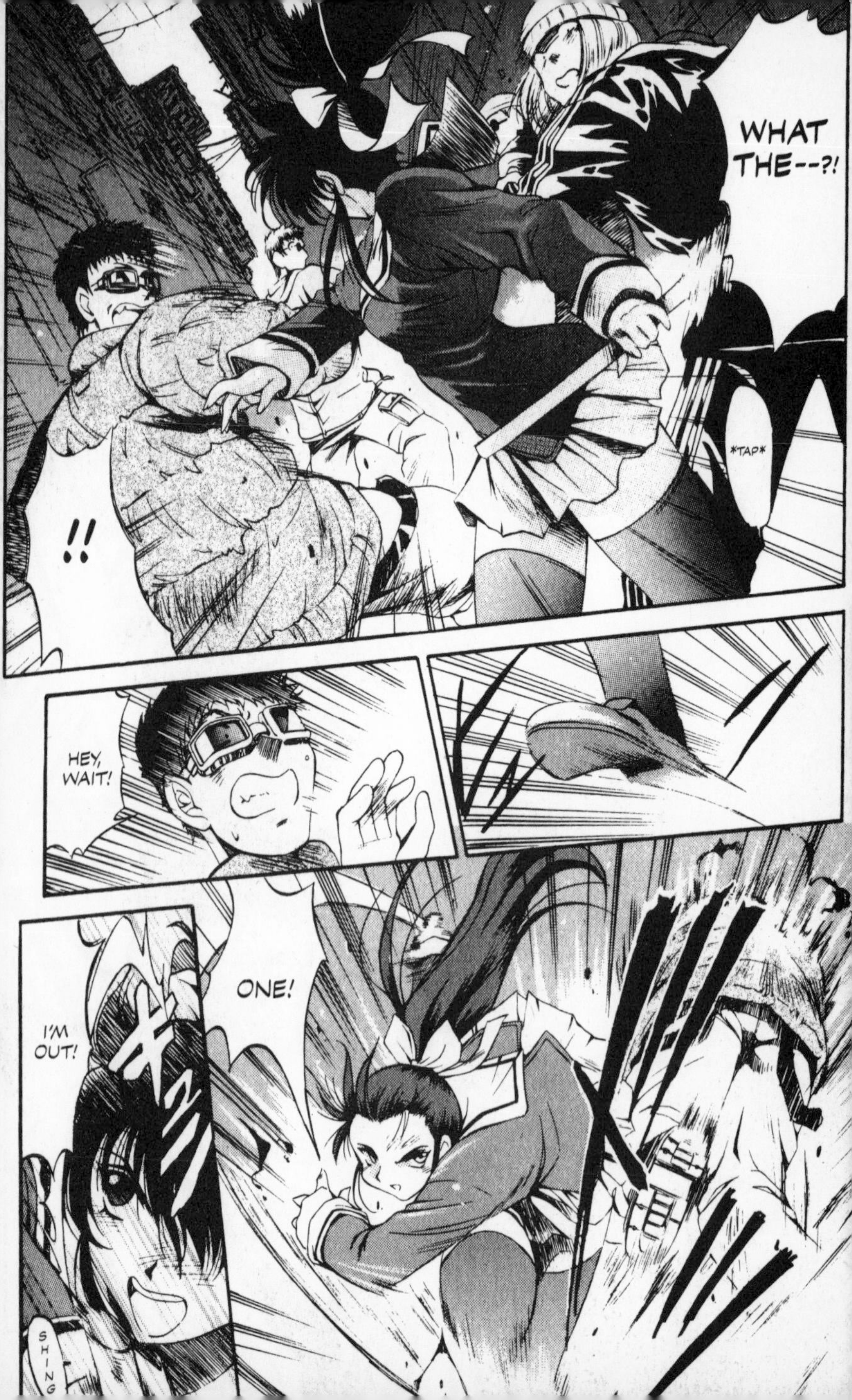
WHAT THE--?!
TAP
!!
HEY, WAIT!
ONE!
I'M OUT!
SHING

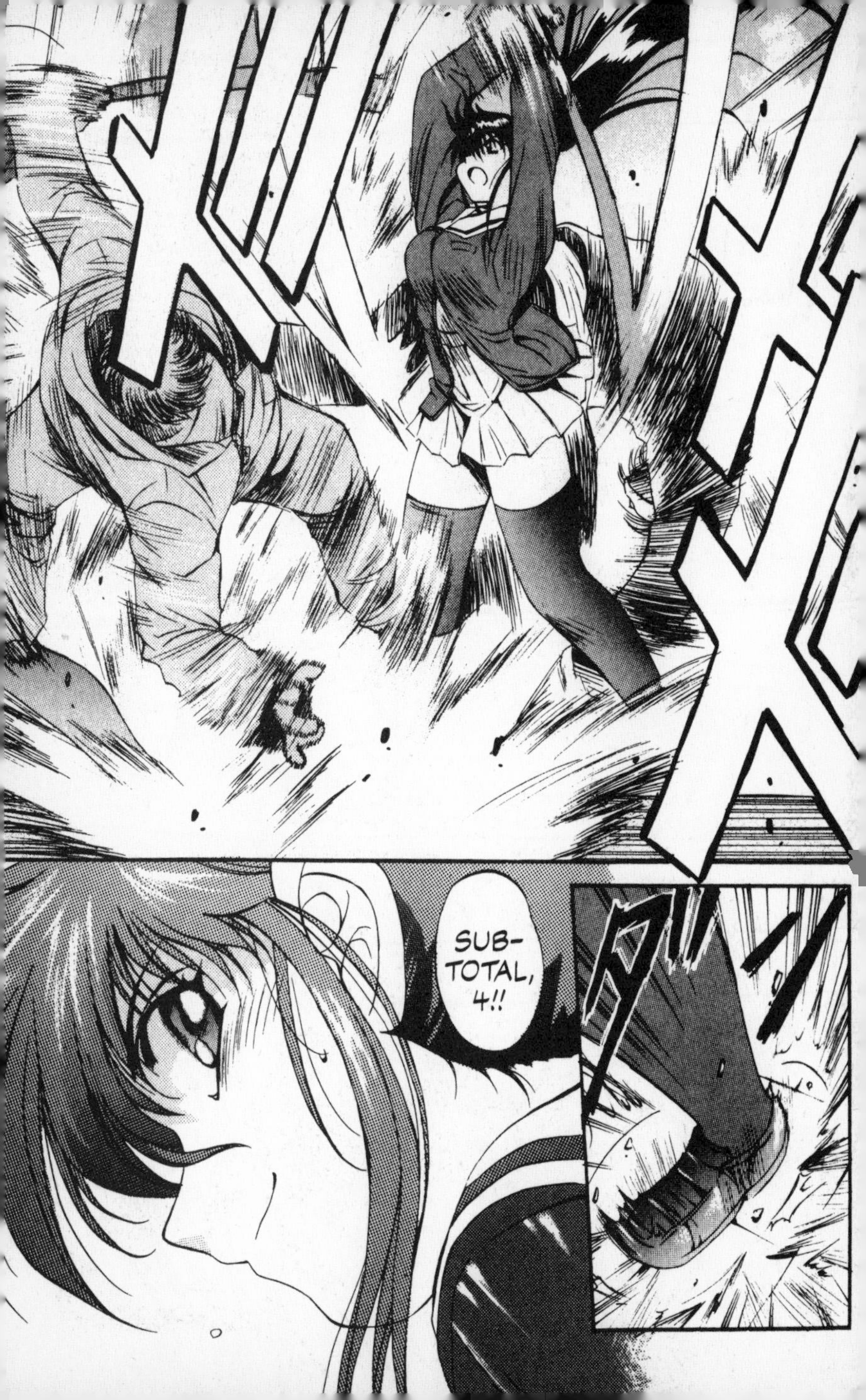
SUB-TOTAL, 4!!

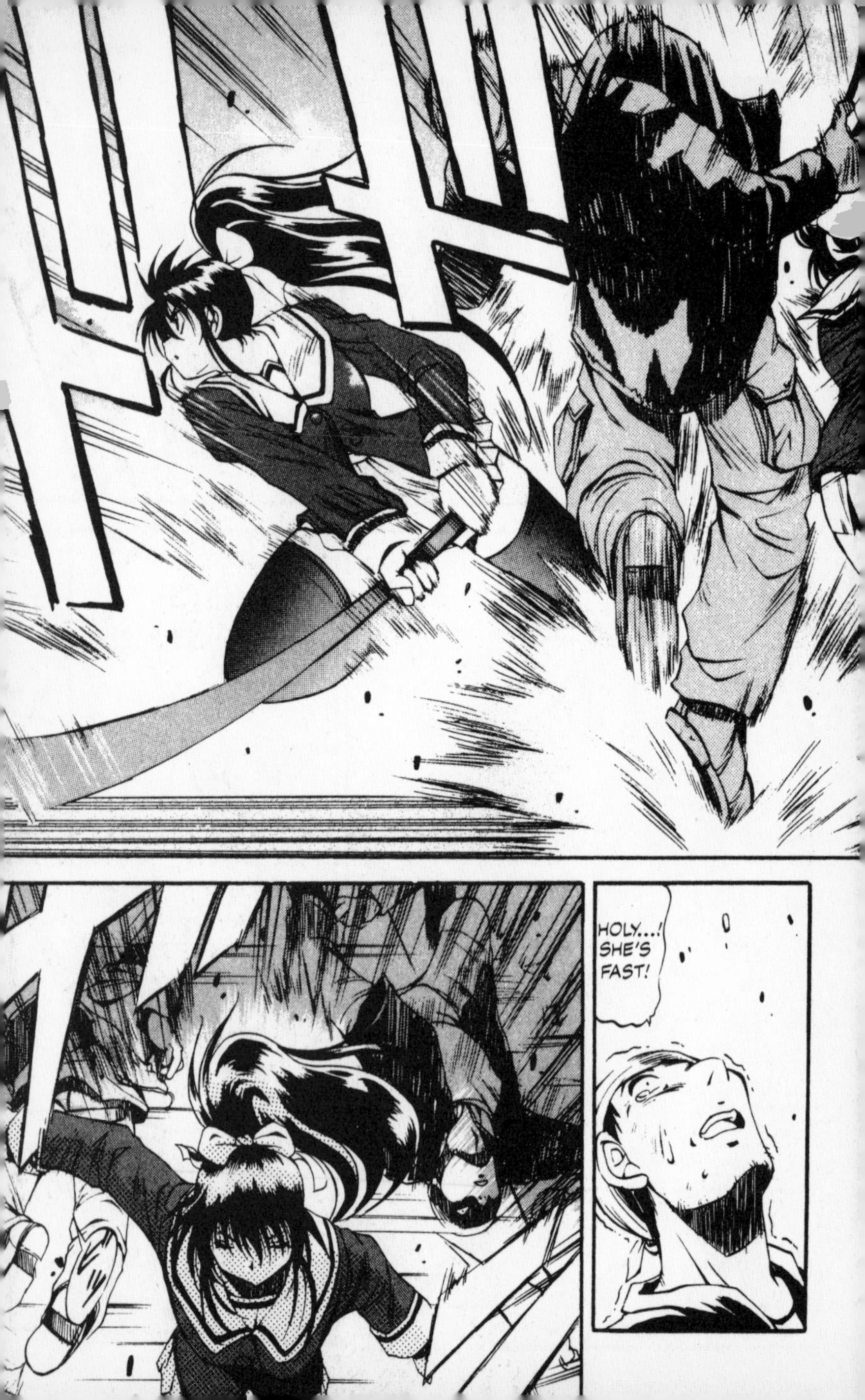
HOLY...! SHE'S FAST!

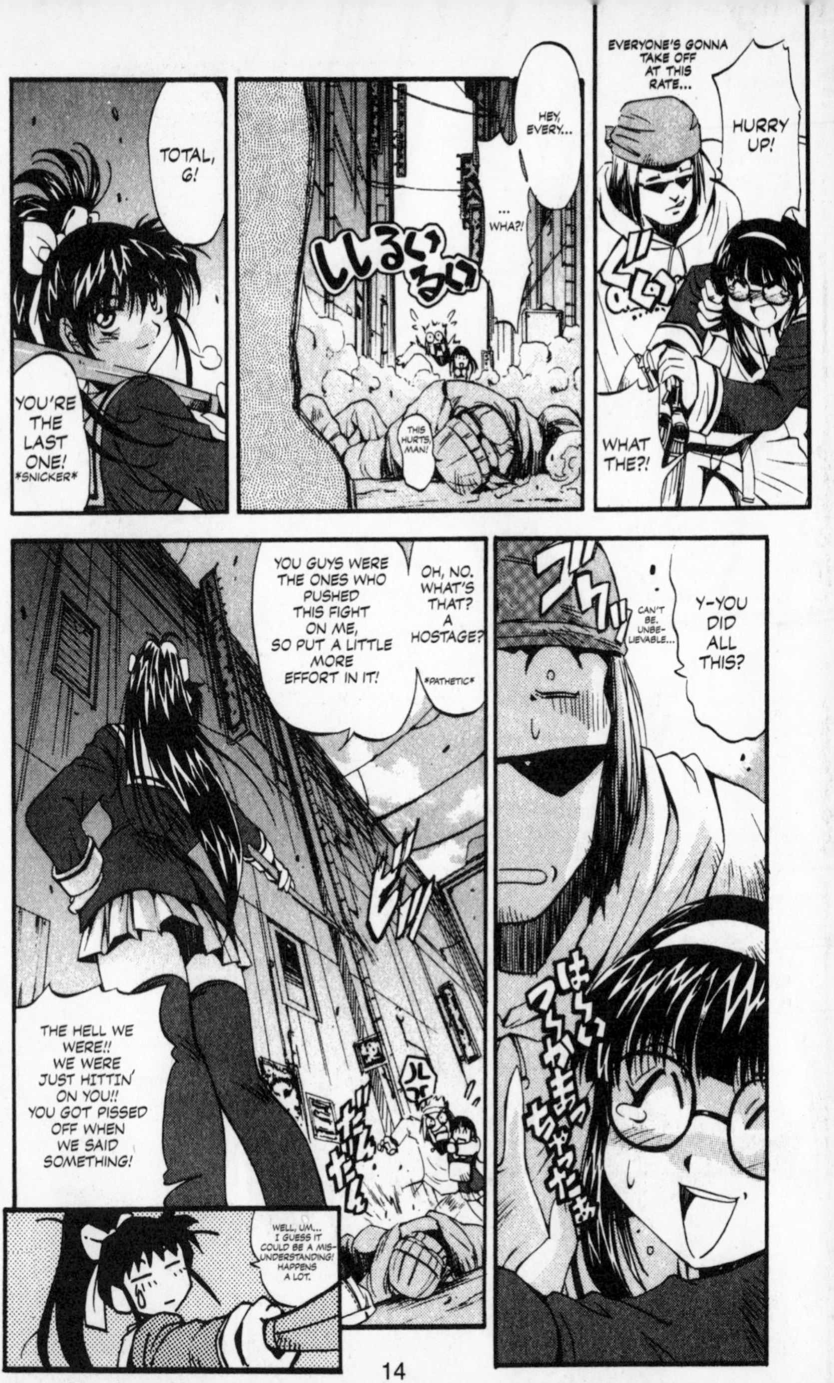
EVERYONE'S GONNA TAKE OFF AT THIS RATE...
HURRY UP!
WHAT THE?!
HEY, EVERY...
... WHA?!
THIS HURTS, MAN!
TOTAL, 6!
YOU'RE THE LAST ONE! *SNICKER*
Y-YOU DID ALL THIS?
CAN'T BE. UNBE-LIEVABLE...
OH, NO. WHAT'S THAT? A HOSTAGE?
PATHETIC
YOU GUYS WERE THE ONES WHO PUSHED THIS FIGHT ON ME, SO PUT A LITTLE MORE EFFORT IN IT!
THE HELL WE WERE!! WE WERE JUST HITTIN' ON YOU!! YOU GOT PISSED OFF WHEN WE SAID SOMETHING!
WELL, UM... I GUESS IT COULD BE A MIS-UNDERSTANDING! HAPPENS A LOT.

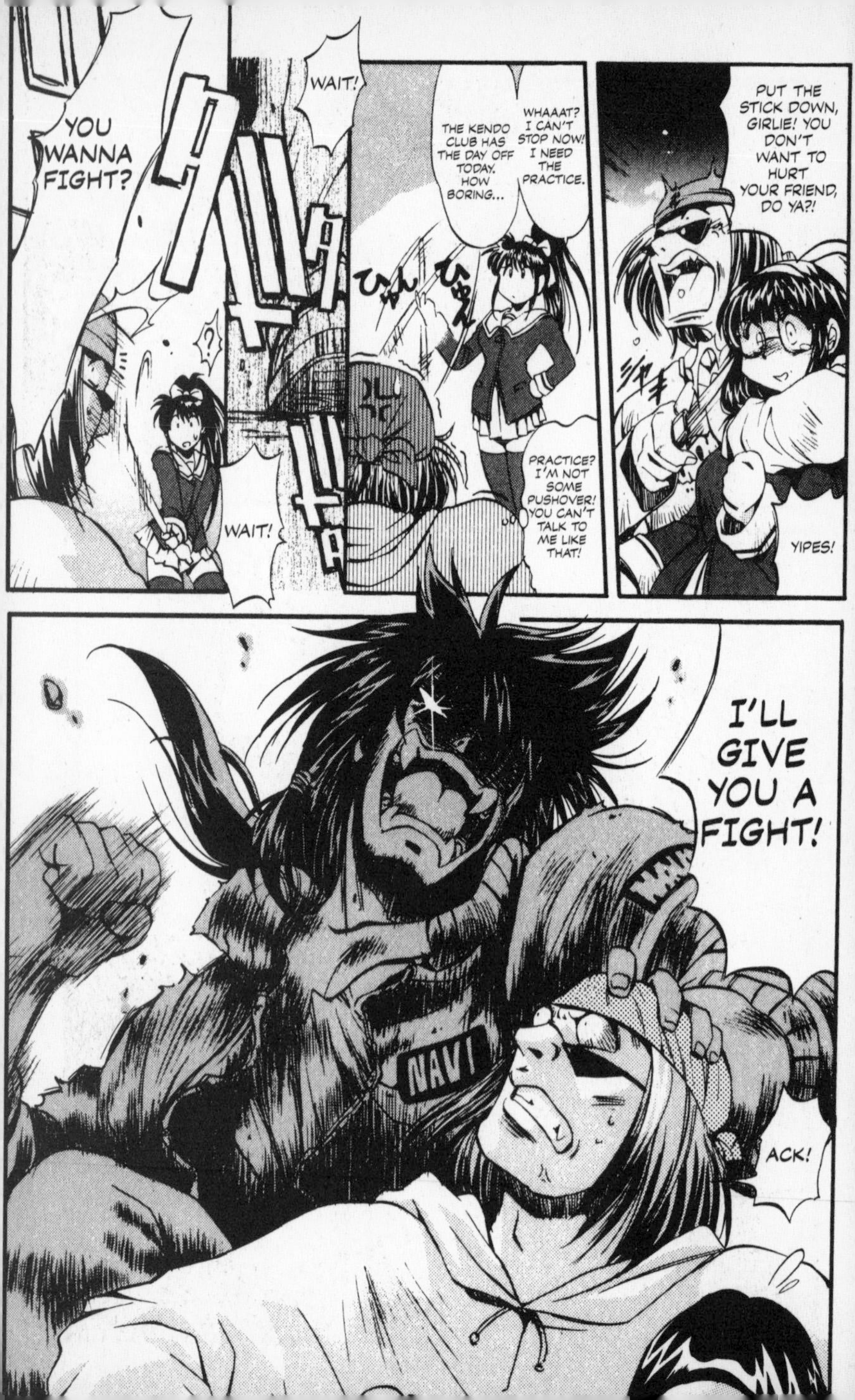
PUT THE STICK DOWN, GIRLIE! YOU DON'T WANT TO HURT YOUR FRIEND, DO YA?!
ジャキ
YIPES!
WHAAAT? I CAN'T STOP NOW! I NEED THE PRACTICE.
THE KENDO CLUB HAS THE DAY OFF TODAY. HOW BORING...
WAIT!
ひゅん ひゅん
PRACTICE? I'M NOT SOME PUSHOVER! YOU CAN'T TALK TO ME LIKE THAT!
YOU WANNA FIGHT?
WAIT!
I'LL GIVE YOU A FIGHT!
NAVI
ACK!

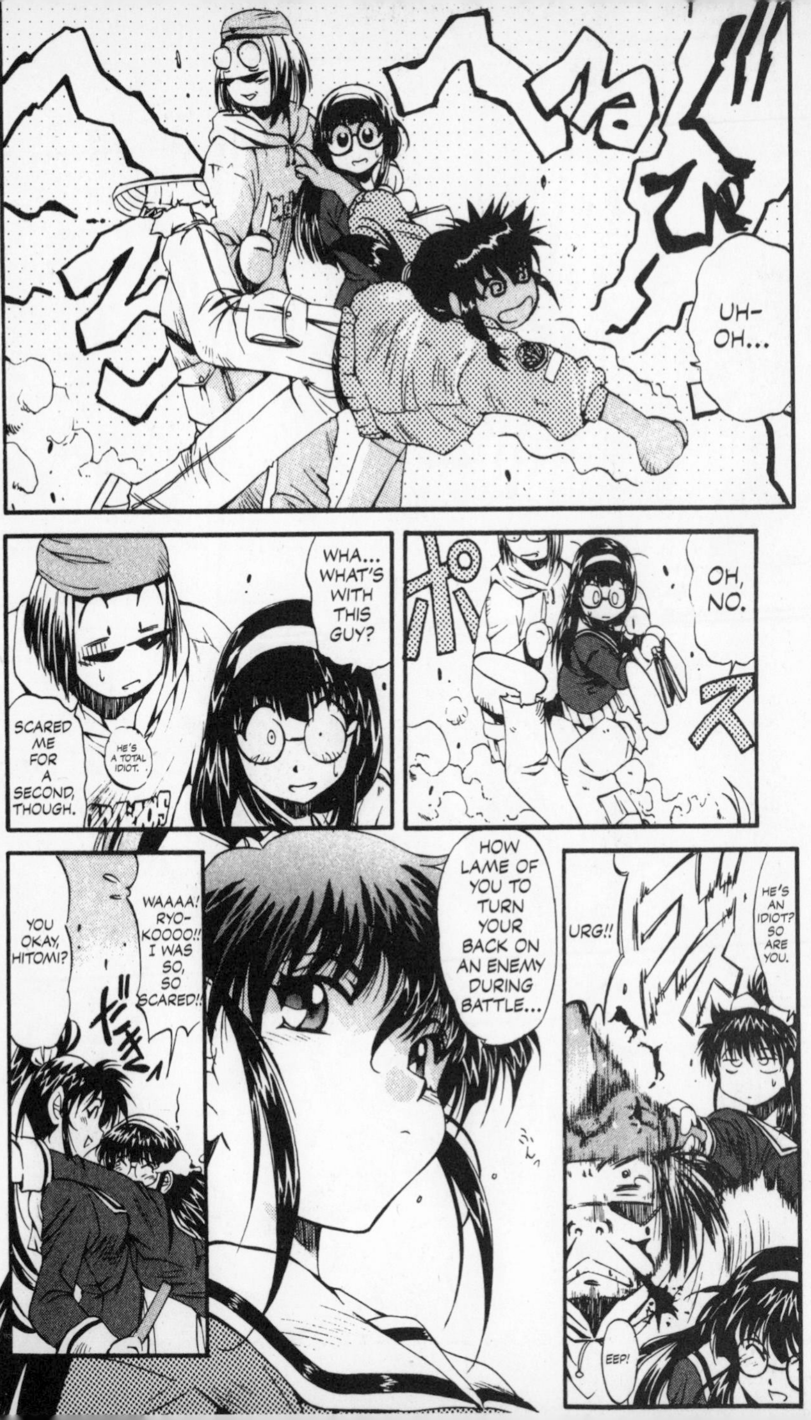
UH-OH...
OH, NO.
WHA... WHAT'S WITH THIS GUY?
HE'S A TOTAL IDIOT.
SCARED ME FOR A SECOND, THOUGH.
HE'S AN IDIOT? SO ARE YOU.
URG!!
EEP!
HOW LAME OF YOU TO TURN YOUR BACK ON AN ENEMY DURING BATTLE...
WAAAA! RYO-KOOOO!! I WAS SO, SO SCARED!!
YOU OKAY, HITOMI?

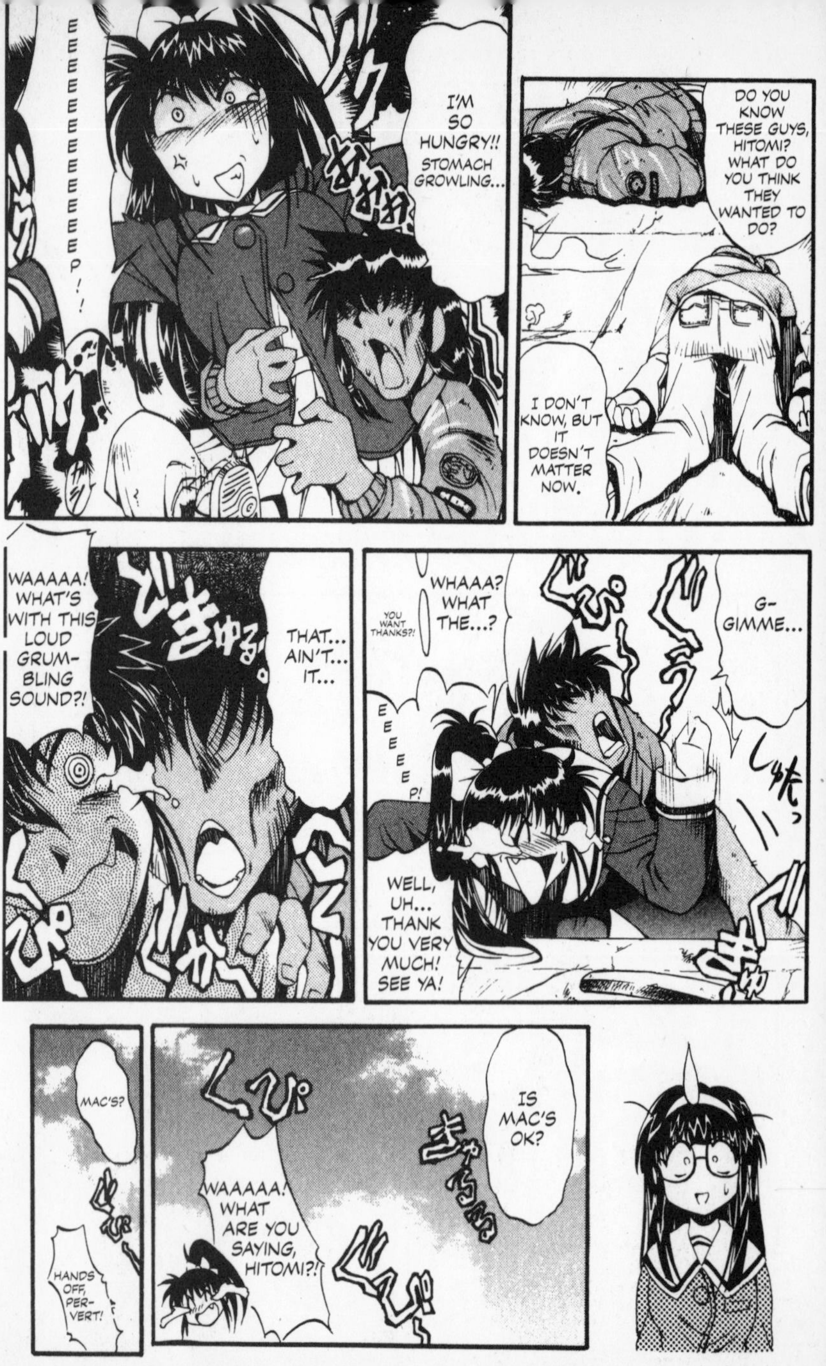
DO YOU KNOW THESE GUYS, HITOMI? WHAT DO YOU THINK THEY WANTED TO DO?
I DON'T KNOW, BUT IT DOESN'T MATTER NOW.
I'M SO HUNGRY!! STOMACH GROWLING...
EEEEEEEEEEEEEEP!!
G-GIMME...
WHAAA? WHAT THE...?
YOU WANT THANKS?!
EEEEEP!
WELL, UH... THANK YOU VERY MUCH! SEE YA!
THAT... AIN'T... IT...
WAAAAA! WHAT'S WITH THIS LOUD GRUMBLING SOUND?!
IS MAC'S OK?
WAAAAA! WHAT ARE YOU SAYING, HITOMI?!
MAC'S?
HANDS OFF, PER-VERT!

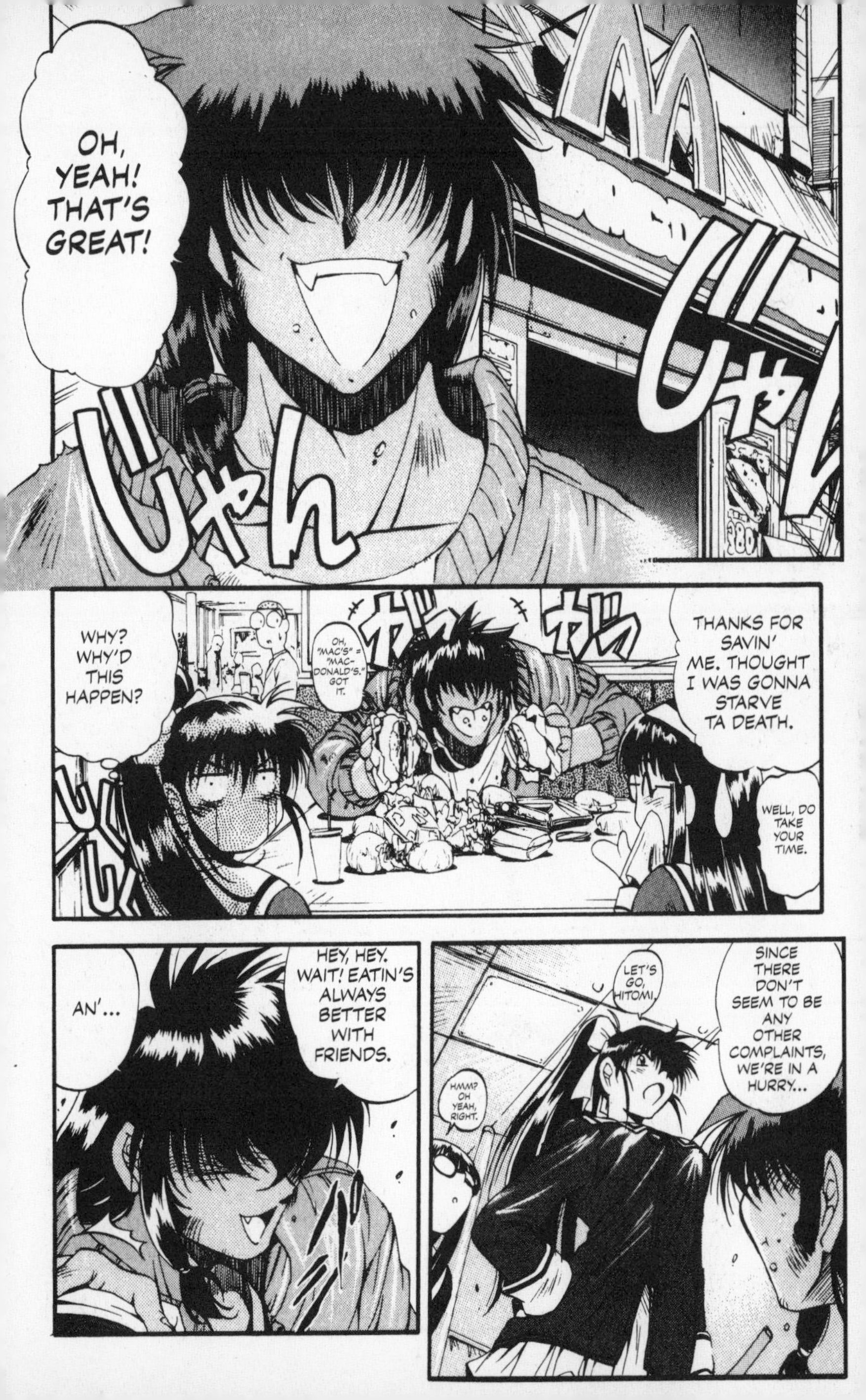
OH, YEAH! THAT'S GREAT!
じゃん
じゃん
THANKS FOR SAVIN' ME. THOUGHT I WAS GONNA STARVE TA DEATH.
WELL, DO TAKE YOUR TIME.
OH, "MAC'S" = "MAC-DONALD'S." GOT IT.
WHY? WHY'D THIS HAPPEN?
SINCE THERE DON'T SEEM TO BE ANY OTHER COMPLAINTS, WE'RE IN A HURRY...
LET'S GO, HITOMI.
HMM? OH YEAH, RIGHT.
HEY, HEY. WAIT! EATIN'S ALWAYS BETTER WITH FRIENDS.
AN'...

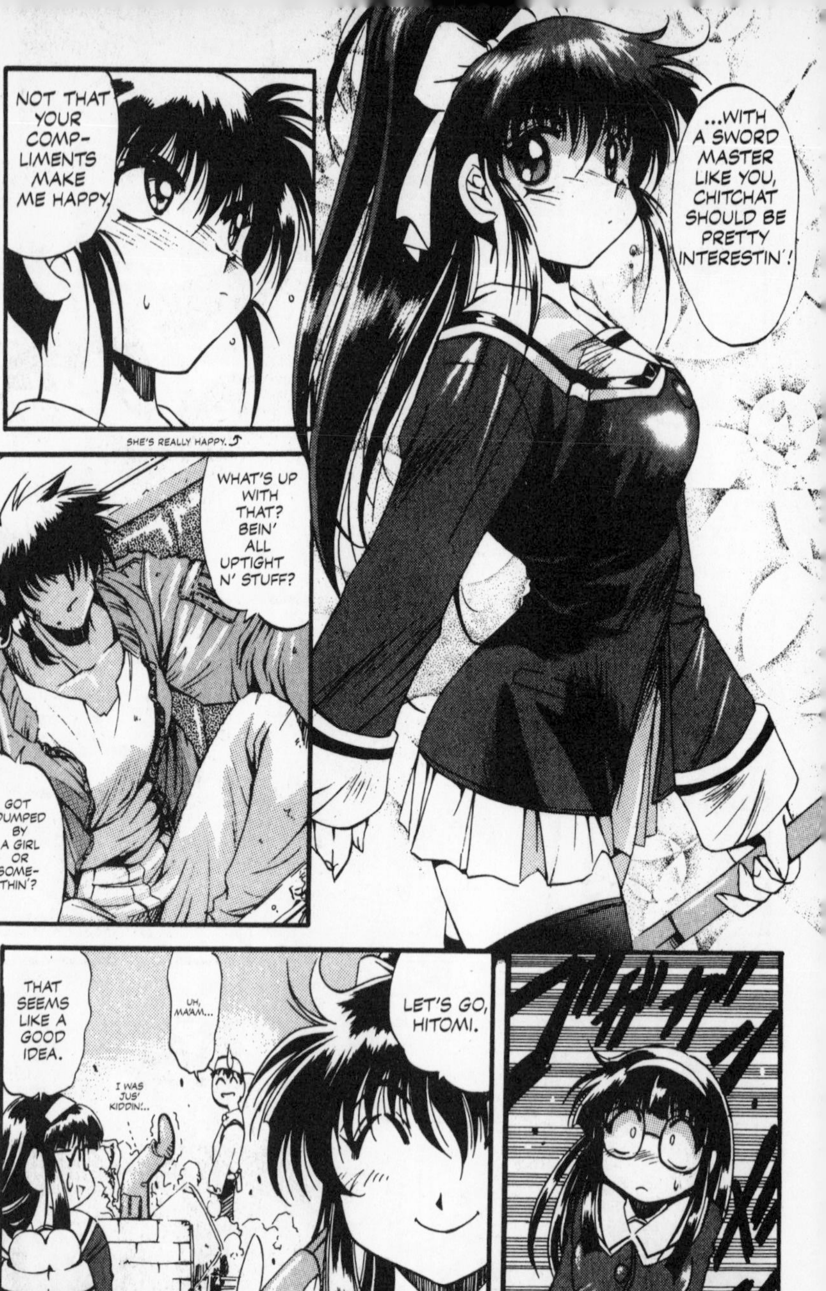
...WITH A SWORD MASTER LIKE YOU, CHITCHAT SHOULD BE PRETTY INTERESTIN'!
NOT THAT YOUR COMPLIMENTS MAKE ME HAPPY.
SHE'S REALLY HAPPY.
WHAT'S UP WITH THAT? BEIN' ALL UPTIGHT N' STUFF?
GOT DUMPED BY A GIRL OR SOMETHIN'?
LET'S GO, HITOMI.
UH, MA'AM...
THAT SEEMS LIKE A GOOD IDEA.
I WAS JUS' KIDDIN'...

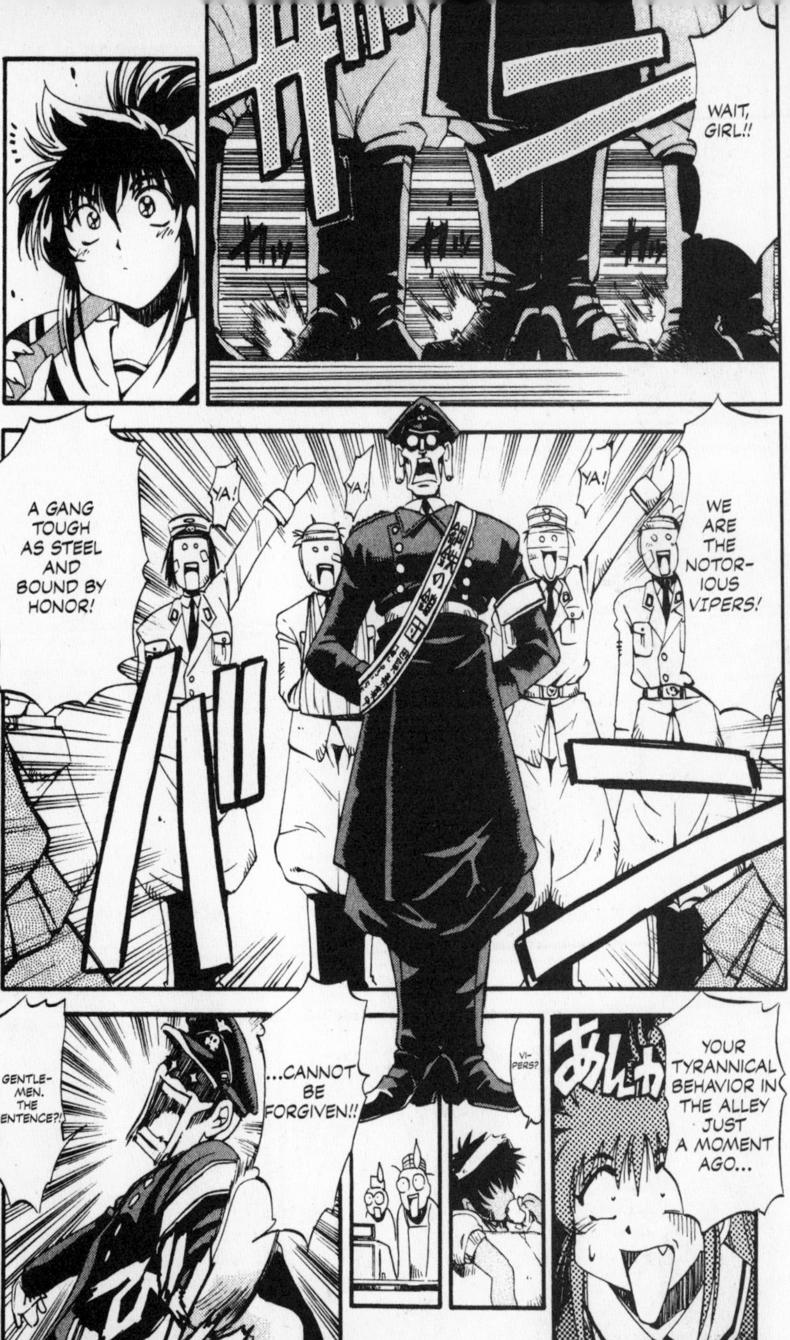
WAIT, GIRL!!
YA!
WE ARE THE NOTORIOUS VIPERS!
YA!
YA!
A GANG TOUGH AS STEEL AND BOUND BY HONOR!
YOUR TYRANNICAL BEHAVIOR IN THE ALLEY JUST A MOMENT AGO...
VIPERS?
...CANNOT BE FORGIVEN!!
GENTLEMEN. THE SENTENCE?!

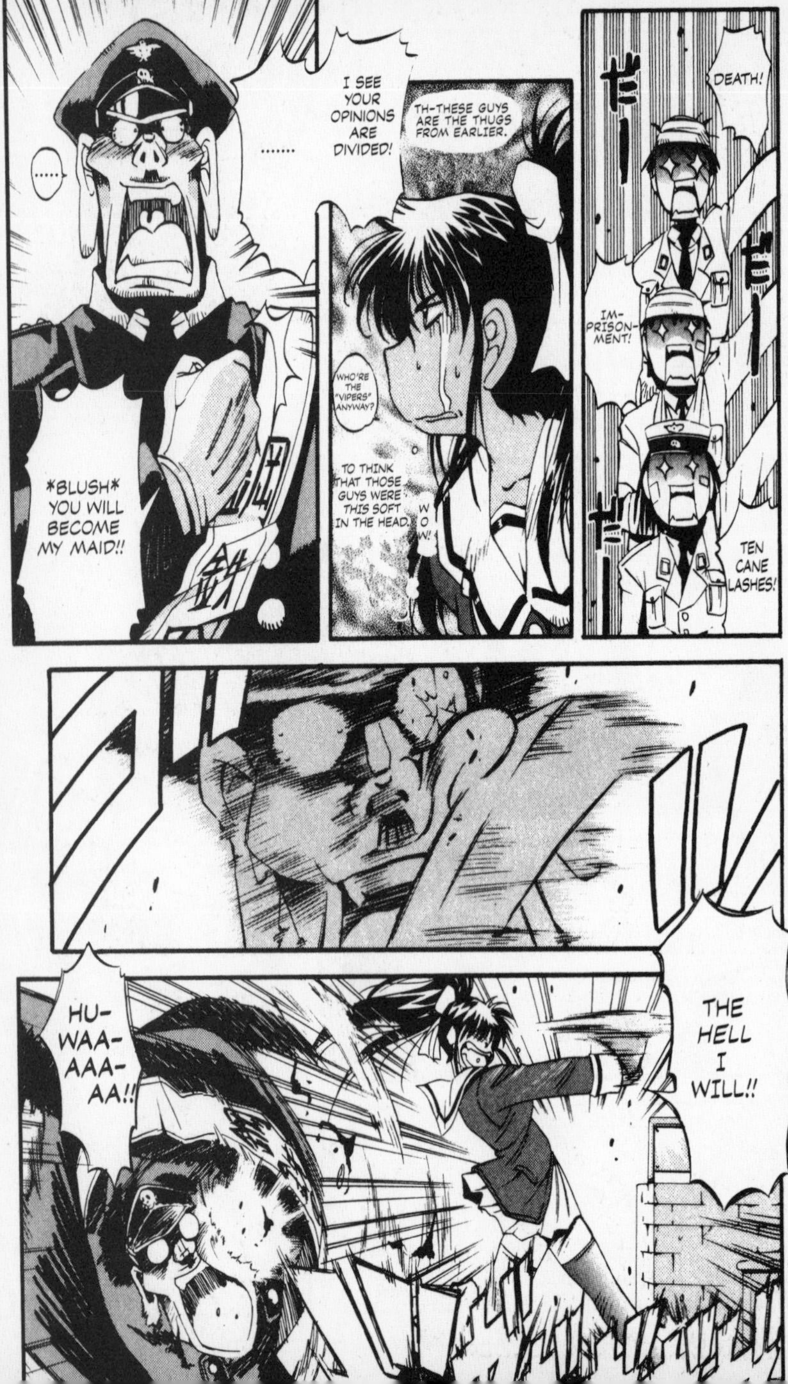

DEATH!
IM-PRISON-MENT!
TEN CANE LASHES!
TH-THESE GUYS ARE THE THUGS FROM EARLIER.
WHO'RE THE "VIPERS" ANYWAY?
TO THINK THAT THOSE GUYS WERE THIS SOFT IN THE HEAD.
WOW!
I SEE YOUR OPINIONS ARE DIVIDED!
......
......
BLUSH YOU WILL BECOME MY MAID!!
THE HELL I WILL!!
HU-WAA-AAA-AA!!

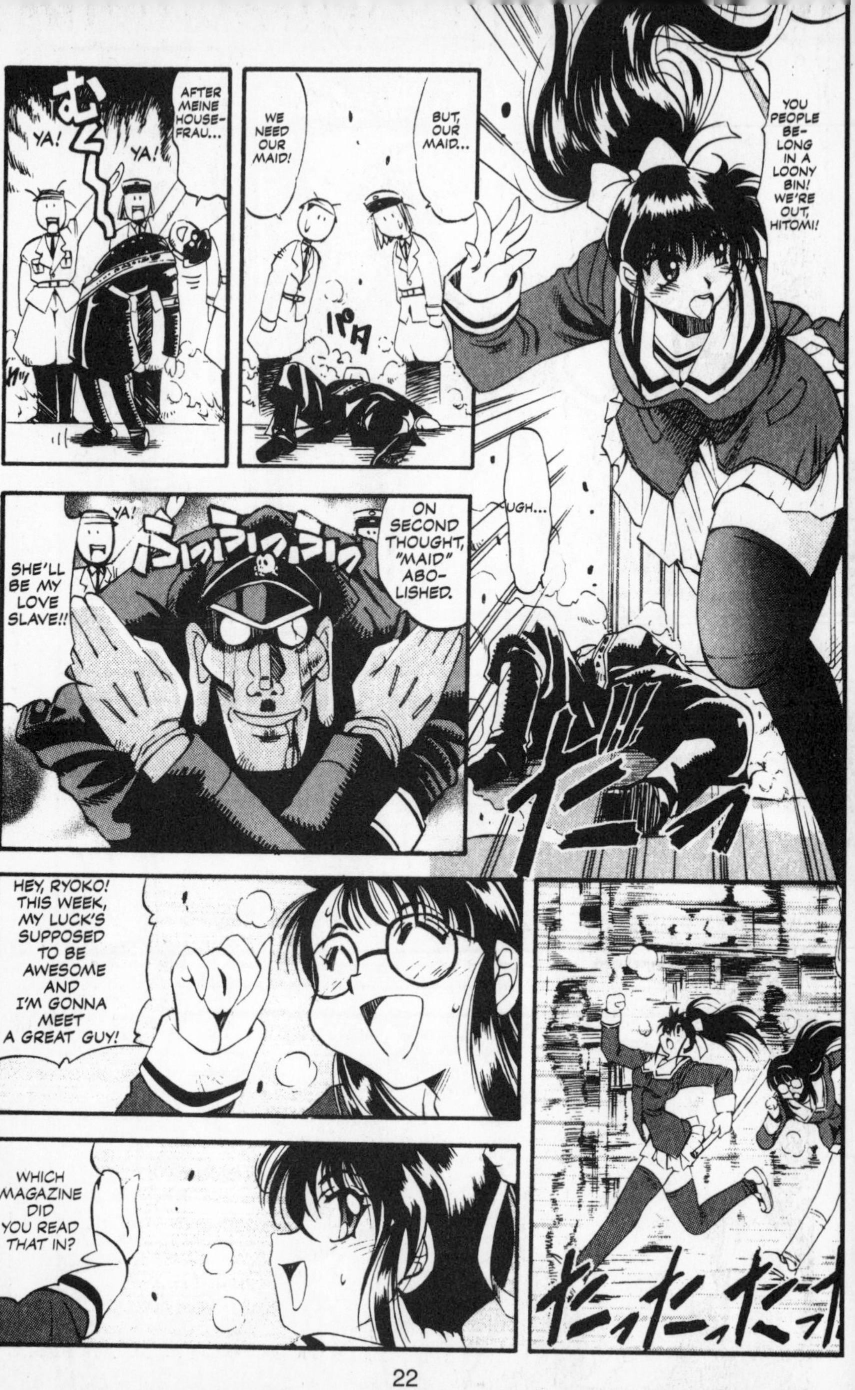
YOU PEOPLE BE-LONG IN A LOONY BIN! WE'RE OUT, HITOMI!
UGH...
BUT, OUR MAID...
WE NEED OUR MAID!
AFTER MEINE HOUSE-FRAU...
YA!
YA!
ON SECOND THOUGHT, "MAID" ABO-LISHED.
YA!
SHE'LL BE MY LOVE SLAVE!!
HEY, RYOKO! THIS WEEK, MY LUCK'S SUPPOSED TO BE AWESOME AND I'M GONNA MEET A GREAT GUY!
WHICH MAGAZINE DID YOU READ THAT IN?

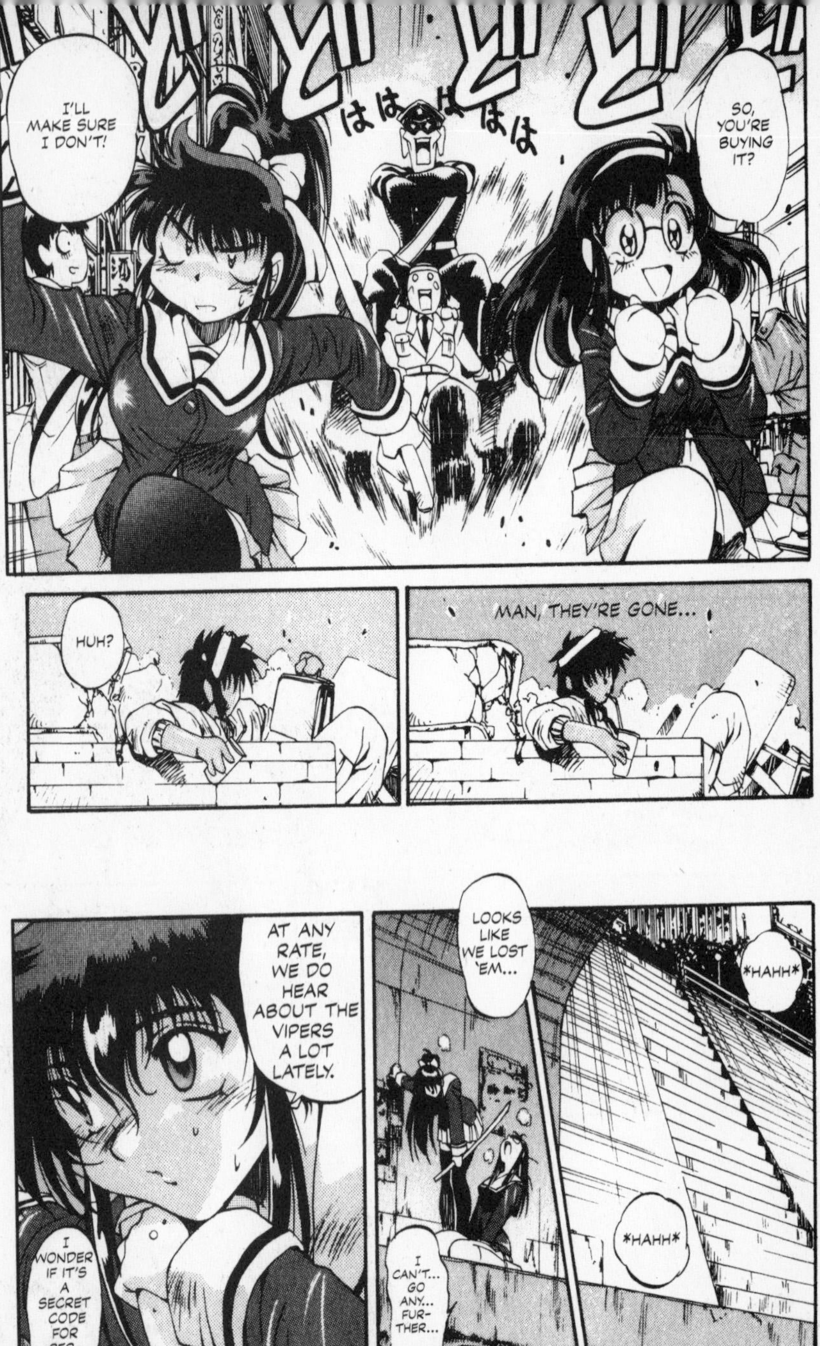
SO, YOU'RE BUYING IT?
はははは
I'LL MAKE SURE I DON'T!
MAN, THEY'RE GONE...
HUH?
HAHH
LOOKS LIKE WE LOST 'EM...
HAHH
I CAN'T... GO ANY... FURTHER...
AT ANY RATE, WE DO HEAR ABOUT THE VIPERS A LOT LATELY.
I WONDER IF IT'S A SECRET CODE FOR PERVERTS?

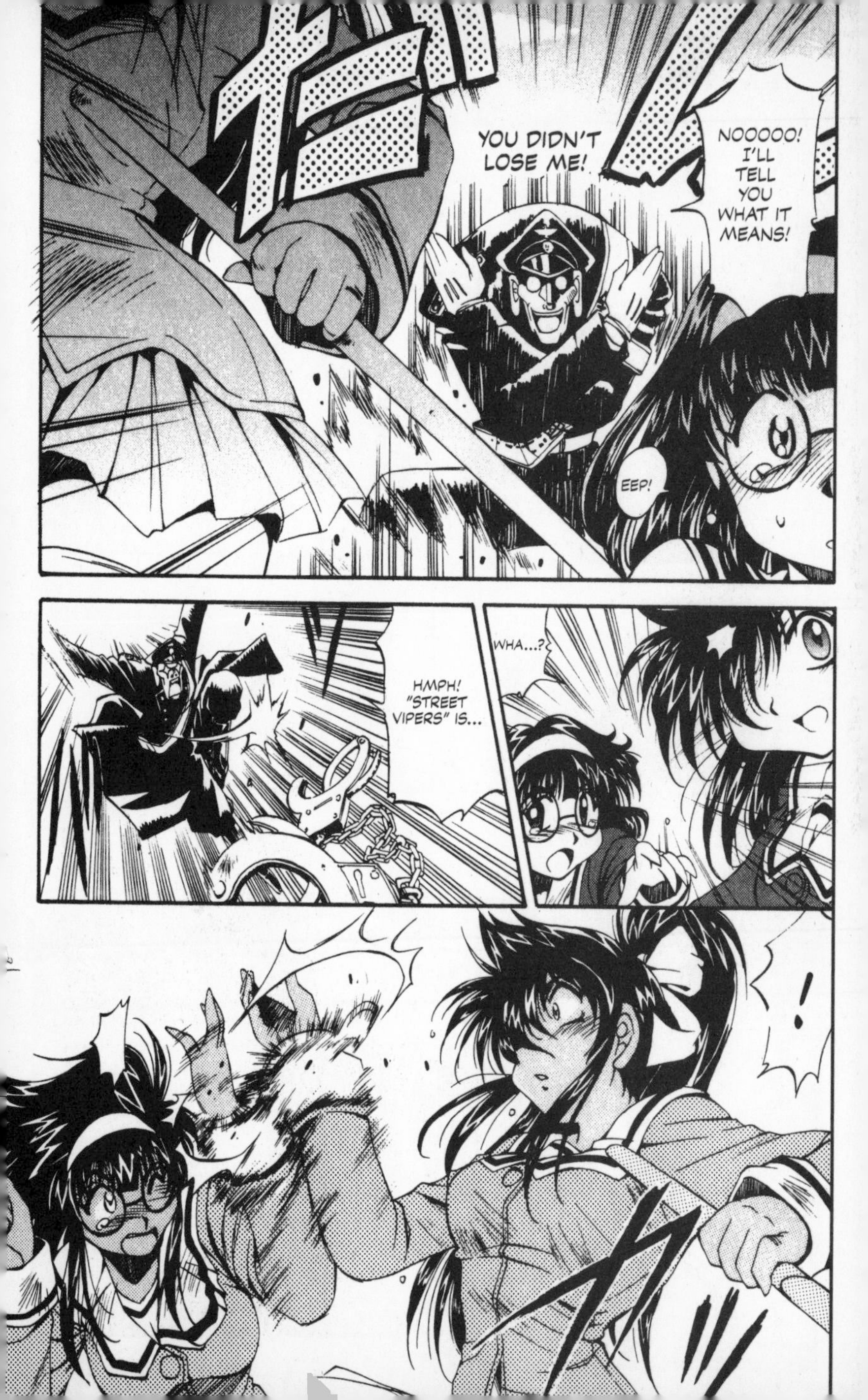
NOOOOO! I'LL TELL YOU WHAT IT MEANS!
YOU DIDN'T LOSE ME!
EEP!
WHA...?
HMPH! "STREET VIPERS" IS...
!

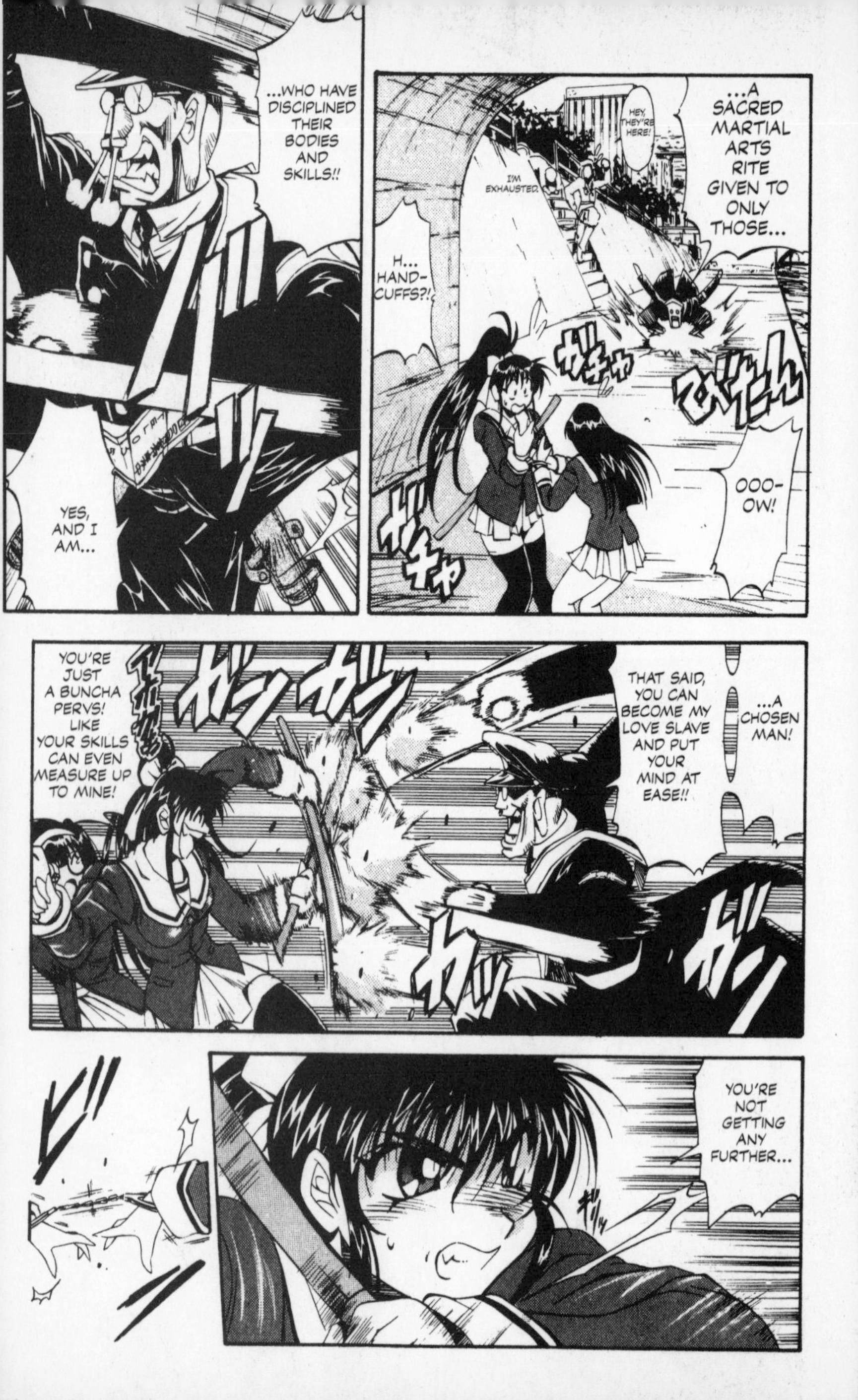
...A SACRED MARTIAL ARTS RITE GIVEN TO ONLY THOSE...
HEY, THEY'RE HERE!
I'M EXHAUSTED.
H... HAND-CUFFS?!
OOO-OW!
...WHO HAVE DISCIPLINED THEIR BODIES AND SKILLS!!
YES, AND I AM...
...A CHOSEN MAN!
THAT SAID, YOU CAN BECOME MY LOVE SLAVE AND PUT YOUR MIND AT EASE!!
YOU'RE JUST A BUNCHA PERVS! LIKE YOUR SKILLS CAN EVEN MEASURE UP TO MINE!
YOU'RE NOT GETTING ANY FURTHER...

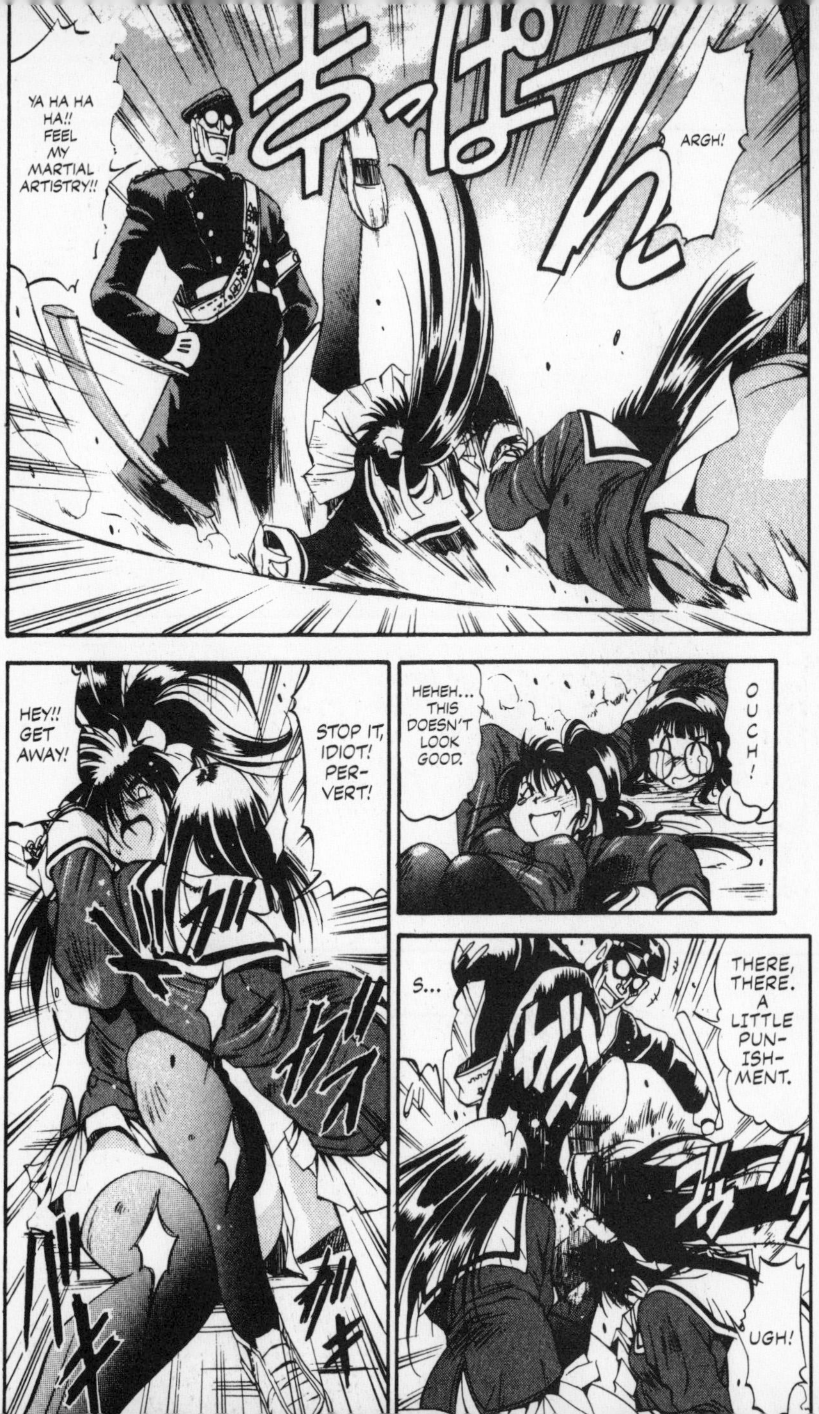
ARGH!
YA HA HA HA!! FEEL MY MARTIAL ARTISTRY!!
OUCH!
HEHEH... THIS DOESN'T LOOK GOOD.
THERE, THERE. A LITTLE PUN-ISH-MENT.
S...
UGH!
STOP IT, IDIOT! PER-VERT!
HEY!! GET AWAY!

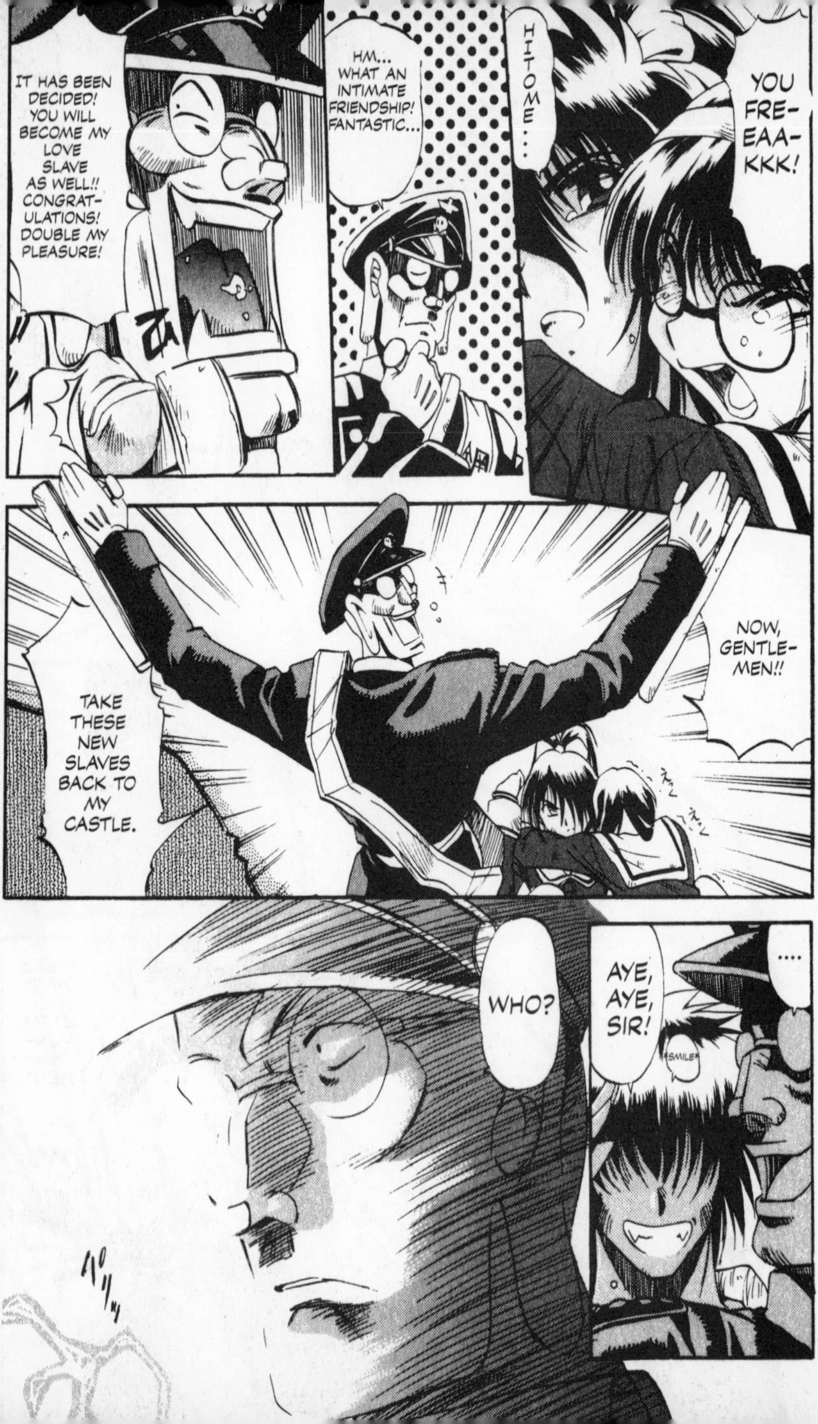
YOU FRE- EAA- KKK!
HITOME...
HM... WHAT AN INTIMATE FRIENDSHIP! FANTASTIC...
IT HAS BEEN DECIDED! YOU WILL BECOME MY LOVE SLAVE AS WELL!! CONGRAT- ULATIONS! DOUBLE MY PLEASURE!
NOW, GENTLE- MEN!!
TAKE THESE NEW SLAVES BACK TO MY CASTLE.
....
AYE, AYE, SIR!
SMILE
WHO?

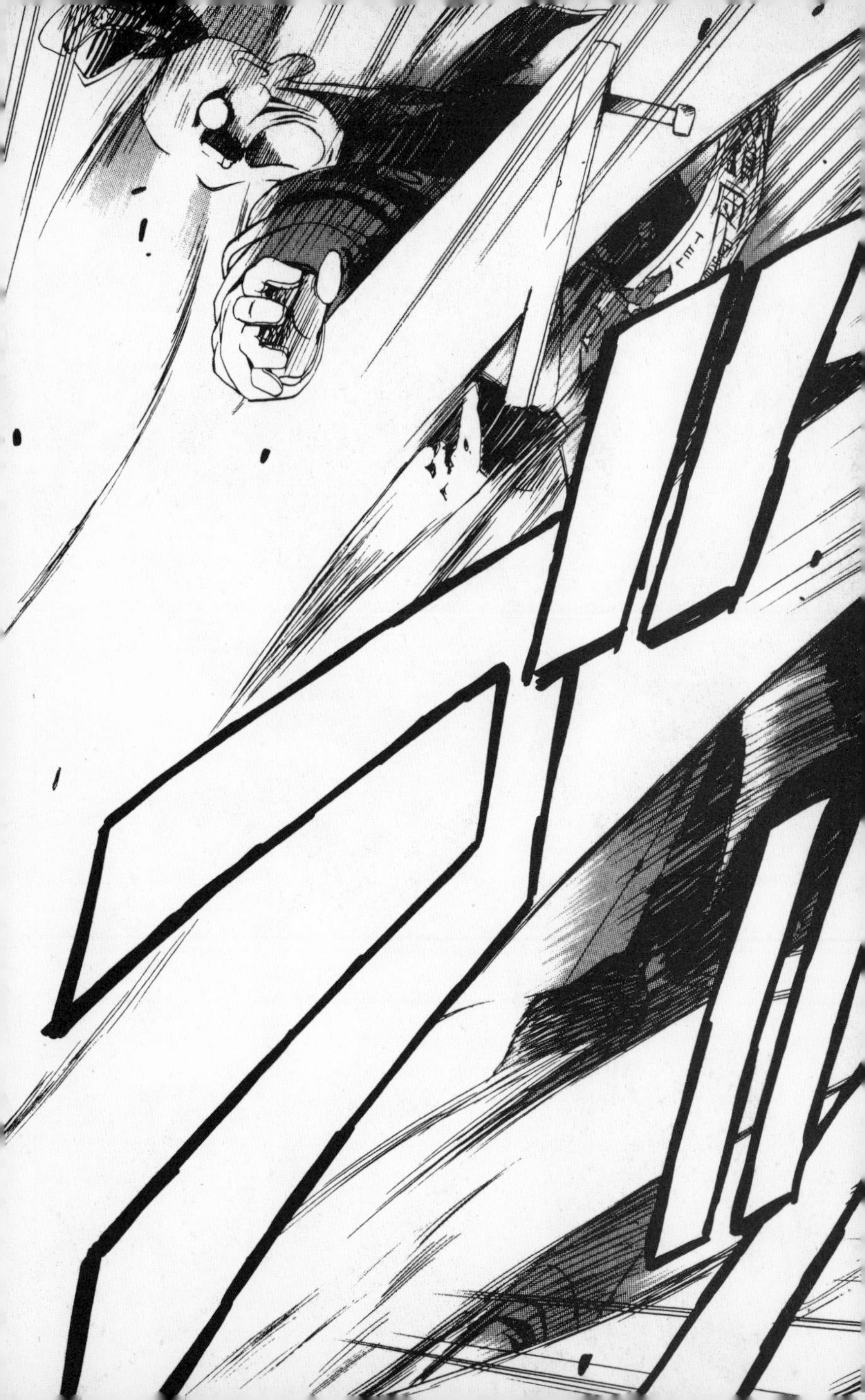

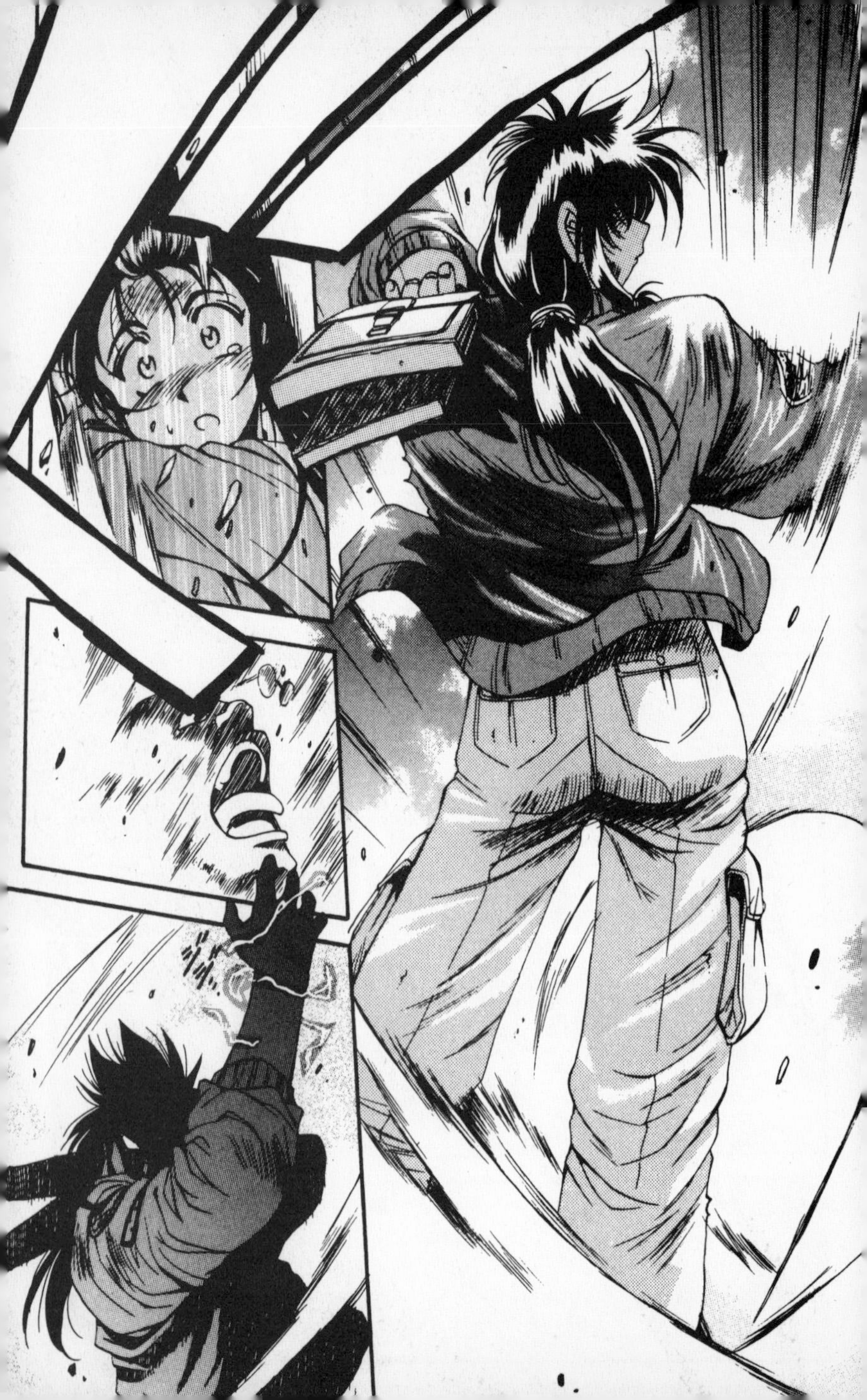

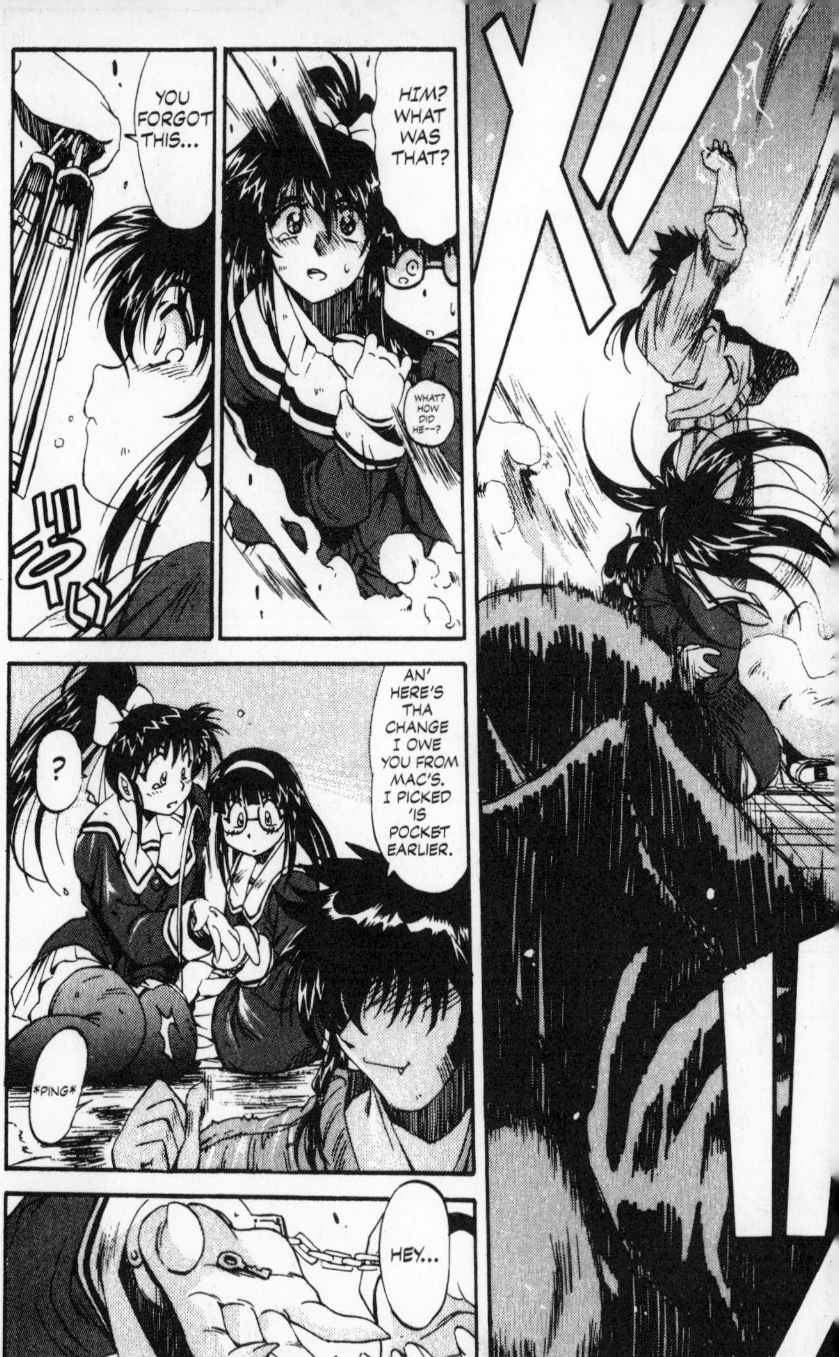
HIM? WHAT WAS THAT?
WHAT? HOW DID HE--?
YOU FORGOT THIS...
AN' HERE'S THA CHANGE I OWE YOU FROM MAC'S. I PICKED 'IS POCKET EARLIER.
?
PING
HEY...

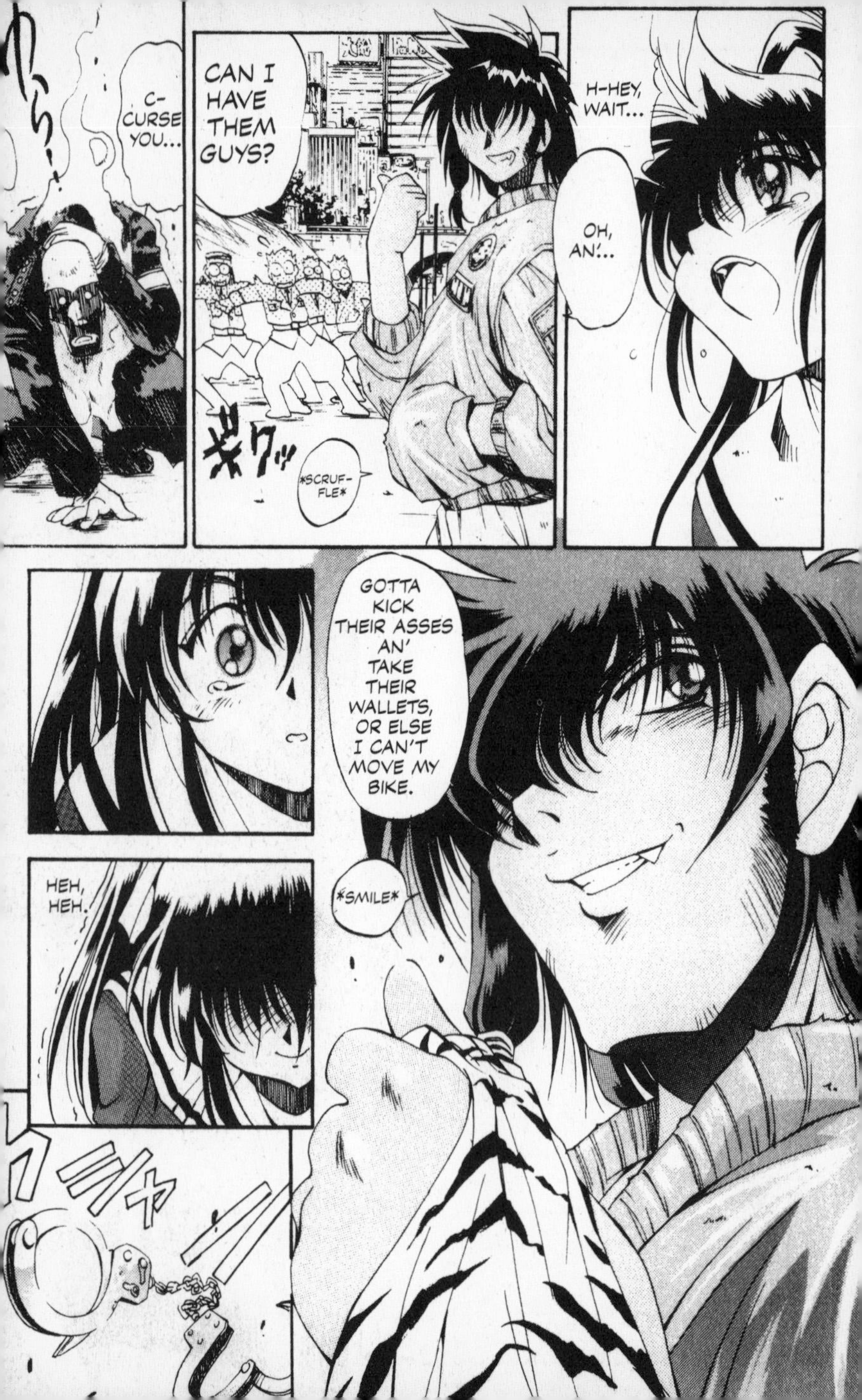
H-HEY, WAIT...
OH, AN'...
CAN I HAVE THEM GUYS?
SCRUFFLE
C-CURSE YOU...
GOTTA KICK THEIR ASSES AN' TAKE THEIR WALLETS, OR ELSE I CAN'T MOVE MY BIKE.
SMILE
HEH, HEH.

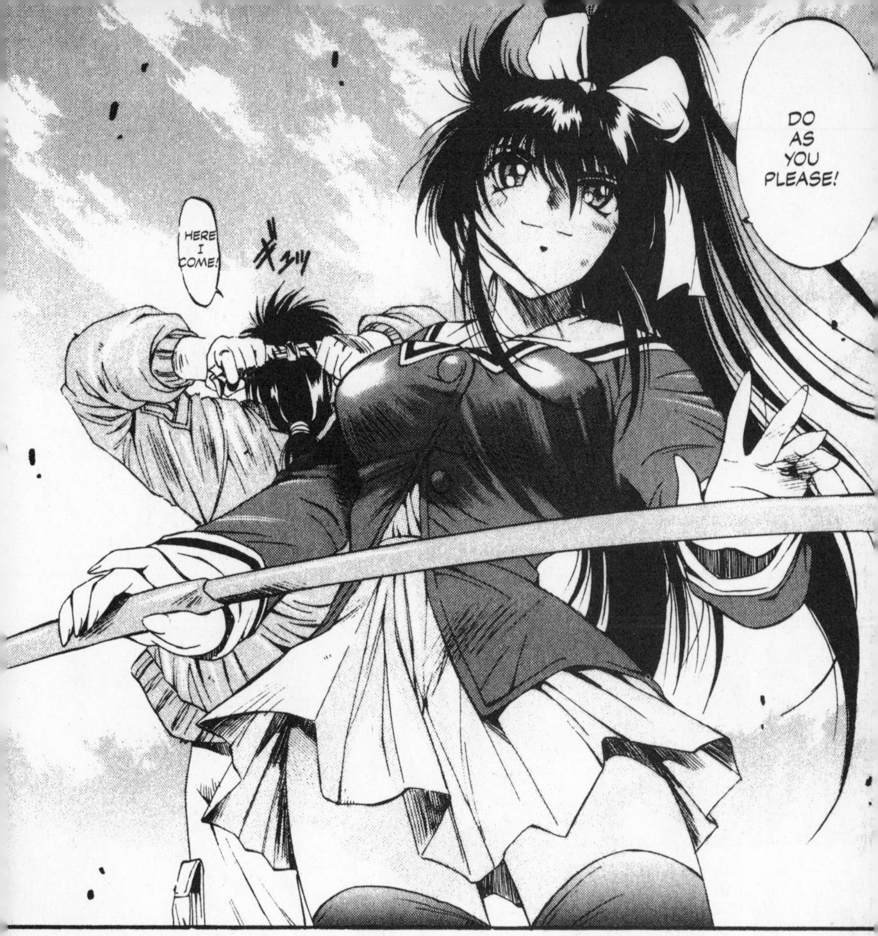
DO AS YOU PLEASE!
HERE I COME!
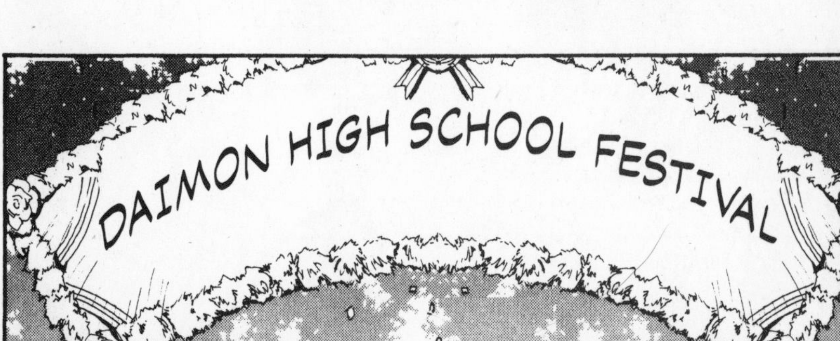
DAIMON HIGH SCHOOL FESTIVAL

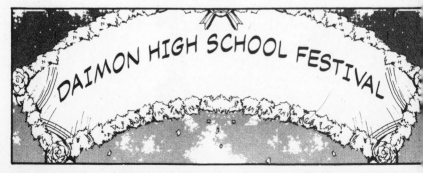

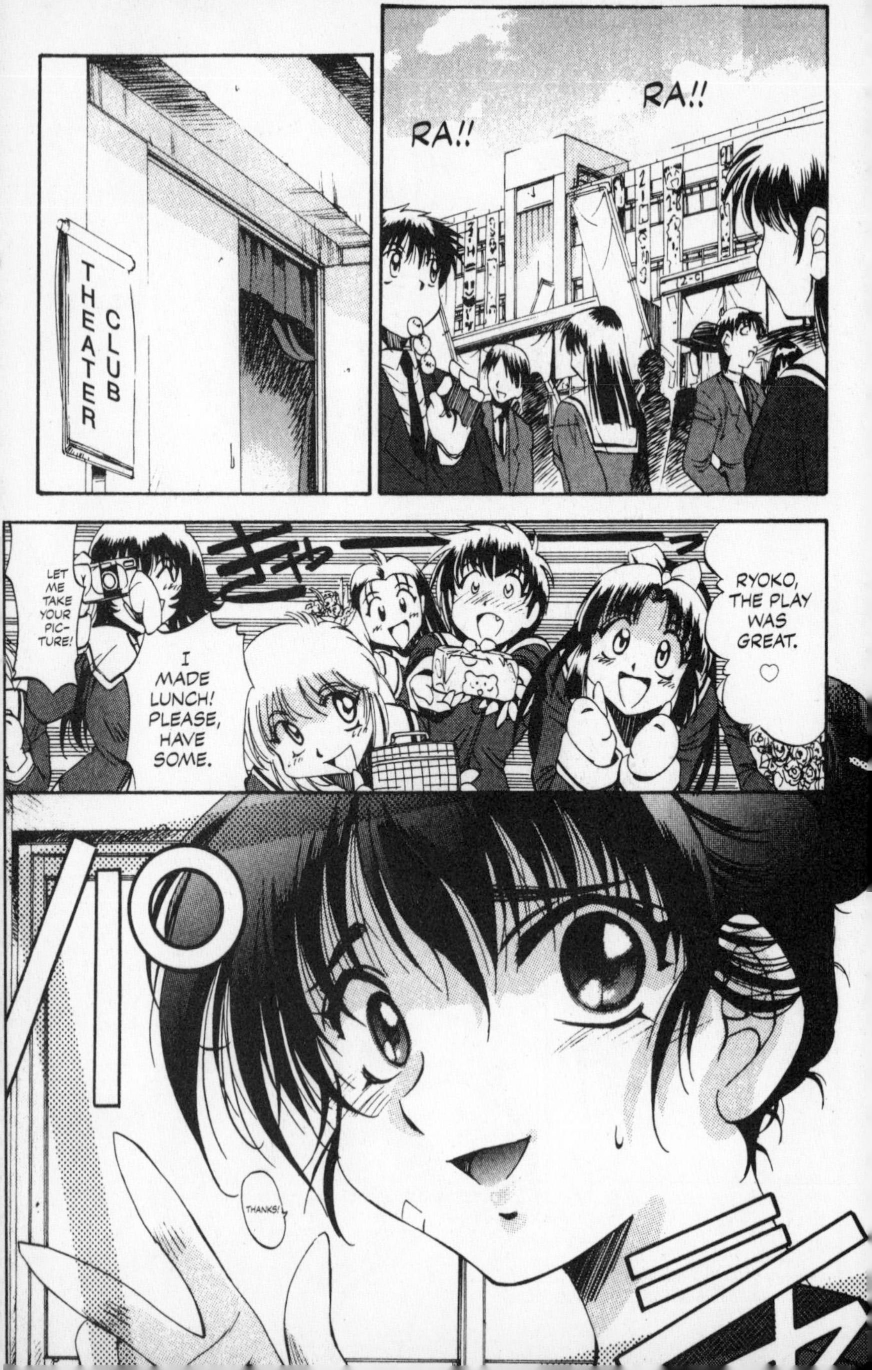
RA!!
RA!!
THEATER CLUB
RYOKO, THE PLAY WAS GREAT. ♡
きゃー
I MADE LUNCH! PLEASE, HAVE SOME.
LET ME TAKE YOUR PICTURE!
THANKS!

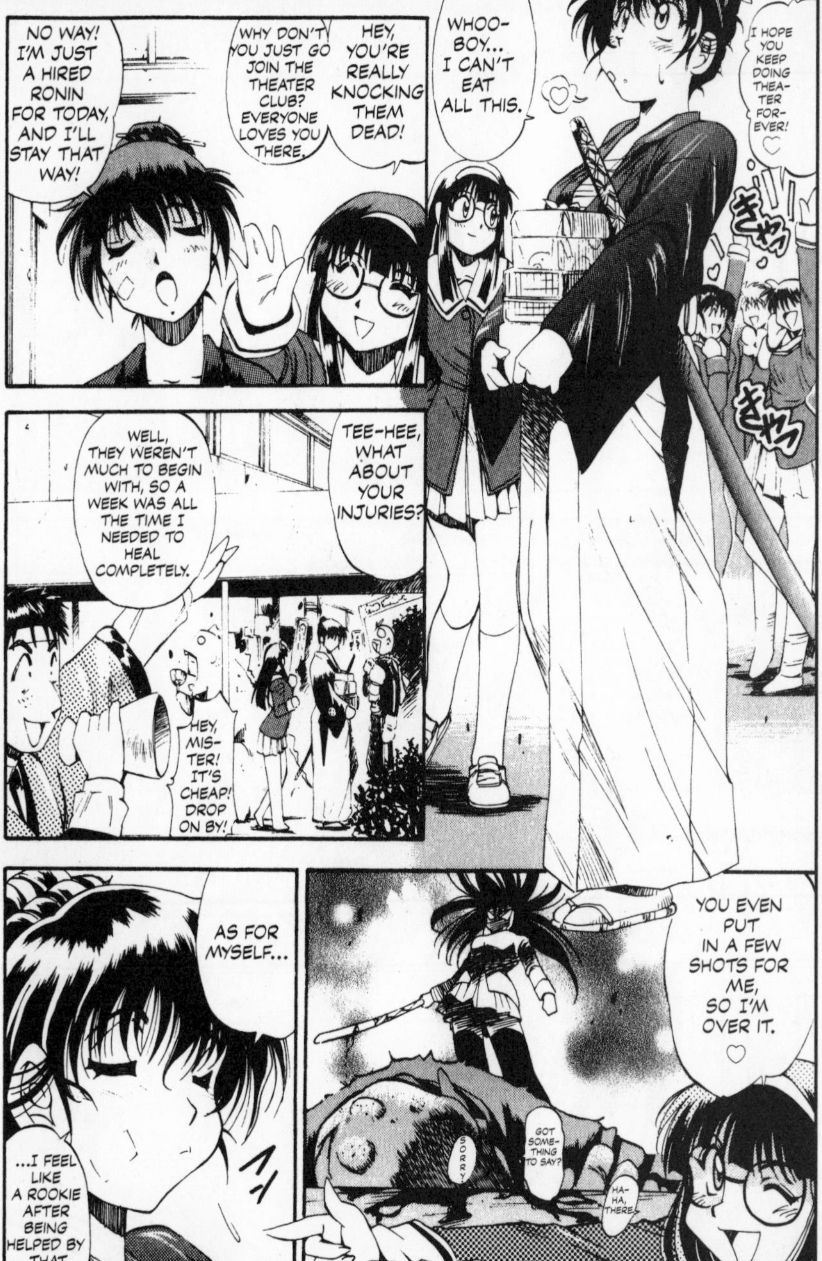
I HOPE YOU KEEP DOING THEATER FOREVER!
きゃっ
きゃっ
WHOO-BOY... I CAN'T EAT ALL THIS.
HEY, YOU'RE REALLY KNOCKING THEM DEAD!
WHY DON'T YOU JUST GO JOIN THE THEATER CLUB? EVERYONE LOVES YOU THERE.
NO WAY! I'M JUST A HIRED RONIN FOR TODAY, AND I'LL STAY THAT WAY!
TEE-HEE, WHAT ABOUT YOUR INJURIES?
WELL, THEY WEREN'T MUCH TO BEGIN WITH, SO A WEEK WAS ALL THE TIME I NEEDED TO HEAL COMPLETELY.
HEY, MISTER! IT'S CHEAP! DROP ON BY!
YOU EVEN PUT IN A FEW SHOTS FOR ME, SO I'M OVER IT.
GOT SOMETHING TO SAY?
SORRY
HA-HA, THERE.
AS FOR MYSELF...
...I FEEL LIKE A ROOKIE AFTER BEING HELPED BY THAT WEIRDO.

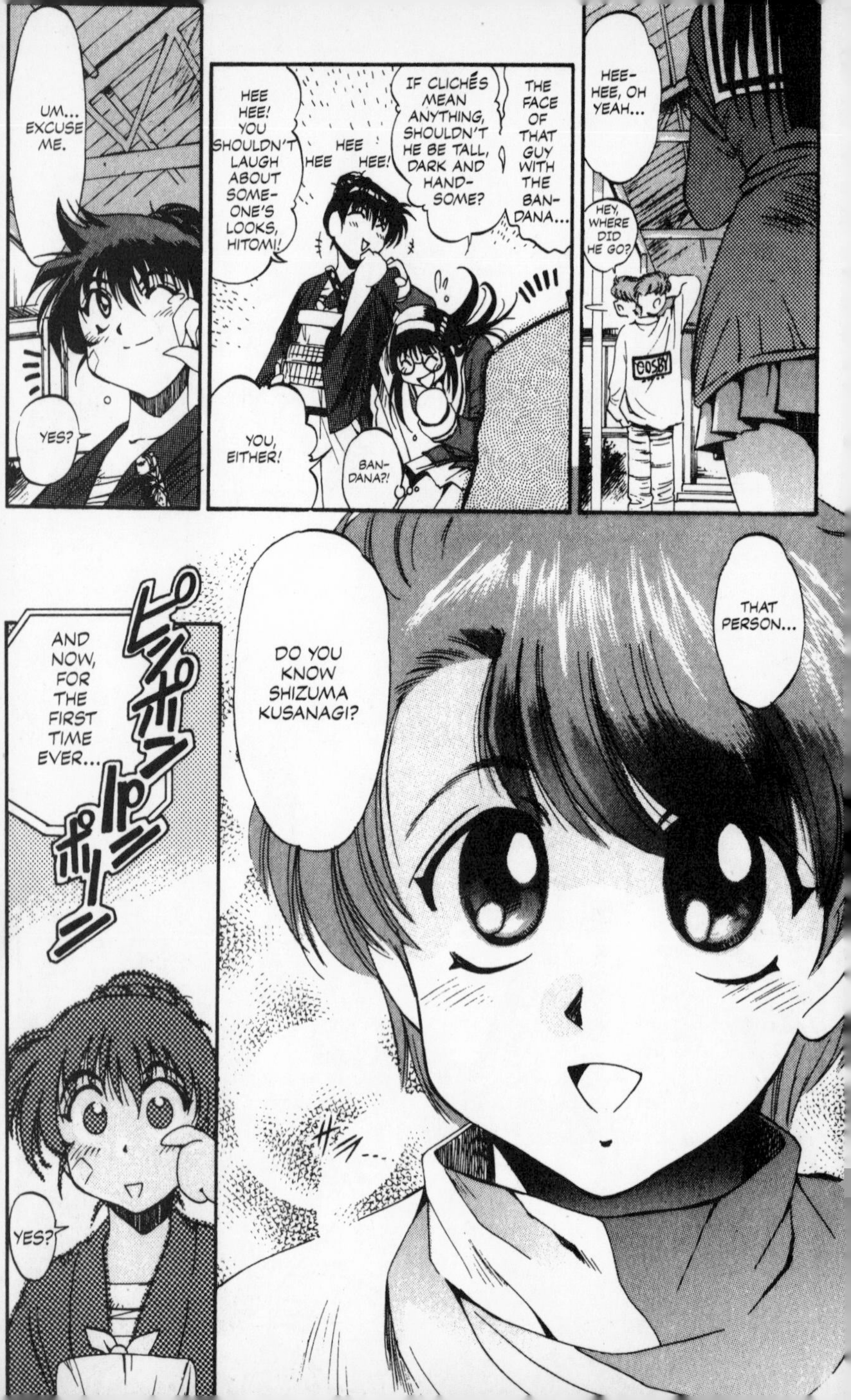
HEE-HEE, OH YEAH...
HEY, WHERE DID HE GO?
THE FACE OF THAT GUY WITH THE BANDANA...
IF CLICHÉS MEAN ANYTHING, SHOULDN'T HE BE TALL, DARK AND HANDSOME?
HEE HEE HEE!
HEE HEE! YOU SHOULDN'T LAUGH ABOUT SOMEONE'S LOOKS, HITOMI!
BANDANA?!
YOU, EITHER!
UM... EXCUSE ME.
YES?
THAT PERSON...
DO YOU KNOW SHIZUMA KUSANAGI?
AND NOW, FOR THE FIRST TIME EVER...
YES?

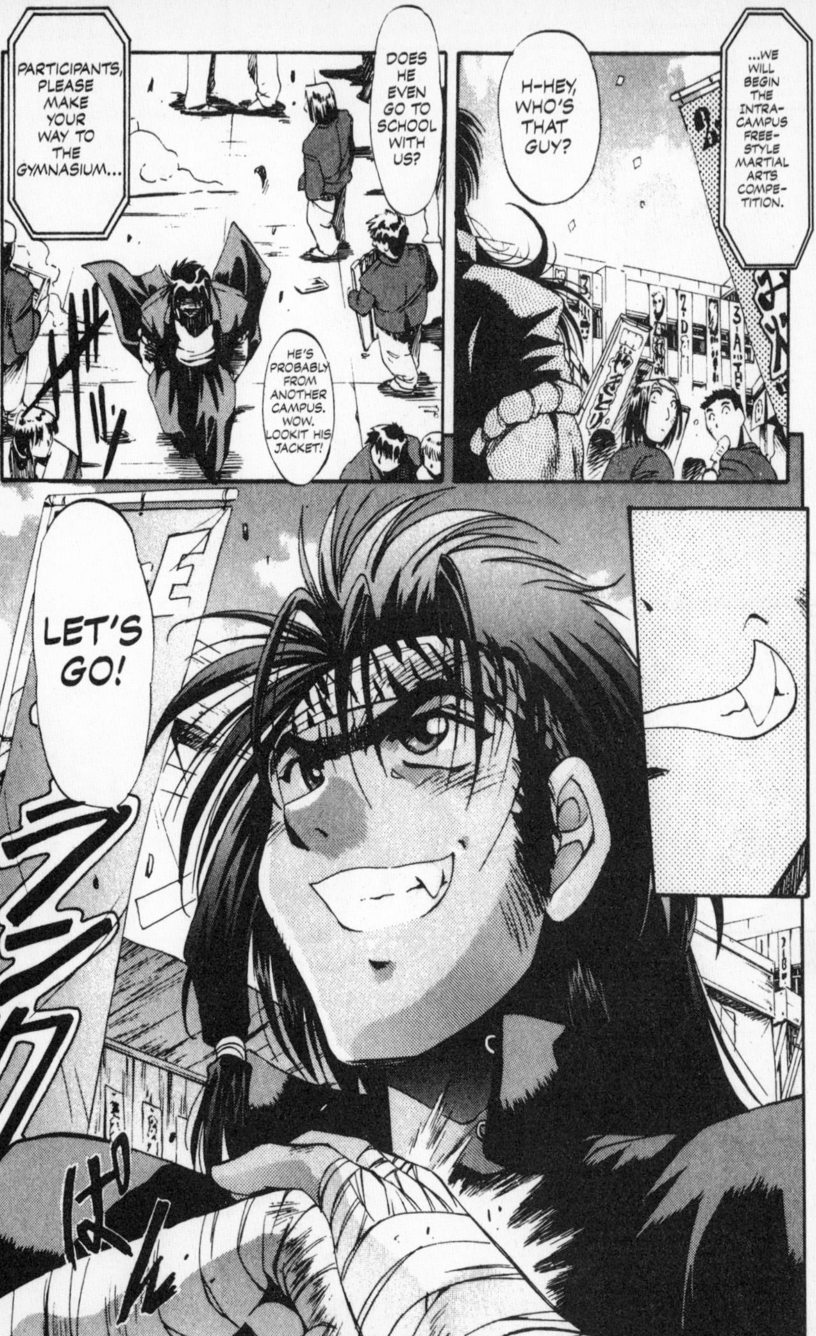
...WE WILL BEGIN THE INTRA-CAMPUS FREE-STYLE MARTIAL ARTS COMPETITION.
H-HEY, WHO'S THAT GUY?
PARTICIPANTS, PLEASE MAKE YOUR WAY TO THE GYMNASIUM...
DOES HE EVEN GO TO SCHOOL WITH US?
HE'S PROBABLY FROM ANOTHER CAMPUS. WOW. LOOKIT HIS JACKET!
LET'S GO!

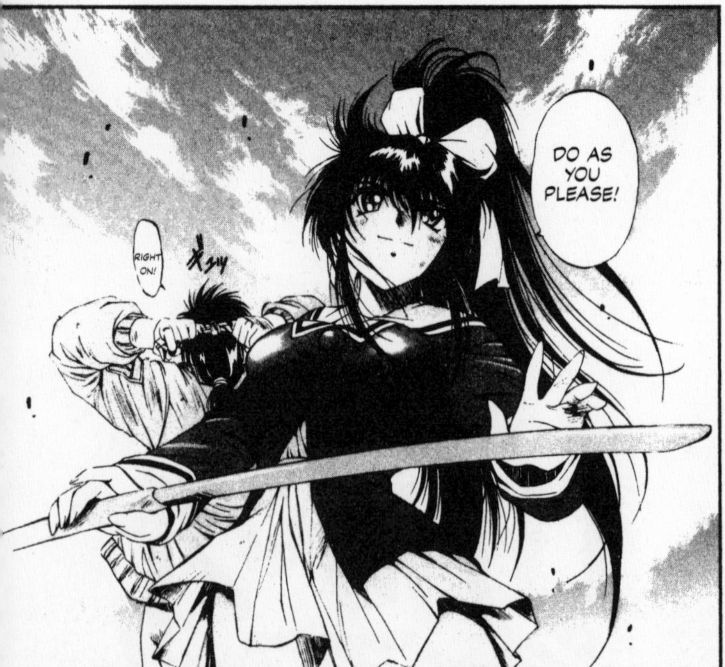
DO AS YOU PLEASE!
RIGHT ON!

REAL BOUT HIGHSCHOOL

リアルバウトハイスクール

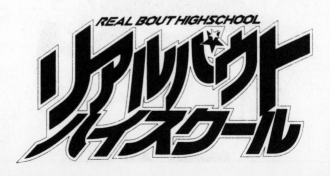

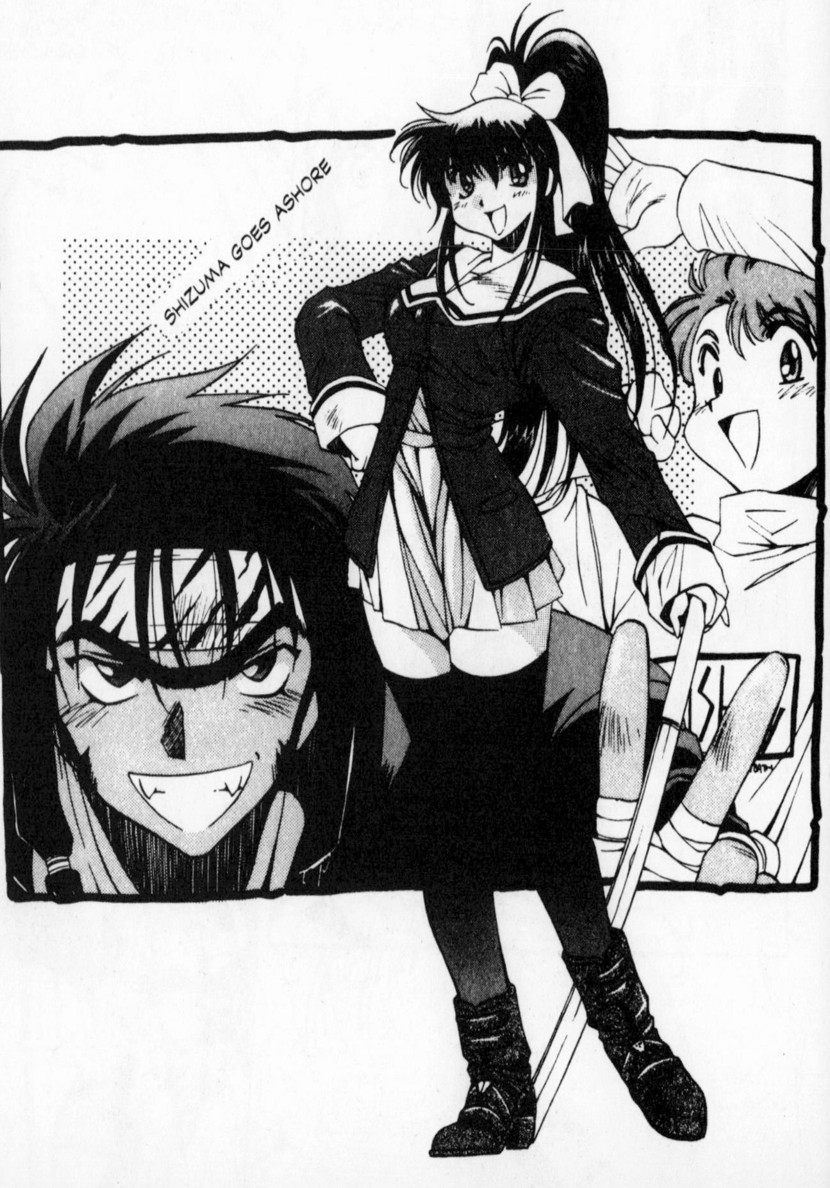
SHIZUMA GOES ASHORE

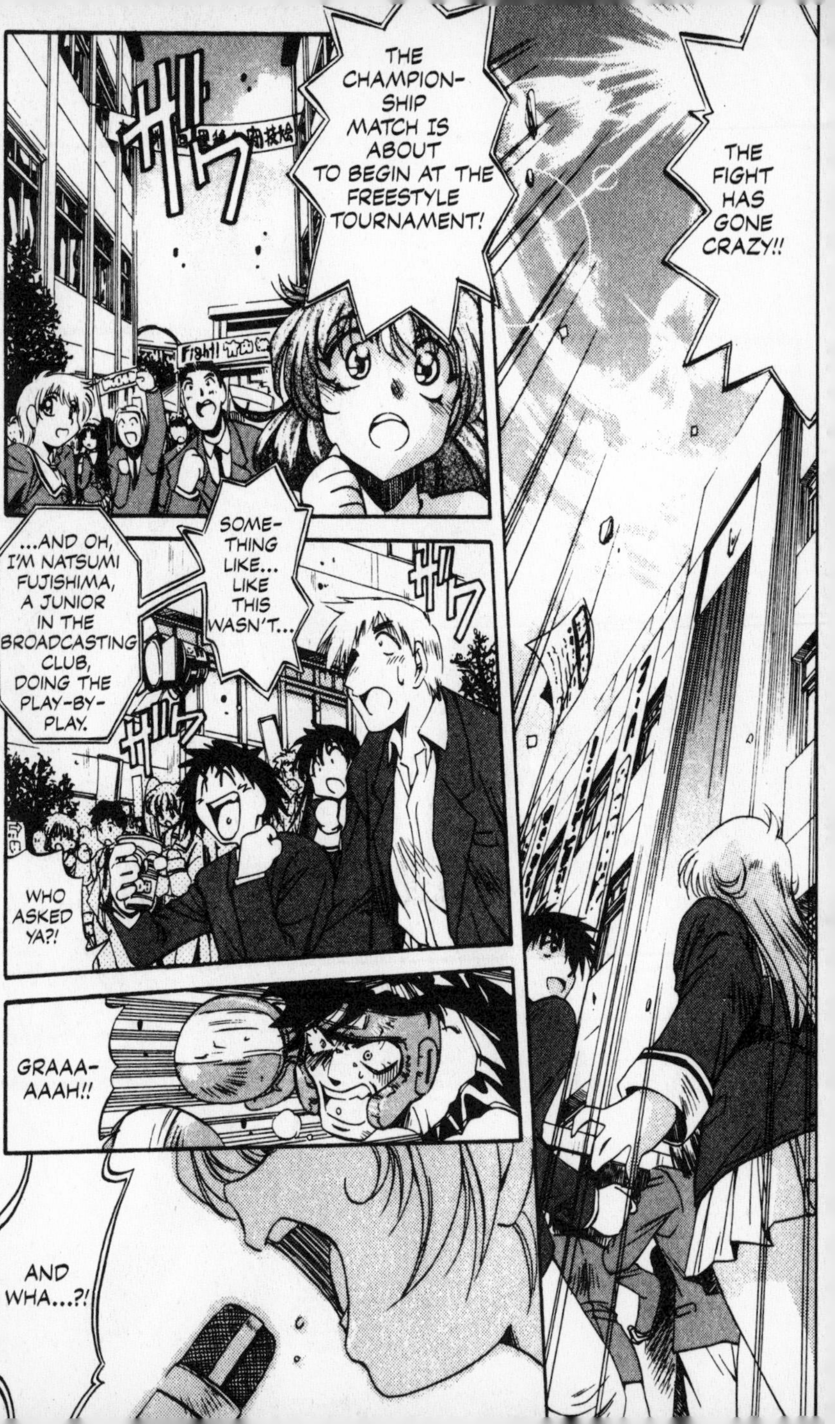

THE FIGHT HAS GONE CRAZY!!
THE CHAMPIONSHIP MATCH IS ABOUT TO BEGIN AT THE FREESTYLE TOURNAMENT!
SOMETHING LIKE... LIKE THIS WASN'T...
...AND OH, I'M NATSUMI FUJISHIMA, A JUNIOR IN THE BROADCASTING CLUB, DOING THE PLAY-BY-PLAY.
WHO ASKED YA?!
GRAAA-AAAH!!
AND WHA...?!

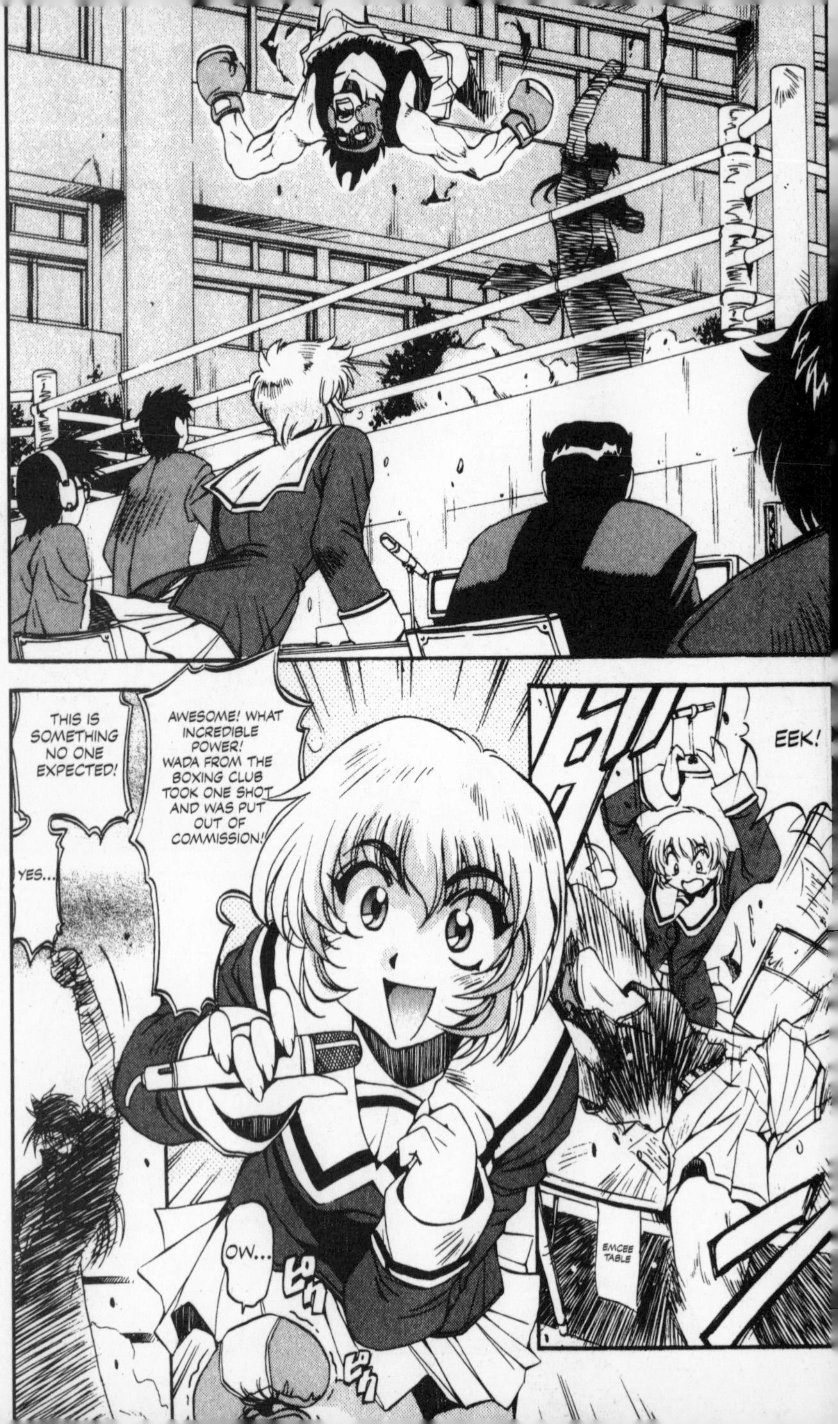
EEK!
AWESOME! WHAT INCREDIBLE POWER! WADA FROM THE BOXING CLUB TOOK ONE SHOT AND WAS PUT OUT OF COMMISSION!
THIS IS SOMETHING NO ONE EXPECTED!
YES...
EMCEE TABLE
OW...

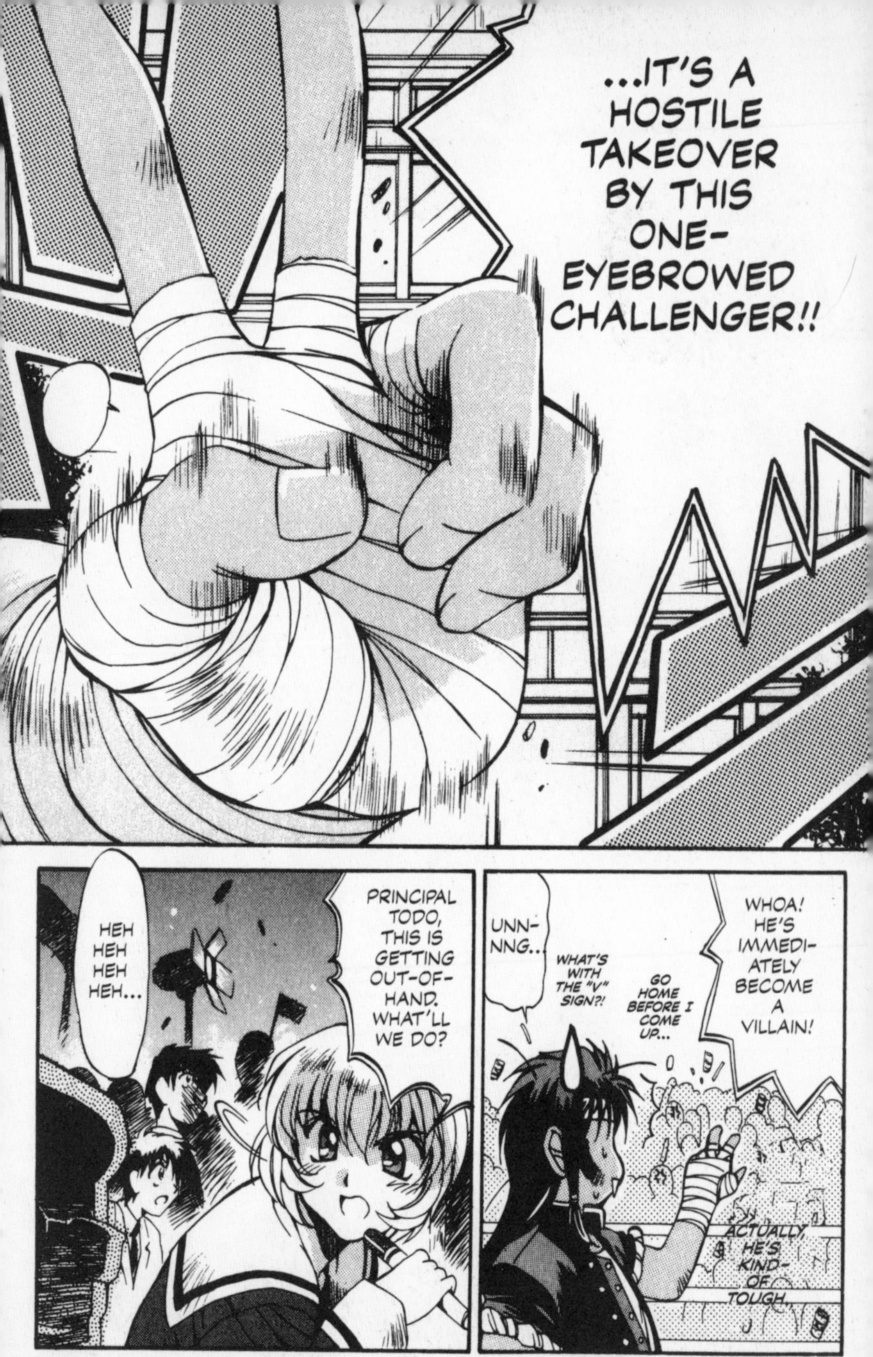
...IT'S A HOSTILE TAKEOVER BY THIS ONE-EYEBROWED CHALLENGER!!
WHOA! HE'S IMMEDIATELY BECOME A VILLAIN!
GO HOME BEFORE I COME UP...
WHAT'S WITH THE "V" SIGN?!
UNNNNG...
ACTUALLY, HE'S KIND-OF TOUGH.
PRINCIPAL TODO, THIS IS GETTING OUT-OF-HAND. WHAT'LL WE DO?
HEH HEH HEH HEH...

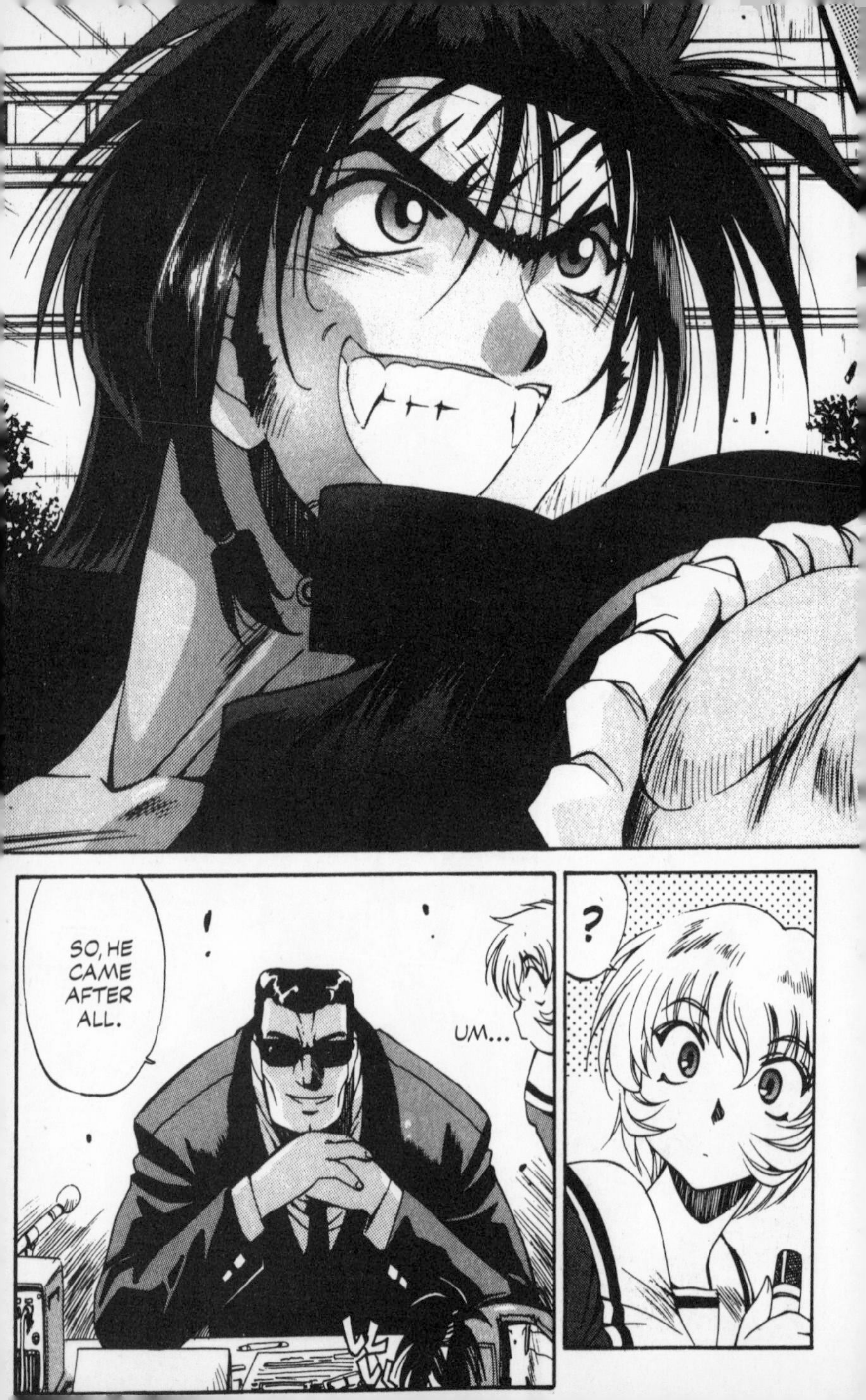
?
!
UM...
SO, HE CAME AFTER ALL.

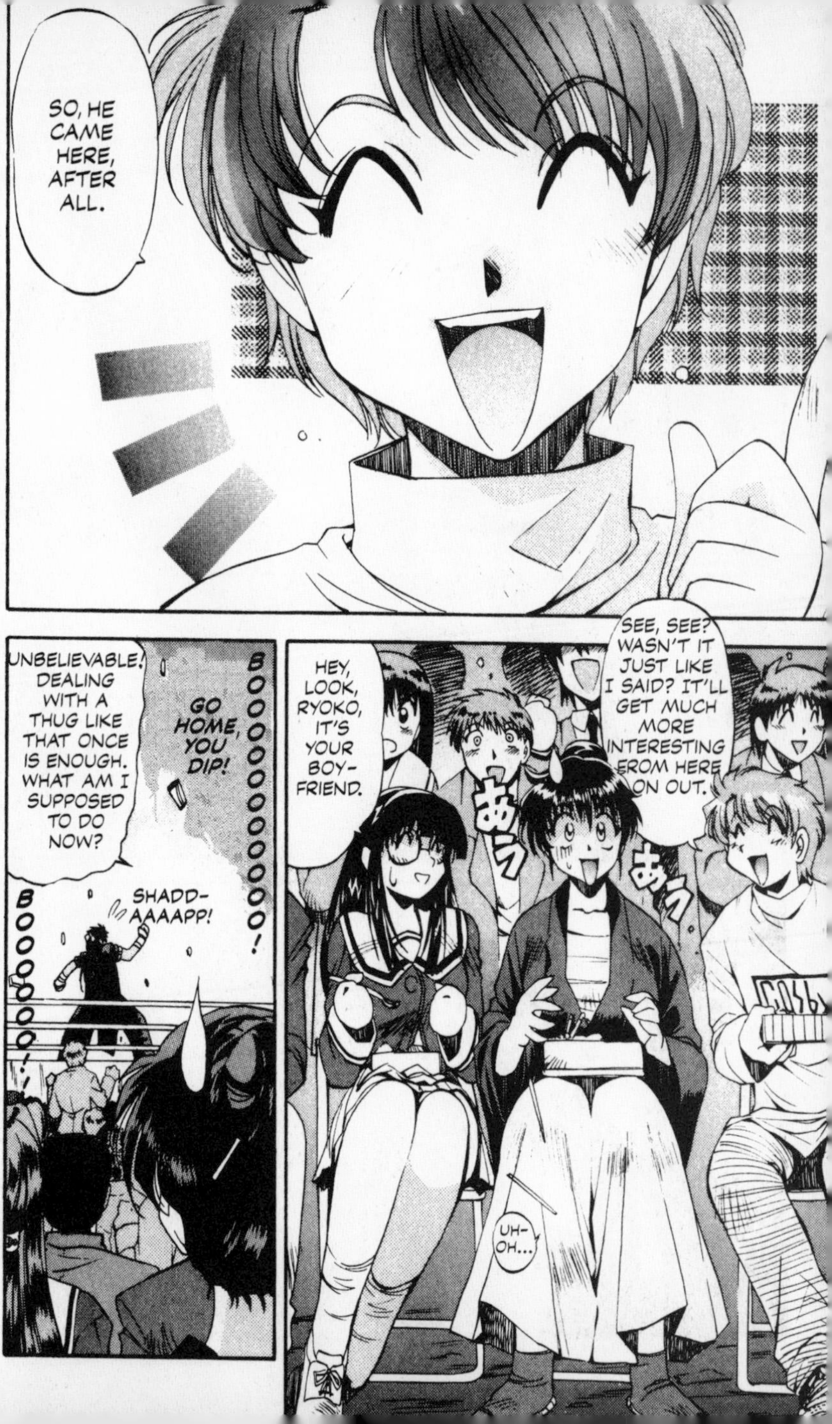

SO, HE CAME HERE, AFTER ALL.
SEE, SEE? WASN'T IT JUST LIKE I SAID? IT'LL GET MUCH MORE INTERESTING FROM HERE ON OUT.
HEY, LOOK, RYOKO, IT'S YOUR BOY-FRIEND.
あう
あう
UH-OH...
BOOOOOOOOOOOOOO!
GO HOME, YOU DIP!
UNBELIEVABLE! DEALING WITH A THUG LIKE THAT ONCE IS ENOUGH. WHAT AM I SUPPOSED TO DO NOW?
SHADD-AAAAPP!
BOOOOOOO!!

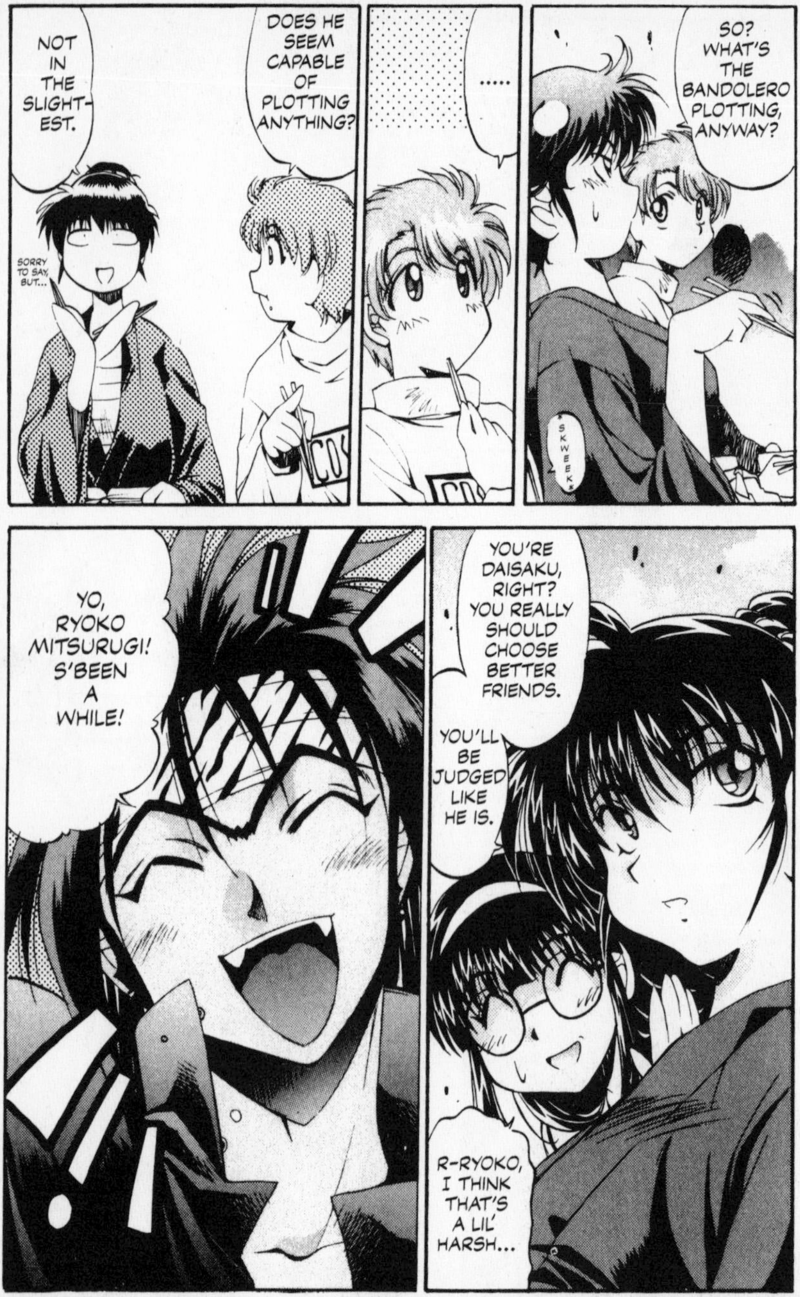
SO? WHAT'S THE BANDOLERO PLOTTING, ANYWAY?
SKWEEK
.....
DOES HE SEEM CAPABLE OF PLOTTING ANYTHING?
NOT IN THE SLIGHTEST.
SORRY TO SAY, BUT...
YOU'RE DAISAKU, RIGHT? YOU REALLY SHOULD CHOOSE BETTER FRIENDS.
YOU'LL BE JUDGED LIKE HE IS.
R-RYOKO, I THINK THAT'S A LIL' HARSH...
YO, RYOKO MITSURUGI! S'BEEN A WHILE!

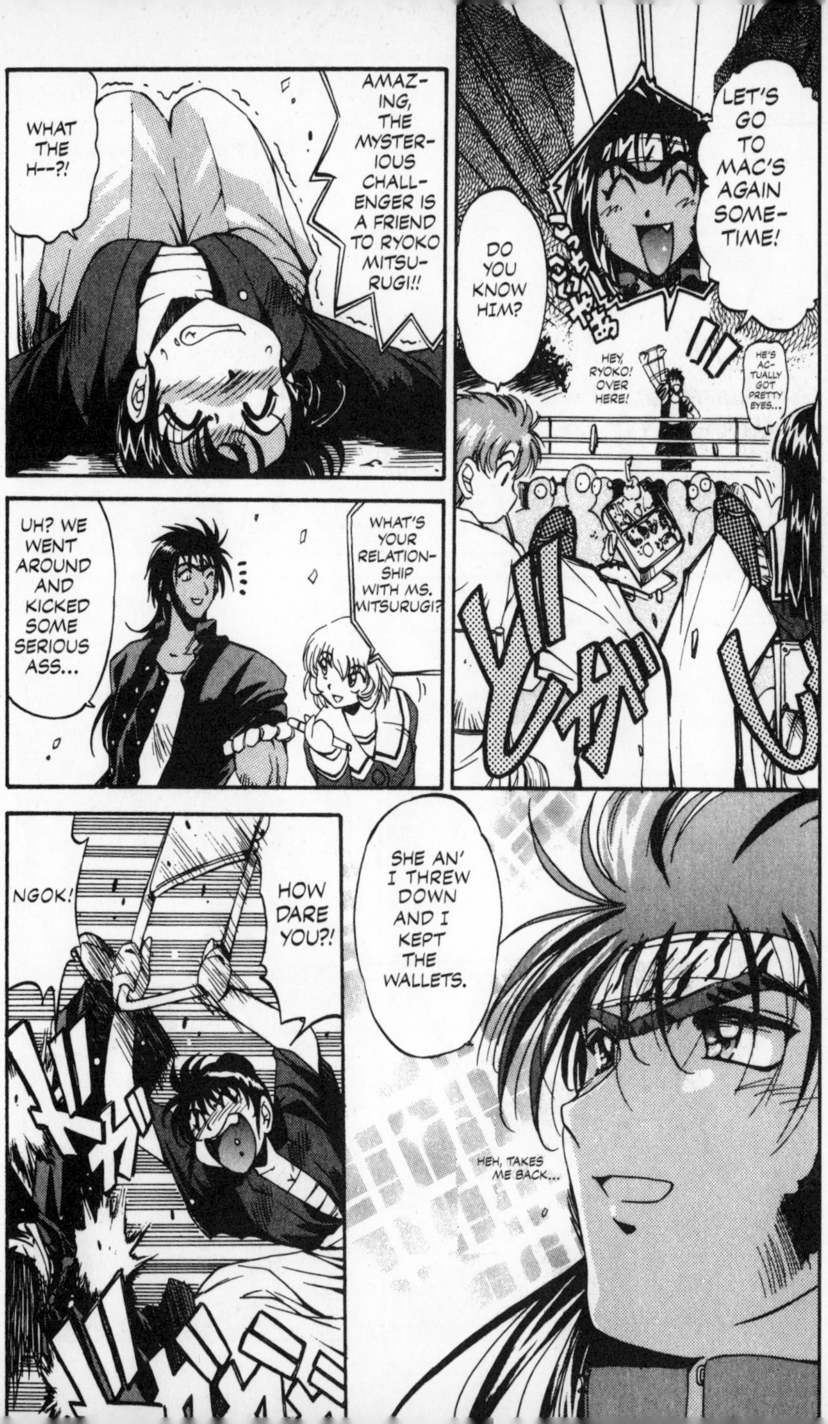
LET'S GO TO MAC'S AGAIN SOMETIME!
DO YOU KNOW HIM?
HEY, RYOKO! OVER HERE!
HE'S ACTUALLY GOT PRETTY EYES...
AMAZING, THE MYSTERIOUS CHALLENGER IS A FRIEND TO RYOKO MITSURUGI!!
WHAT THE H--?!
WHAT'S YOUR RELATIONSHIP WITH MS. MITSURUGI?
UH? WE WENT AROUND AND KICKED SOME SERIOUS ASS...
SHE AN' I THREW DOWN AND I KEPT THE WALLETS.
HEH, TAKES ME BACK...
HOW DARE YOU?!
NGOK!

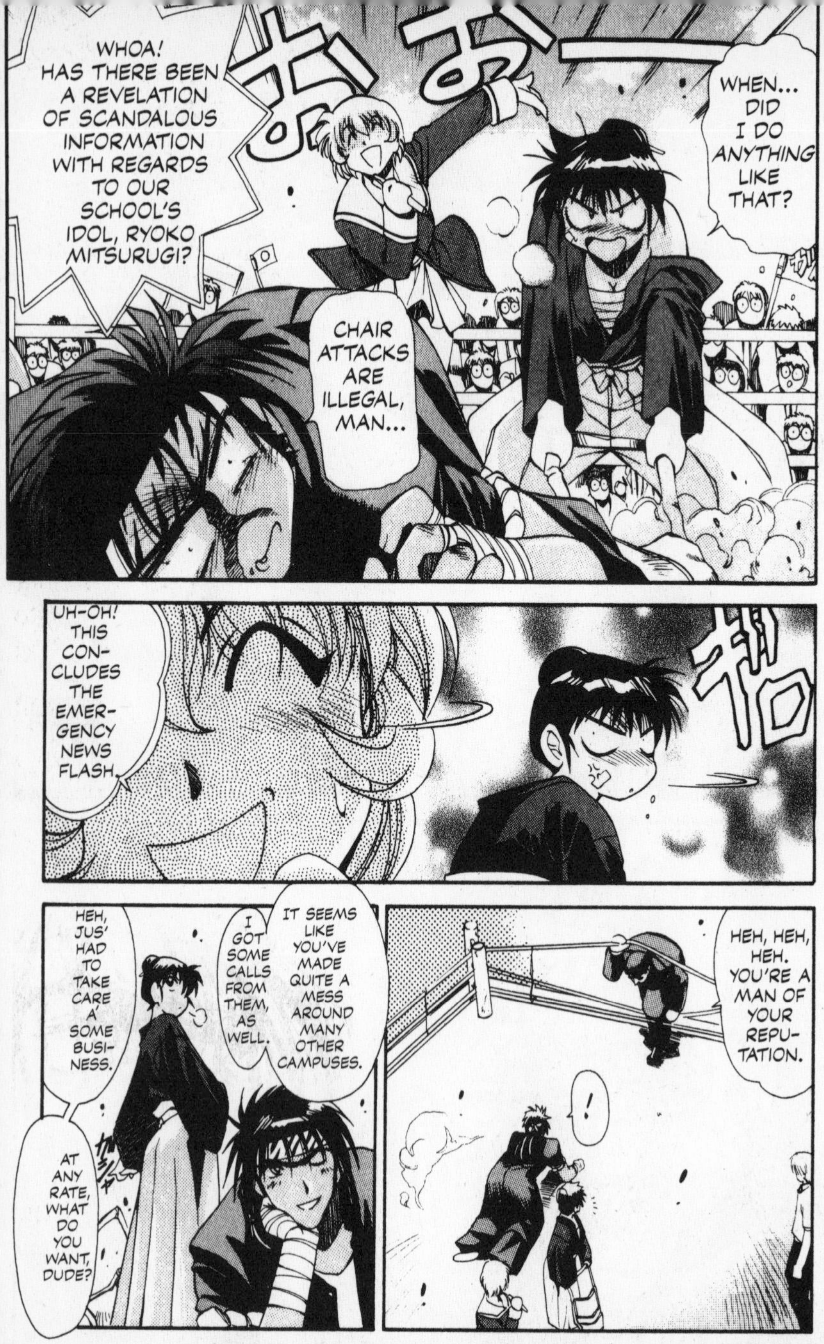
おぉー
WHOA! HAS THERE BEEN A REVELATION OF SCANDALOUS INFORMATION WITH REGARDS TO OUR SCHOOL'S IDOL, RYOKO MITSURUGI?
WHEN... DID I DO ANYTHING LIKE THAT?
CHAIR ATTACKS ARE ILLEGAL, MAN...
ギロ
UH-OH! THIS CONCLUDES THE EMERGENCY NEWS FLASH.
HEH, HEH, HEH. YOU'RE A MAN OF YOUR REPUTATION.
!
IT SEEMS LIKE YOU'VE MADE QUITE A MESS AROUND MANY OTHER CAMPUSES.
I GOT SOME CALLS FROM THEM, AS WELL.
HEH, JUS' HAD TO TAKE CARE A' SOME BUSINESS.
AT ANY RATE, WHAT DO YOU WANT, DUDE?

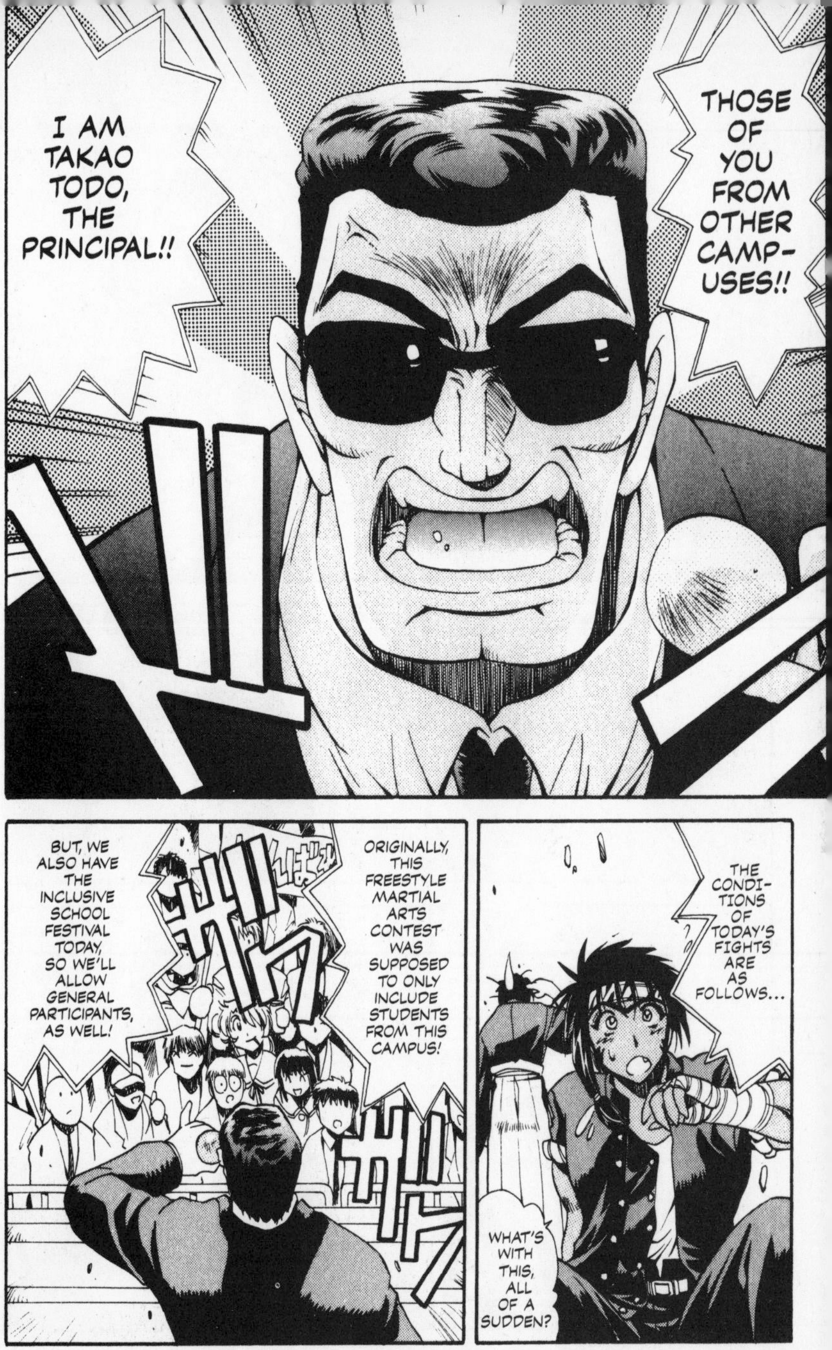
THOSE OF YOU FROM OTHER CAMP-USES!!
I AM TAKAO TODO, THE PRINCIPAL!!
THE CONDI-TIONS OF TODAY'S FIGHTS ARE AS FOLLOWS...
WHAT'S WITH THIS, ALL OF A SUDDEN?
ORIGINALLY, THIS FREESTYLE MARTIAL ARTS CONTEST WAS SUPPOSED TO ONLY INCLUDE STUDENTS FROM THIS CAMPUS!
BUT, WE ALSO HAVE THE INCLUSIVE SCHOOL FESTIVAL TODAY, SO WE'LL ALLOW GENERAL PARTICIPANTS, AS WELL!

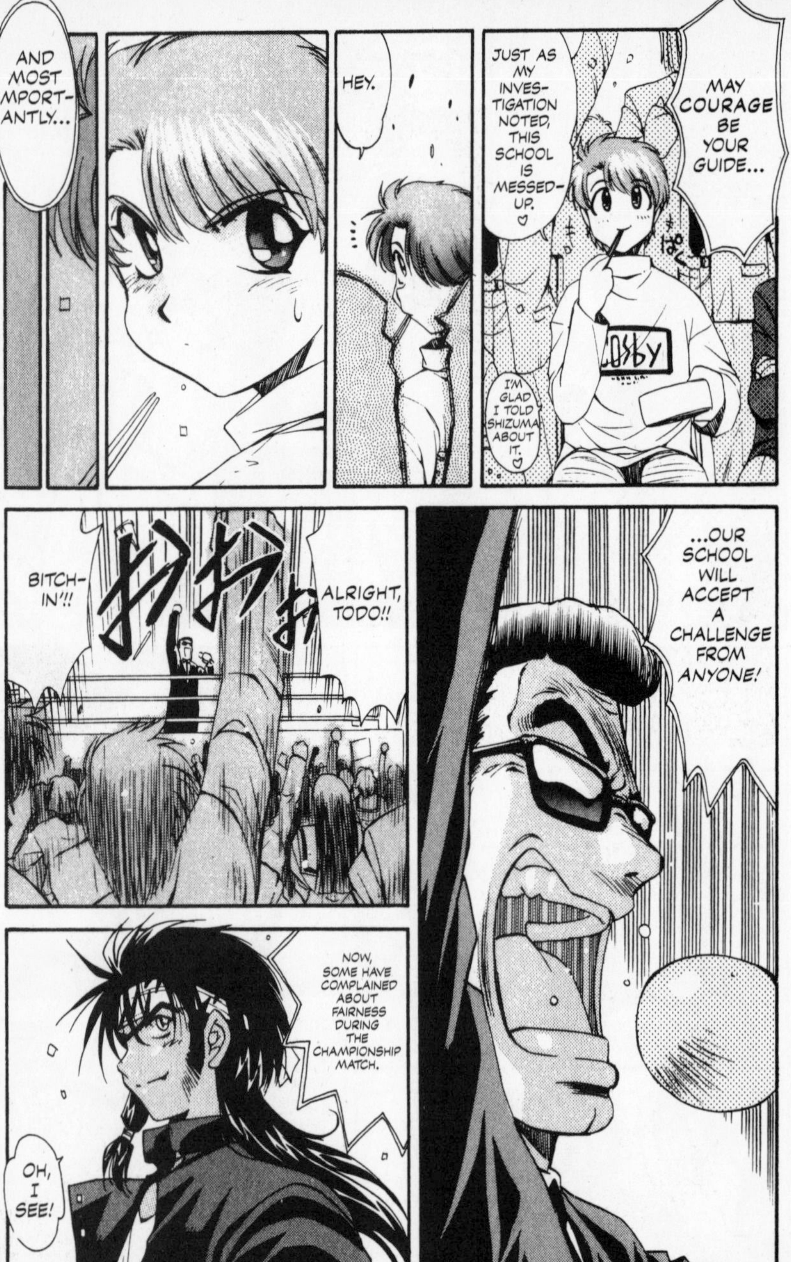
MAY COURAGE BE YOUR GUIDE...
JUST AS MY INVES-TIGATION NOTED, THIS SCHOOL IS MESSED-UP. ♡
I'M GLAD I TOLD SHIZUMA ABOUT IT. ♡
HEY.
AND MOST IMPORT-ANTLY...
...OUR SCHOOL WILL ACCEPT A CHALLENGE FROM ANYONE!
ALRIGHT, TODO!!
おおぉ
BITCH-IN'!!
NOW, SOME HAVE COMPLAINED ABOUT FAIRNESS DURING THE CHAMPIONSHIP MATCH.
OH, I SEE!

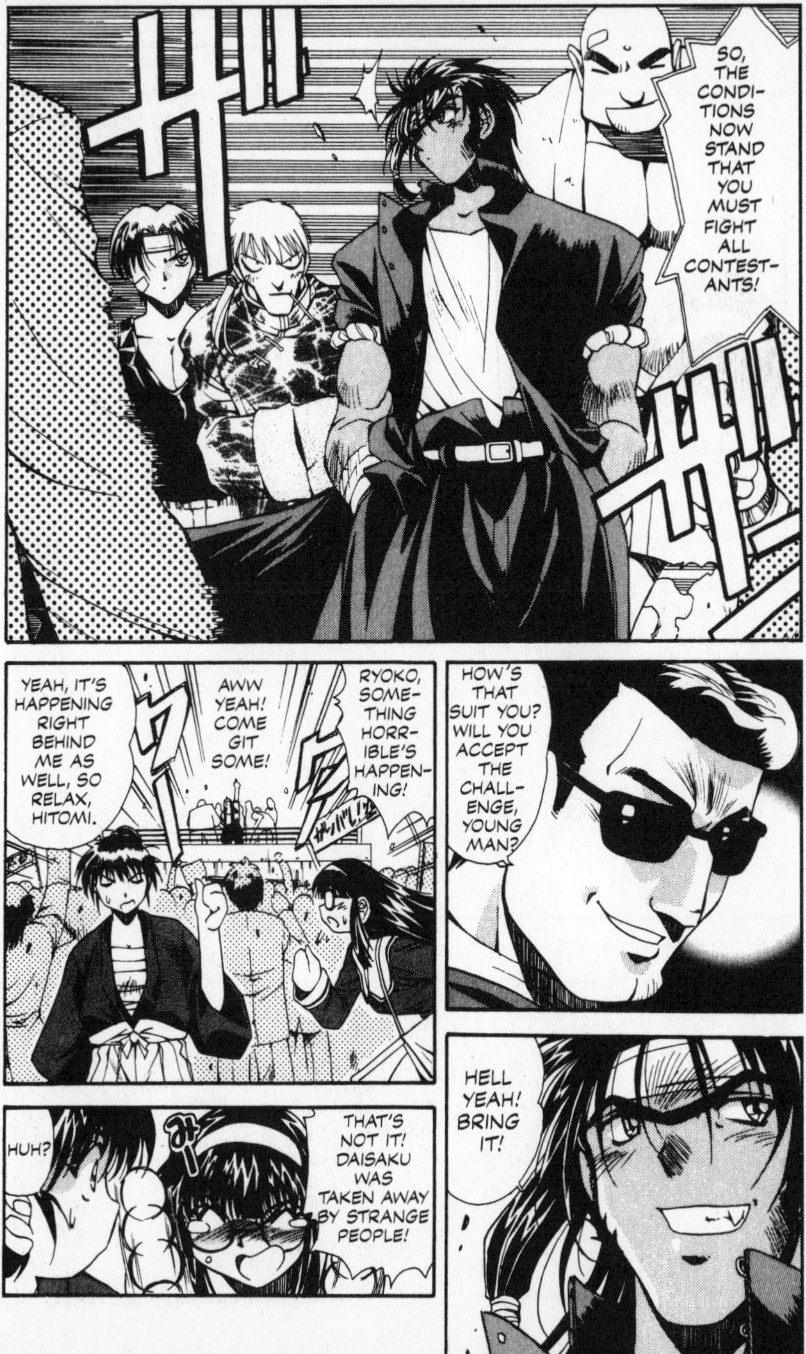
SO, THE CONDITIONS NOW STAND THAT YOU MUST FIGHT ALL CONTESTANTS!
HOW'S THAT SUIT YOU? WILL YOU ACCEPT THE CHALLENGE, YOUNG MAN?
RYOKO, SOMETHING HORRIBLE'S HAPPENING!
AWW YEAH! COME GIT SOME!
YEAH, IT'S HAPPENING RIGHT BEHIND ME AS WELL, SO RELAX, HITOMI.
HELL YEAH! BRING IT!
THAT'S NOT IT! DAISAKU WAS TAKEN AWAY BY STRANGE PEOPLE!
HUH?

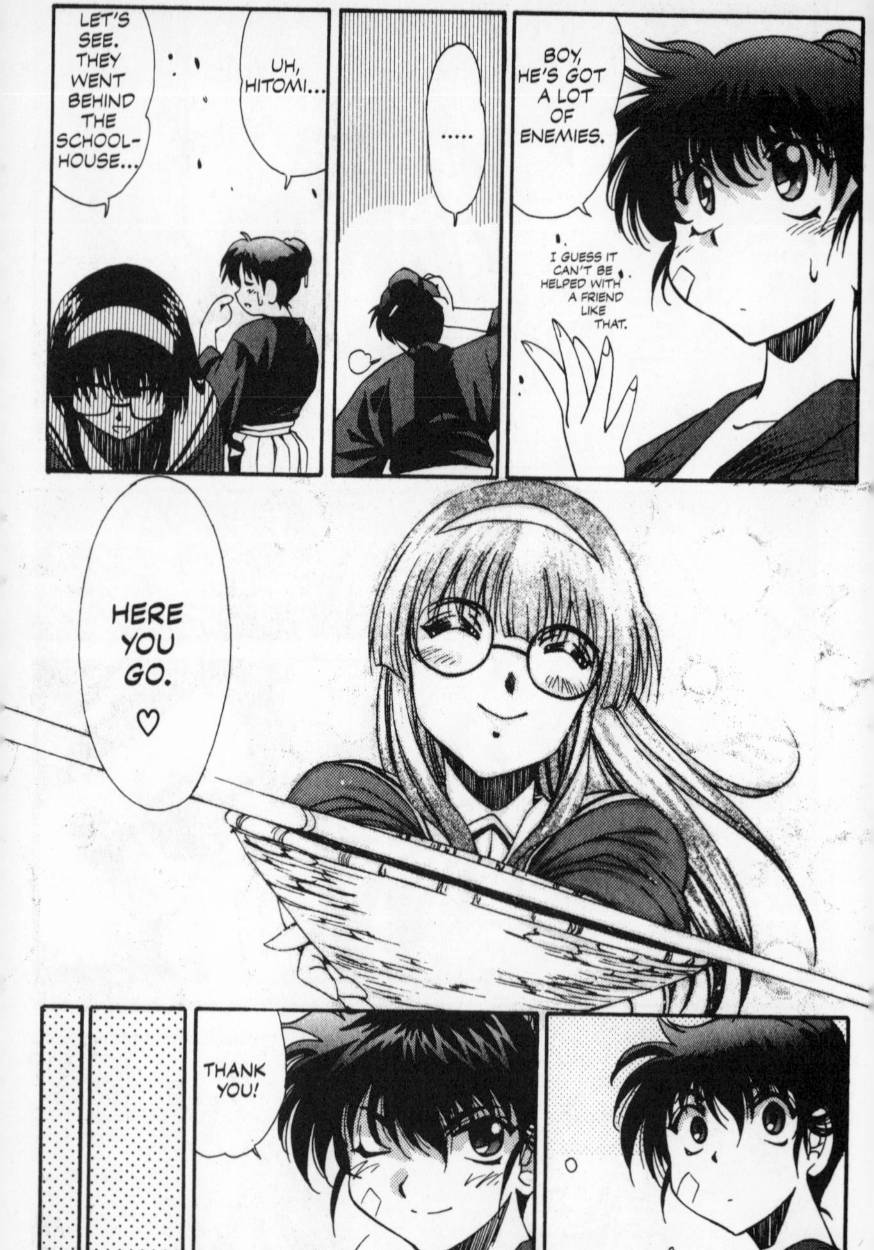
BOY, HE'S GOT A LOT OF ENEMIES.
I GUESS IT CAN'T BE HELPED WITH A FRIEND LIKE THAT.
.....
UH, HITOMI...
LET'S SEE. THEY WENT BEHIND THE SCHOOL-HOUSE...
HERE YOU GO. ♡
THANK YOU!

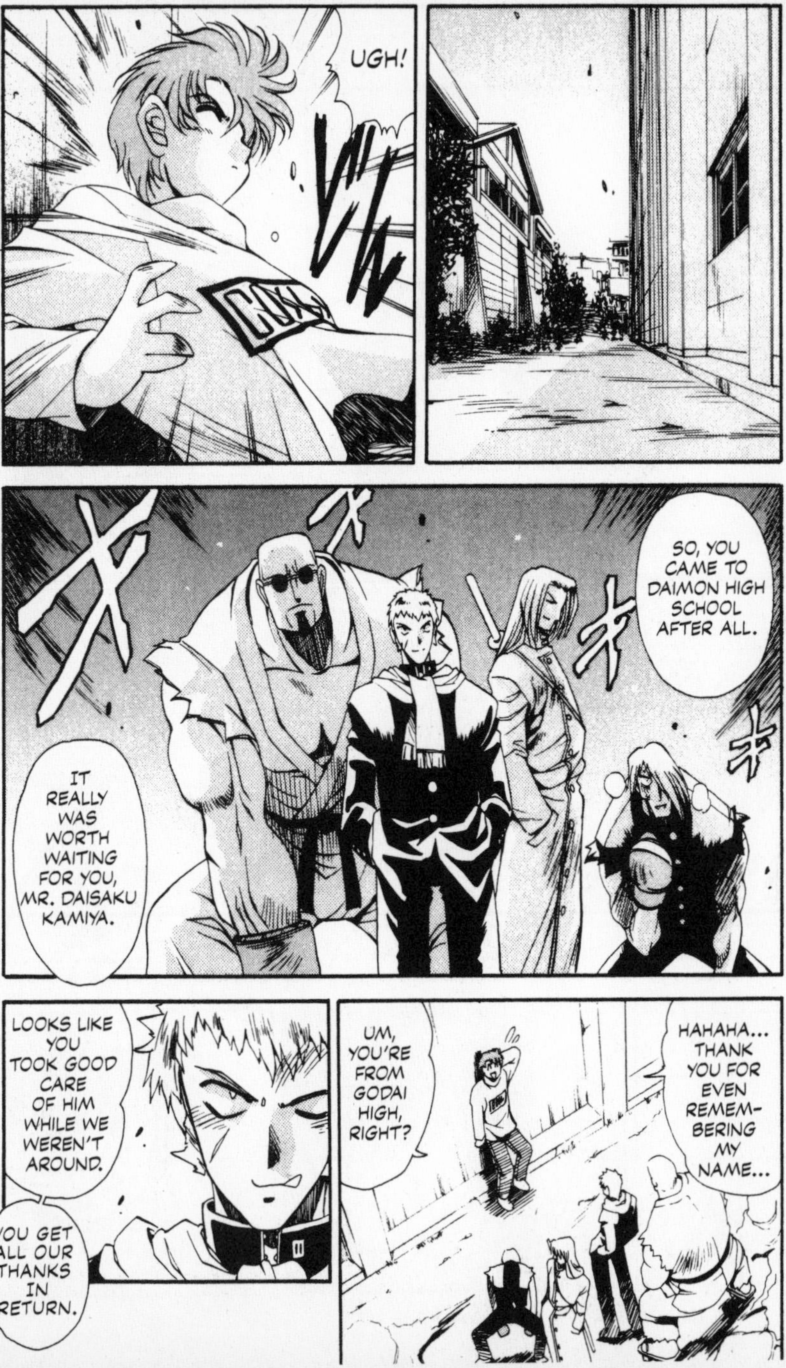
UGH!
SO, YOU CAME TO DAIMON HIGH SCHOOL AFTER ALL.
IT REALLY WAS WORTH WAITING FOR YOU, MR. DAISAKU KAMIYA.
HAHAHA... THANK YOU FOR EVEN REMEM-BERING MY NAME...
UM, YOU'RE FROM GODAI HIGH, RIGHT?
LOOKS LIKE YOU TOOK GOOD CARE OF HIM WHILE WE WEREN'T AROUND.
YOU GET ALL OUR THANKS IN RETURN.

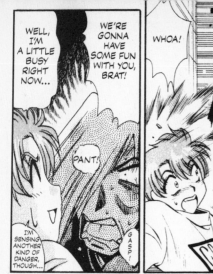

AW, THIS IS IRRITATING, DAMN IT!
WHOA!
WE'RE GONNA HAVE SOME FUN WITH YOU, BRAT!
WELL, I'M A LITTLE BUSY RIGHT NOW...
PANT!
GASP!
I'M SENSING ANOTHER KIND OF DANGER, THOUGH...
YOUR PLANS HAVE ALL BEEN CAN-CELED!
AAAAAA! OW! OW! SOMEBODY HELP MEEE!
HEH HEH HEH, KUSA-NAGI...
HEH, IT LOOKS LIKE WE HAVE A VISITOR.
WHAT?! IS IT KUSA-NAGI?!

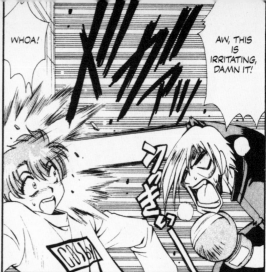

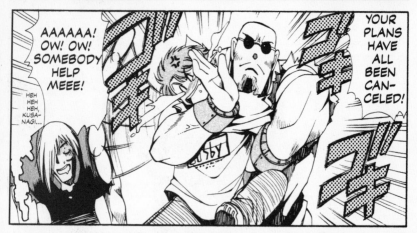

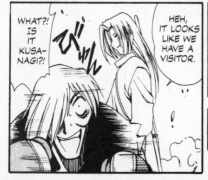

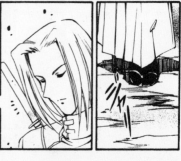

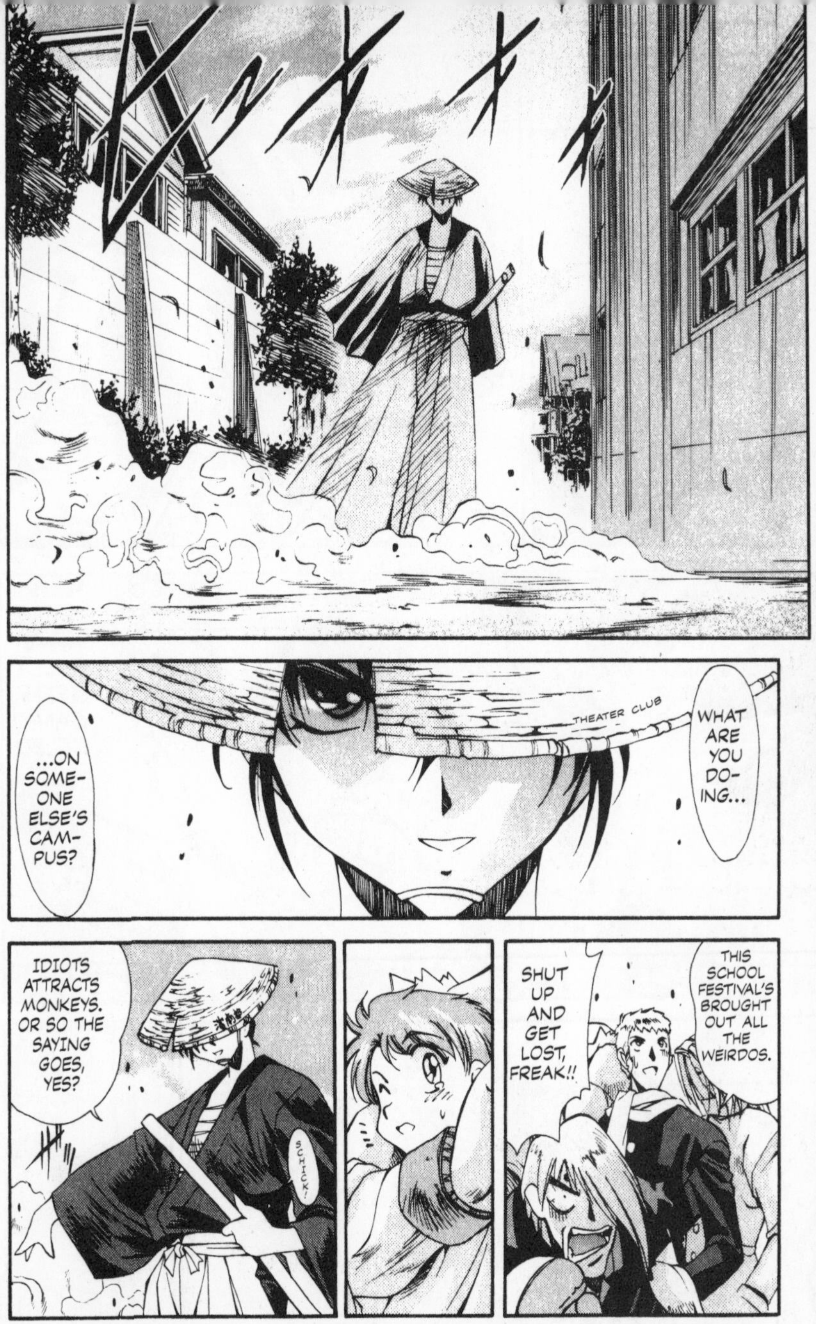
WHAT ARE YOU DOING...
THEATER CLUB
...ON SOMEONE ELSE'S CAMPUS?
THIS SCHOOL FESTIVAL'S BROUGHT OUT ALL THE WEIRDOS.
SHUT UP AND GET LOST, FREAK!!
IDIOTS ATTRACTS MONKEYS. OR SO THE SAYING GOES, YES?
SCHICK!

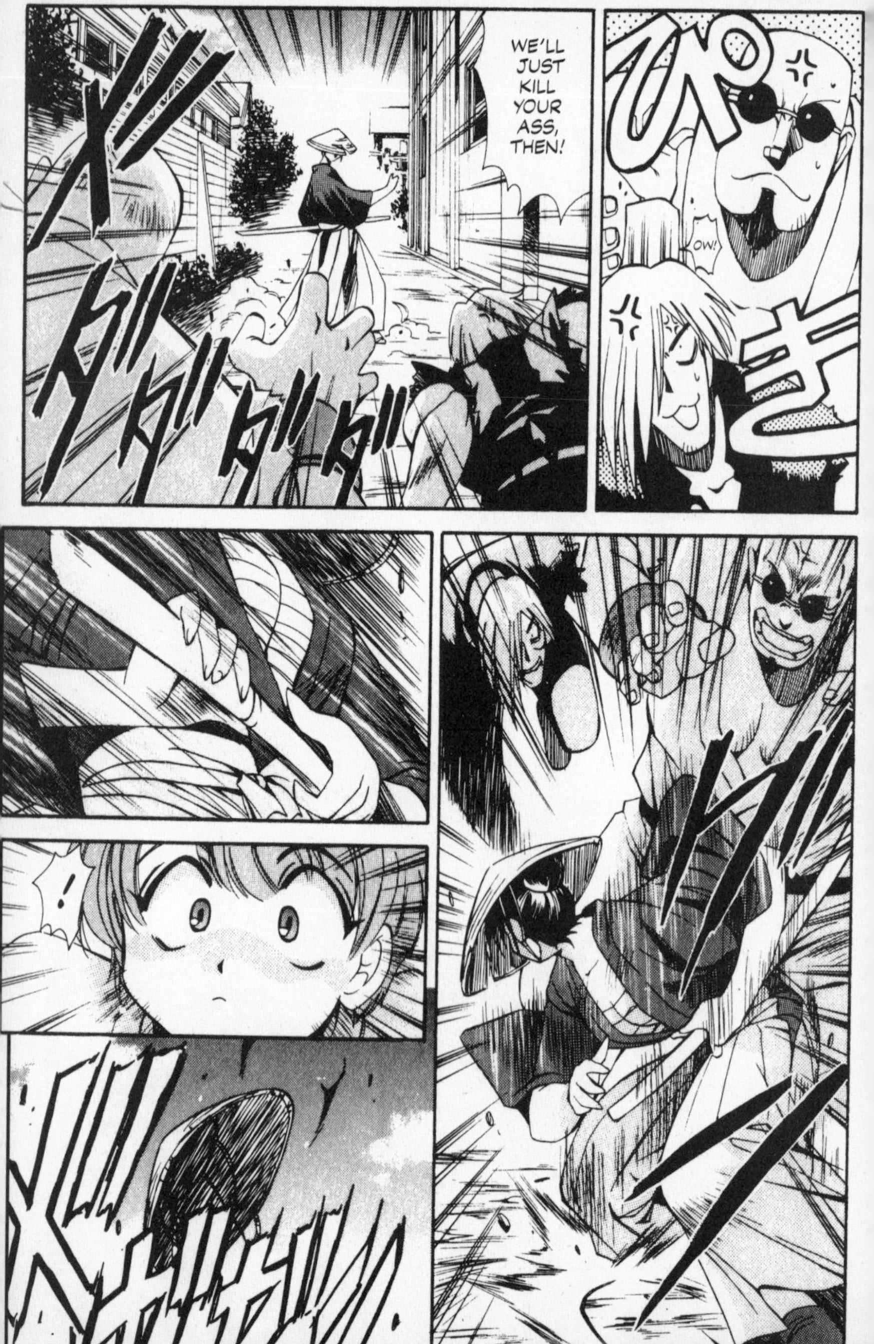
OW!
WE'LL JUST KILL YOUR ASS, THEN!
!

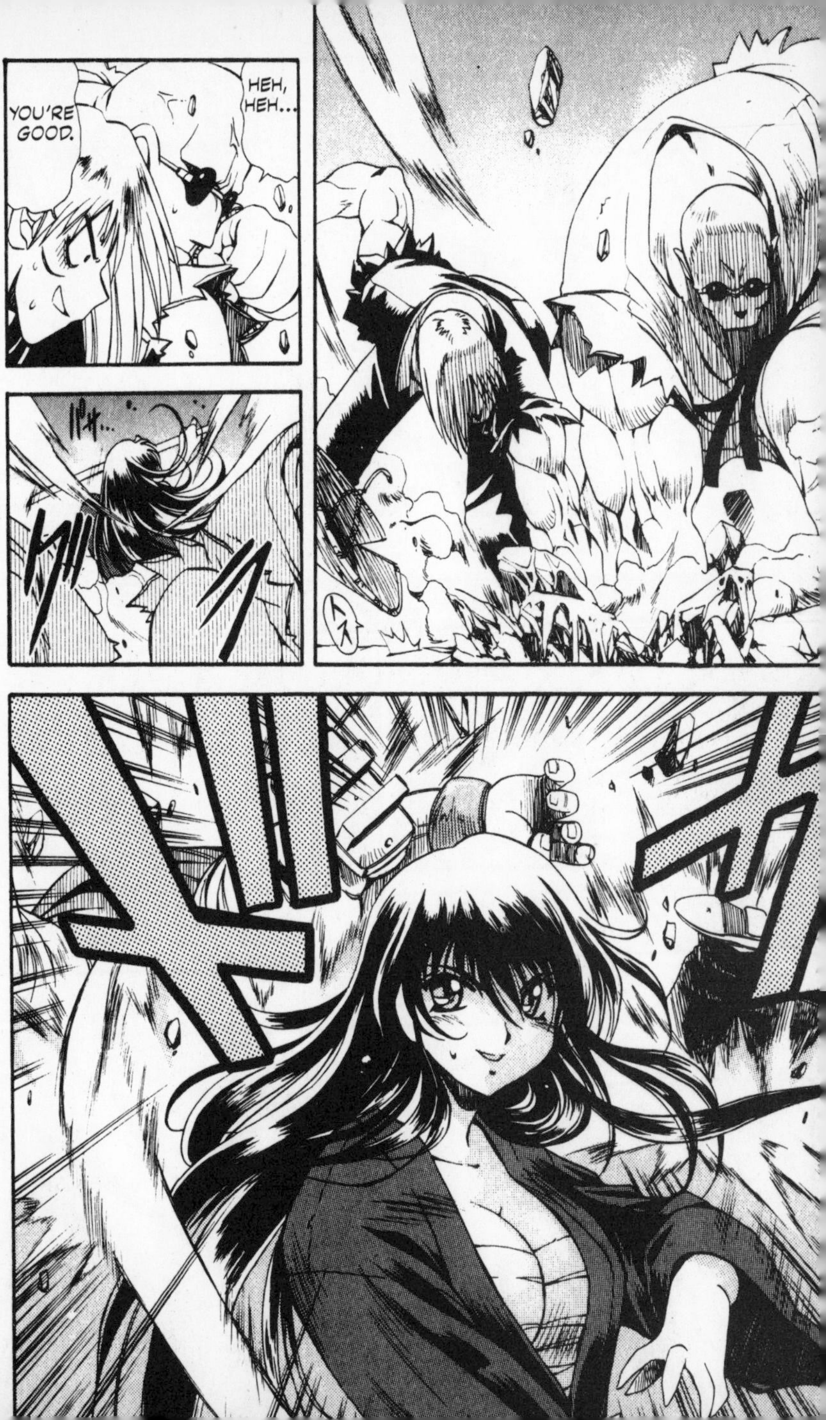
HEH, HEH...
YOU'RE GOOD.

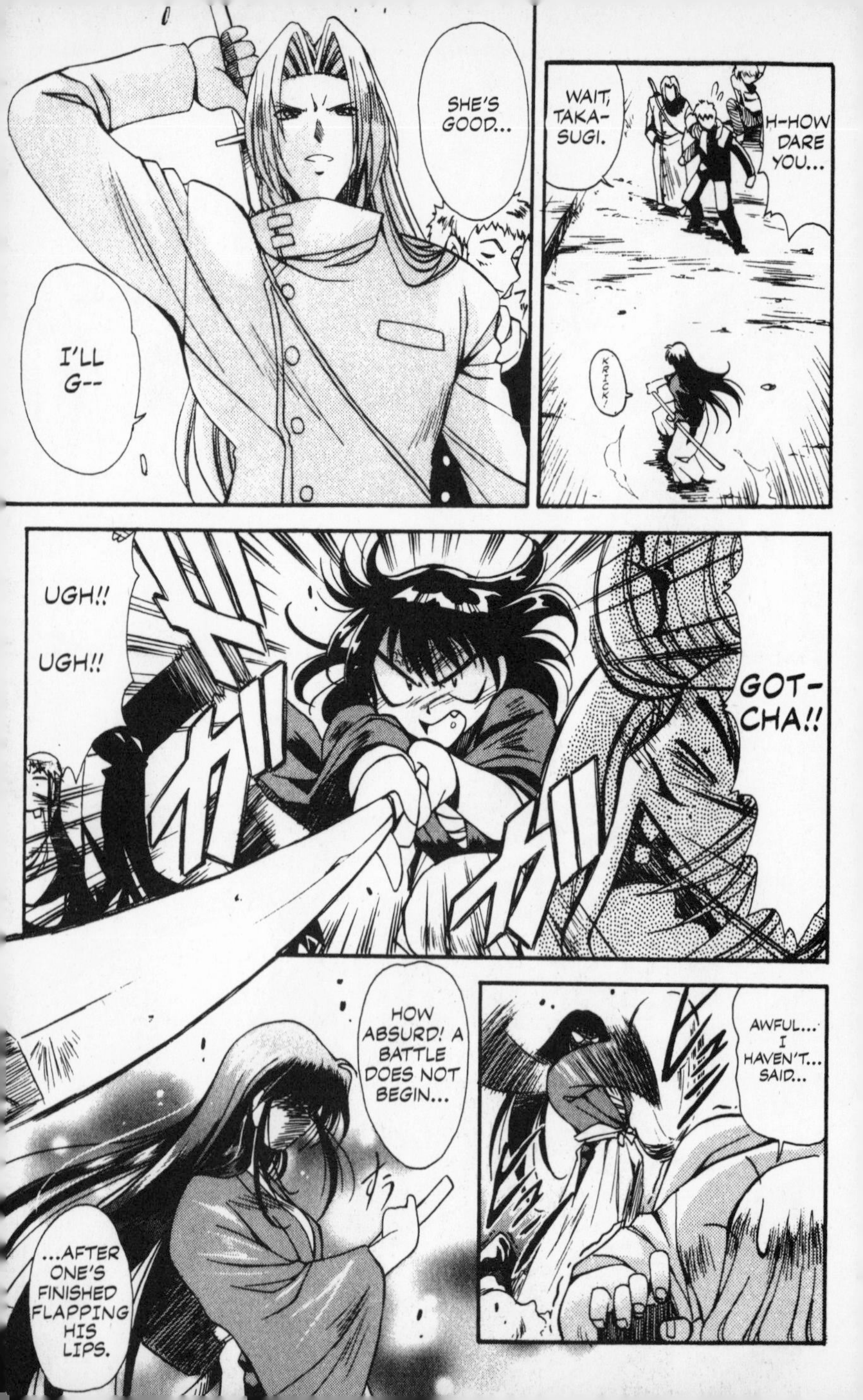
H-HOW DARE YOU...
WAIT, TAKA-SUGI.
KRICK!
SHE'S GOOD...
I'LL G--
GOT-CHA!!
UGH!!
UGH!!
AWFUL... I HAVEN'T... SAID...
HOW ABSURD! A BATTLE DOES NOT BEGIN...
...AFTER ONE'S FINISHED FLAPPING HIS LIPS.

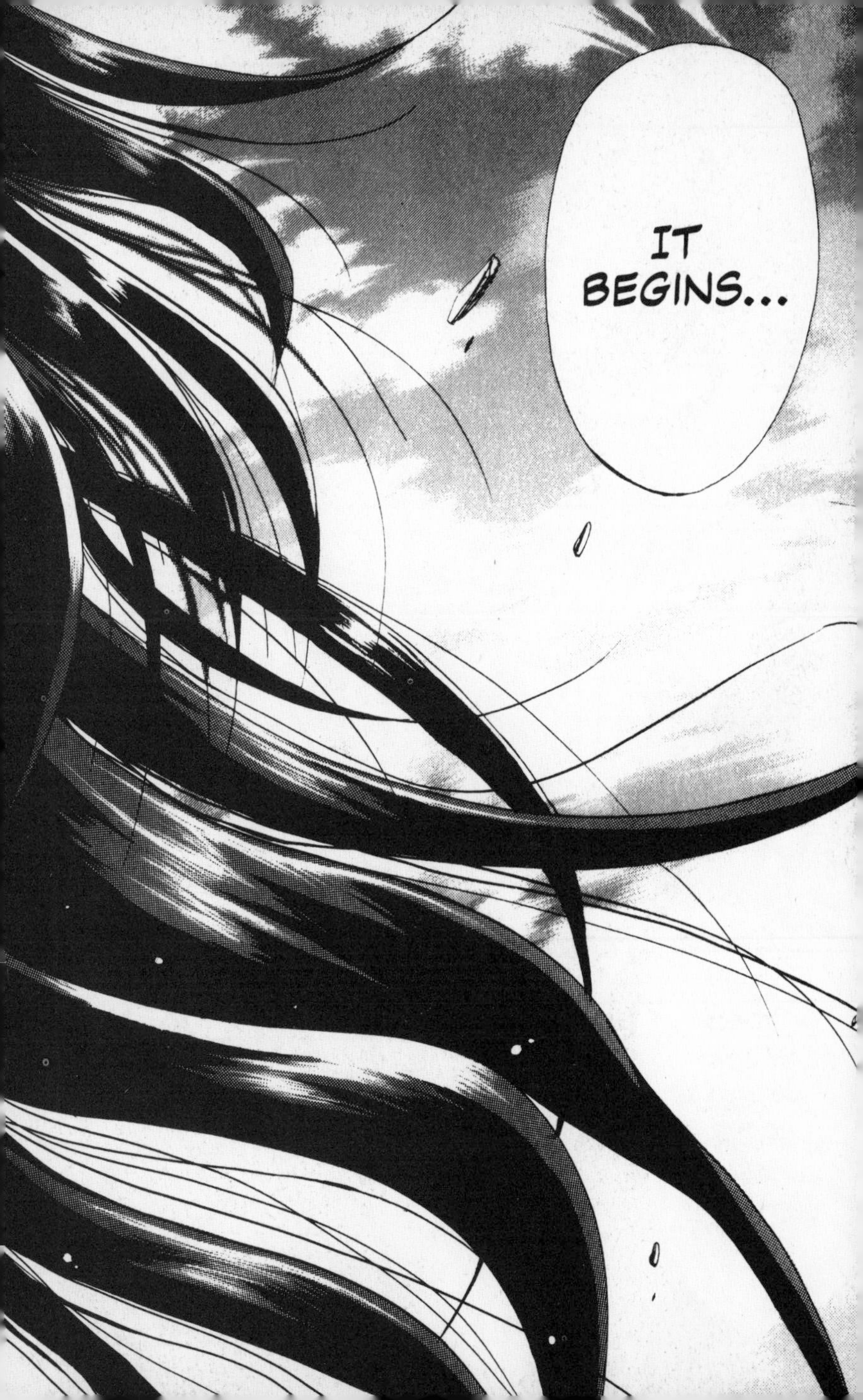
IT BEGINS...

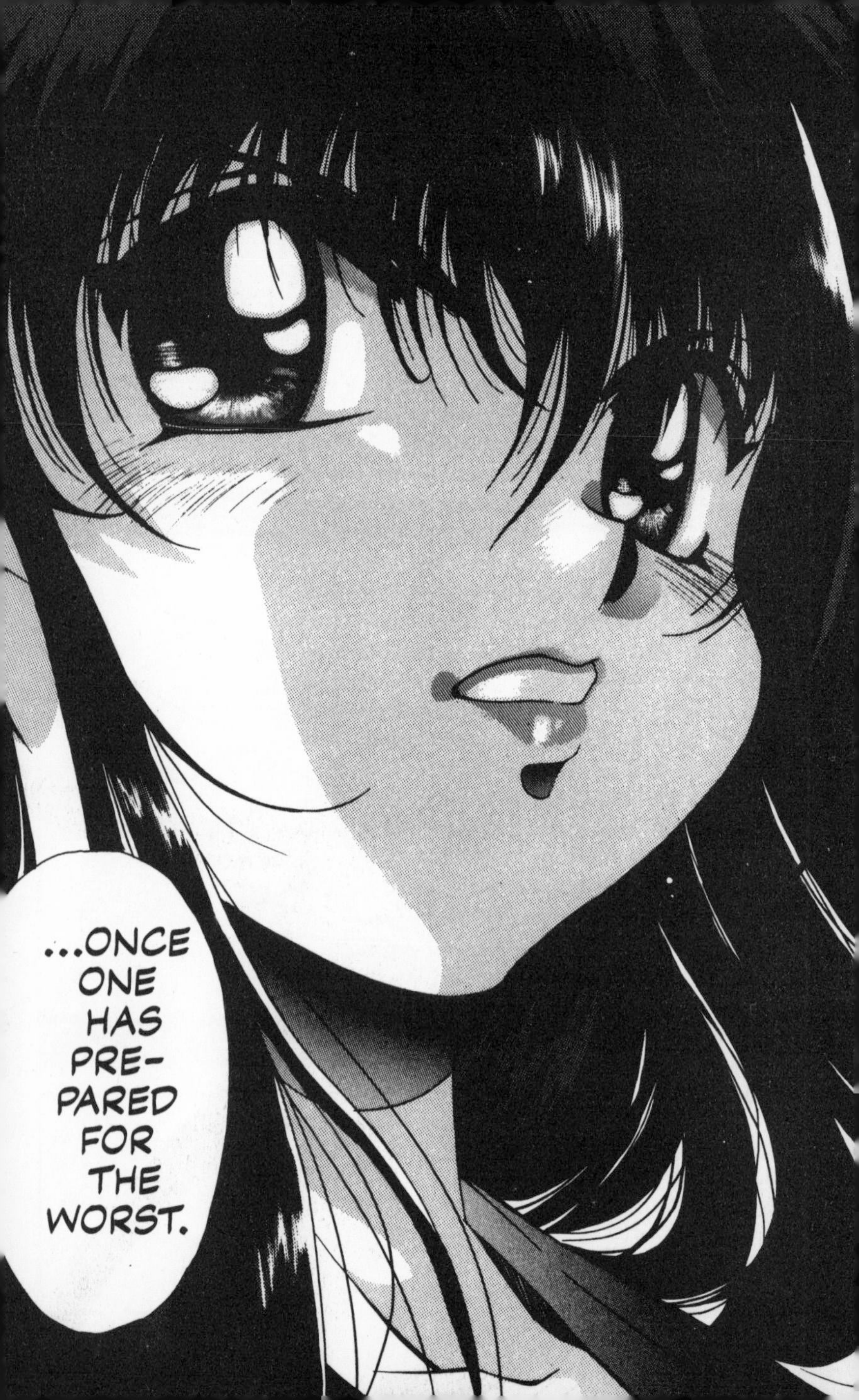
...ONCE ONE HAS PRE-PARED FOR THE WORST.

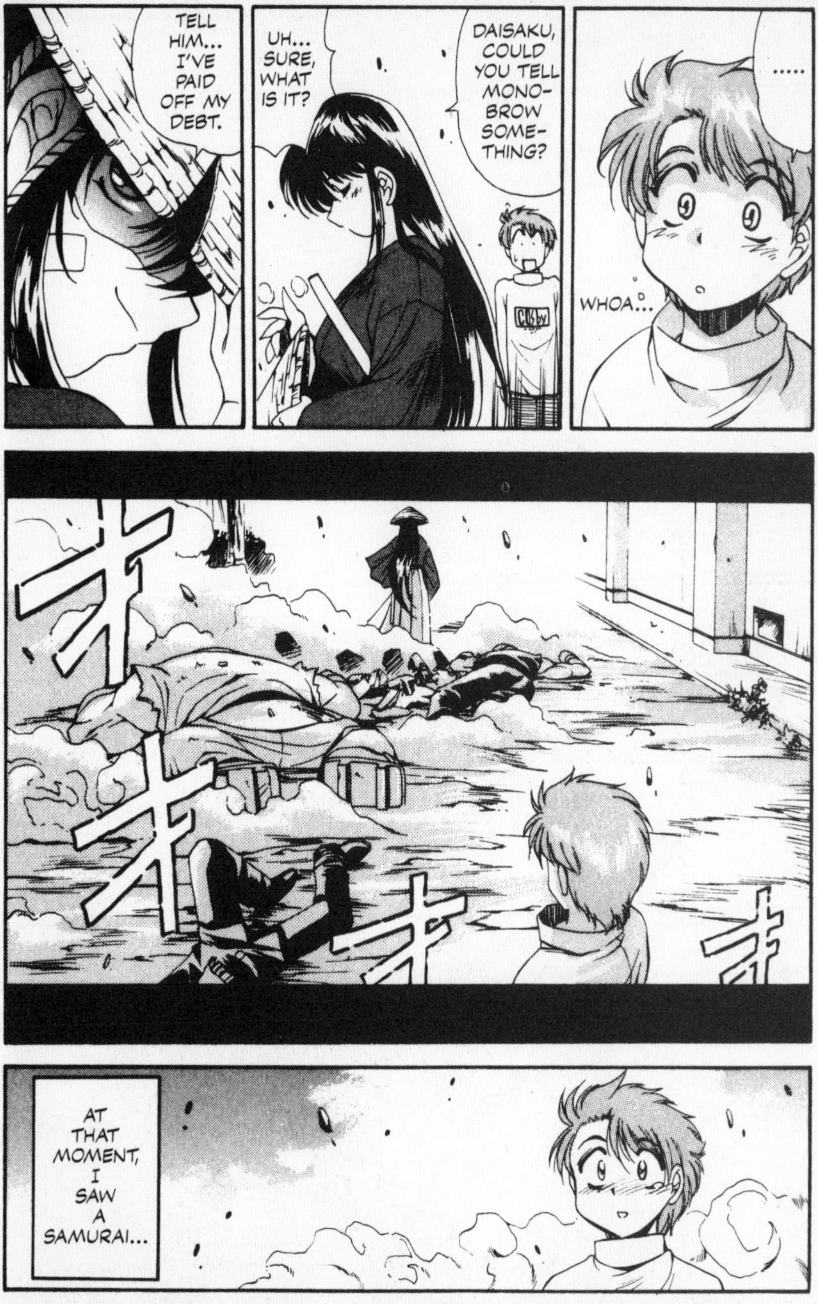
.....
WHOA...
DAISAKU, COULD YOU TELL MONO-BROW SOMETHING?
UH... SURE, WHAT IS IT?
TELL HIM... I'VE PAID OFF MY DEBT.
AT THAT MOMENT, I SAW A SAMURAI...

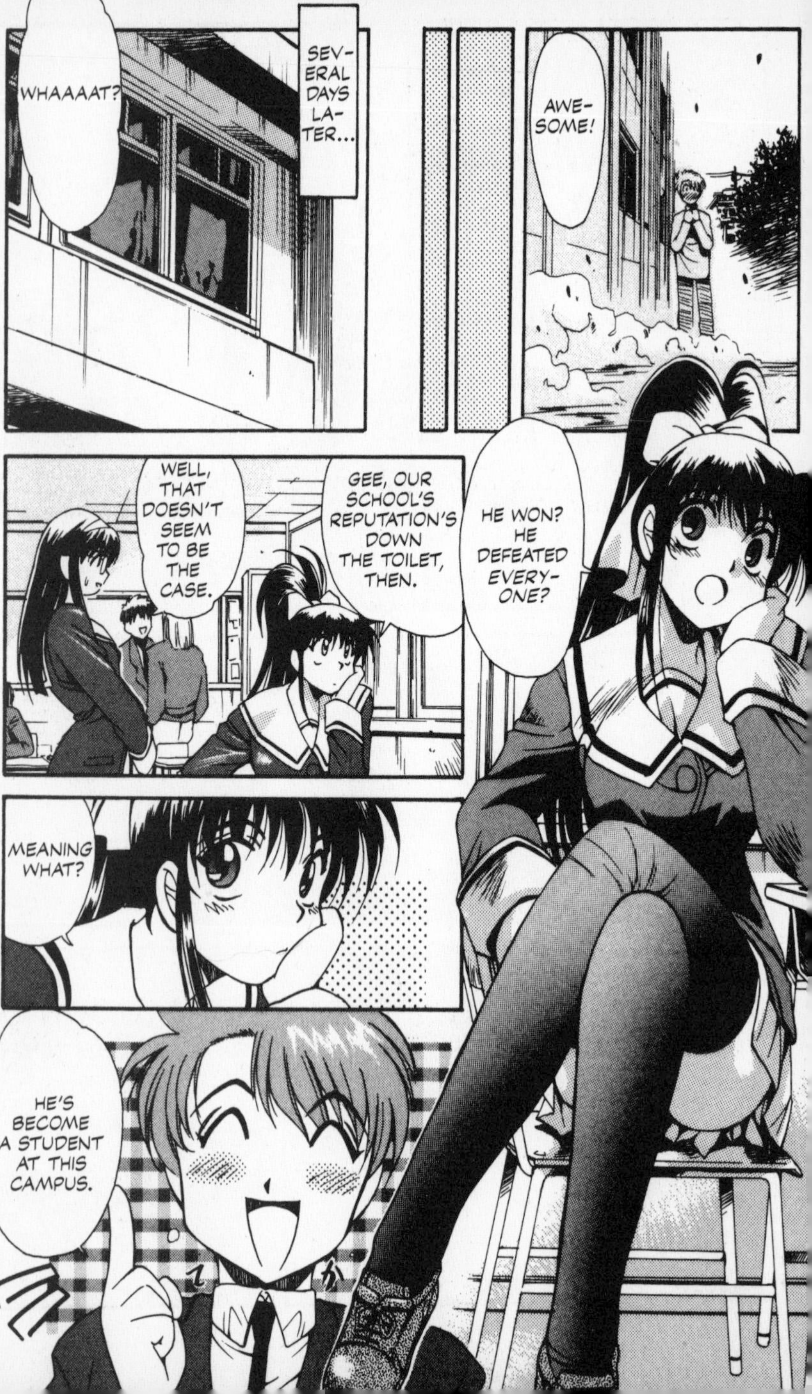
AWE-SOME!
SEV-ERAL DAYS LA-TER...
WHAAAAT?
HE WON? HE DEFEATED EVERY-ONE?
GEE, OUR SCHOOL'S REPUTATION'S DOWN THE TOILET, THEN.
WELL, THAT DOESN'T SEEM TO BE THE CASE.
MEANING WHAT?
HE'S BECOME A STUDENT AT THIS CAMPUS.

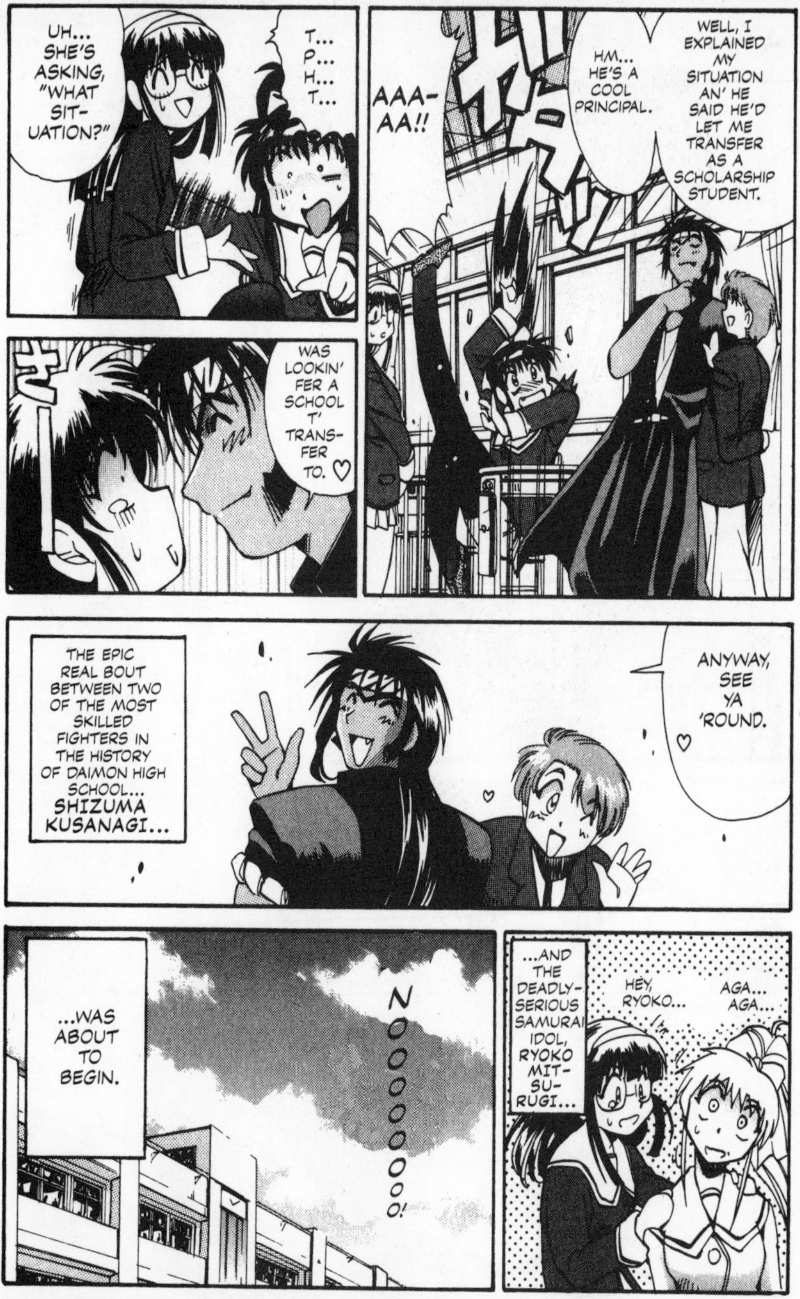
WELL, I EXPLAINED MY SITUATION AN' HE SAID HE'D LET ME TRANSFER AS A SCHOLARSHIP STUDENT.
HM... HE'S A COOL PRINCIPAL.
AAA-AA!!
T... P... H... T...
UH... SHE'S ASKING, "WHAT SIT-UATION?"
WAS LOOKIN' FER A SCHOOL T' TRANS-FER TO. ♡
ANYWAY, SEE YA 'ROUND. ♡
THE EPIC REAL BOUT BETWEEN TWO OF THE MOST SKILLED FIGHTERS IN THE HISTORY OF DAIMON HIGH SCHOOL... **SHIZUMA KUSANAGI...**
AGA... AGA...
HEY, RYOKO...
...AND THE DEADLY-SERIOUS SAMURAI IDOL, RYOKO MIT-SU-RUGI...
NOOOOOOOOOO!
...WAS ABOUT TO BEGIN.

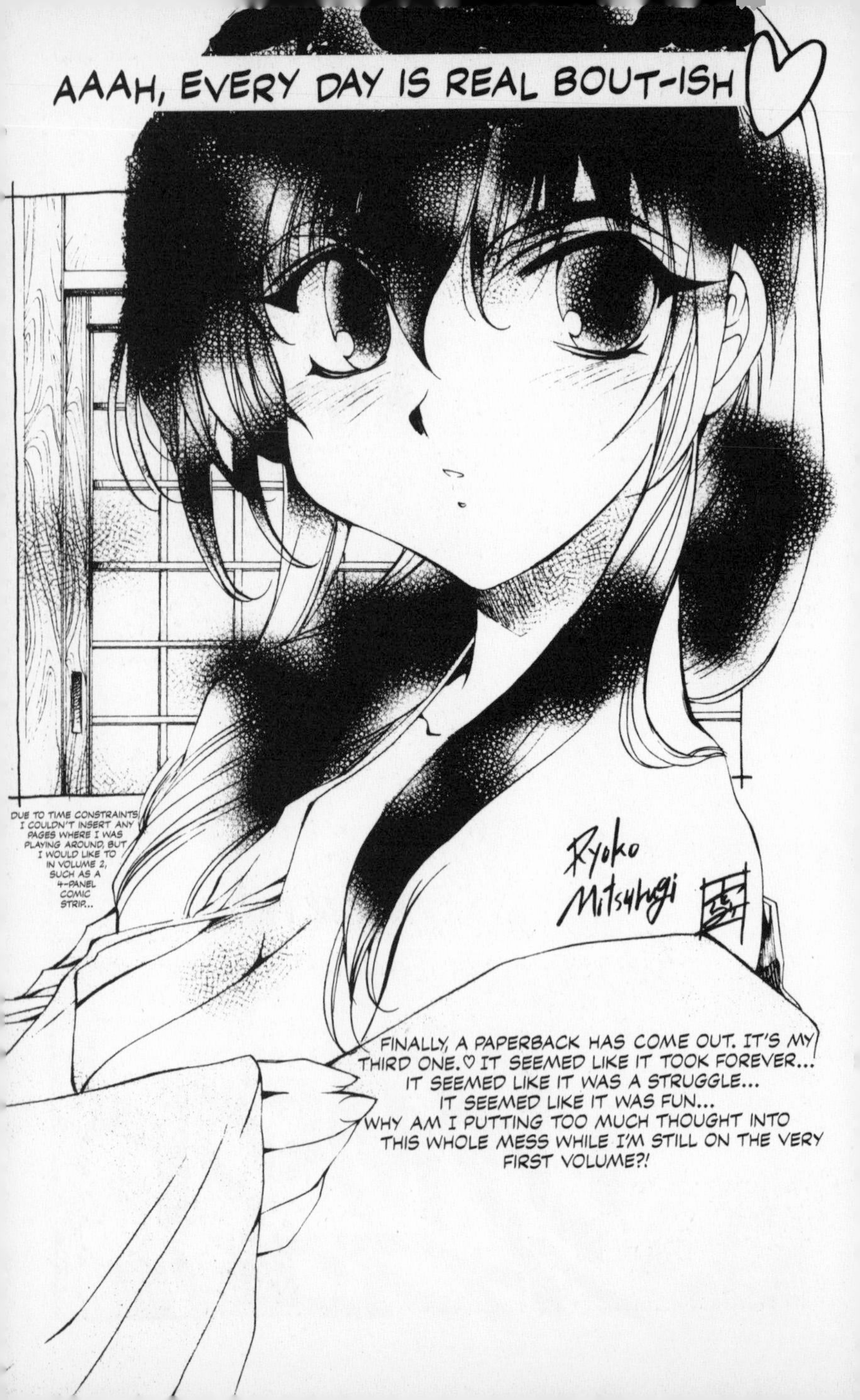
AAAH, EVERY DAY IS REAL BOUT-ISH ♡
FINALLY, A PAPERBACK HAS COME OUT. IT'S MY THIRD ONE.♡ IT SEEMED LIKE IT TOOK FOREVER... IT SEEMED LIKE IT WAS A STRUGGLE... IT SEEMED LIKE IT WAS FUN... WHY AM I PUTTING TOO MUCH THOUGHT INTO THIS WHOLE MESS WHILE I'M STILL ON THE VERY FIRST VOLUME?!
DUE TO TIME CONSTRAINTS, I COULDN'T INSERT ANY PAGES WHERE I WAS PLAYING AROUND, BUT I WOULD LIKE TO IN VOLUME 2, SUCH AS A 4-PANEL COMIC STRIP...
Ryoko Mitsurugi

REAL BOUT HIGHSCHOOL

リアルバウトハイスクール

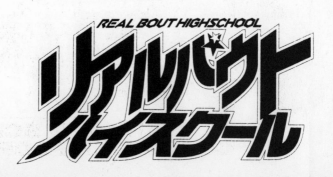

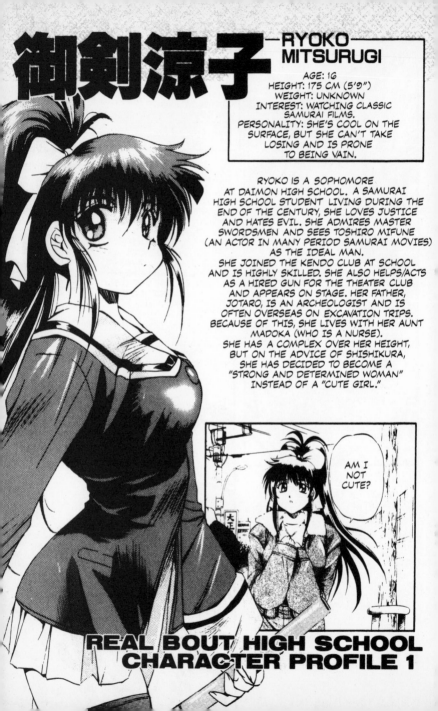

御剣涼子 RYOKO MITSURUGI

AGE: 16
HEIGHT: 175 CM (5'9")
WEIGHT: UNKNOWN
INTEREST: WATCHING CLASSIC SAMURAI FILMS.
PERSONALITY: SHE'S COOL ON THE SURFACE, BUT SHE CAN'T TAKE LOSING AND IS PRONE TO BEING VAIN.

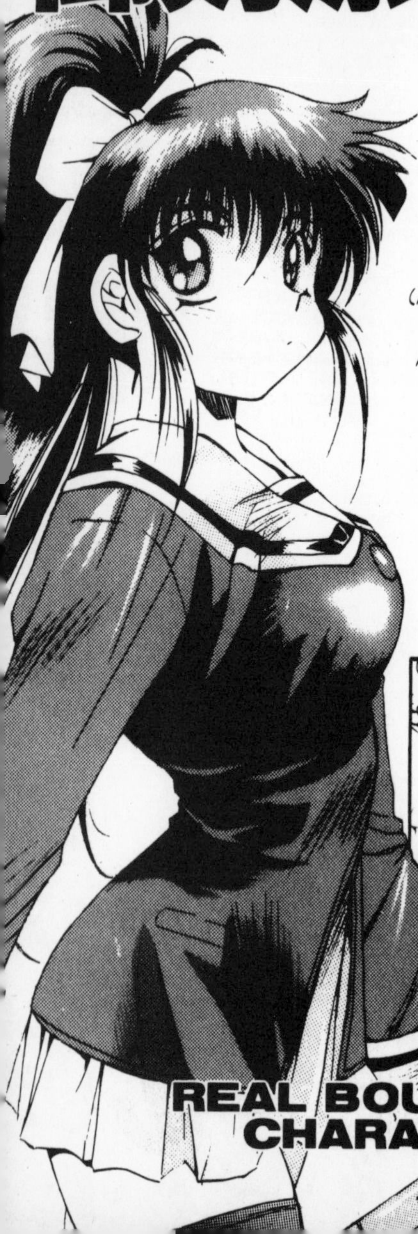

RYOKO IS A SOPHOMORE AT DAIMON HIGH SCHOOL. A SAMURAI HIGH SCHOOL STUDENT LIVING DURING THE END OF THE CENTURY, SHE LOVES JUSTICE AND HATES EVIL. SHE ADMIRES MASTER SWORDSMEN AND SEES TOSHIRO MIFUNE (AN ACTOR IN MANY PERIOD SAMURAI MOVIES) AS THE IDEAL MAN.

SHE JOINED THE KENDO CLUB AT SCHOOL AND IS HIGHLY SKILLED. SHE ALSO HELPS/ACTS AS A HIRED GUN FOR THE THEATER CLUB AND APPEARS ON STAGE. HER FATHER, JOTARO, IS AN ARCHEOLOGIST AND IS OFTEN OVERSEAS ON EXCAVATION TRIPS. BECAUSE OF THIS, SHE LIVES WITH HER AUNT MADOKA (WHO IS A NURSE).

SHE HAS A COMPLEX OVER HER HEIGHT, BUT ON THE ADVICE OF SHISHIKURA, SHE HAS DECIDED TO BECOME A "STRONG AND DETERMINED WOMAN" INSTEAD OF A "CUTE GIRL."

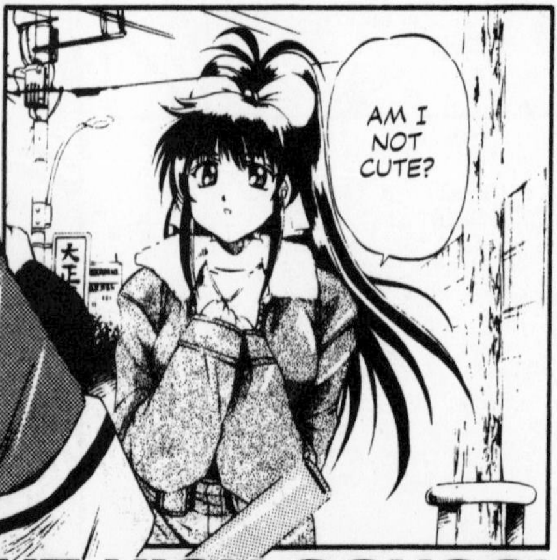
AM I NOT CUTE?

REAL BOUT HIGH SCHOOL CHARACTER PROFILE 1

草薙静馬

SHIZUMA KUSANAGI

AGE:16
HEIGHT: 184 CM (6' 0.5")
WEIGHT: 72KG (158 POUNDS)
INTERESTS: BAND, MOTORCYCLING
PERSONALITY: VERY RUDE AND QUESTIONS AUTHORITY. GETS CARRIED AWAY.

SHIZUMA IS A RUFFIAN WHO CAME FROM WESTERN JAPAN. HE FORCEFULLY ENTERED THE FREE-STYLE MARTIAL ARTS TOURNAMENT DURING THE SCHOOL FESTIVAL AND WON EASILY. AS HIS PRIZE, HE IS ALLOWED TO TRANSFER TO DAIMON HIGH SCHOOL AS A SCHOLARSHIP STUDENT. THERE APPEAR TO BE SECRETS BEHIND HIS STRENGTH...

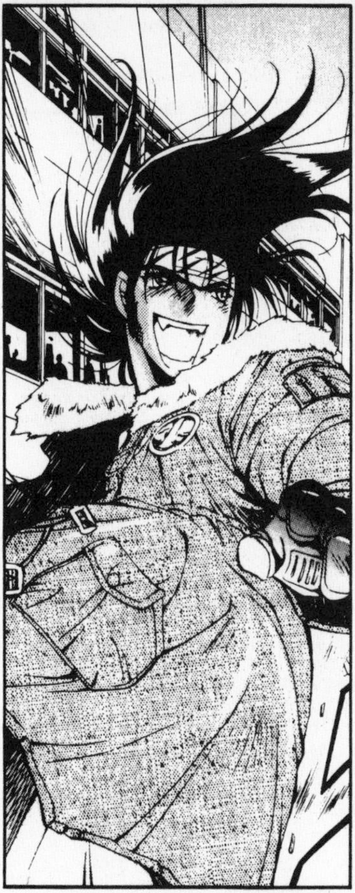

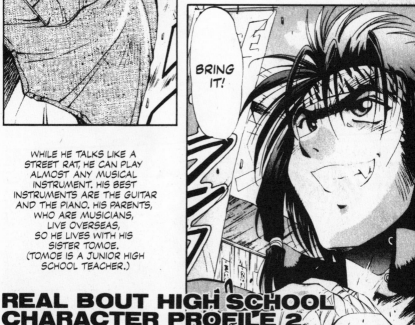

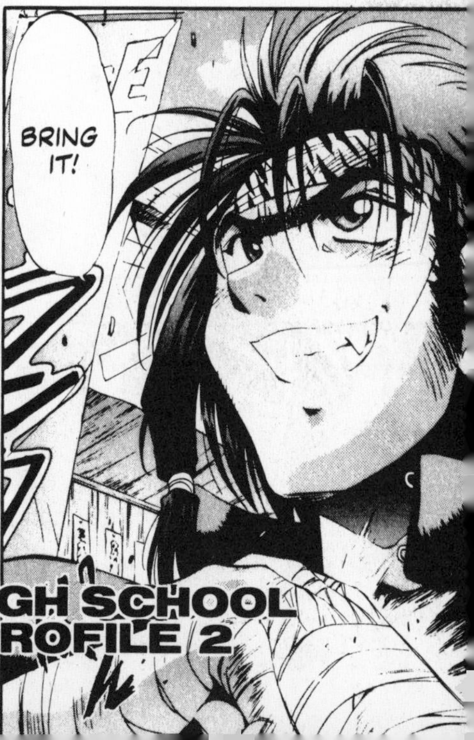
BRING IT!

WHILE HE TALKS LIKE A STREET RAT, HE CAN PLAY ALMOST ANY MUSICAL INSTRUMENT. HIS BEST INSTRUMENTS ARE THE GUITAR AND THE PIANO. HIS PARENTS, WHO ARE MUSICIANS, LIVE OVERSEAS, SO HE LIVES WITH HIS SISTER TOMOE. (TOMOE IS A JUNIOR HIGH SCHOOL TEACHER.)

REAL BOUT HIGH SCHOOL CHARACTER PROFILE 2

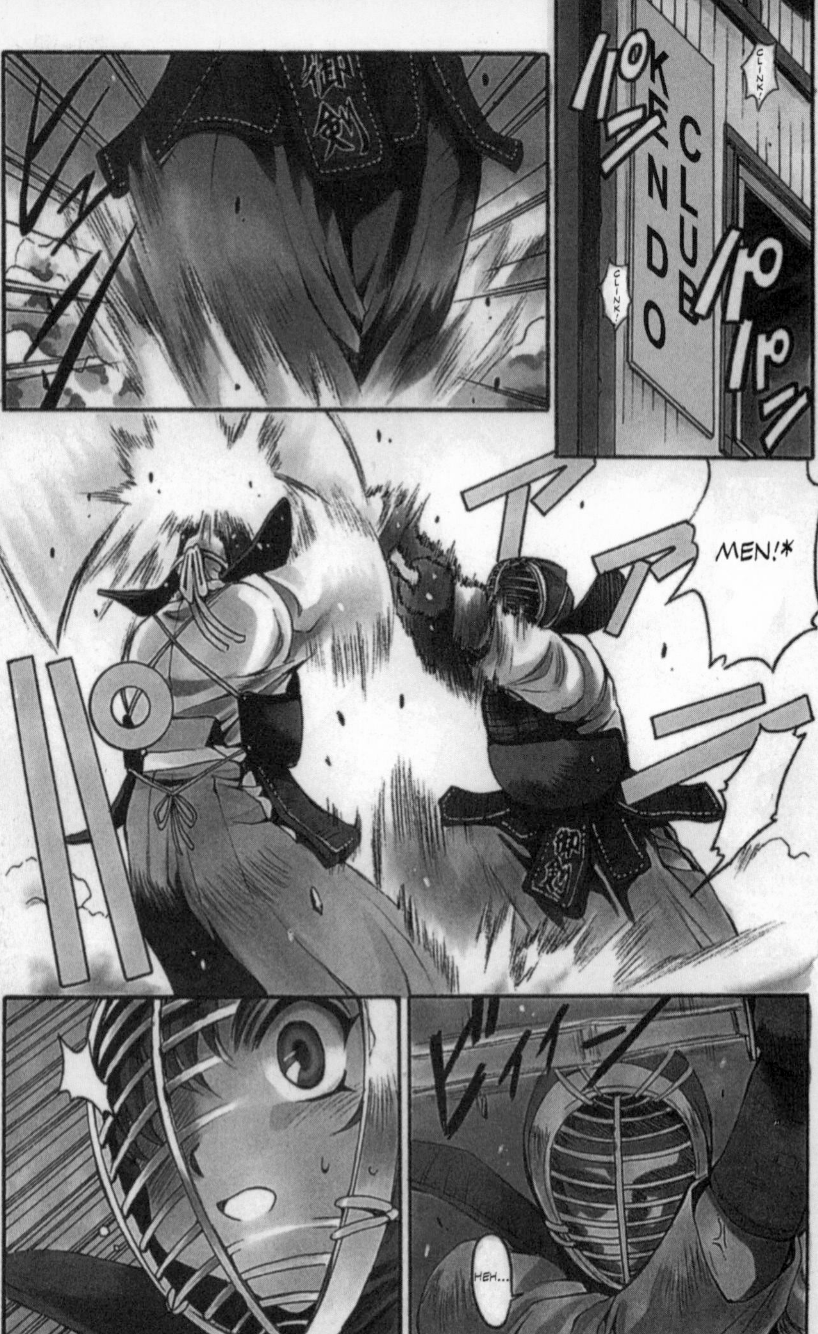
CLINK!
KENDO CLUB
CLINK!
MEN!*
HEH...

*MEN: A TRADITIONAL KENDO CRY FOR AN ATTACK TO THE HEAD.

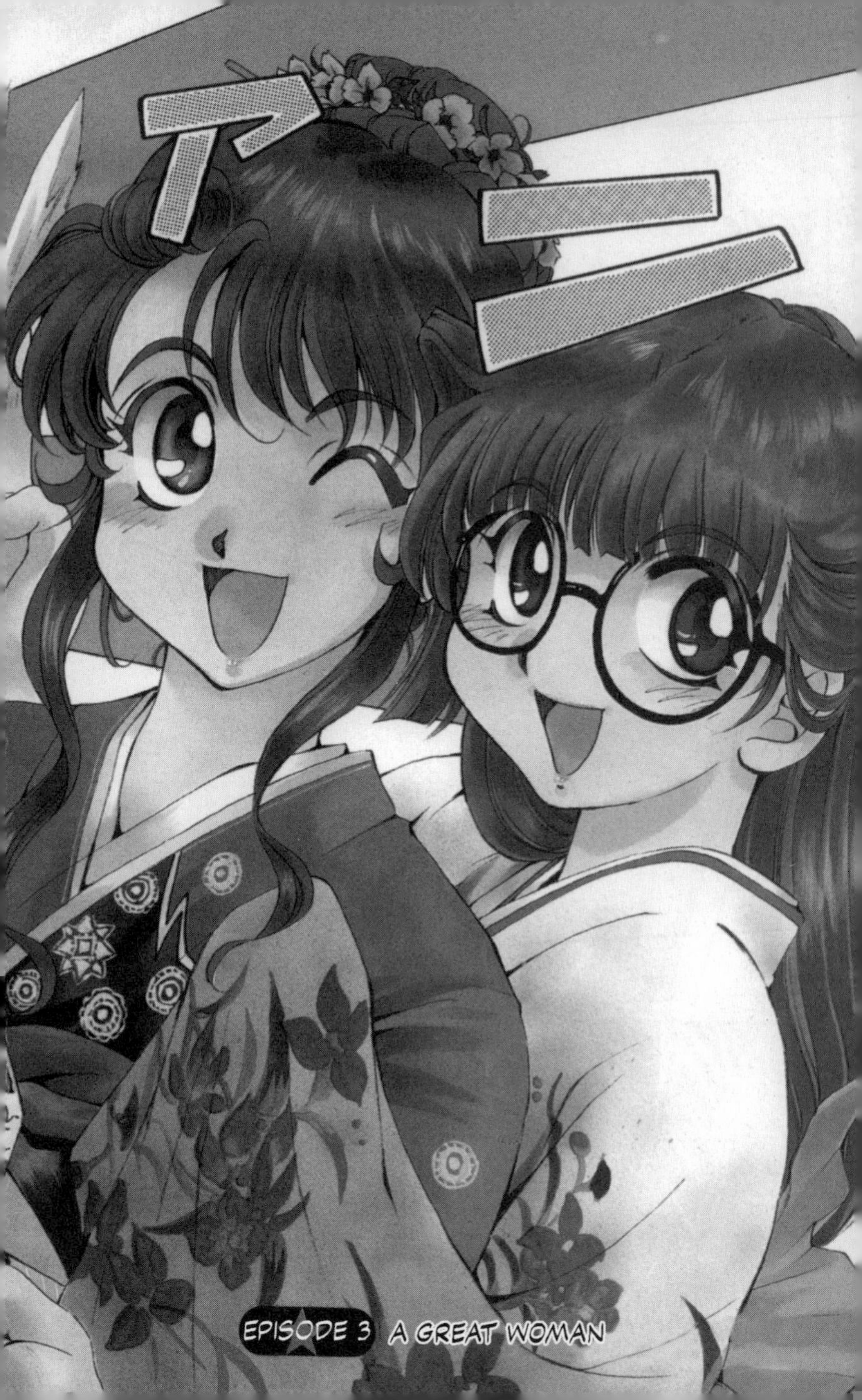
EPISODE 3 A GREAT WOMAN

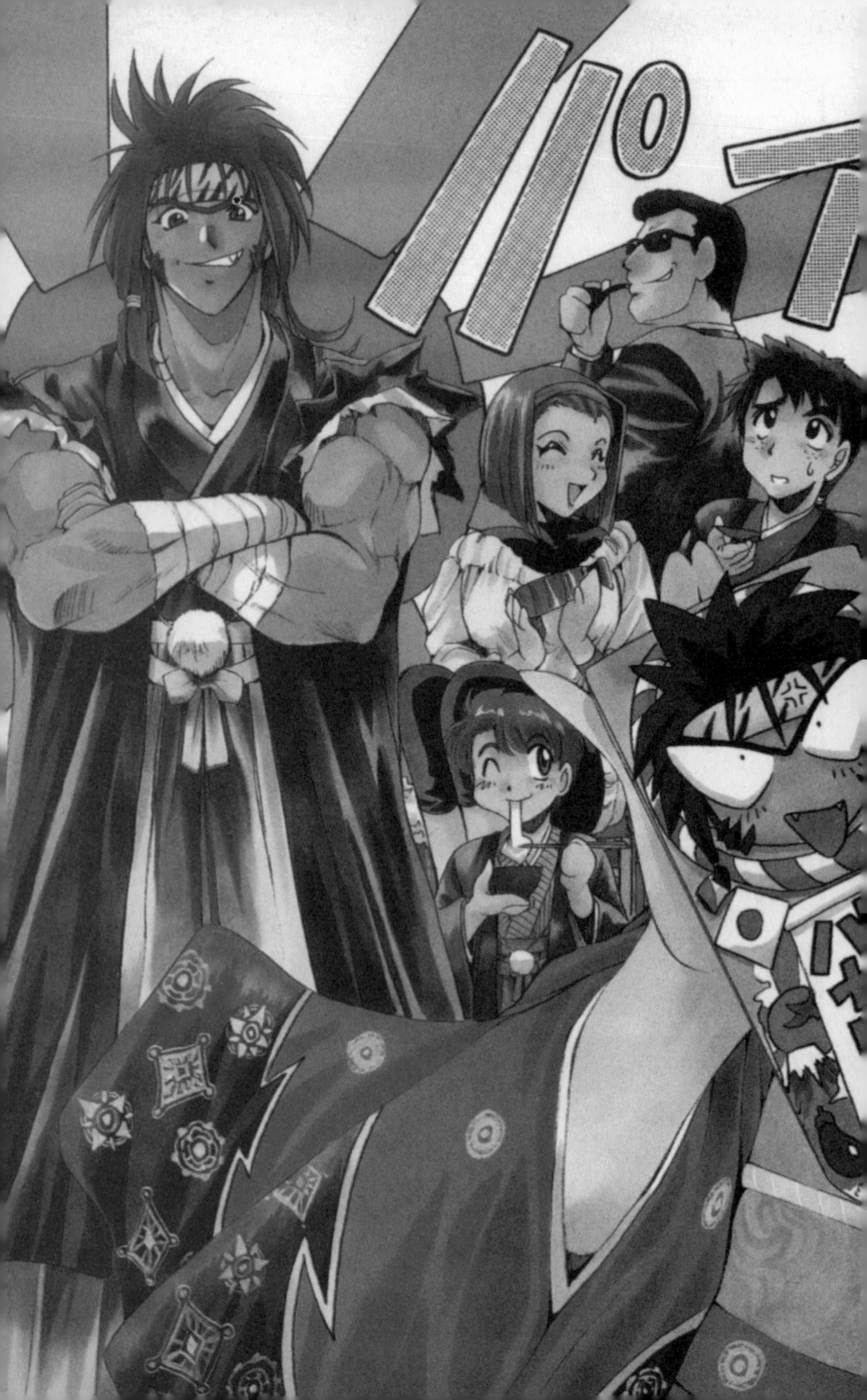
パー

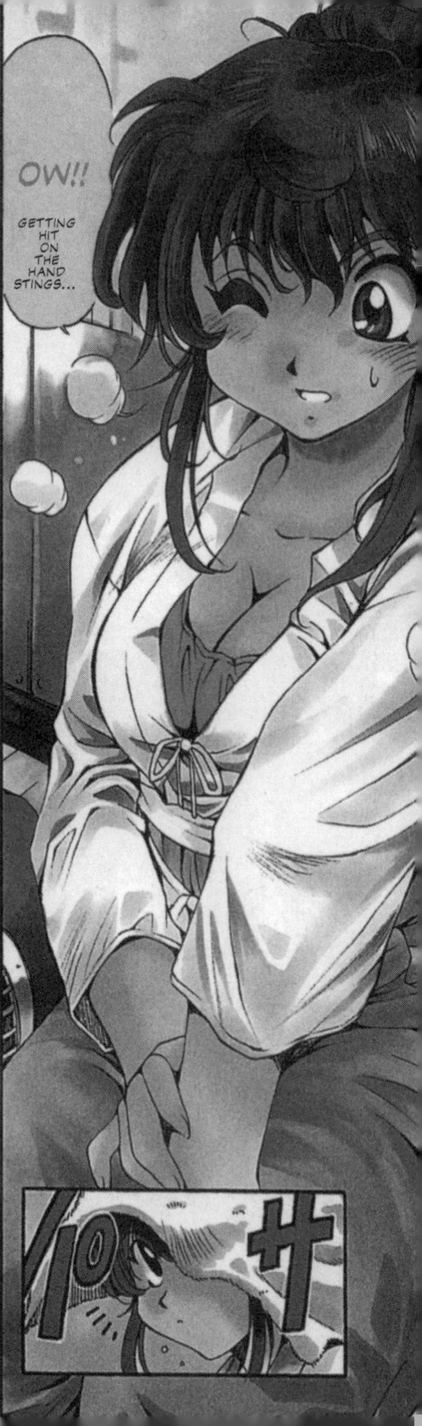
OW!!
GETTING HIT ON THE HAND STINGS...

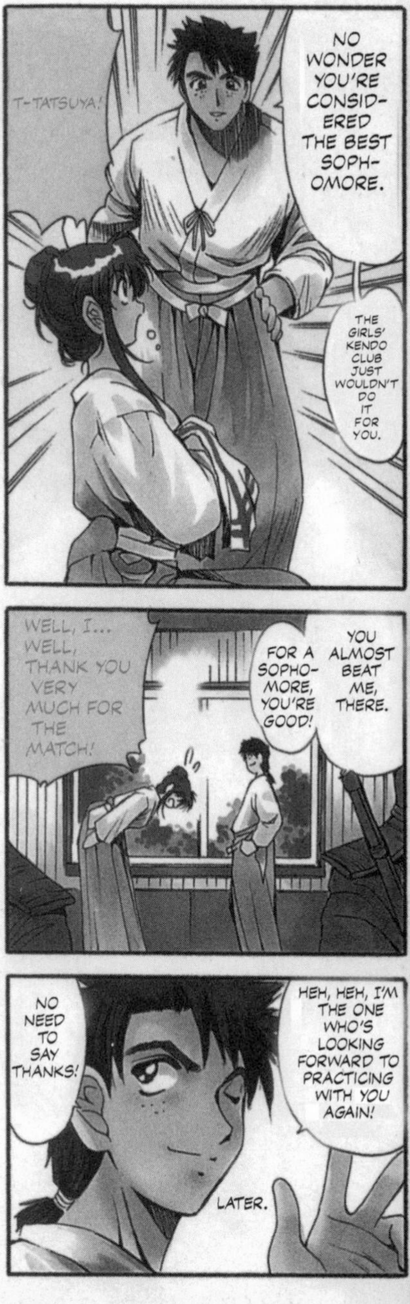
NO WONDER YOU'RE CONSID-ERED THE BEST SOPH-OMORE.
T-TATSUYA!
THE GIRLS' KENDO CLUB JUST WOULDN'T DO IT FOR YOU.
YOU ALMOST BEAT ME, THERE.
FOR A SOPHO-MORE, YOU'RE GOOD!
WELL, I... WELL, THANK YOU VERY MUCH FOR THE MATCH!
HEH, HEH, I'M THE ONE WHO'S LOOKING FORWARD TO PRACTICING WITH YOU AGAIN!
NO NEED TO SAY THANKS!
LATER.

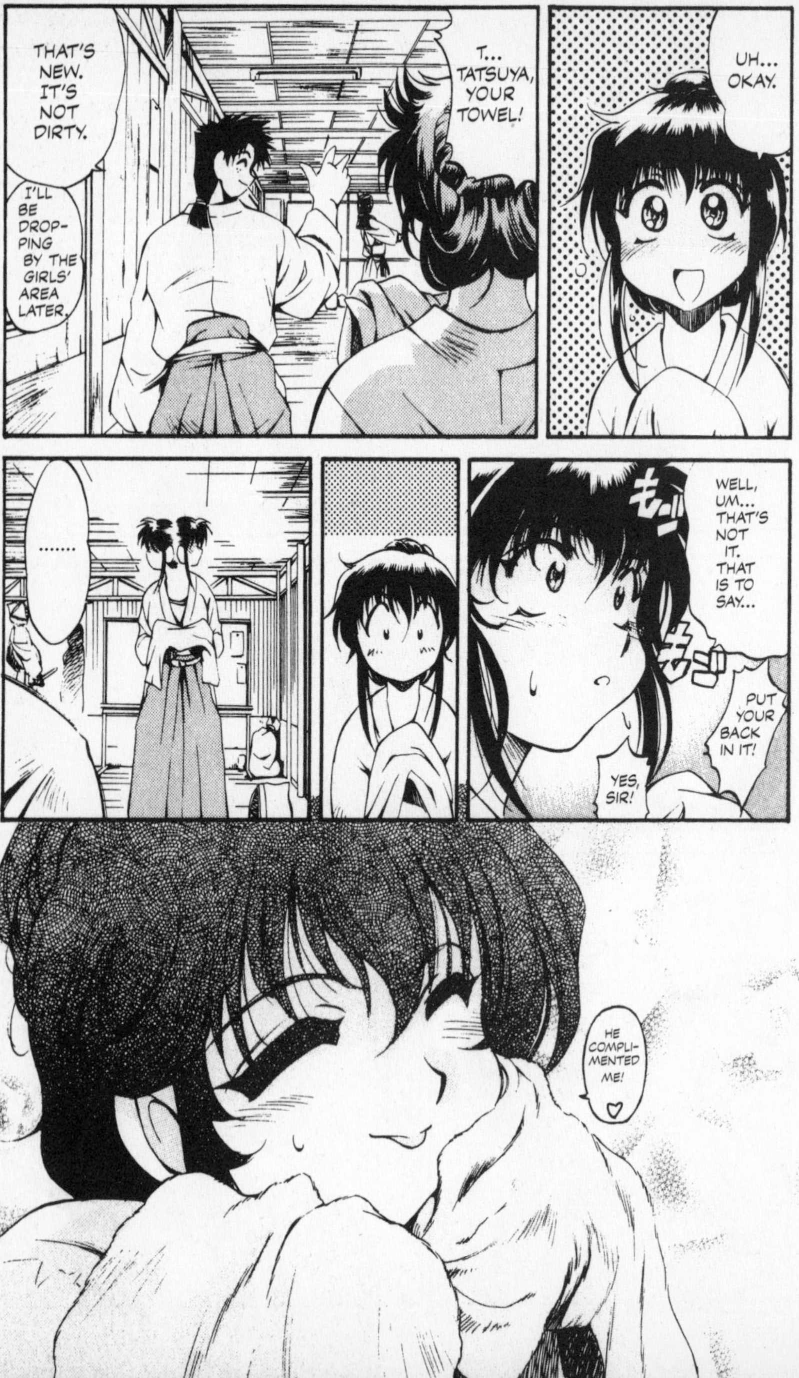
UH... OKAY.
T... TATSUYA, YOUR TOWEL!
THAT'S NEW. IT'S NOT DIRTY.
I'LL BE DROPPING BY THE GIRLS' AREA LATER.
WELL, UM... THAT'S NOT IT. THAT IS TO SAY...
もじ
もじ
PUT YOUR BACK IN IT!
YES, SIR!
....
HE COMPLIMENTED ME! ♥

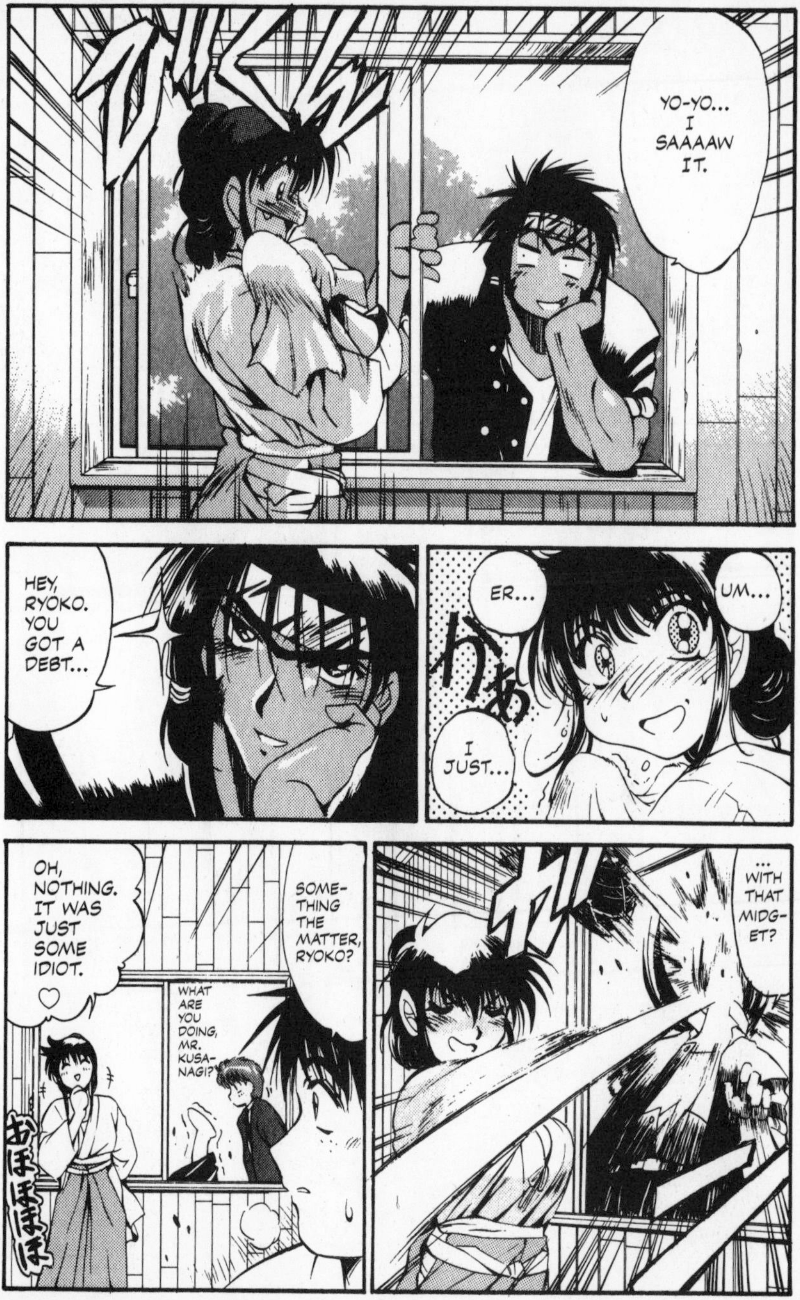
YO-YO... I SAAAAW IT.
UM...
ER...
I JUST...
HEY, RYOKO. YOU GOT A DEBT...
...WITH THAT MIDGET?
SOMETHING THE MATTER, RYOKO?
OH, NOTHING. IT WAS JUST SOME IDIOT. ♡
WHAT ARE YOU DOING, MR. KUSANAGI?

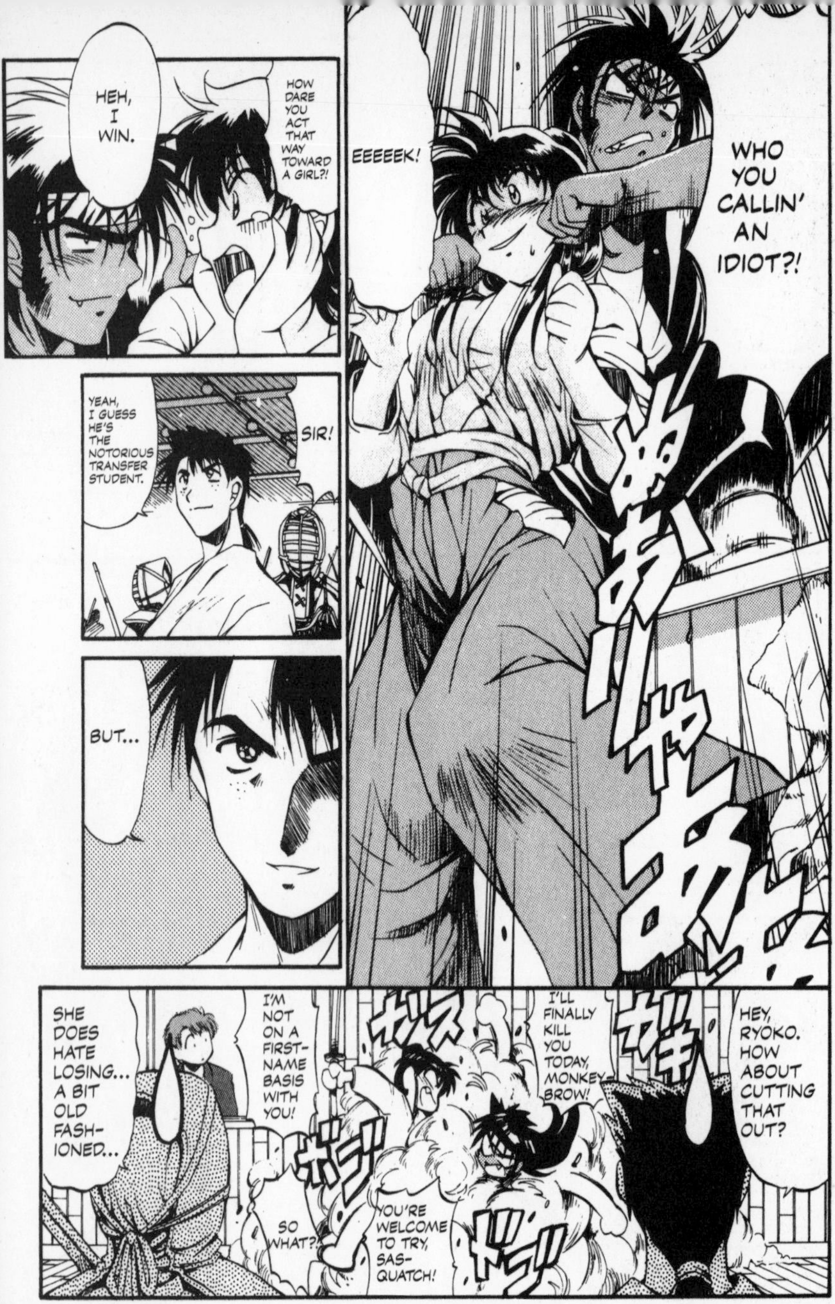
WHO YOU CALLIN' AN IDIOT?!
EEEEEK!
HOW DARE YOU ACT THAT WAY TOWARD A GIRL?!
HEH, I WIN.
SIR!
YEAH, I GUESS HE'S THE NOTORIOUS TRANSFER STUDENT.
BUT...
HEY, RYOKO. HOW ABOUT CUTTING THAT OUT?
I'LL FINALLY KILL YOU TODAY, MONKEY-BROW!
YOU'RE WELCOME TO TRY, SAS-QUATCH!
I'M NOT ON A FIRST-NAME BASIS WITH YOU!
SO WHAT?!
SHE DOES HATE LOSING... A BIT OLD FASH-IONED...

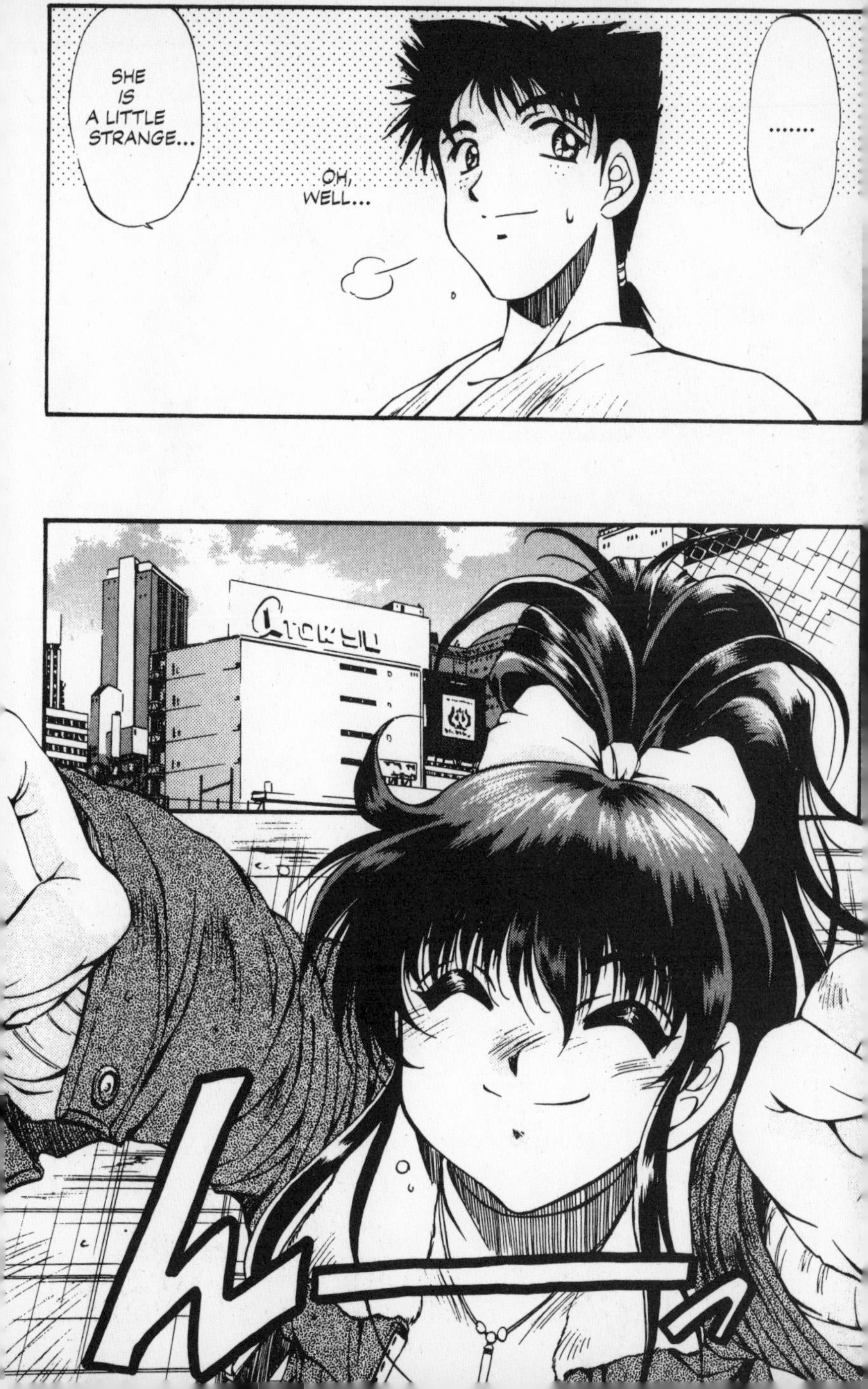
....
OH, WELL...
SHE IS A LITTLE STRANGE...

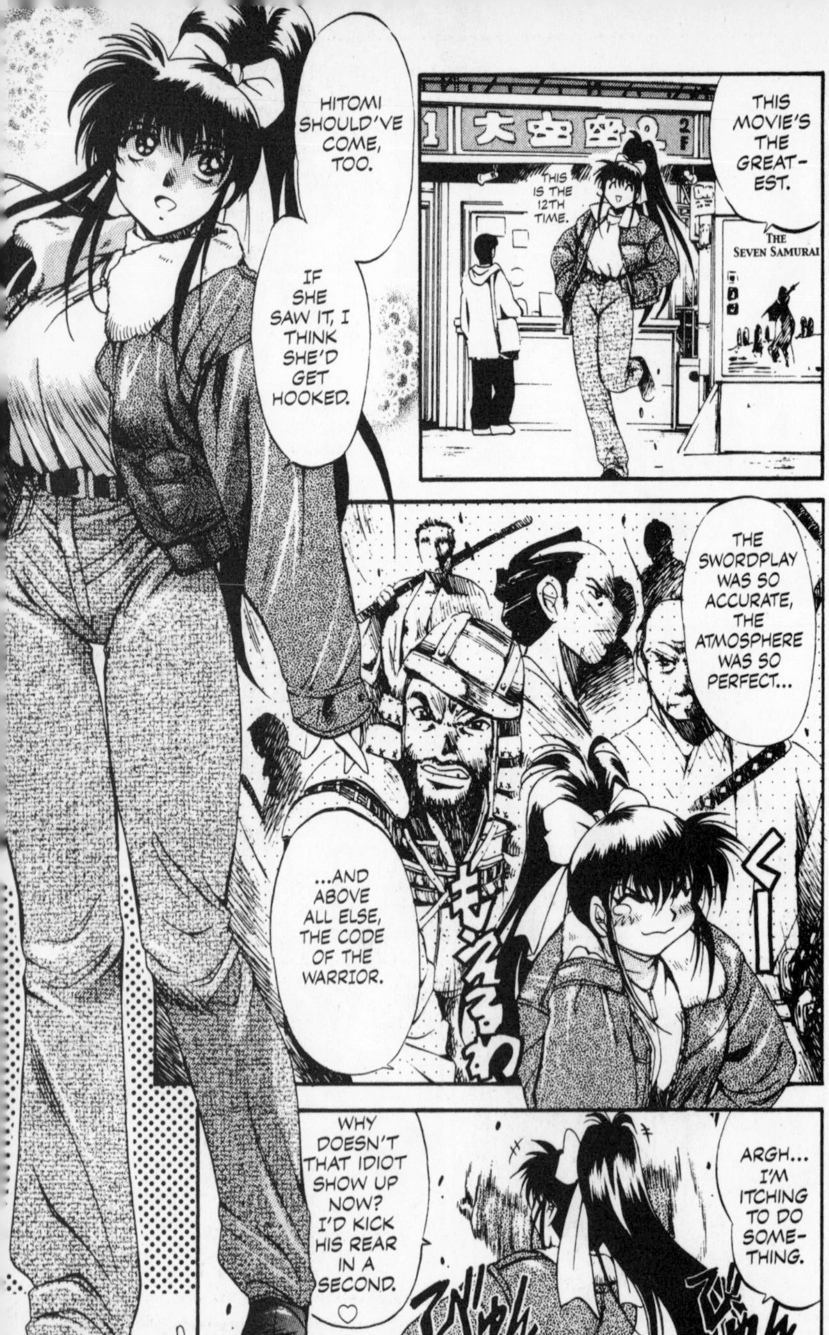
THIS MOVIE'S THE GREAT-EST.
THIS IS THE 12TH TIME.
THE SEVEN SAMURAI
THE SWORDPLAY WAS SO ACCURATE, THE ATMOSPHERE WAS SO PERFECT...
...AND ABOVE ALL ELSE, THE CODE OF THE WARRIOR.
ARGH... I'M ITCHING TO DO SOME-THING.
WHY DOESN'T THAT IDIOT SHOW UP NOW? I'D KICK HIS REAR IN A SECOND. ♡
HITOMI SHOULD'VE COME, TOO.
IF SHE SAW IT, I THINK SHE'D GET HOOKED.

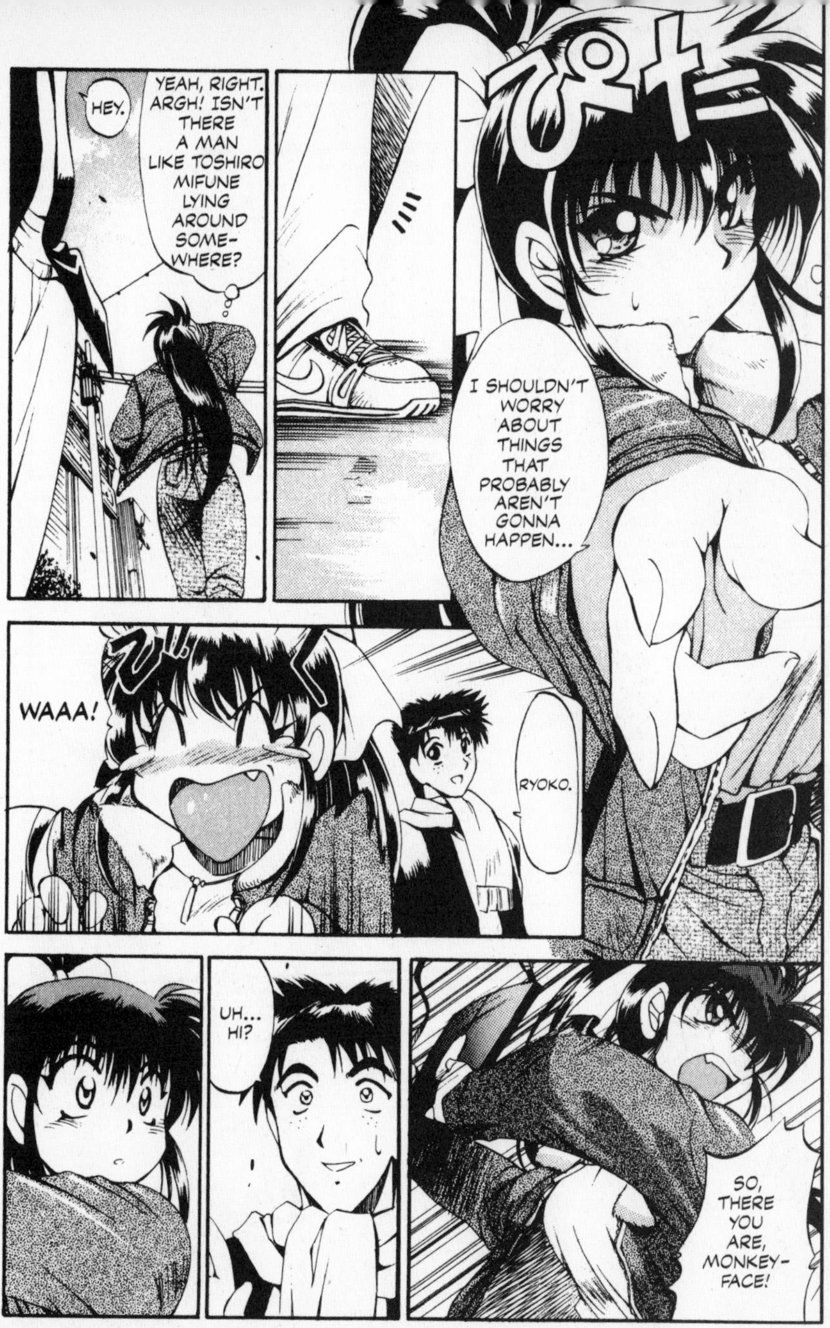
I SHOULDN'T WORRY ABOUT THINGS THAT PROBABLY AREN'T GONNA HAPPEN...
YEAH, RIGHT. ARGH! ISN'T THERE A MAN LIKE TOSHIRO MIFUNE LYING AROUND SOME-WHERE?
HEY.
RYOKO.
WAAA!
SO, THERE YOU ARE, MONKEY-FACE!
UH... HI?

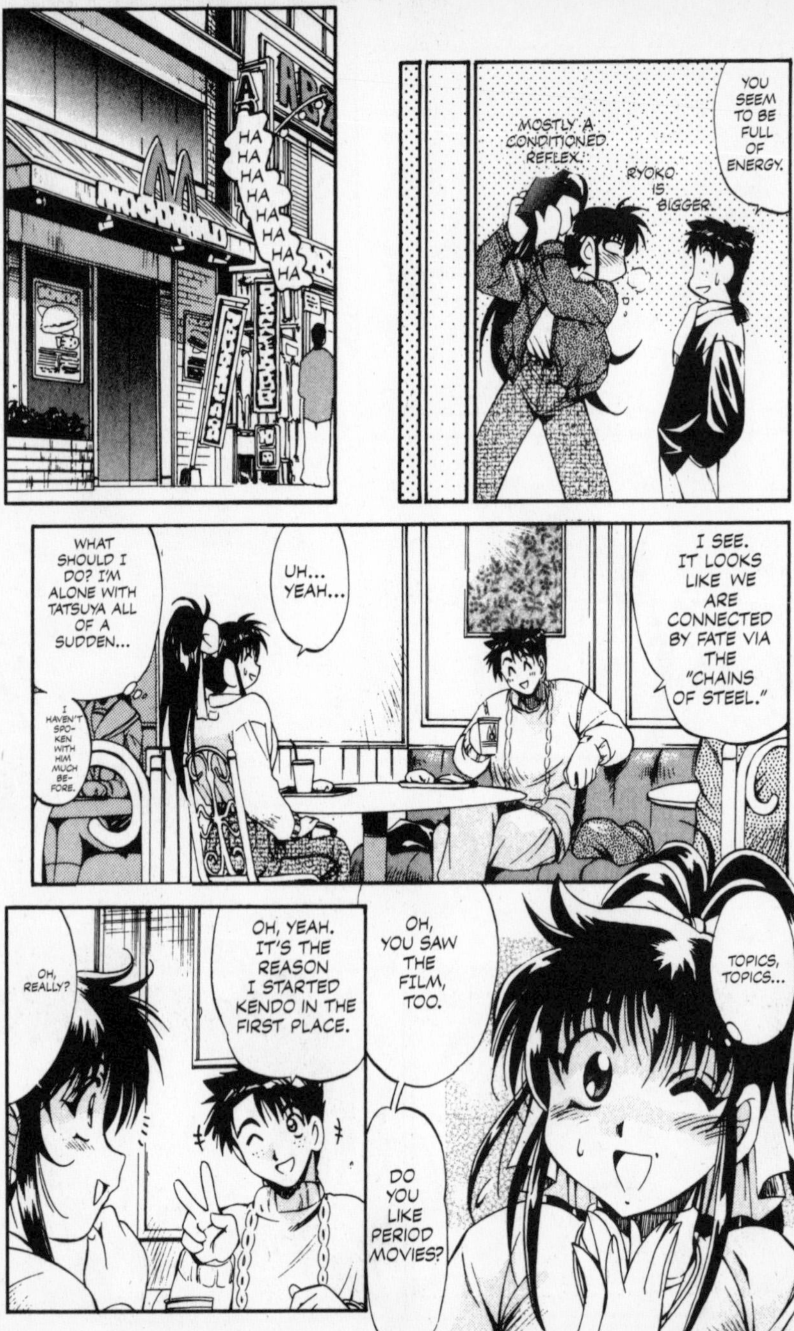

YOU SEEM TO BE FULL OF ENERGY.
RYOKO IS BIGGER.
MOSTLY A CONDITIONED REFLEX.
HA HA HA HA HA HA HA HA
I SEE. IT LOOKS LIKE WE ARE CONNECTED BY FATE VIA THE "CHAINS OF STEEL."
UH... YEAH...
WHAT SHOULD I DO? I'M ALONE WITH TATSUYA ALL OF A SUDDEN...
I HAVEN'T SPO-KEN WITH HIM MUCH BE-FORE.
TOPICS, TOPICS...
DO YOU LIKE PERIOD MOVIES?
OH, YOU SAW THE FILM, TOO.
OH, YEAH. IT'S THE REASON I STARTED KENDO IN THE FIRST PLACE.
OH, REALLY?

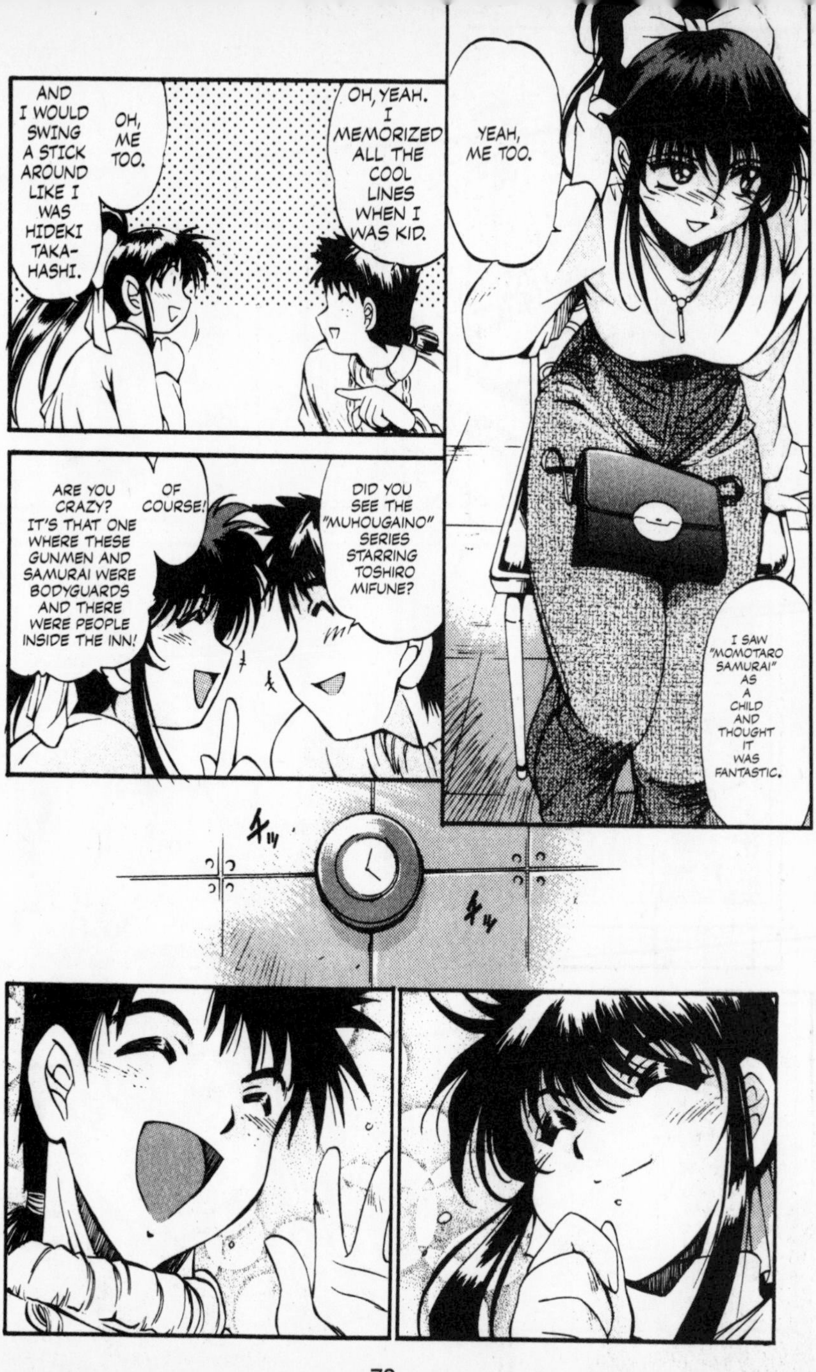
YEAH, ME TOO.
I SAW "MOMOTARO SAMURAI" AS A CHILD AND THOUGHT IT WAS FANTASTIC.
OH, YEAH. I MEMORIZED ALL THE COOL LINES WHEN I WAS KID.
OH, ME TOO.
AND I WOULD SWING A STICK AROUND LIKE I WAS HIDEKI TAKA-HASHI.
DID YOU SEE THE "MUHOUGAINO" SERIES STARRING TOSHIRO MIFUNE?
OF COURSE!
ARE YOU CRAZY? IT'S THAT ONE WHERE THESE GUNMEN AND SAMURAI WERE BODYGUARDS AND THERE WERE PEOPLE INSIDE THE INN!

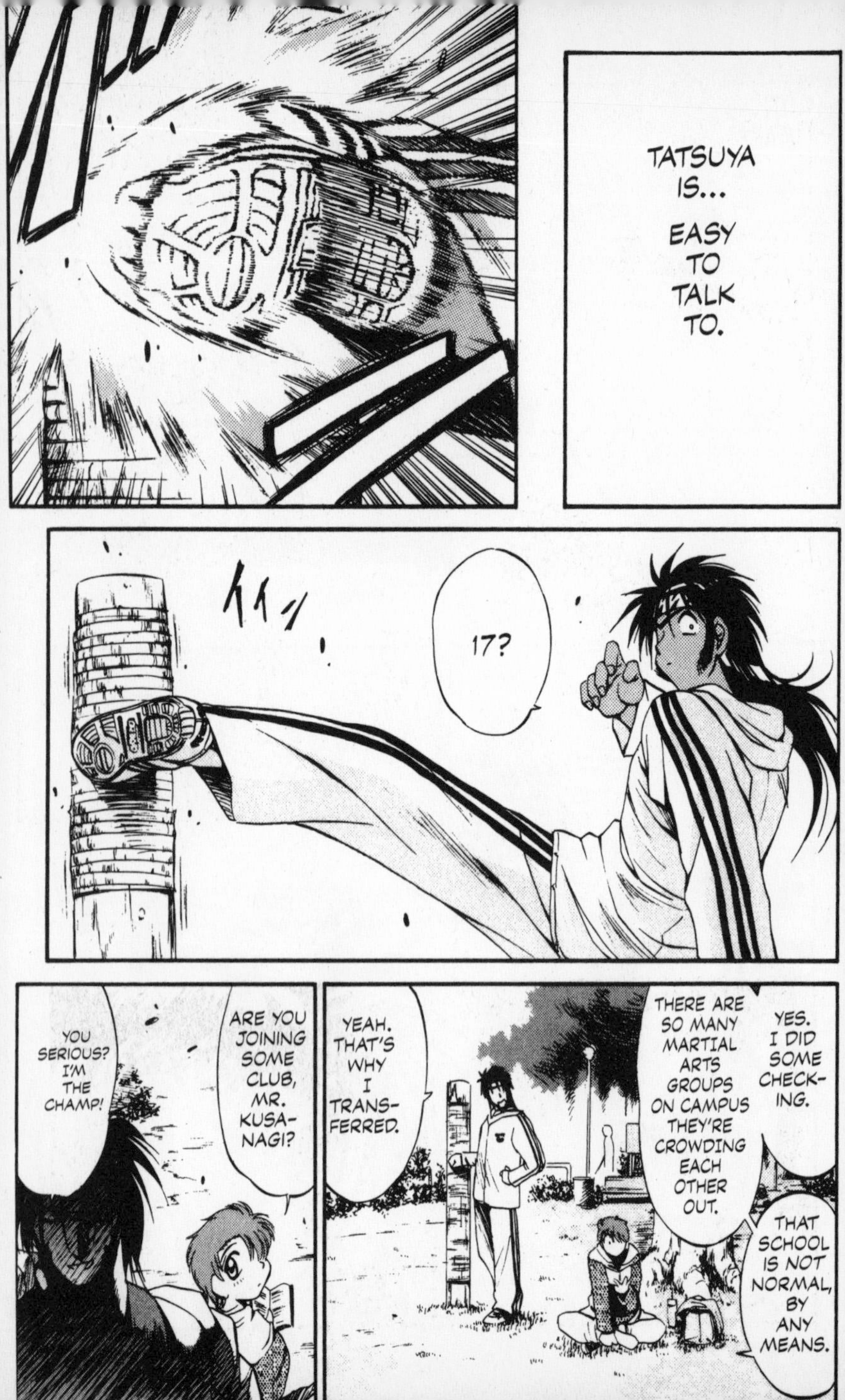
TATSUYA IS... EASY TO TALK TO.
17?
YES. I DID SOME CHECK-ING.
THERE ARE SO MANY MARTIAL ARTS GROUPS ON CAMPUS THEY'RE CROWDING EACH OTHER OUT.
THAT SCHOOL IS NOT NORMAL, BY ANY MEANS.
YEAH. THAT'S WHY I TRANS-FERRED.
ARE YOU JOINING SOME CLUB, MR. KUSA-NAGI?
YOU SERIOUS? I'M THE CHAMP!

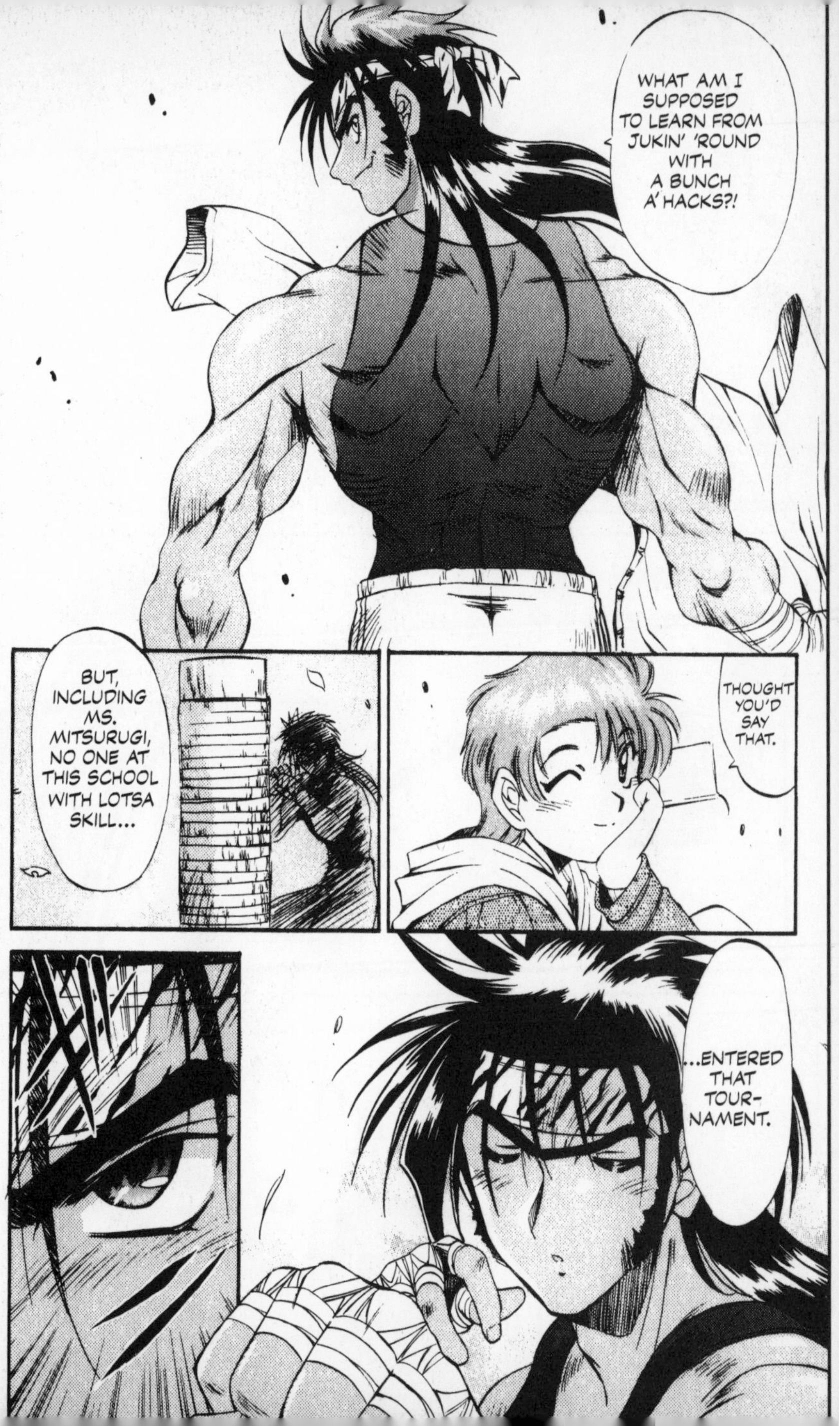
WHAT AM I SUPPOSED TO LEARN FROM JUKIN' 'ROUND WITH A BUNCH A' HACKS?!
THOUGHT YOU'D SAY THAT.
BUT, INCLUDING MS. MITSURUGI, NO ONE AT THIS SCHOOL WITH LOTSA SKILL...
...ENTERED THAT TOUR-NAMENT.

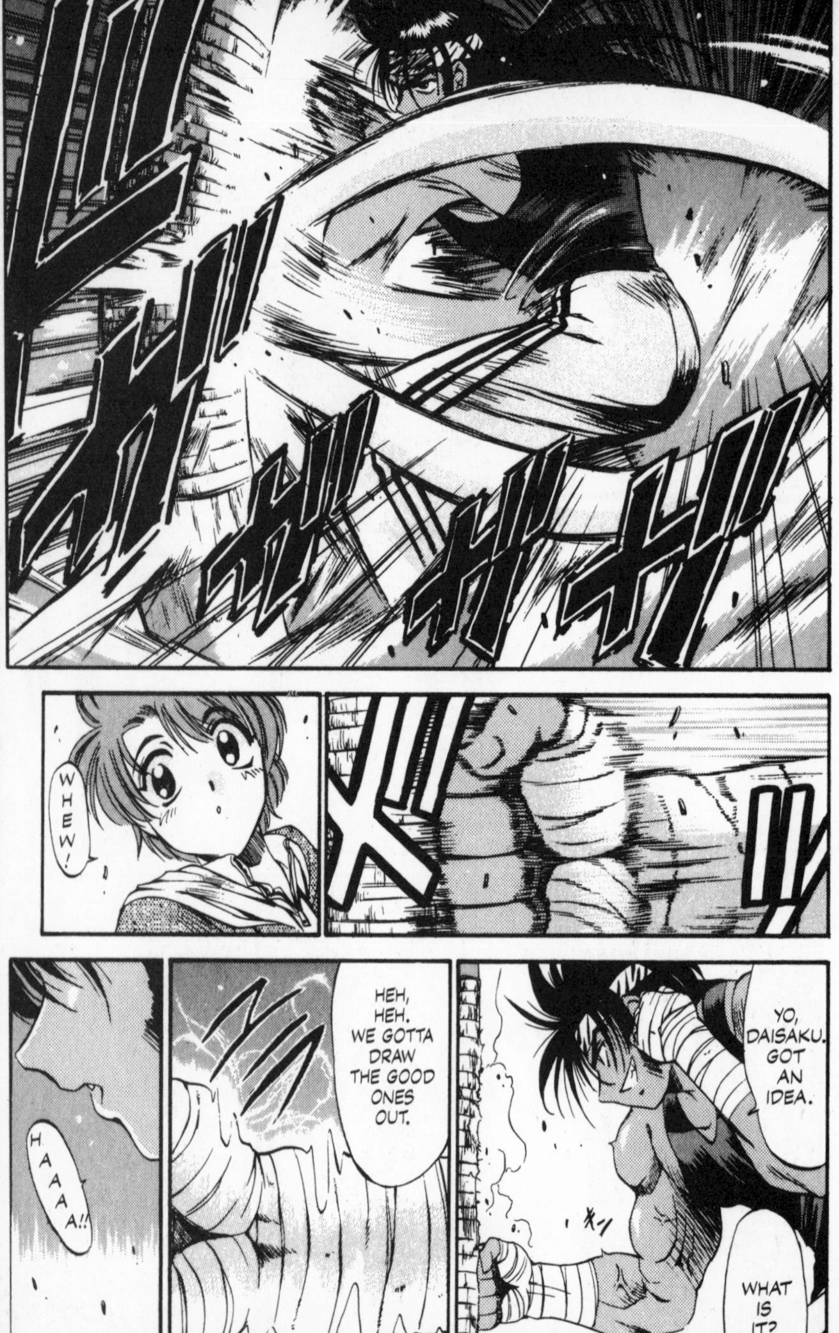
WHEW!
YO, DAISAKU. GOT AN IDEA.
WHAT IS IT?
HEH, HEH. WE GOTTA DRAW THE GOOD ONES OUT.
HAAAA!!

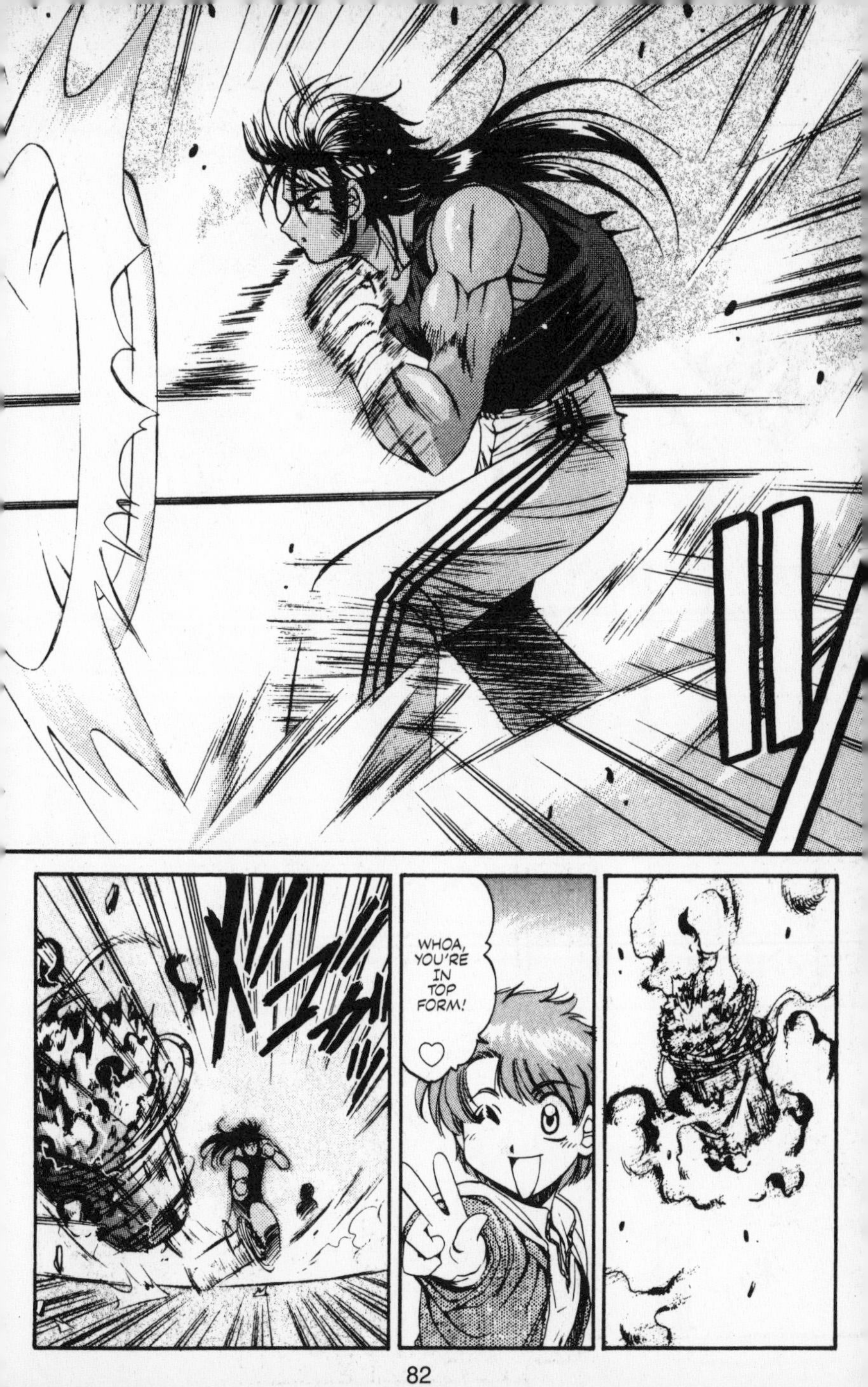
WHOA, YOU'RE IN TOP FORM!

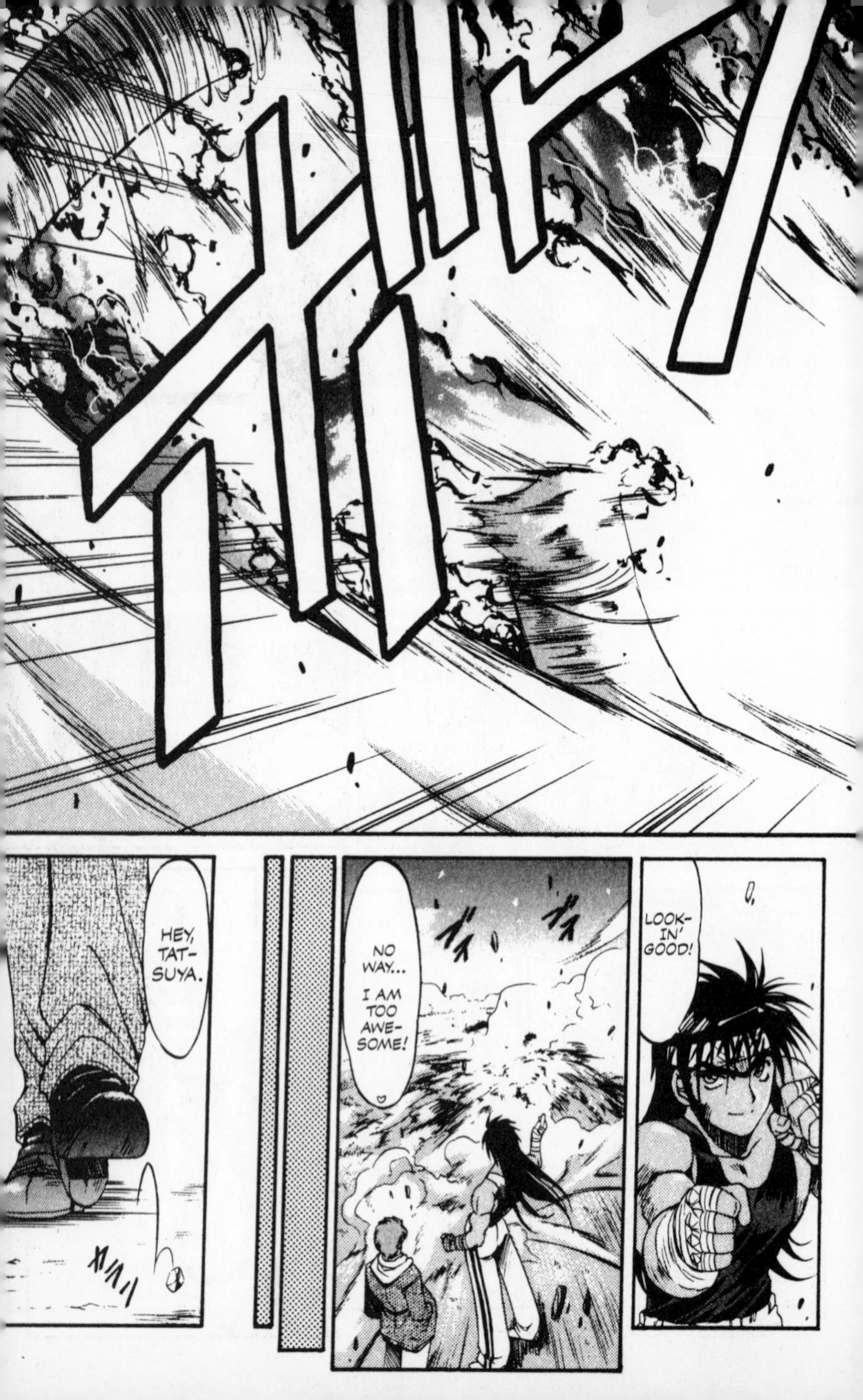
LOOK-IN' GOOD!
NO WAY... I AM TOO AWE-SOME!
HEY, TAT-SUYA.

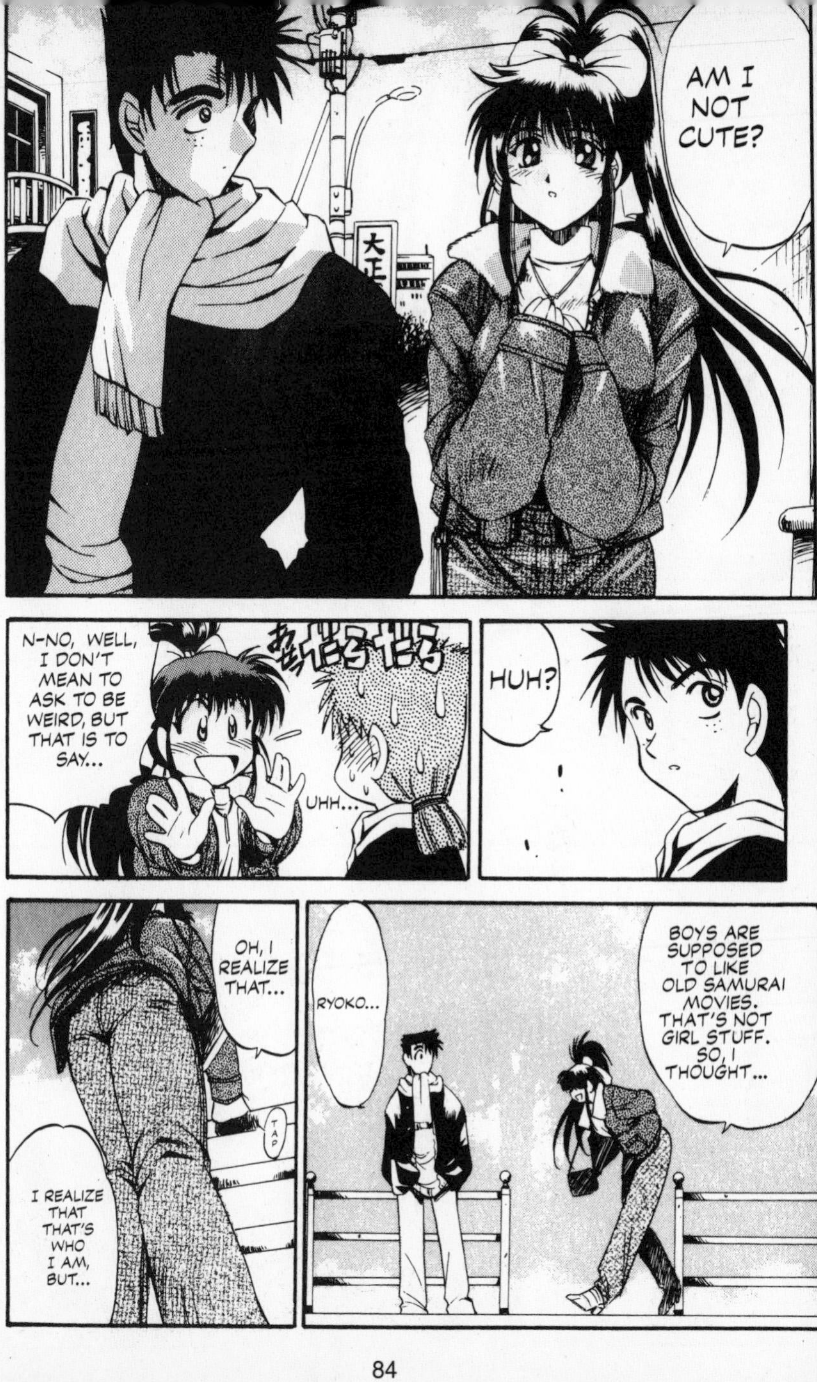
AM I NOT CUTE?
HUH?
N-NO, WELL, I DON'T MEAN TO ASK TO BE WEIRD, BUT THAT IS TO SAY...
UHH...
BOYS ARE SUPPOSED TO LIKE OLD SAMURAI MOVIES. THAT'S NOT GIRL STUFF. SO, I THOUGHT...
RYOKO...
OH, I REALIZE THAT...
TAP
I REALIZE THAT THAT'S WHO I AM, BUT...

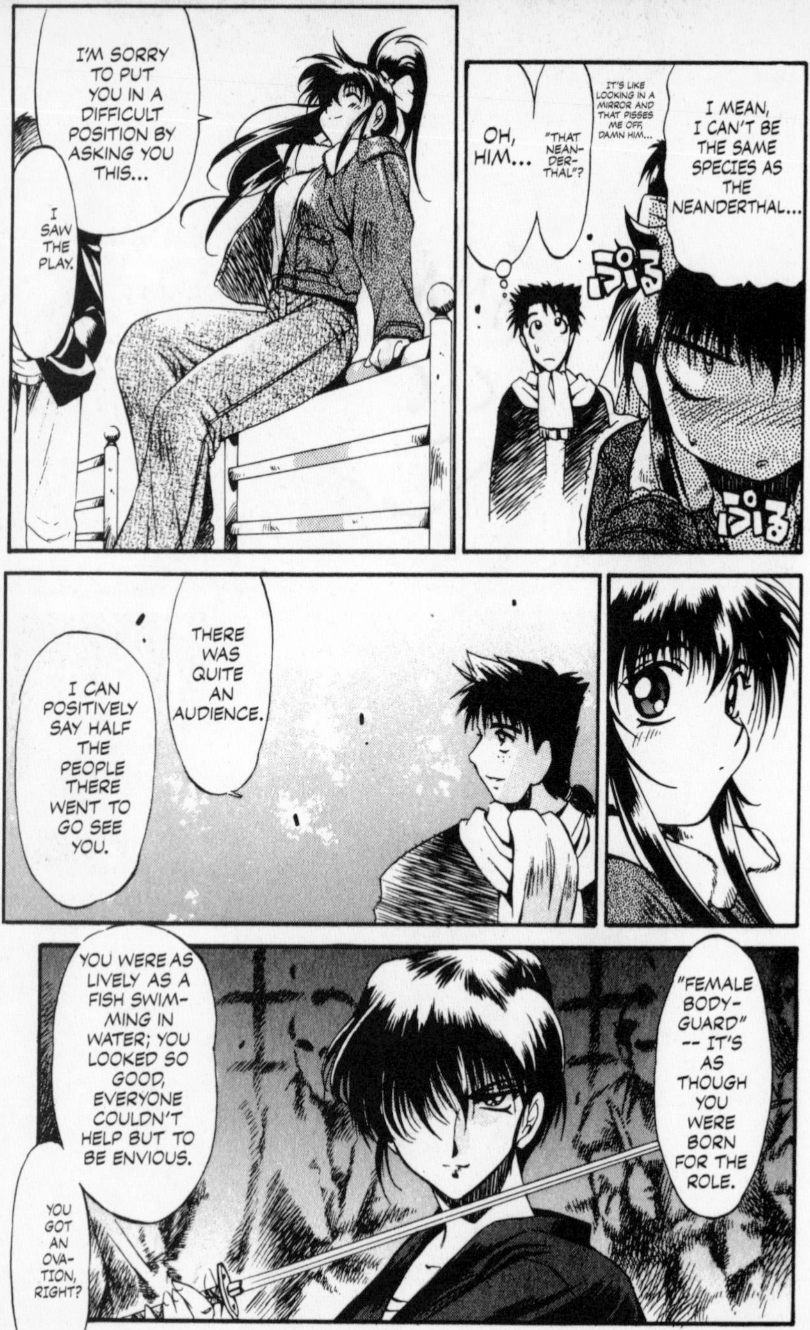
I MEAN, I CAN'T BE THE SAME SPECIES AS THE NEANDERTHAL...
ぷる
IT'S LIKE LOOKING IN A MIRROR AND THAT PISSES ME OFF, DAMN HIM...
"THAT NEAN-DER-THAL"?
OH, HIM...
ぷる
I'M SORRY TO PUT YOU IN A DIFFICULT POSITION BY ASKING YOU THIS...
I SAW THE PLAY.
THERE WAS QUITE AN AUDIENCE.
I CAN POSITIVELY SAY HALF THE PEOPLE THERE WENT TO GO SEE YOU.
"FEMALE BODY-GUARD" -- IT'S AS THOUGH YOU WERE BORN FOR THE ROLE.
YOU WERE AS LIVELY AS A FISH SWIM-MING IN WATER; YOU LOOKED SO GOOD, EVERYONE COULDN'T HELP BUT TO BE ENVIOUS.
YOU GOT AN OVA-TION, RIGHT?

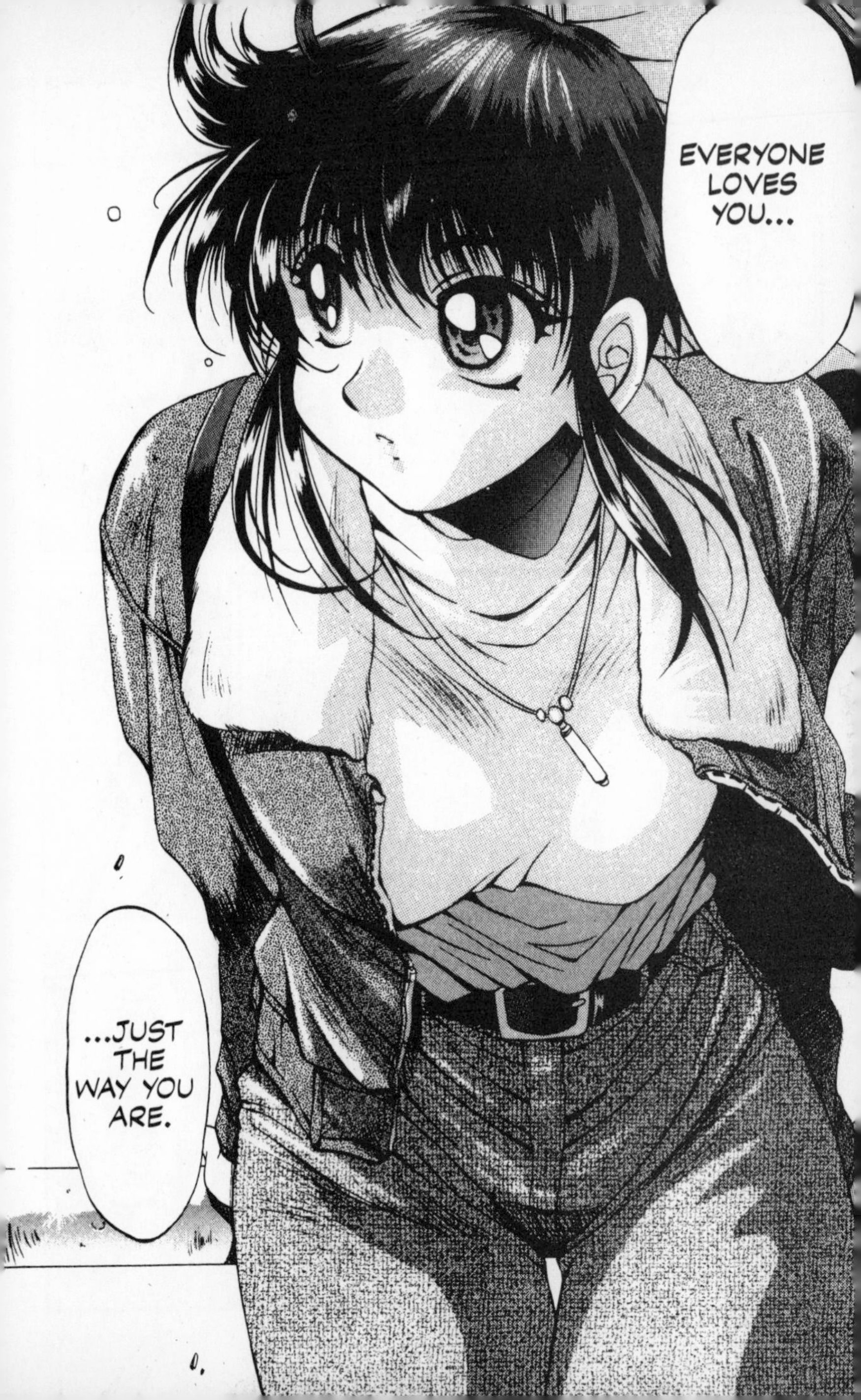
EVERYONE LOVES YOU...
...JUST THE WAY YOU ARE.

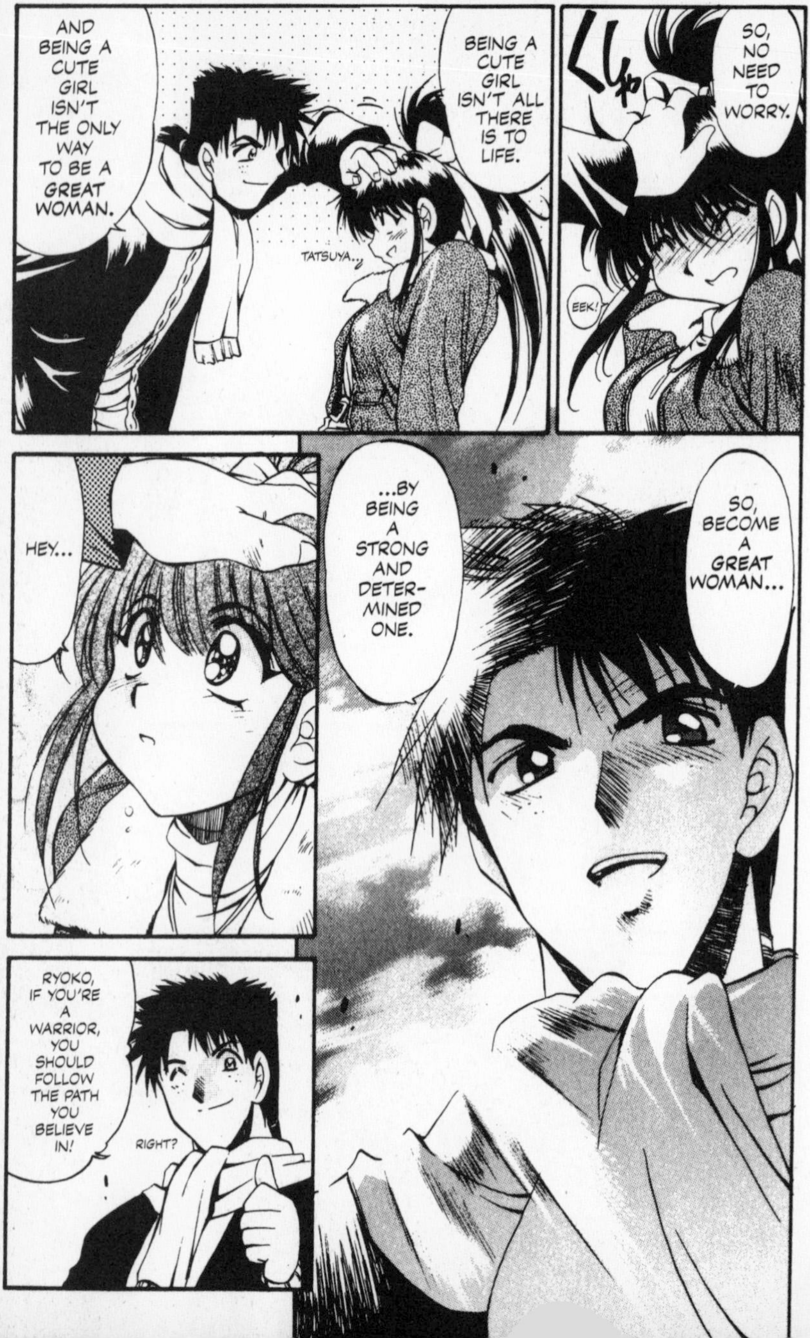
SO, NO NEED TO WORRY.
くしゃ
EEK!
BEING A CUTE GIRL ISN'T ALL THERE IS TO LIFE.
AND BEING A CUTE GIRL ISN'T THE ONLY WAY TO BE A GREAT WOMAN.
TATSUYA...
SO, BECOME A GREAT WOMAN...
...BY BEING A STRONG AND DETERMINED ONE.
HEY...
RYOKO, IF YOU'RE A WARRIOR, YOU SHOULD FOLLOW THE PATH YOU BELIEVE IN!
RIGHT?

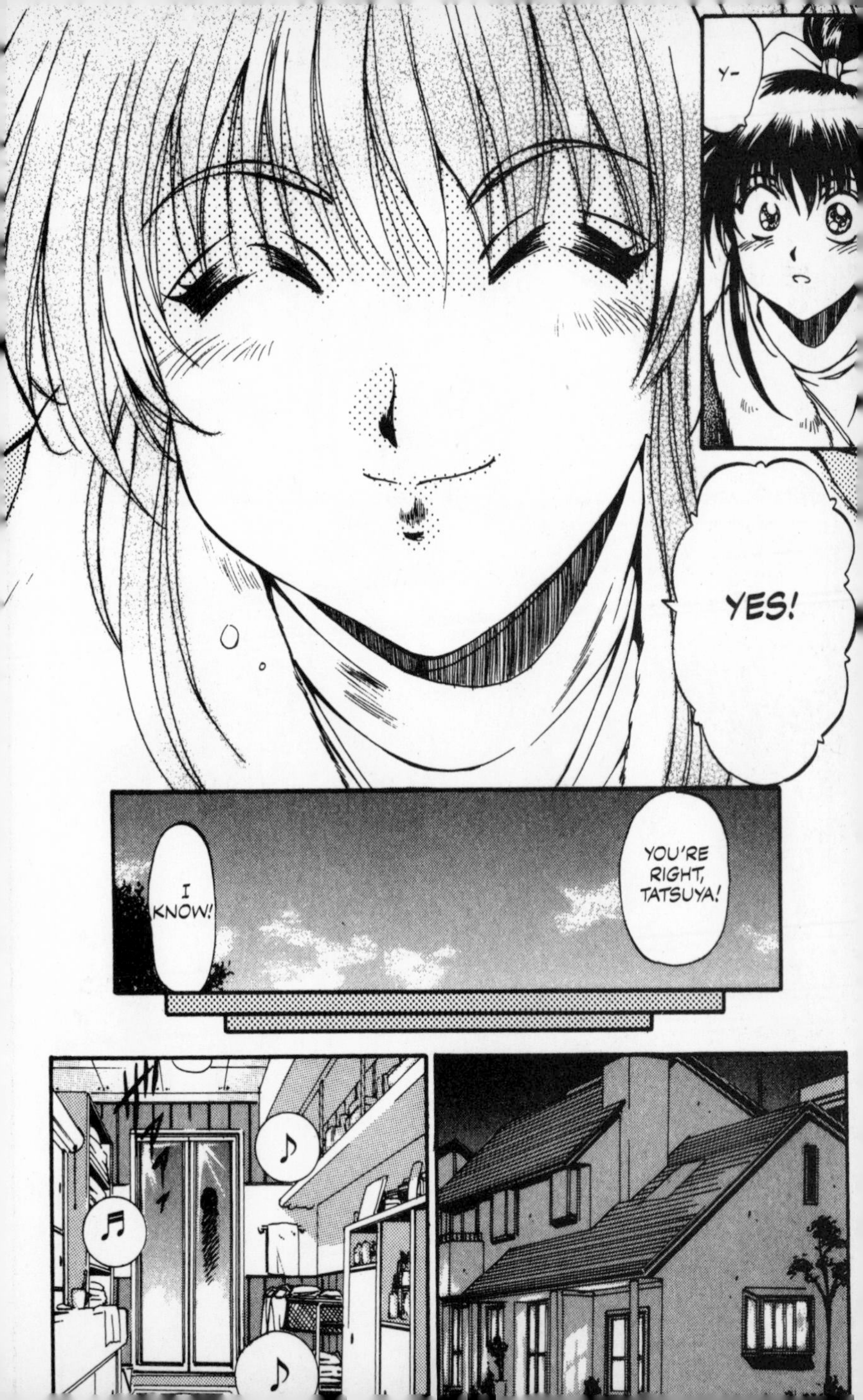
Y-
YES!
YOU'RE RIGHT, TATSUYA!
I KNOW!

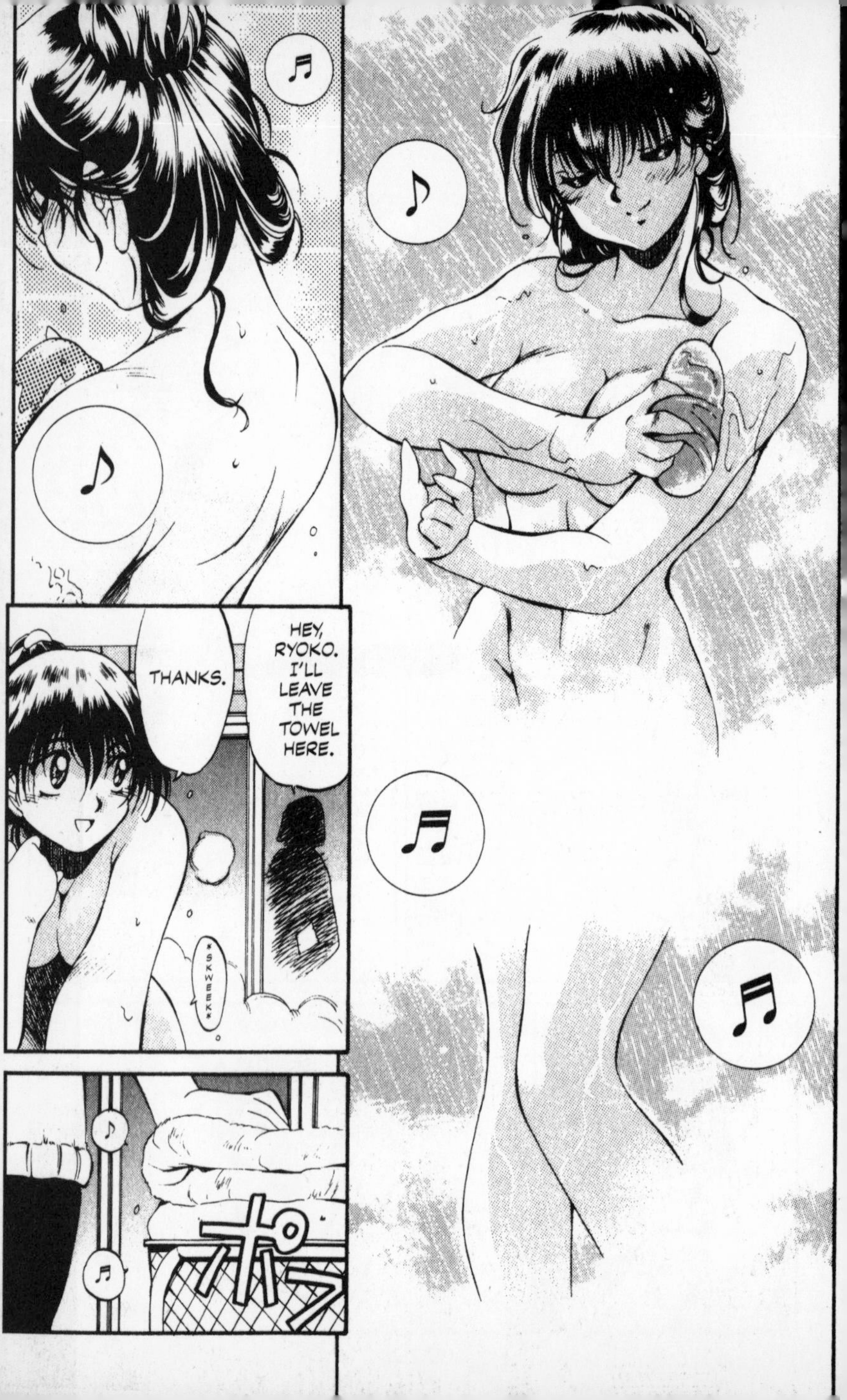
HEY, RYOKO. I'LL LEAVE THE TOWEL HERE.
THANKS.
SKWEEK
ポフ

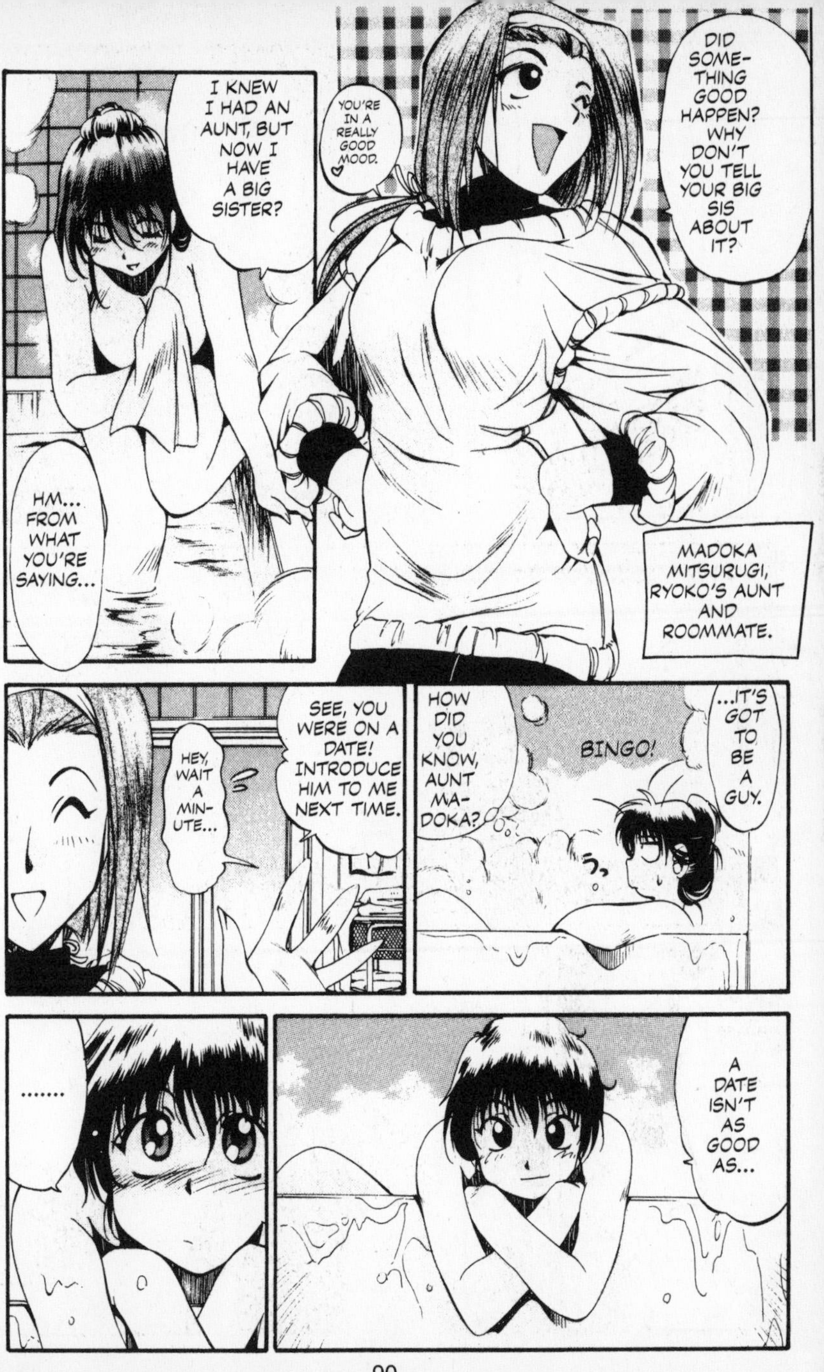
DID SOME-THING GOOD HAPPEN? WHY DON'T YOU TELL YOUR BIG SIS ABOUT IT?
YOU'RE IN A REALLY GOOD MOOD. ♡
MADOKA MITSURUGI, RYOKO'S AUNT AND ROOMMATE.
I KNEW I HAD AN AUNT, BUT NOW I HAVE A BIG SISTER?
HM... FROM WHAT YOU'RE SAYING...
...IT'S GOT TO BE A GUY.
BINGO!
HOW DID YOU KNOW, AUNT MA-DOKA?
SEE, YOU WERE ON A DATE! INTRODUCE HIM TO ME NEXT TIME.
HEY, WAIT A MIN-UTE...
A DATE ISN'T AS GOOD AS...
....

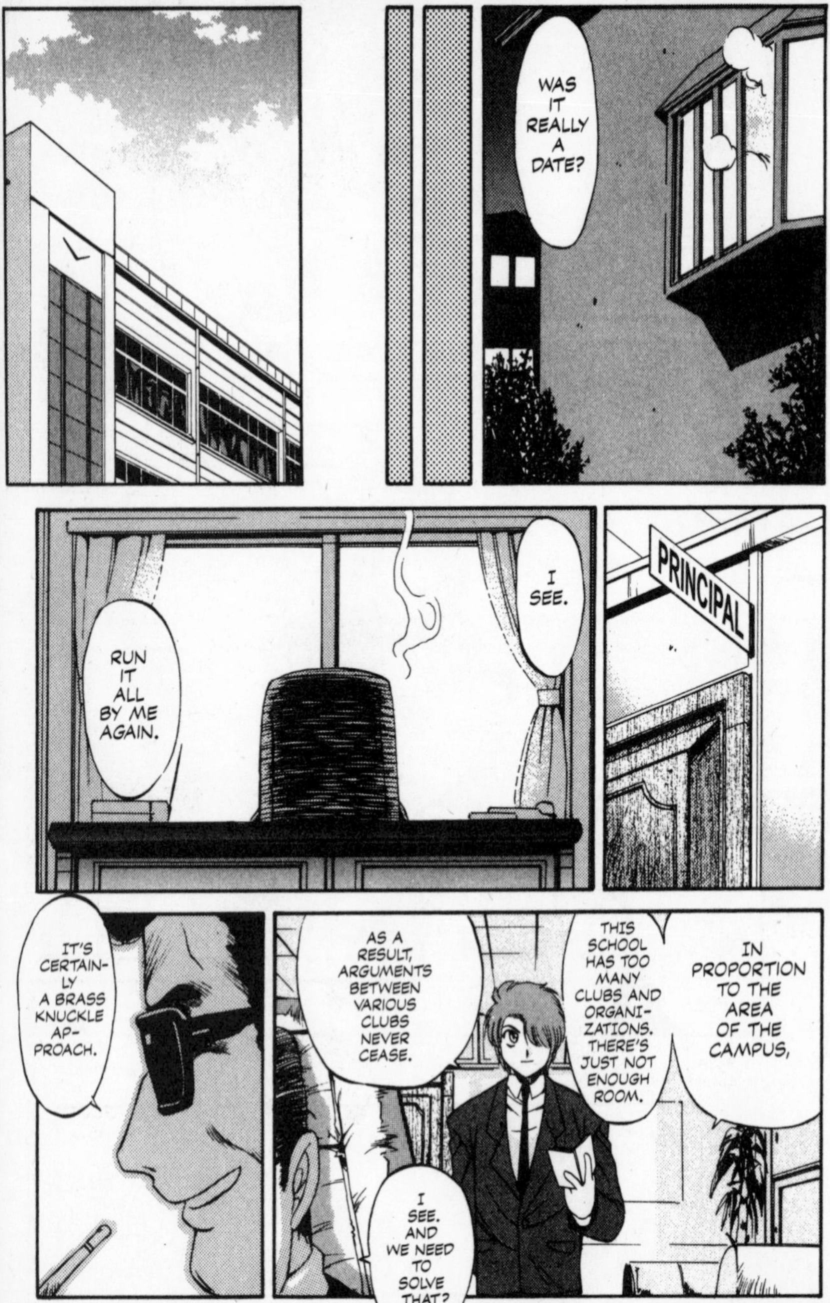
WAS IT REALLY A DATE?
PRINCIPAL
I SEE.
RUN IT ALL BY ME AGAIN.
IN PROPORTION TO THE AREA OF THE CAMPUS,
THIS SCHOOL HAS TOO MANY CLUBS AND ORGANI-ZATIONS. THERE'S JUST NOT ENOUGH ROOM.
AS A RESULT, ARGUMENTS BETWEEN VARIOUS CLUBS NEVER CEASE.
I SEE. AND WE NEED TO SOLVE THAT?
IT'S CERTAIN-LY A BRASS KNUCKLE AP-PROACH.

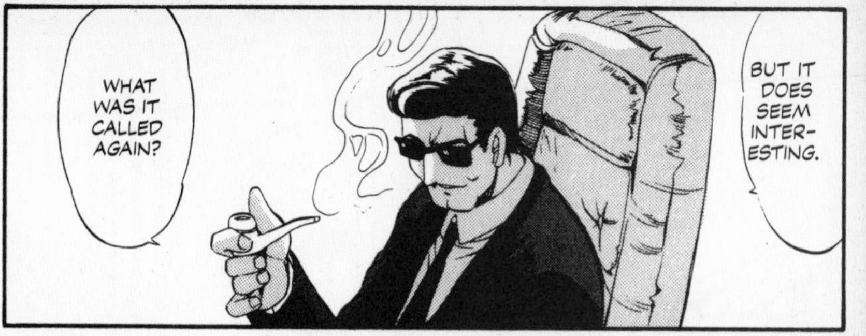
BUT IT DOES SEEM INTER-ESTING.
WHAT WAS IT CALLED AGAIN?

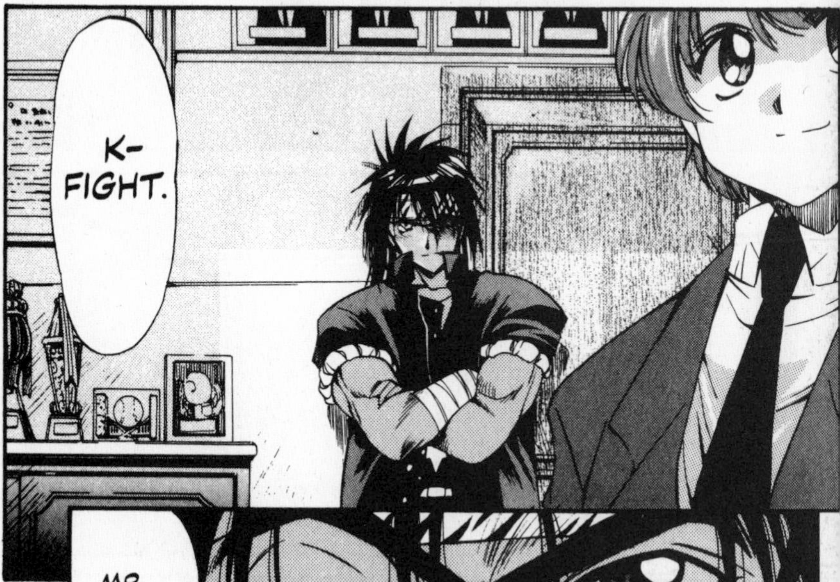
K-FIGHT.

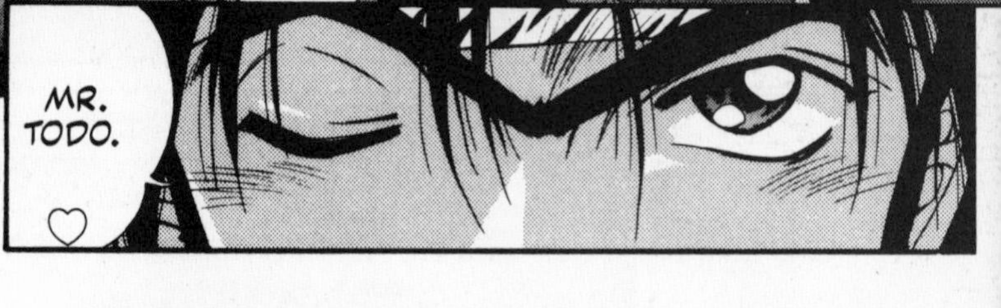
MR. TODO.

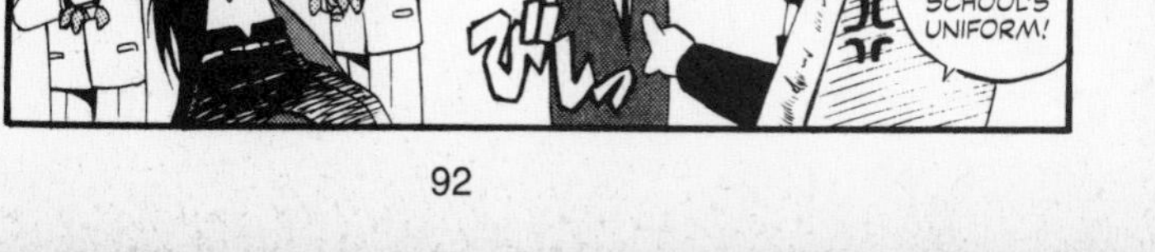
BEFORE I DO ANYTHING ELSE, WEAR OUR SCHOOL'S UNIFORM!
EDUCATIONAL CONFORMITY CLUB, GO!
びしっ
COME HERE!
WHA?!

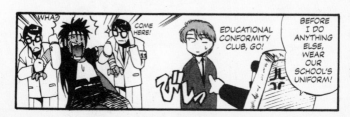

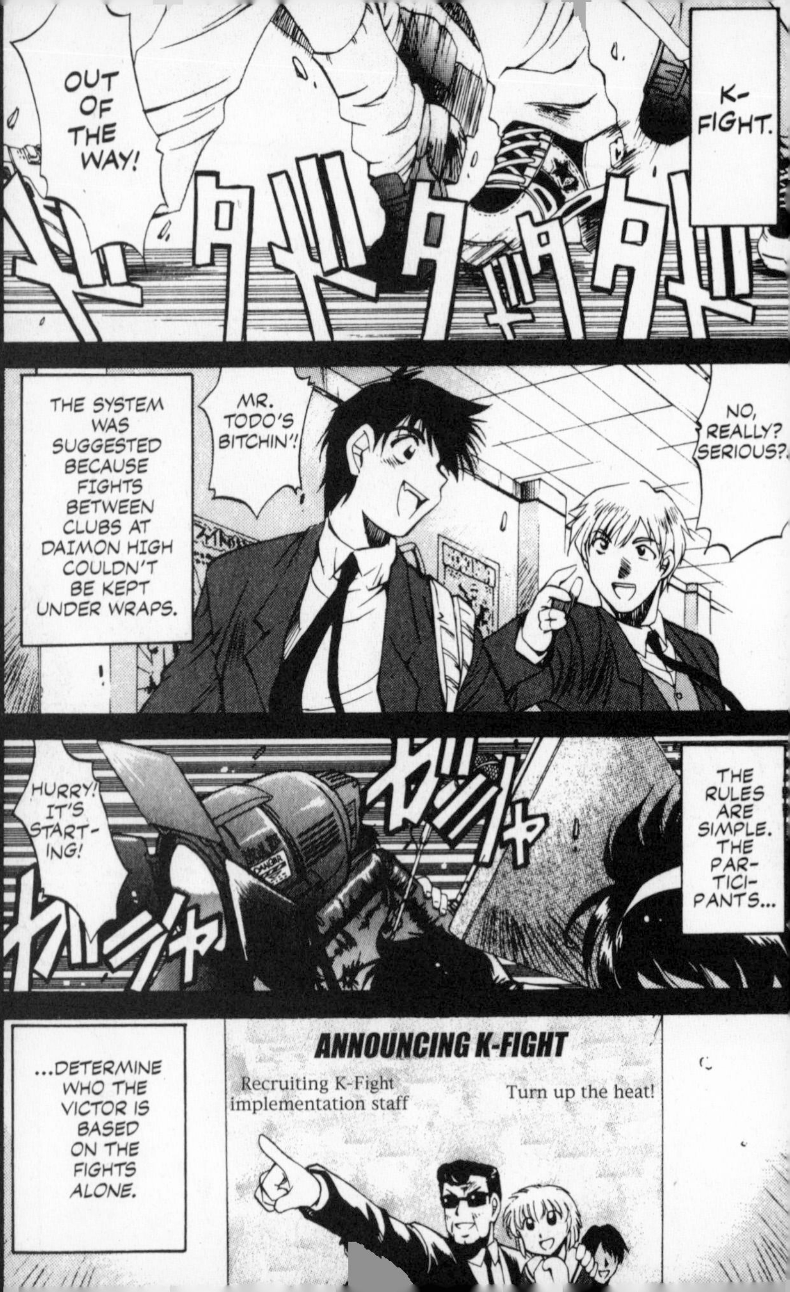
K-FIGHT.
OUT OF THE WAY!
NO, REALLY? SERIOUS?.
MR. TODO'S BITCHIN'!
THE SYSTEM WAS SUGGESTED BECAUSE FIGHTS BETWEEN CLUBS AT DAIMON HIGH COULDN'T BE KEPT UNDER WRAPS.
THE RULES ARE SIMPLE. THE PARTICIPANTS...
HURRY! IT'S STARTING!
ANNOUNCING K-FIGHT
Turn up the heat!
Recruiting K-Fight implementation staff
...DETERMINE WHO THE VICTOR IS BASED ON THE FIGHTS ALONE.

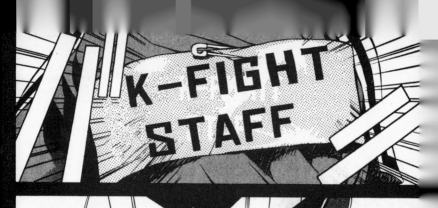

K-FIGHT STAFF
LADIES AND GENTLEMEN!
THE FIRST K-FIGHT TOURNAMENT IS ABOUT TO START!
PLUS, THERE WAS A DISTURBING DEVELOPMENT TODAY.
HUH?

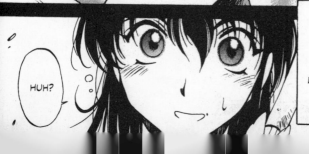

Episode 4 The Duel, Official Announcement

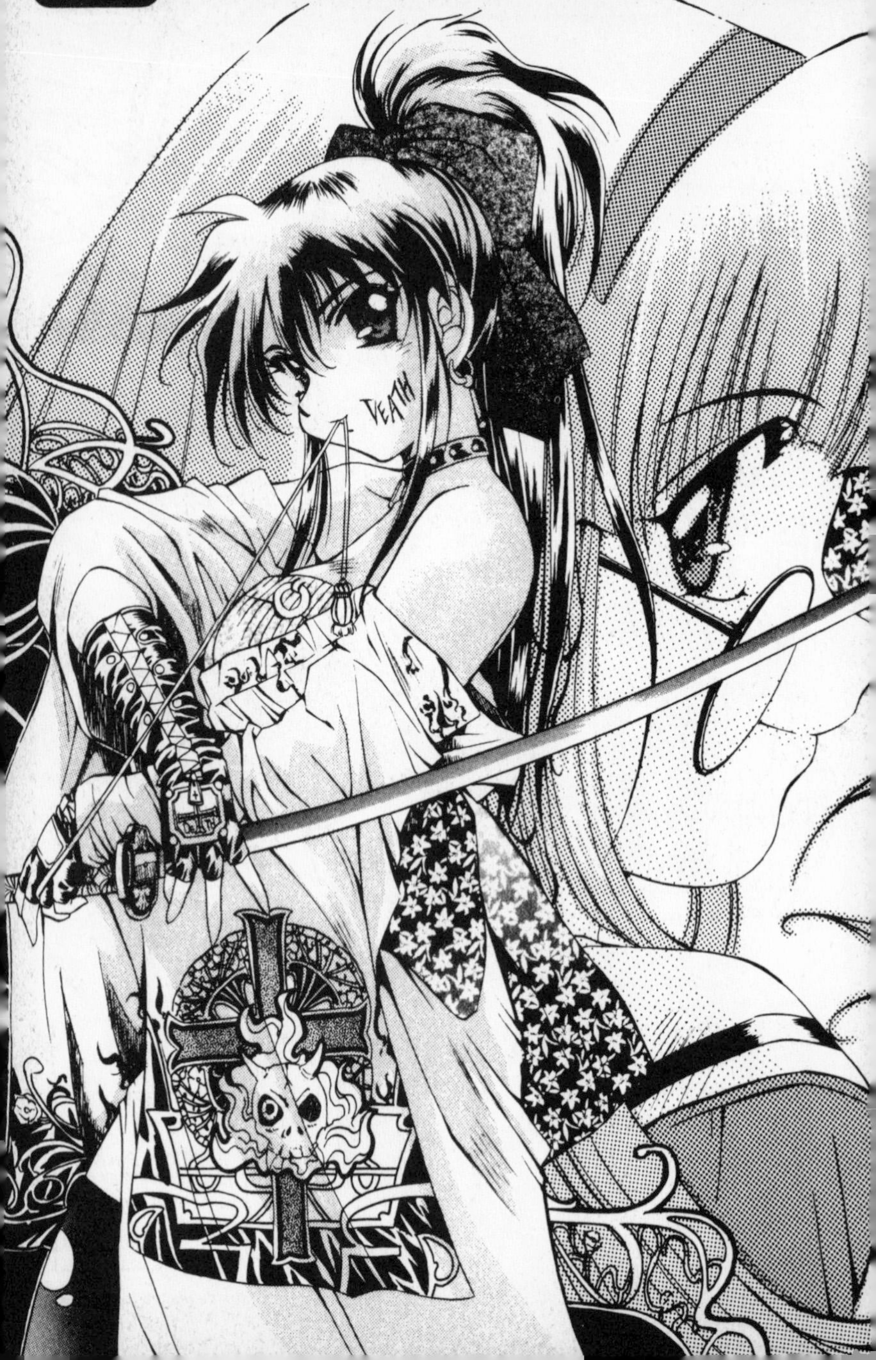
DEATH

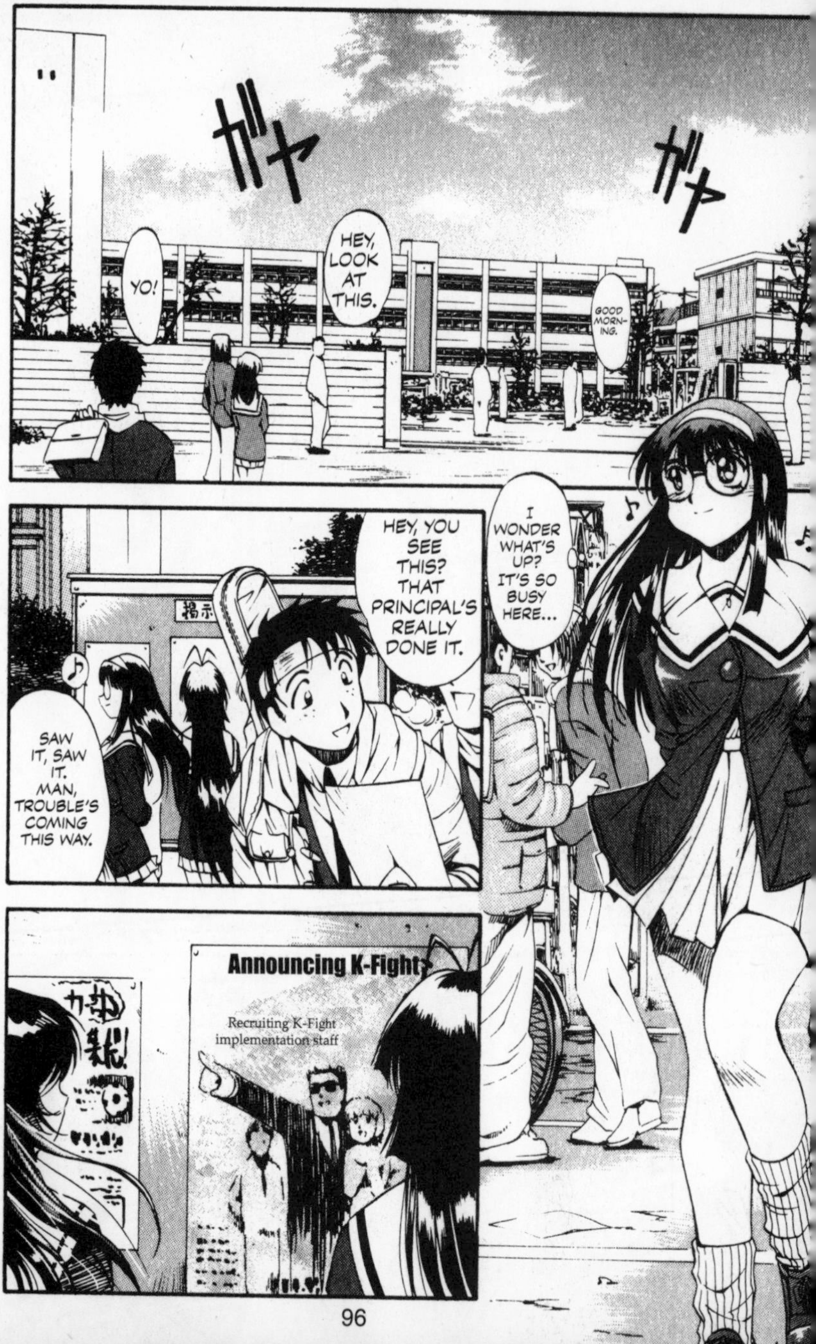
ガヤ
ガヤ
GOOD MORNING.
HEY, LOOK AT THIS.
YO!
I WONDER WHAT'S UP? IT'S SO BUSY HERE...
HEY, YOU SEE THIS? THAT PRINCIPAL'S REALLY DONE IT.
掲示
SAW IT, SAW IT. MAN, TROUBLE'S COMING THIS WAY.
Announcing K-Fight
Recruiting K-Fight implementation staff

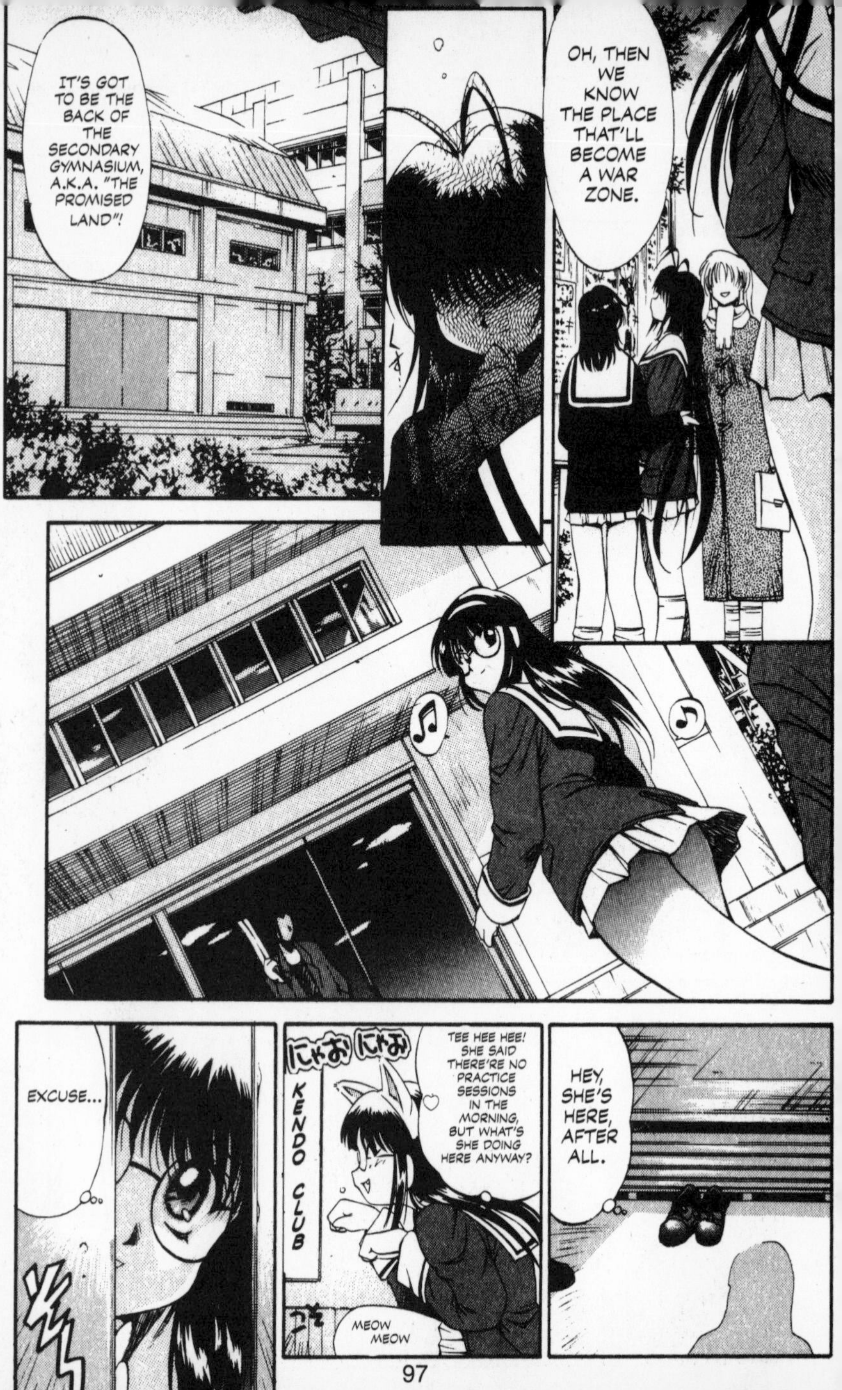
OH, THEN WE KNOW THE PLACE THAT'LL BECOME A WAR ZONE.
IT'S GOT TO BE THE BACK OF THE SECONDARY GYMNASIUM, A.K.A. "THE PROMISED LAND"!
HEY, SHE'S HERE, AFTER ALL.
にゃお にゃお
TEE HEE HEE! SHE SAID THERE'RE NO PRACTICE SESSIONS IN THE MORNING, BUT WHAT'S SHE DOING HERE ANYWAY?
KENDO CLUB
MEOW MEOW
EXCUSE...

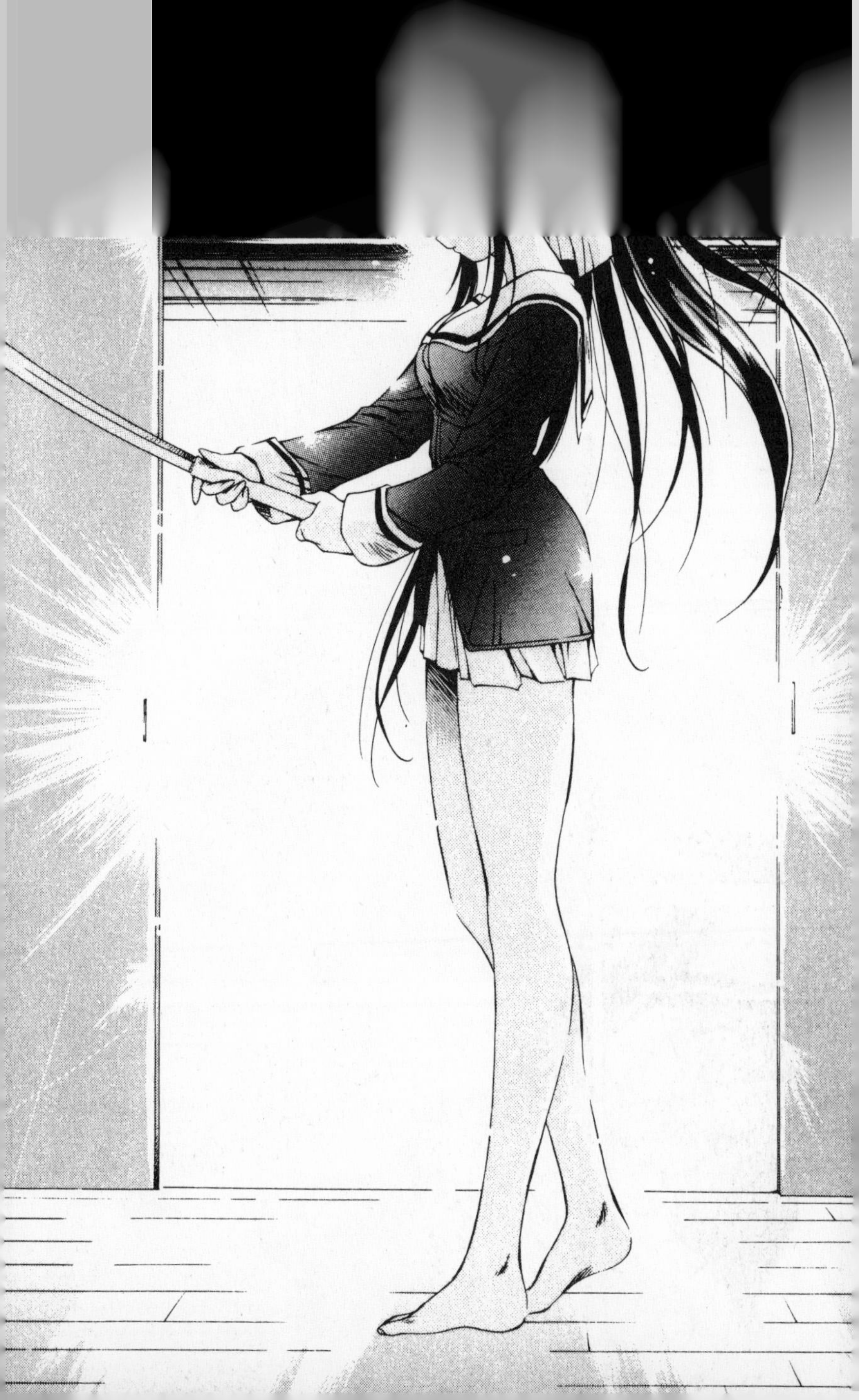

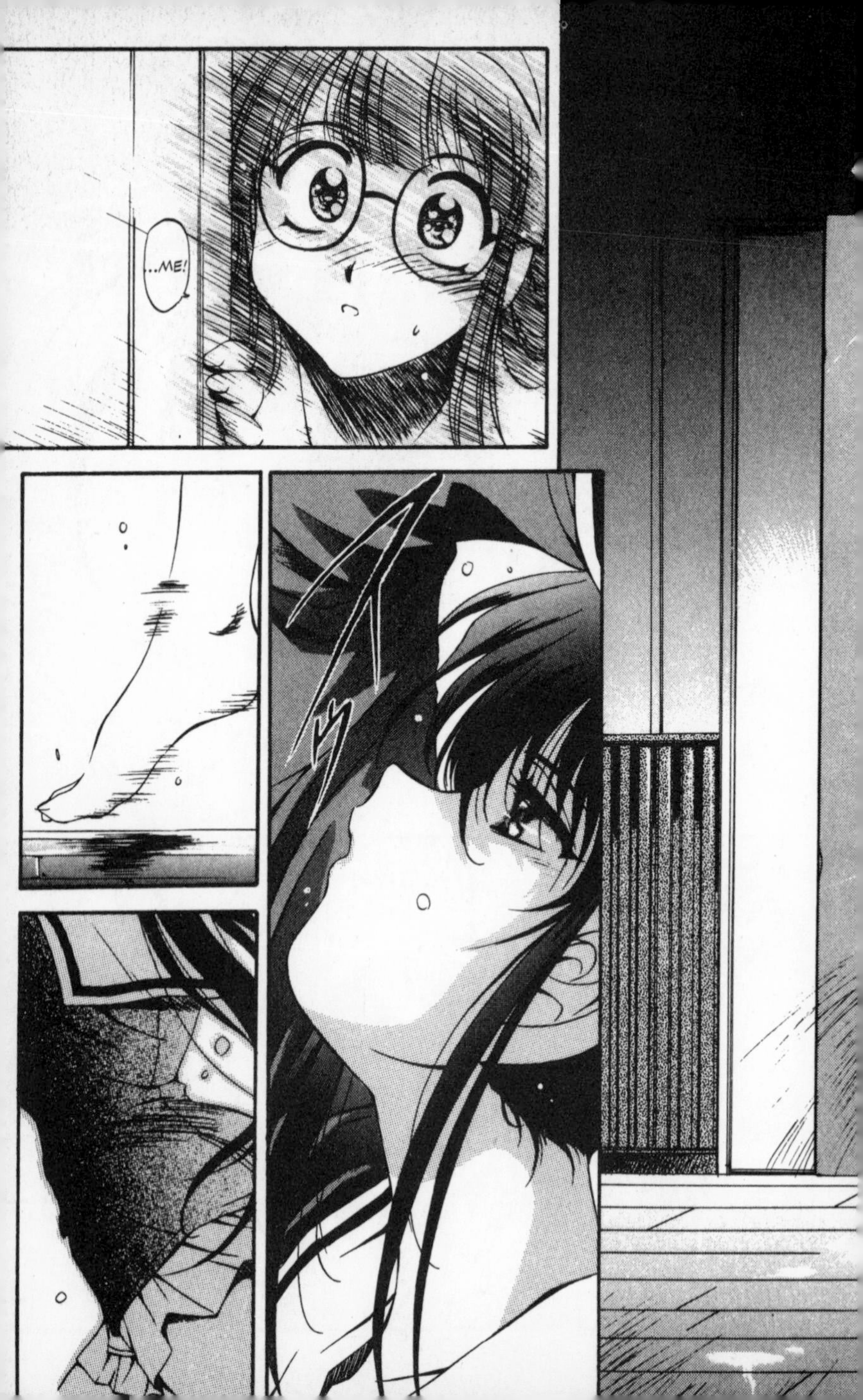
...ME!

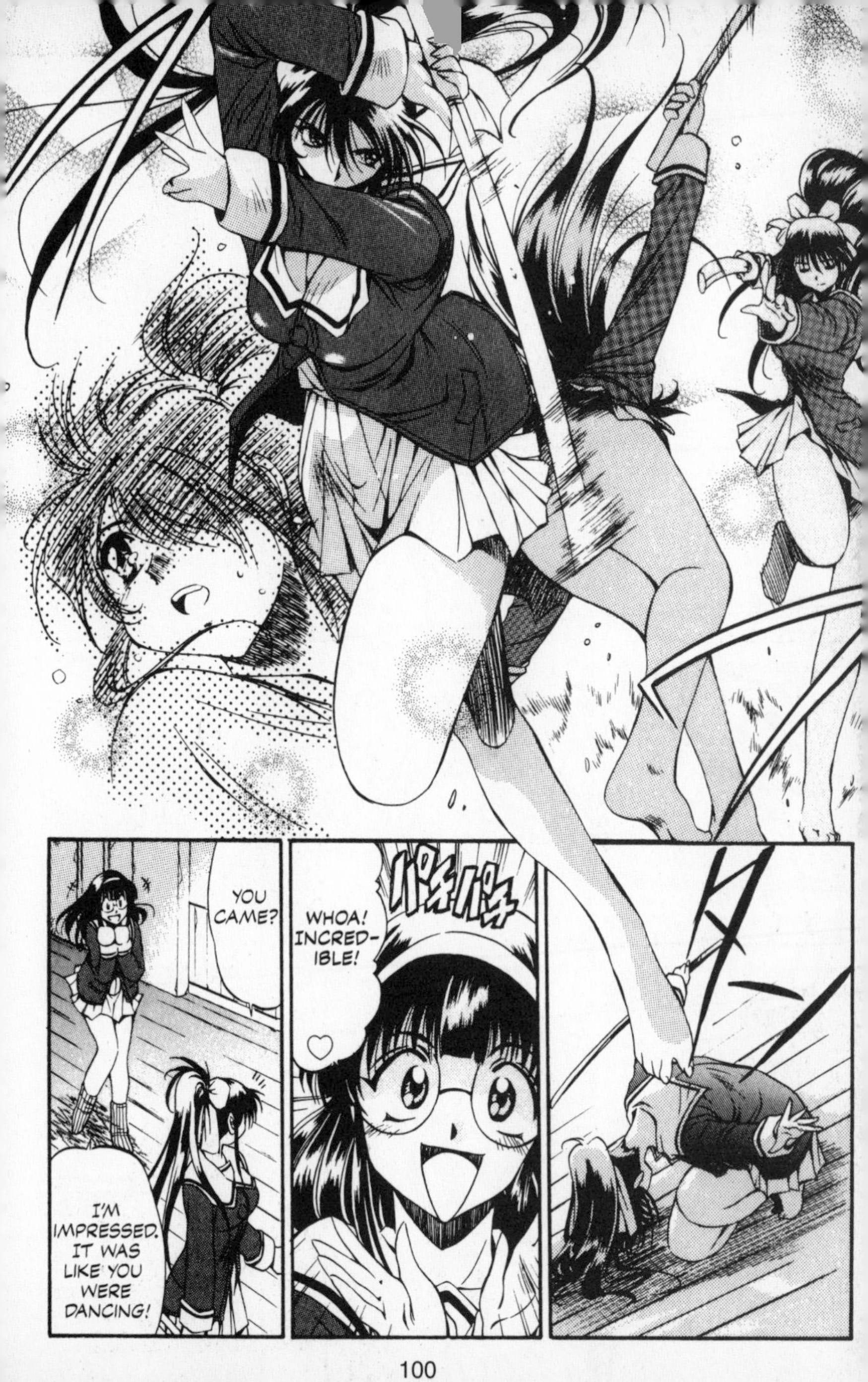
パチパチ
WHOA! INCREDIBLE!
YOU CAME?
I'M IMPRESSED. IT WAS LIKE YOU WERE DANCING!

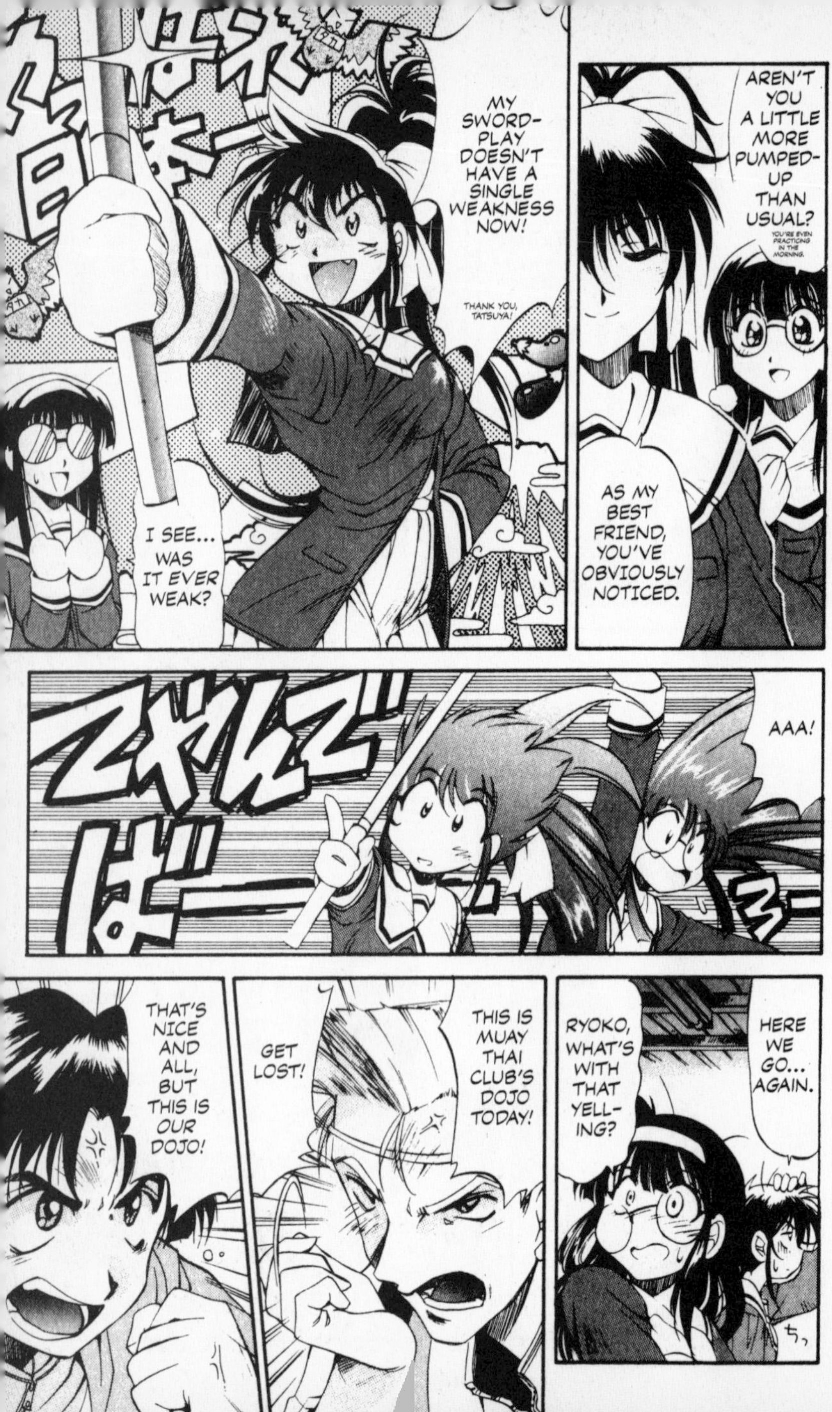
AREN'T YOU A LITTLE MORE PUMPED-UP THAN USUAL?
YOU'RE EVEN PRACTICING IN THE MORNING.
AS MY BEST FRIEND, YOU'VE OBVIOUSLY NOTICED.
MY SWORD-PLAY DOESN'T HAVE A SINGLE WEAKNESS NOW!
THANK YOU, TATSUYA!
I SEE... WAS IT EVER WEAK?
AAA!
HERE WE GO... AGAIN.
RYOKO, WHAT'S WITH THAT YELLING?
THIS IS MUAY THAI CLUB'S DOJO TODAY!
GET LOST!
THAT'S NICE AND ALL, BUT THIS IS OUR DOJO!

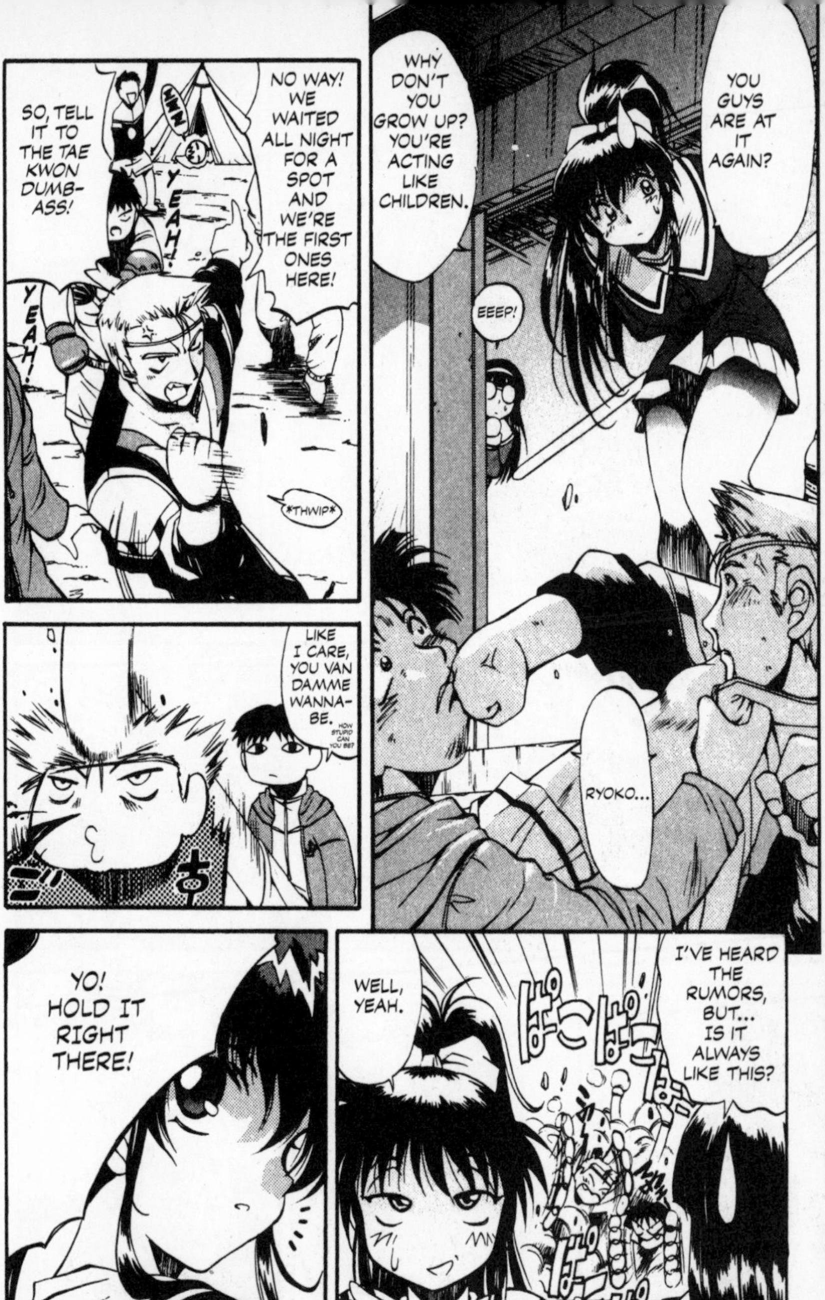
YOU GUYS ARE AT IT AGAIN?
WHY DON'T YOU GROW UP? YOU'RE ACTING LIKE CHILDREN.
EEEP!
RYOKO...
NO WAY! WE WAITED ALL NIGHT FOR A SPOT AND WE'RE THE FIRST ONES HERE!
SO, TELL IT TO THE TAE KWON DUMB-ASS!
YEAH!
YEAH!
THWIP
LIKE I CARE, YOU VAN DAMME WANNA-BE.
HOW STUPID CAN YOU BE?
I'VE HEARD THE RUMORS, BUT... IS IT ALWAYS LIKE THIS?
WELL, YEAH.
YO! HOLD IT RIGHT THERE!

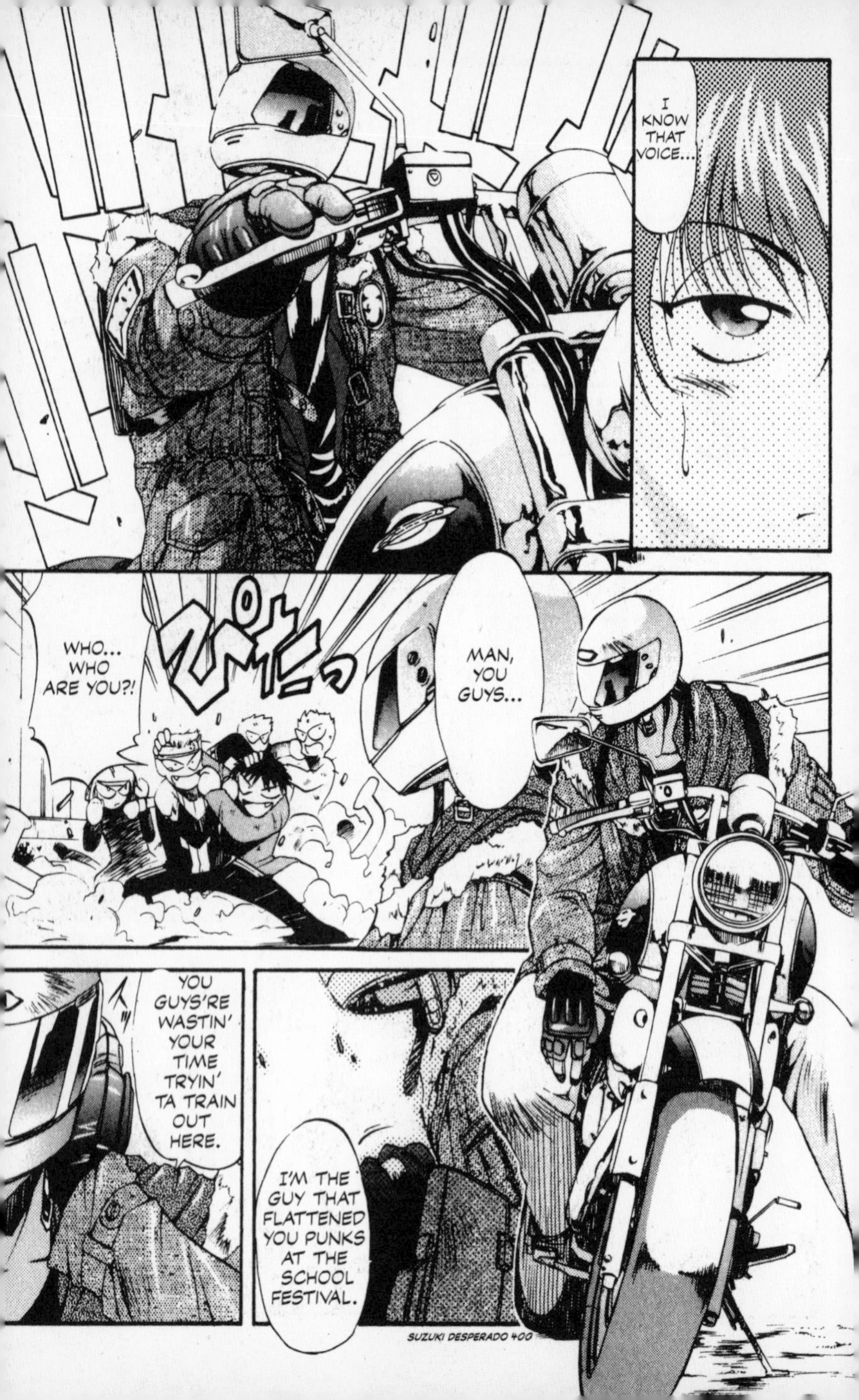
I KNOW THAT VOICE...
MAN, YOU GUYS...
WHO... WHO ARE YOU?!
I'M THE GUY THAT FLATTENED YOU PUNKS AT THE SCHOOL FESTIVAL.
SUZUKI DESPERADO 400
YOU GUYS'RE WASTIN' YOUR TIME TRYIN' TA TRAIN OUT HERE.

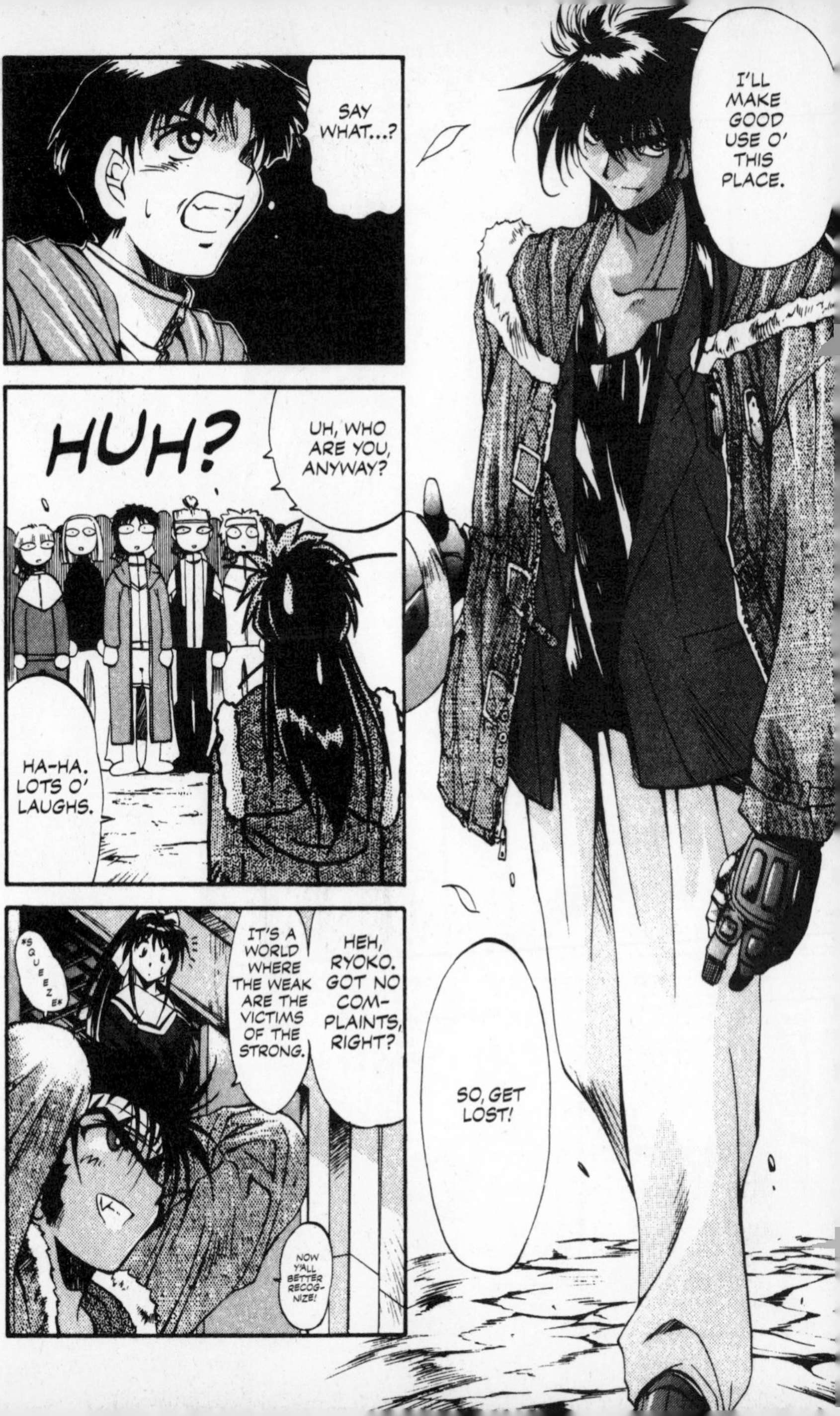

I'LL MAKE GOOD USE O' THIS PLACE.
SO, GET LOST!
SAY WHAT...?
UH, WHO ARE YOU, ANYWAY?
HUH?
HA-HA. LOTS O' LAUGHS.
HEH, RYOKO. GOT NO COM-PLAINTS, RIGHT?
IT'S A WORLD WHERE THE WEAK ARE THE VICTIMS OF THE STRONG.
SQUEEZE
NOW Y'ALL BETTER RECOG-NIZE!

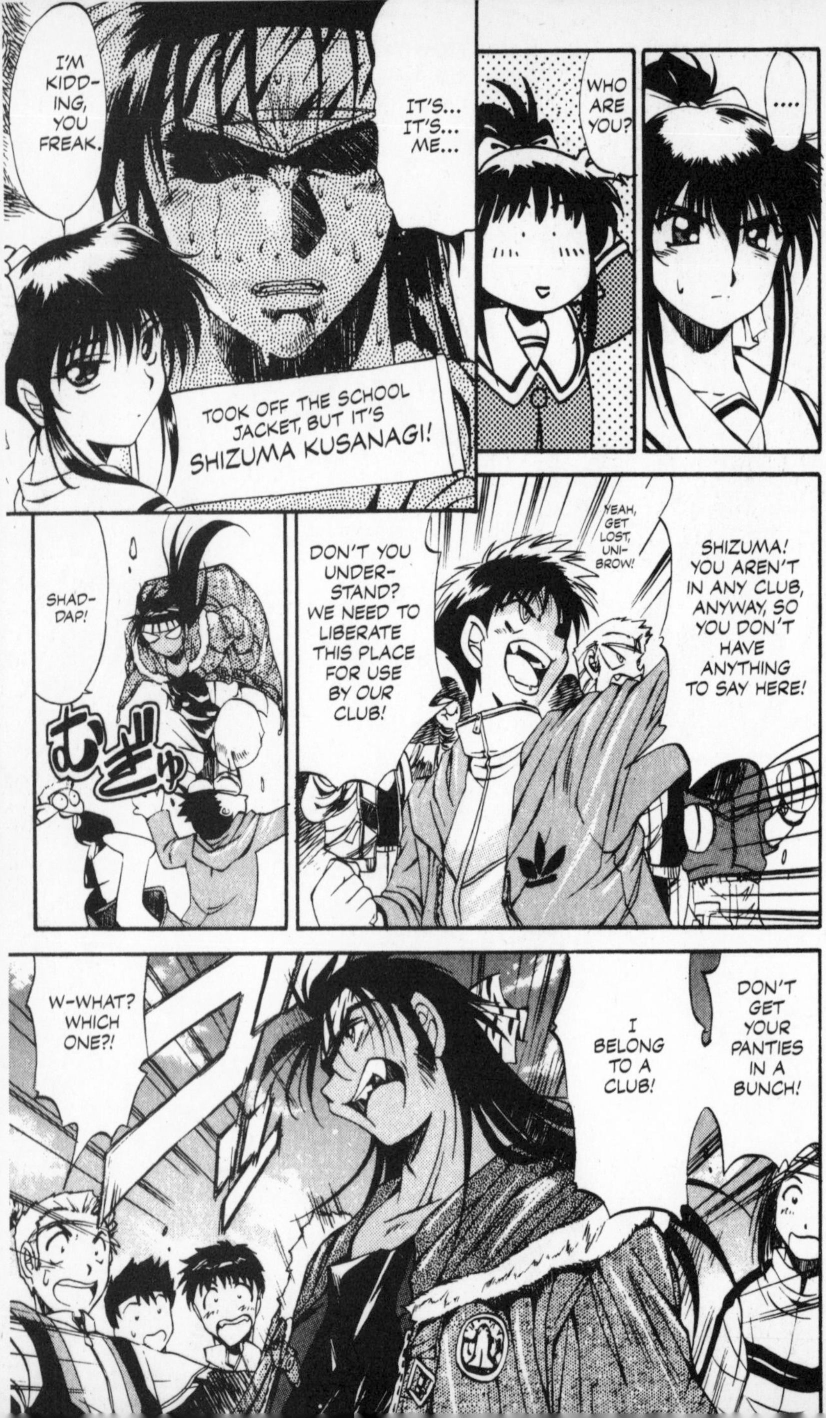
....
WHO ARE YOU?
IT'S... IT'S... ME...
I'M KIDDING, YOU FREAK.
TOOK OFF THE SCHOOL JACKET, BUT IT'S SHIZUMA KUSANAGI!
SHIZUMA! YOU AREN'T IN ANY CLUB, ANYWAY, SO YOU DON'T HAVE ANYTHING TO SAY HERE!
YEAH, GET LOST, UNI-BROW!
DON'T YOU UNDER-STAND? WE NEED TO LIBERATE THIS PLACE FOR USE BY OUR CLUB!
SHAD-DAP!
むぎゅ
DON'T GET YOUR PANTIES IN A BUNCH!
I BELONG TO A CLUB!
W-WHAT? WHICH ONE?!

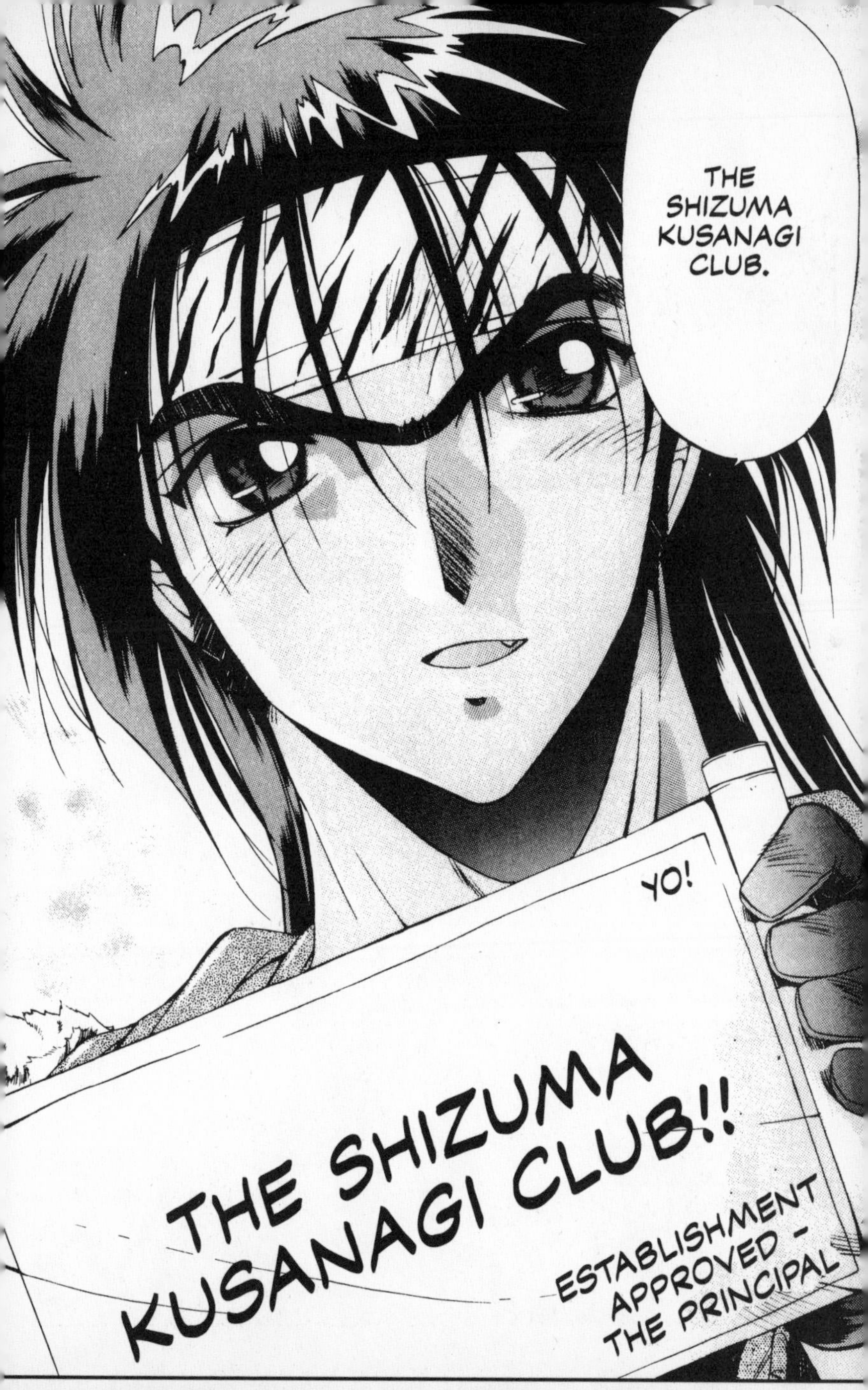
THE SHIZUMA KUSANAGI CLUB.
YO!
THE SHIZUMA KUSANAGI CLUB!!
ESTABLISHMENT APPROVED - THE PRINCIPAL

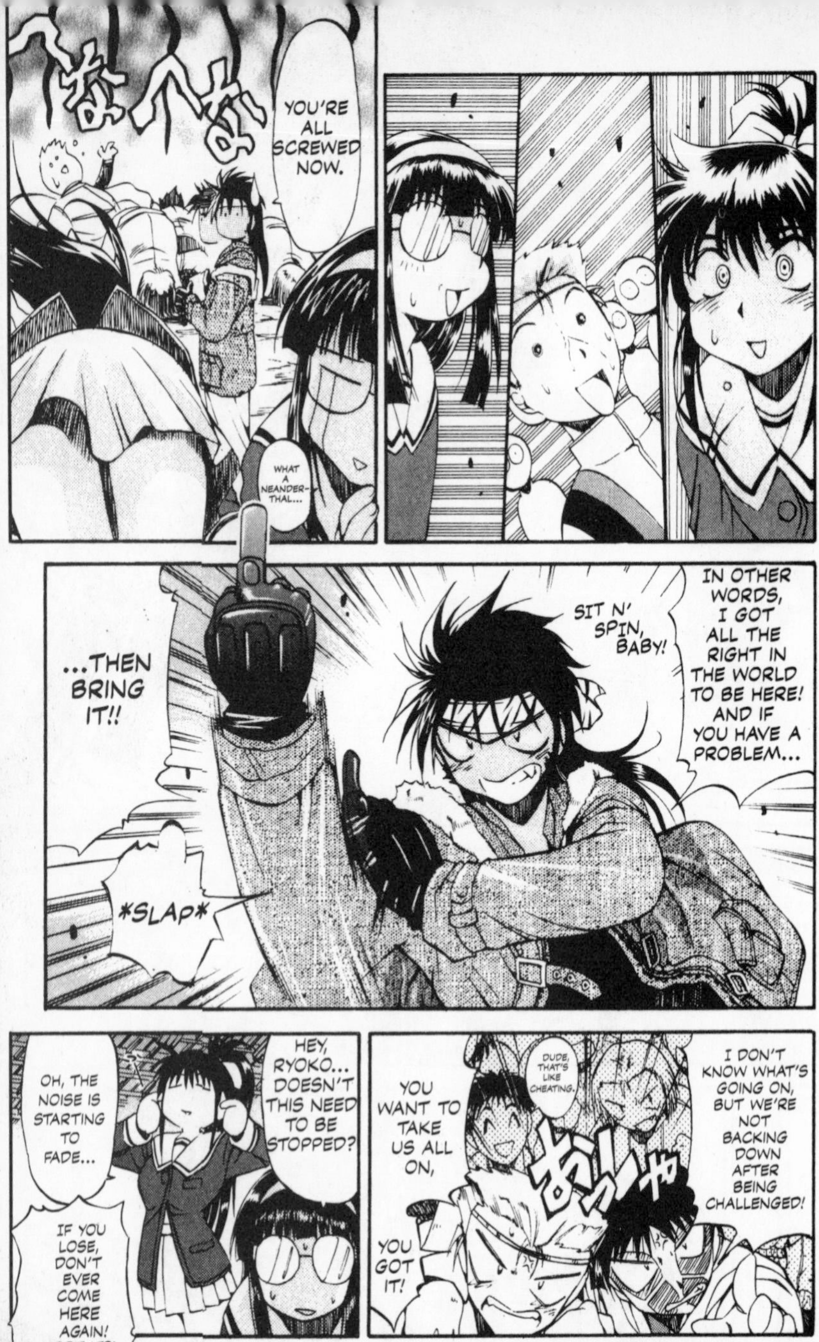
YOU'RE ALL SCREWED NOW.
WHAT A NEANDERTHAL...
IN OTHER WORDS, I GOT ALL THE RIGHT IN THE WORLD TO BE HERE! AND IF YOU HAVE A PROBLEM...
SIT N' SPIN, BABY!
...THEN BRING IT!!
SLAP
I DON'T KNOW WHAT'S GOING ON, BUT WE'RE NOT BACKING DOWN AFTER BEING CHALLENGED!
DUDE, THAT'S LIKE CHEATING.
YOU WANT TO TAKE US ALL ON,
YOU GOT IT!
HEY, RYOKO... DOESN'T THIS NEED TO BE STOPPED?
OH, THE NOISE IS STARTING TO FADE...
IF YOU LOSE, DON'T EVER COME HERE AGAIN! GOT IT?!

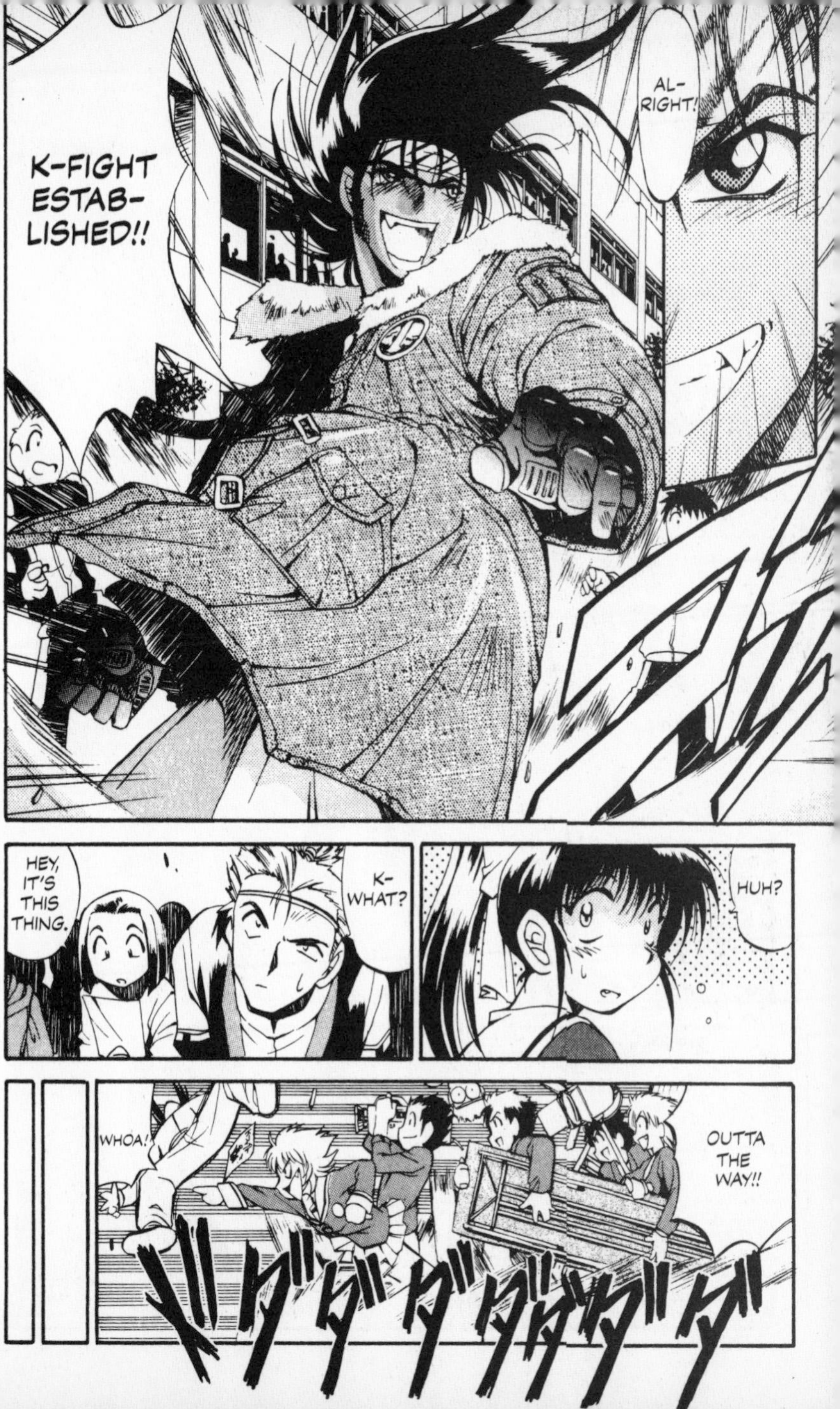
AL-RIGHT!
K-FIGHT ESTAB-LISHED!!
HUH?
K-WHAT?
HEY, IT'S THIS THING.
OUTTA THE WAY!!
WHOA!

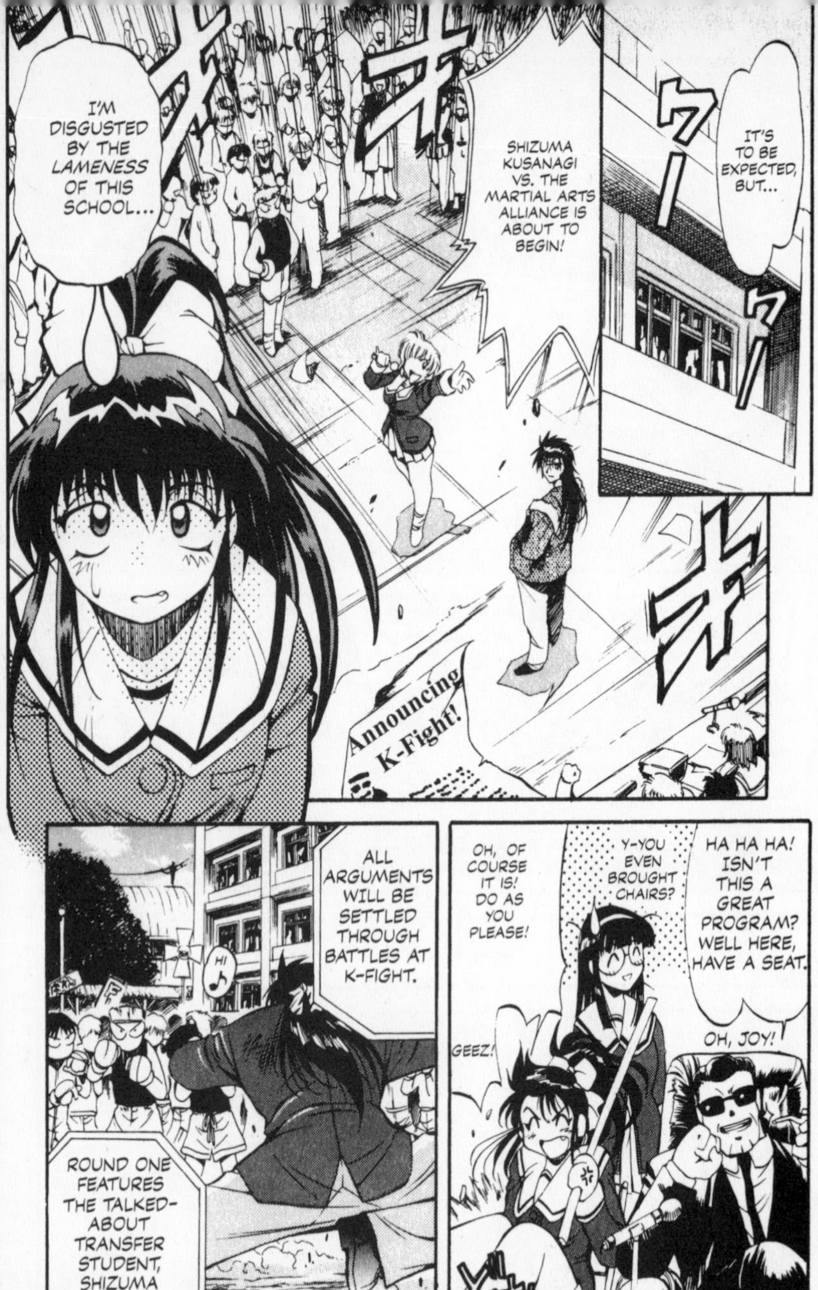
IT'S TO BE EXPECTED, BUT...
SHIZUMA KUSANAGI VS. THE MARTIAL ARTS ALLIANCE IS ABOUT TO BEGIN!
I'M DISGUSTED BY THE LAMENESS OF THIS SCHOOL...
Announcing K-Fight!
HA HA HA! ISN'T THIS A GREAT PROGRAM? WELL HERE, HAVE A SEAT.
Y-YOU EVEN BROUGHT CHAIRS?
OH, OF COURSE IT IS! DO AS YOU PLEASE!
OH, JOY!
GEEZ!
commentator
ALL ARGUMENTS WILL BE SETTLED THROUGH BATTLES AT K-FIGHT.
HI ♪
ROUND ONE FEATURES THE TALKED-ABOUT TRANSFER STUDENT, SHIZUMA KUSANAGI! LET'S START...

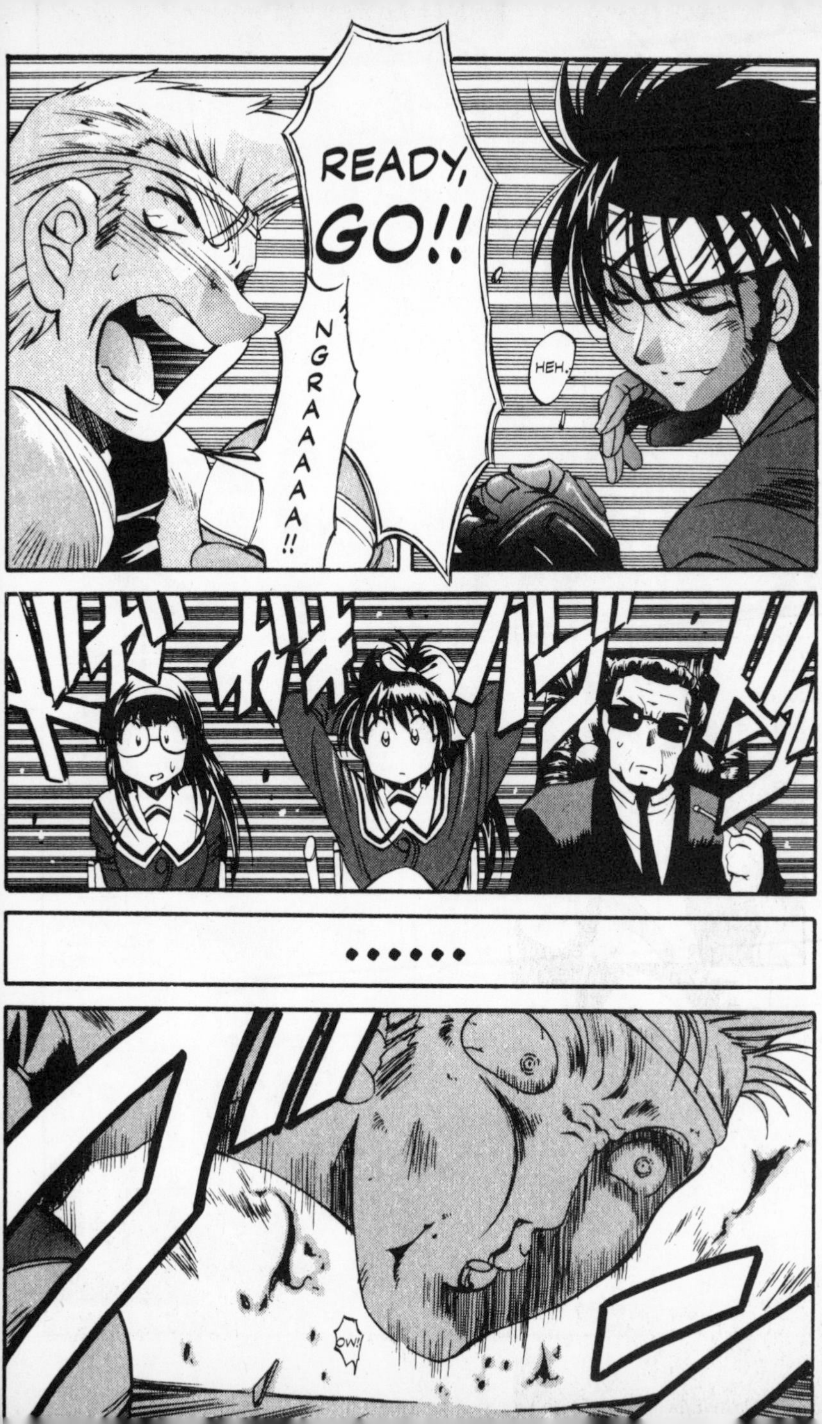
HEH.
READY, GO!!
NGRAAAAAA!!
••••••
OW!!

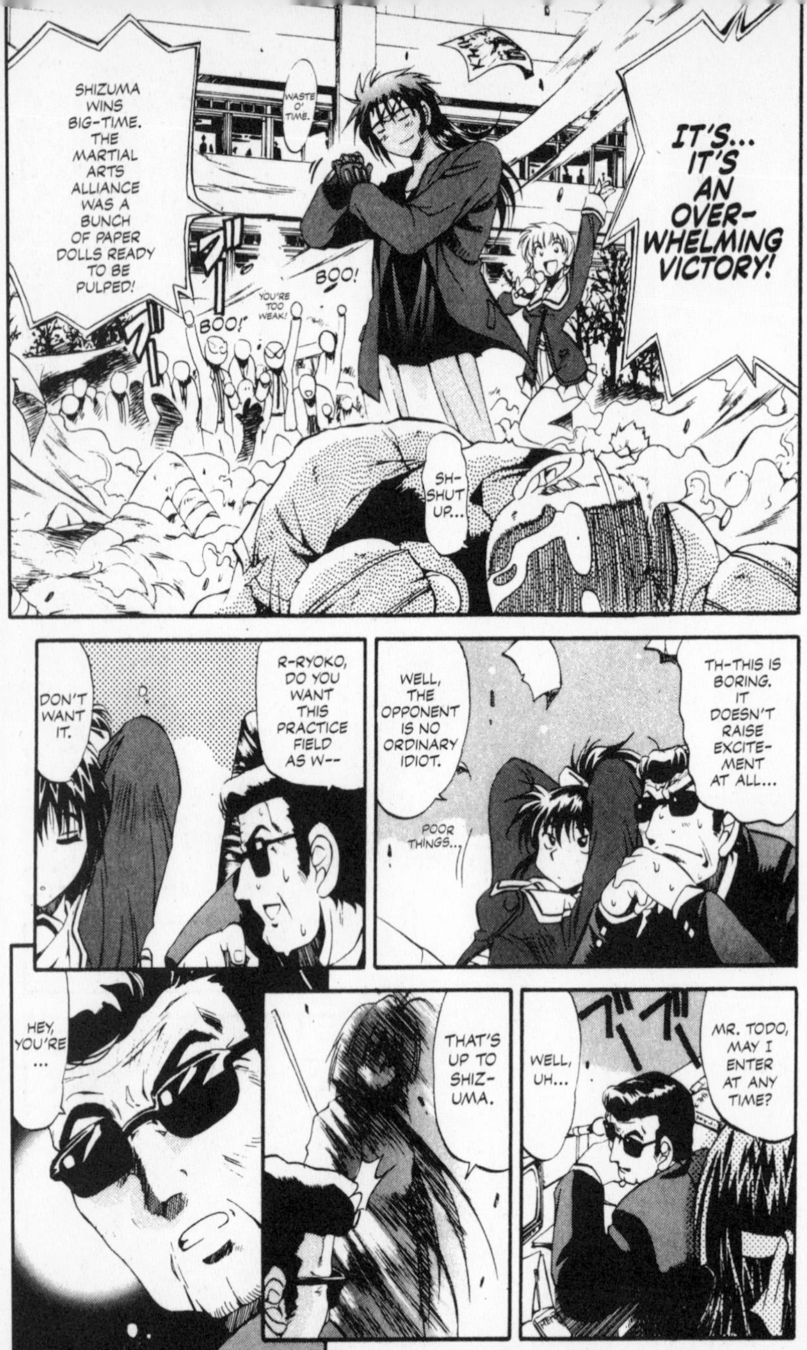
IT'S... IT'S AN OVER-WHELMING VICTORY!
WASTE O' TIME.
SHIZUMA WINS BIG-TIME. THE MARTIAL ARTS ALLIANCE WAS A BUNCH OF PAPER DOLLS READY TO BE PULPED!
BOO!
YOU'RE TOO WEAK!
BOO!
SH-SHUT UP...
TH-THIS IS BORING. IT DOESN'T RAISE EXCITE-MENT AT ALL...
WELL, THE OPPONENT IS NO ORDINARY IDIOT.
POOR THINGS...
R-RYOKO, DO YOU WANT THIS PRACTICE FIELD AS W--
DON'T WANT IT.
MR. TODO, MAY I ENTER AT ANY TIME?
WELL, UH...
THAT'S UP TO SHIZ-UMA.
HEY, YOU'RE ...

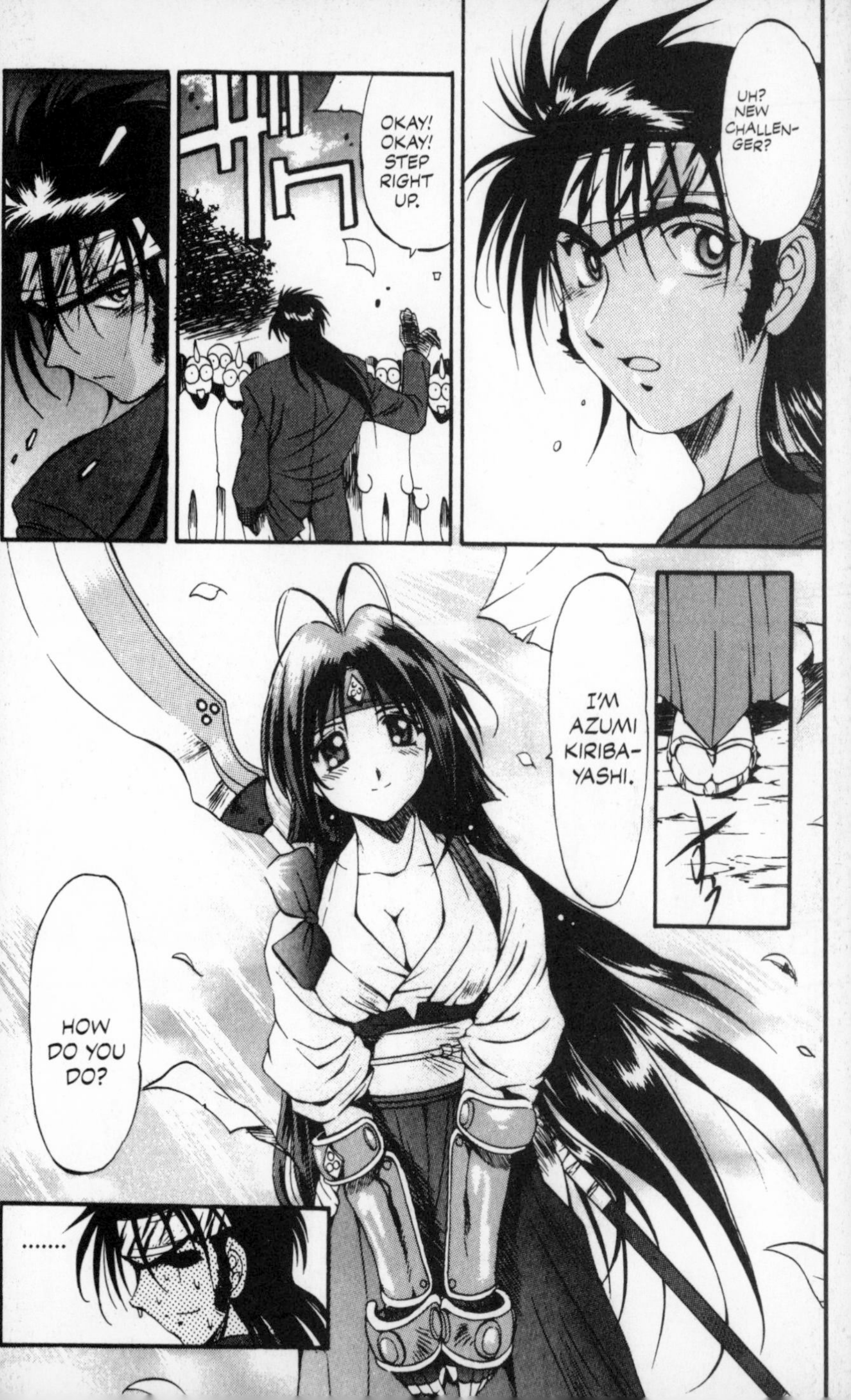
UH? NEW CHALLEN-GER?
ザッ
OKAY! OKAY! STEP RIGHT UP.
I'M AZUMI KIRIBA-YASHI.
HOW DO YOU DO?
....

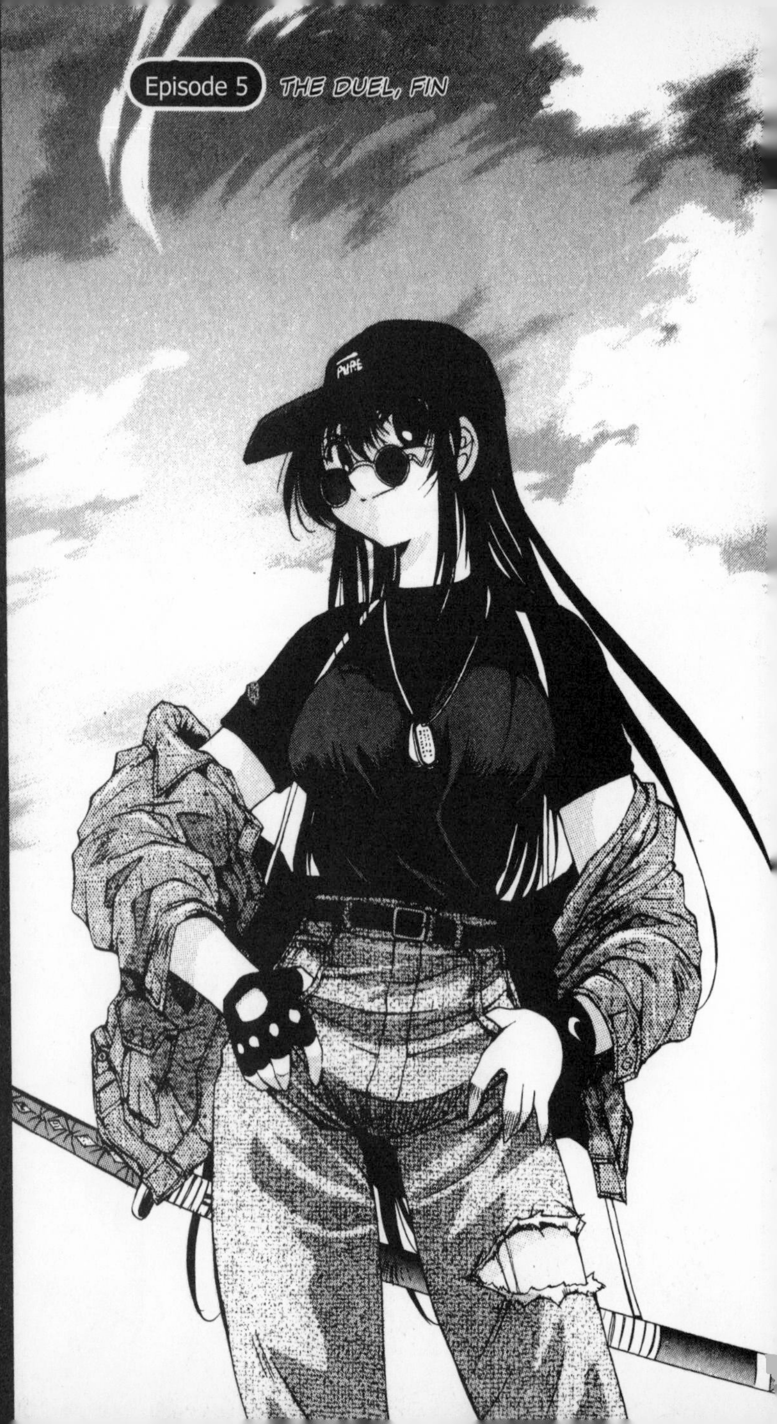
Episode 5
THE DUEL, FIN
PURE

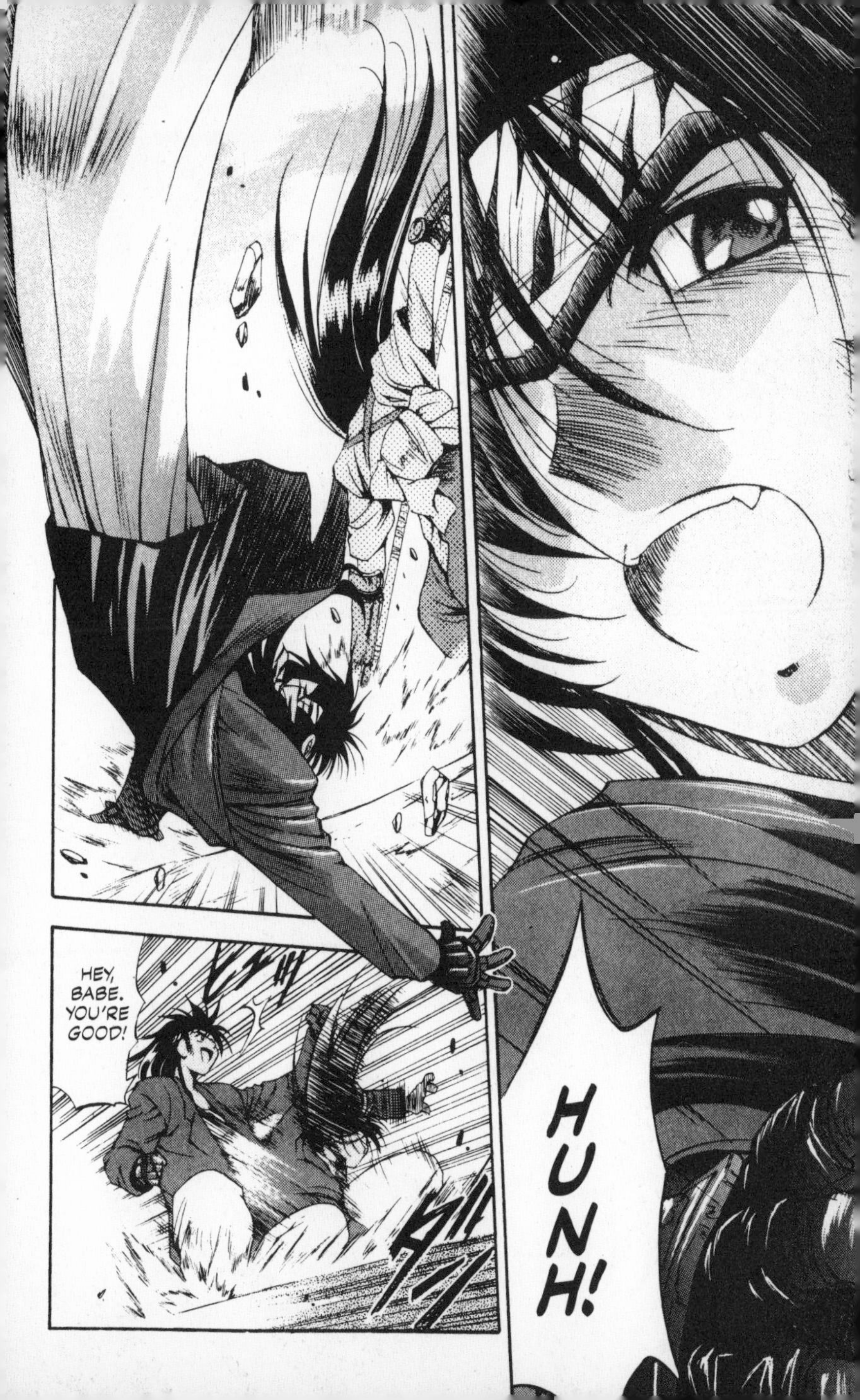
HUNH!
HEY, BABE. YOU'RE GOOD!

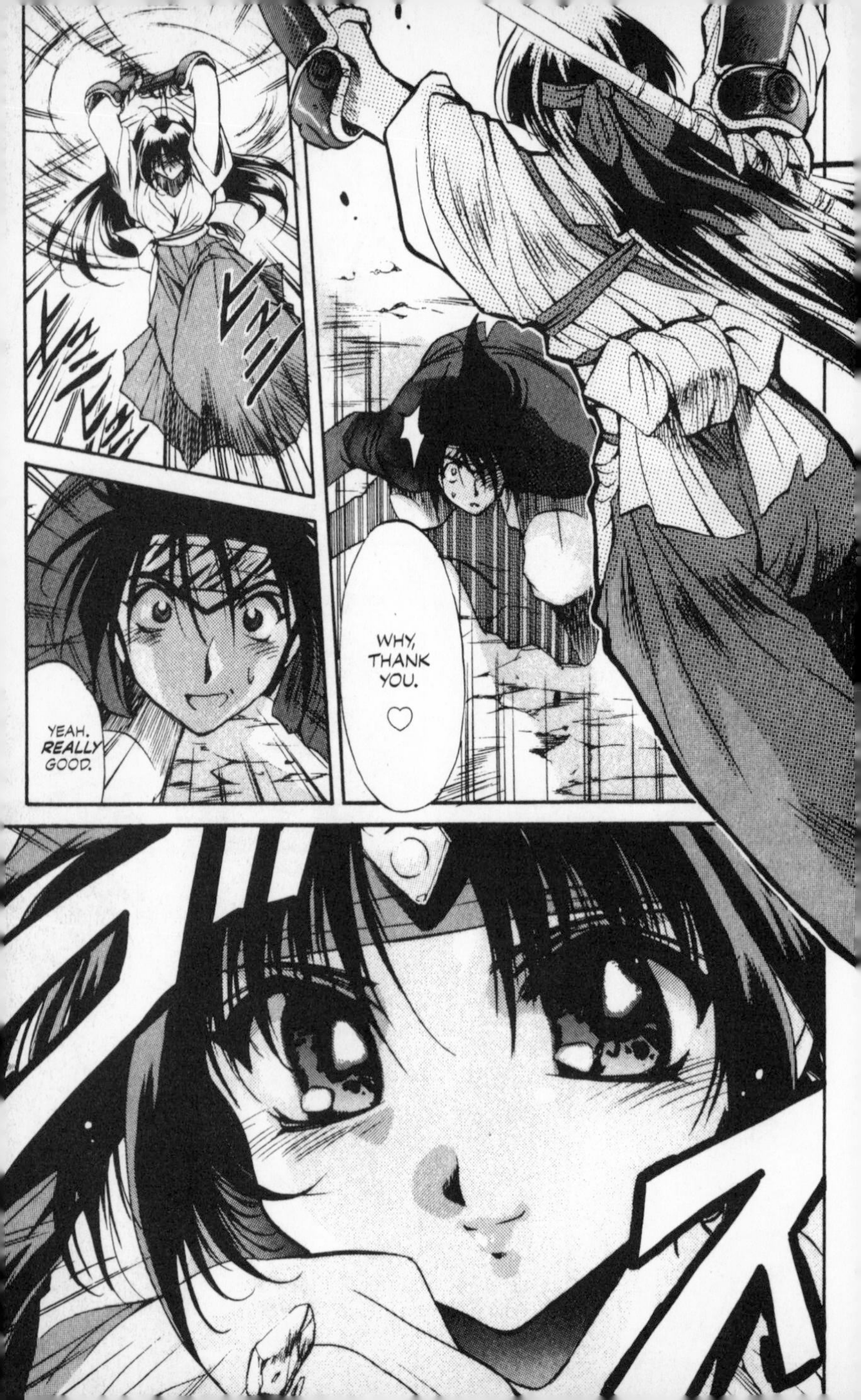
WHY, THANK YOU. ♡
YEAH. REALLY GOOD.

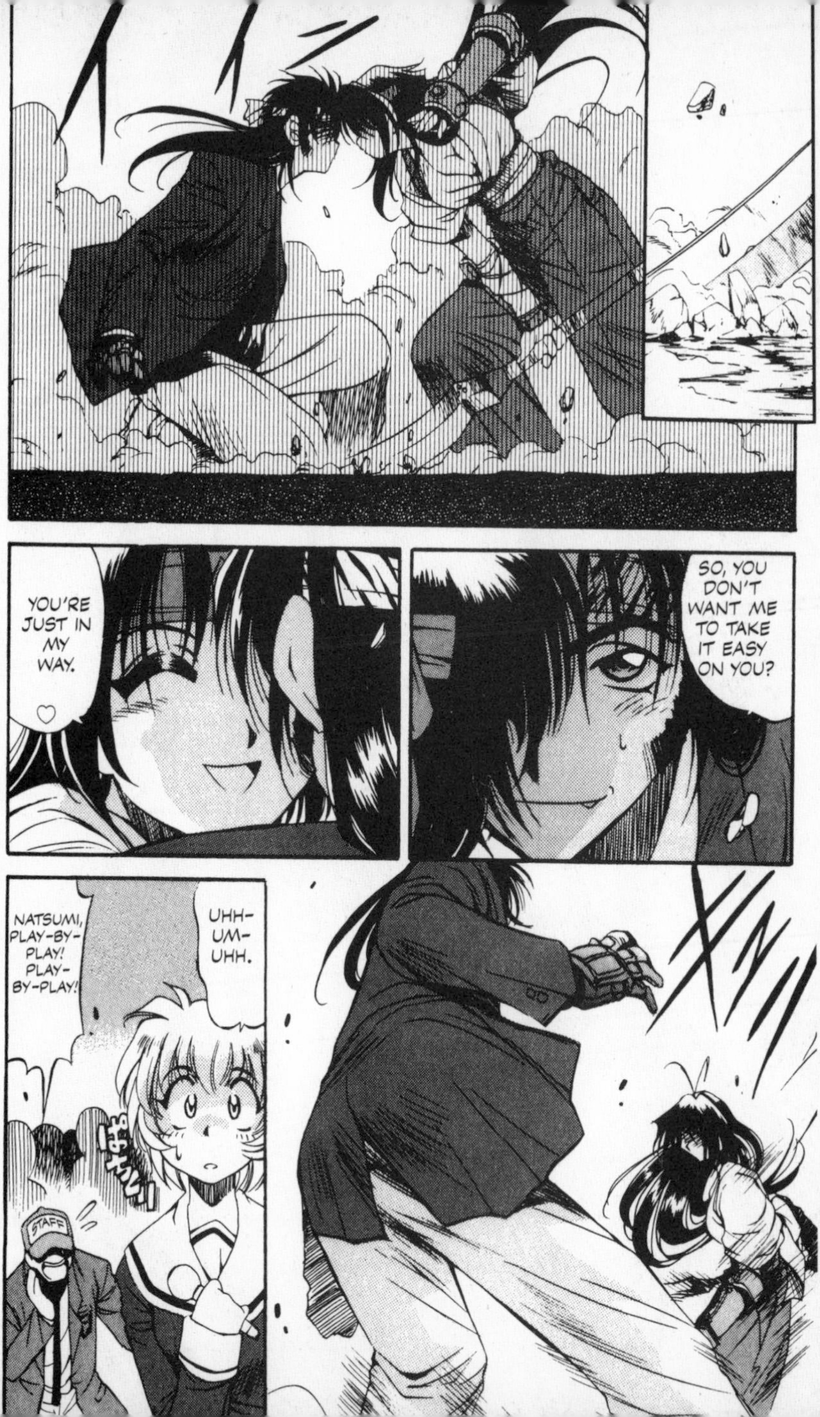
SO, YOU DON'T WANT ME TO TAKE IT EASY ON YOU?
YOU'RE JUST IN MY WAY.
UHH-UM-UHH.
NATSUMI, PLAY-BY-PLAY! PLAY-BY-PLAY!
STAFF

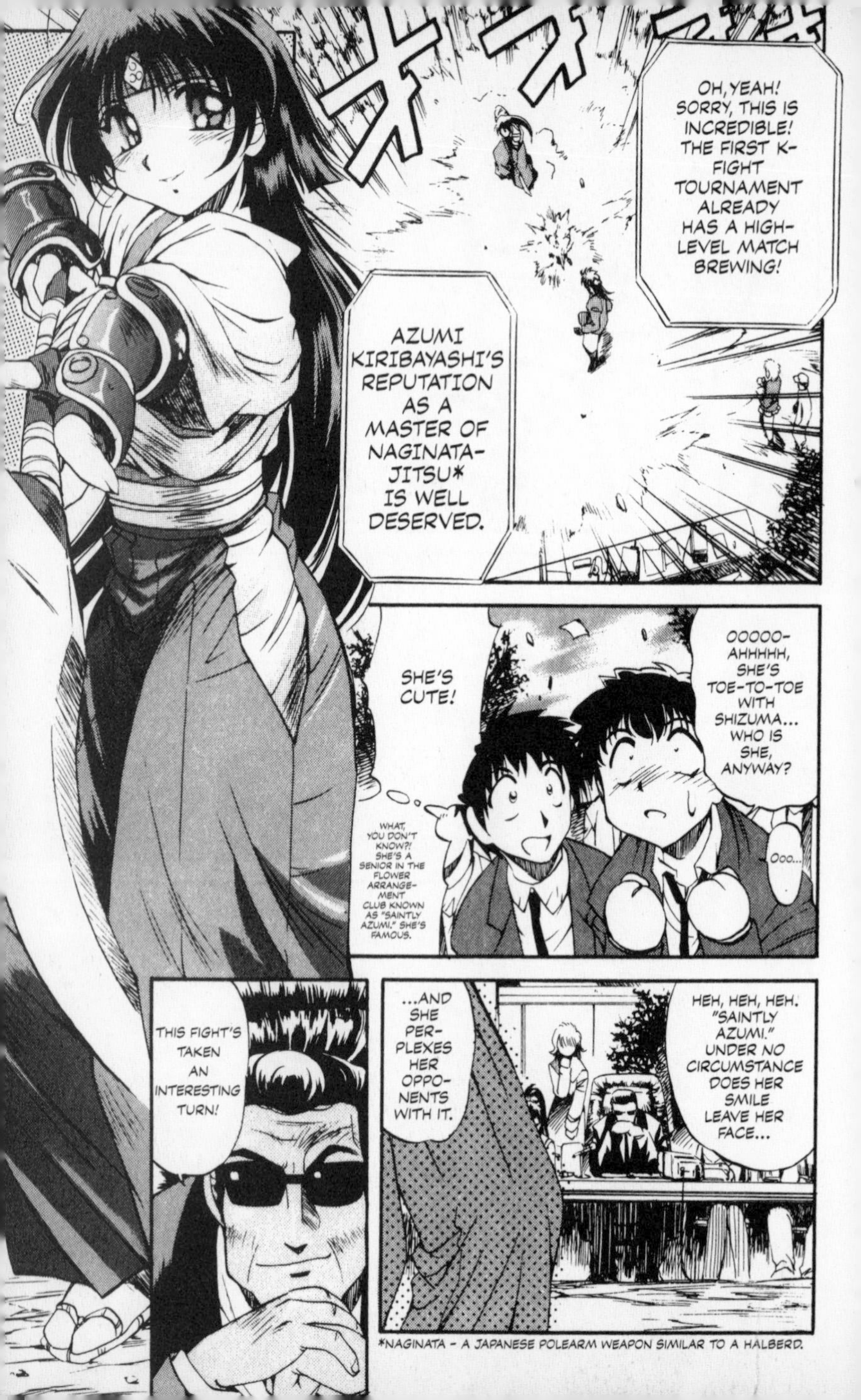
OH, YEAH! SORRY, THIS IS INCREDIBLE! THE FIRST K-FIGHT TOURNAMENT ALREADY HAS A HIGH-LEVEL MATCH BREWING!
AZUMI KIRIBAYASHI'S REPUTATION AS A MASTER OF NAGINATA-JITSU* IS WELL DESERVED.
OOOOO-AHHHHH, SHE'S TOE-TO-TOE WITH SHIZUMA... WHO IS SHE, ANYWAY?
Ooo...
SHE'S CUTE!
WHAT, YOU DON'T KNOW?! SHE'S A SENIOR IN THE FLOWER ARRANGEMENT CLUB KNOWN AS "SAINTLY AZUMI." SHE'S FAMOUS.
HEH, HEH, HEH. "SAINTLY AZUMI." UNDER NO CIRCUMSTANCE DOES HER SMILE LEAVE HER FACE...
...AND SHE PERPLEXES HER OPPONENTS WITH IT.
THIS FIGHT'S TAKEN AN INTERESTING TURN!
*NAGINATA - A JAPANESE POLEARM WEAPON SIMILAR TO A HALBERD.

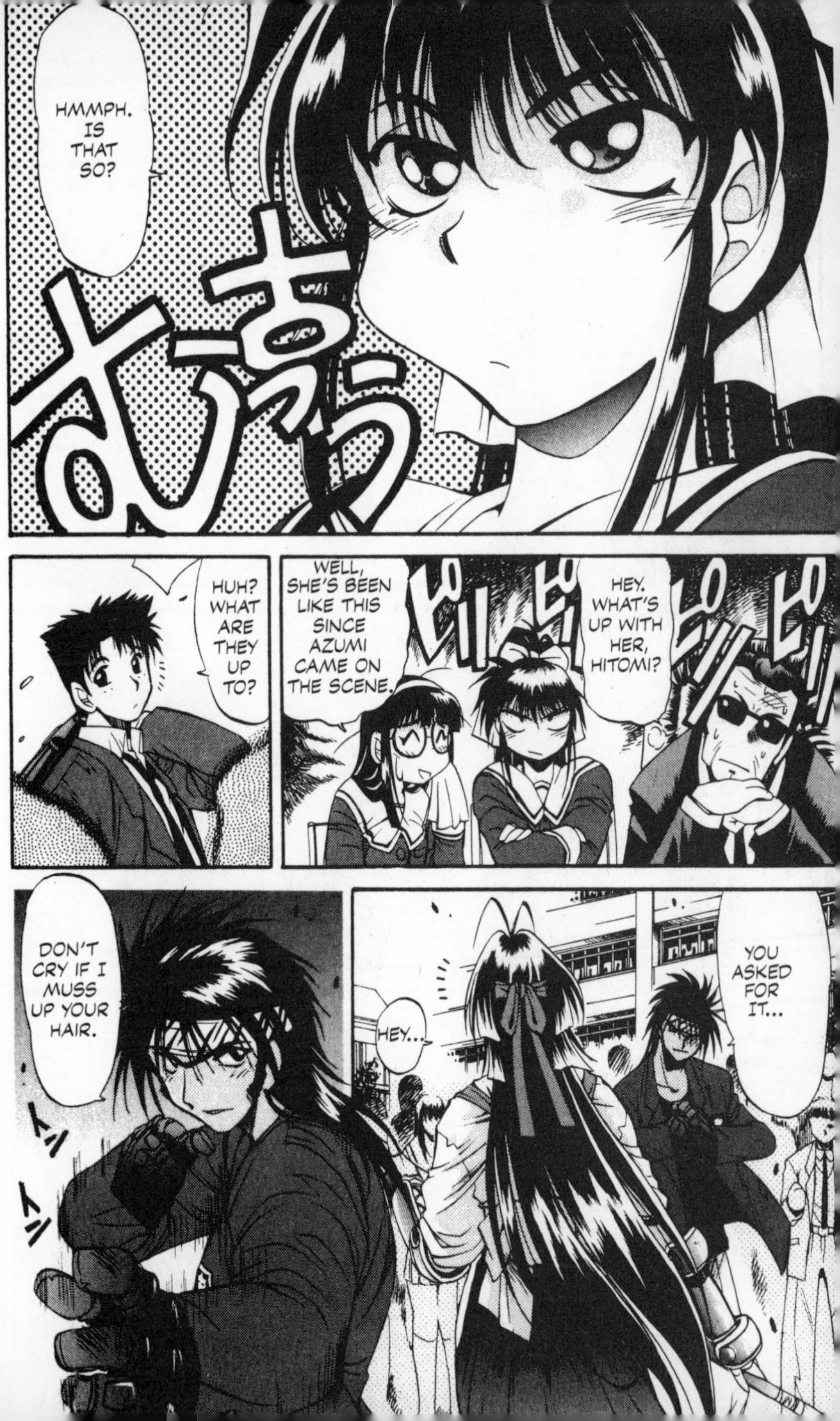
HMMPH. IS THAT SO?
HEY. WHAT'S UP WITH HER, HITOMI?
WELL, SHE'S BEEN LIKE THIS SINCE AZUMI CAME ON THE SCENE.
HUH? WHAT ARE THEY UP TO?
YOU ASKED FOR IT...
HEY...
DON'T CRY IF I MUSS UP YOUR HAIR.

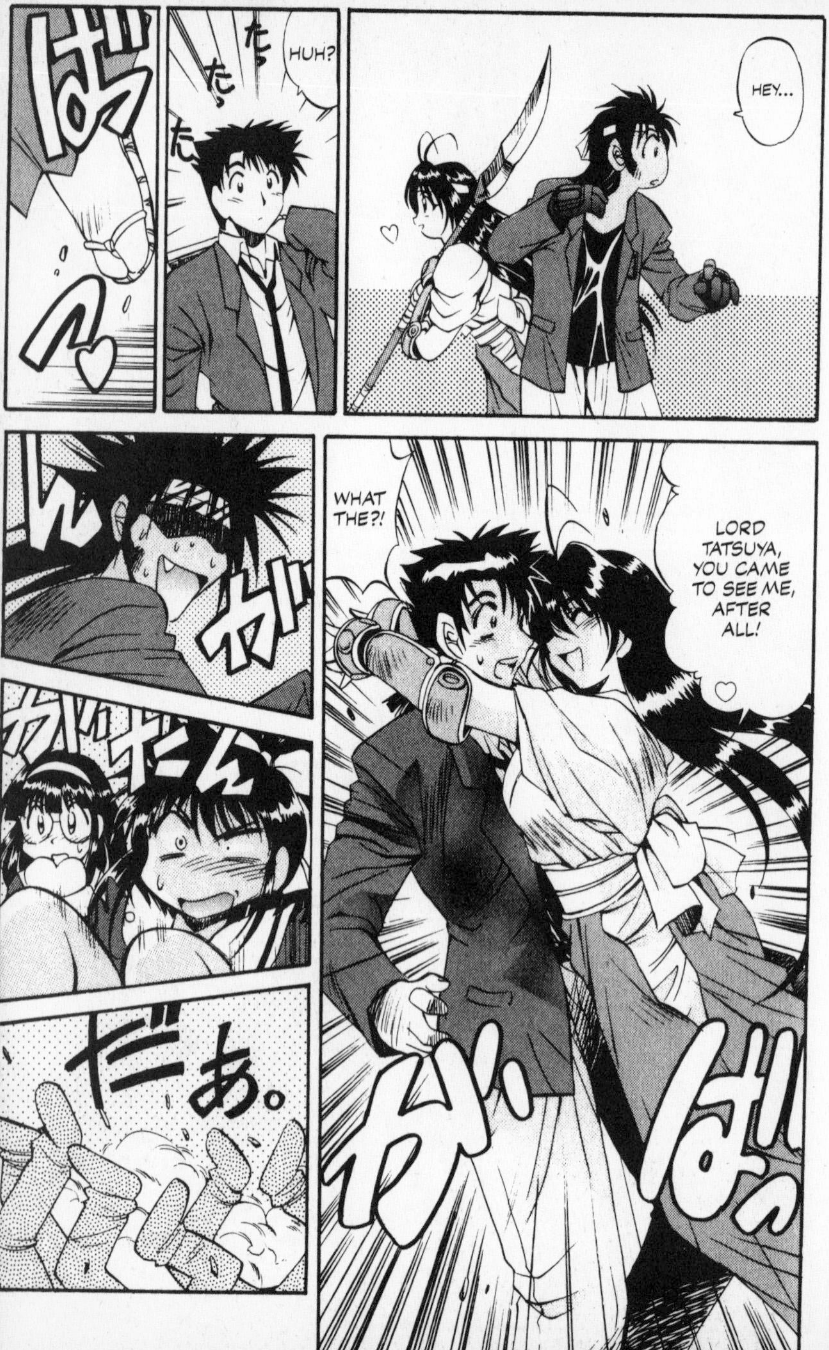
HEY...
HUH?
LORD TATSUYA, YOU CAME TO SEE ME, AFTER ALL!
WHAT THE?!

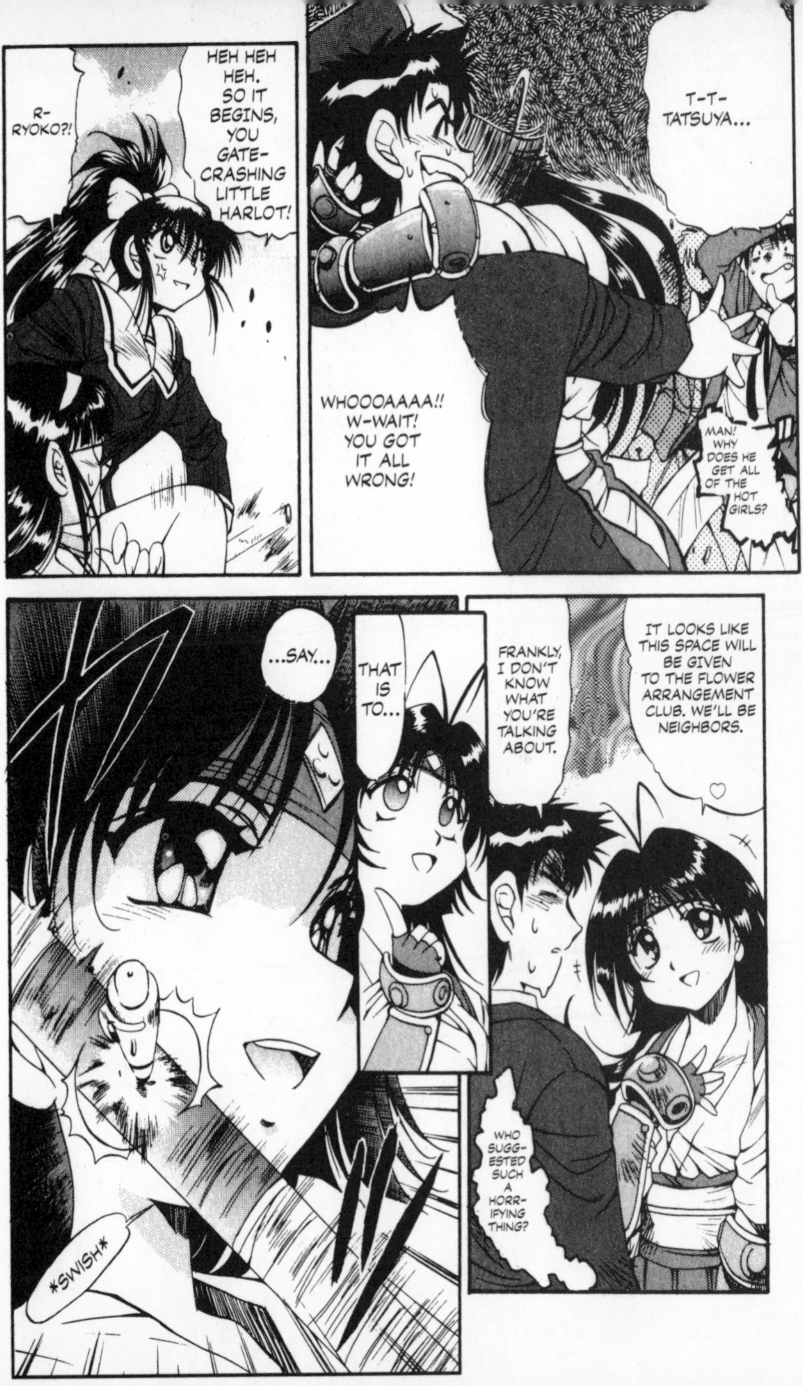
T-T-TATSUYA...
WHOOOAAAA!! W-WAIT! YOU GOT IT ALL WRONG!
MAN! WHY DOES HE GET ALL OF THE HOT GIRLS?
HEH HEH HEH. SO IT BEGINS, YOU GATE-CRASHING LITTLE HARLOT!
R-RYOKO?!
IT LOOKS LIKE THIS SPACE WILL BE GIVEN TO THE FLOWER ARRANGEMENT CLUB. WE'LL BE NEIGHBORS. ♡
FRANKLY, I DON'T KNOW WHAT YOU'RE TALKING ABOUT.
WHO SUGG-ESTED SUCH A HORR-IFYING THING?
THAT IS TO...
...SAY...
SWISH

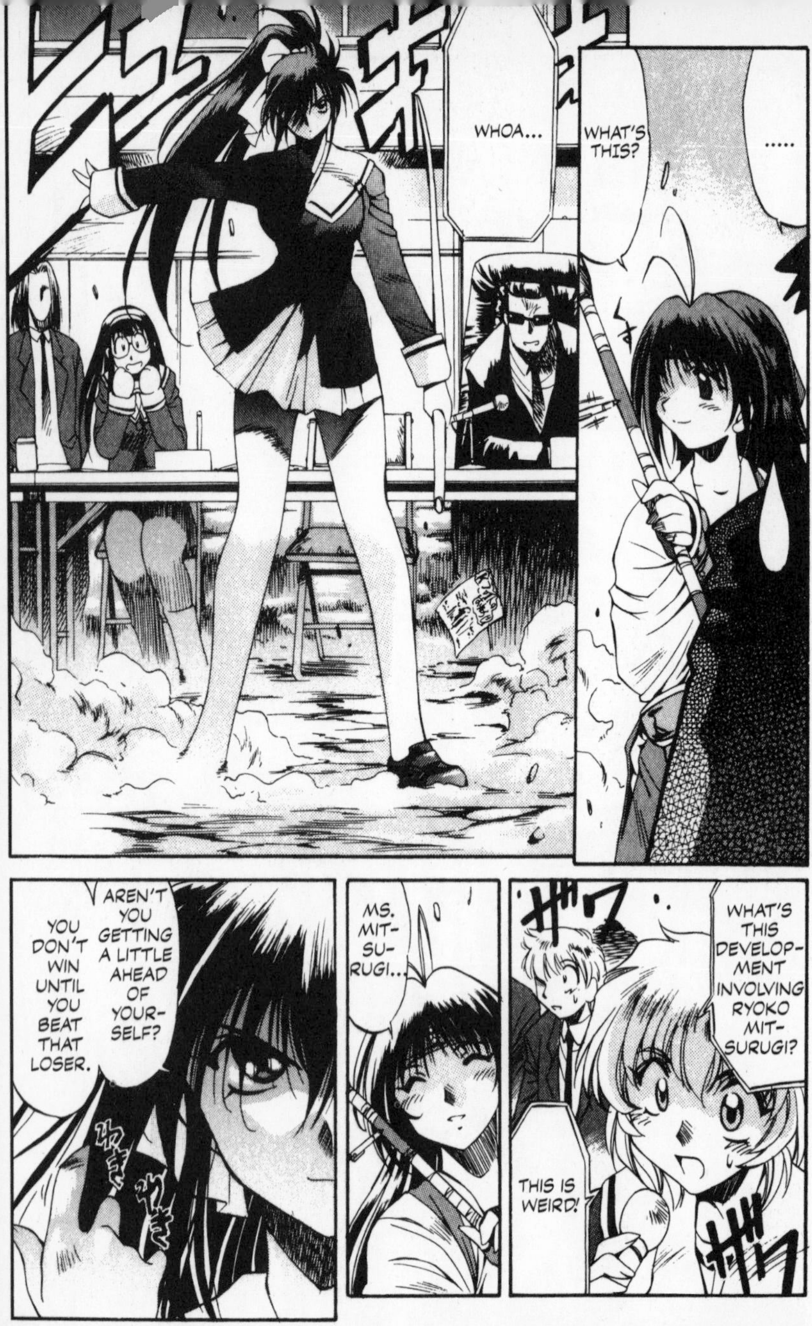
.....
WHAT'S THIS?
WHOA...
WHAT'S THIS DEVELOPMENT INVOLVING RYOKO MIT-SURUGI?
THIS IS WEIRD!
MS. MIT-SU-RUGI...
AREN'T YOU GETTING A LITTLE AHEAD OF YOURSELF?
YOU DON'T WIN UNTIL YOU BEAT THAT LOSER.

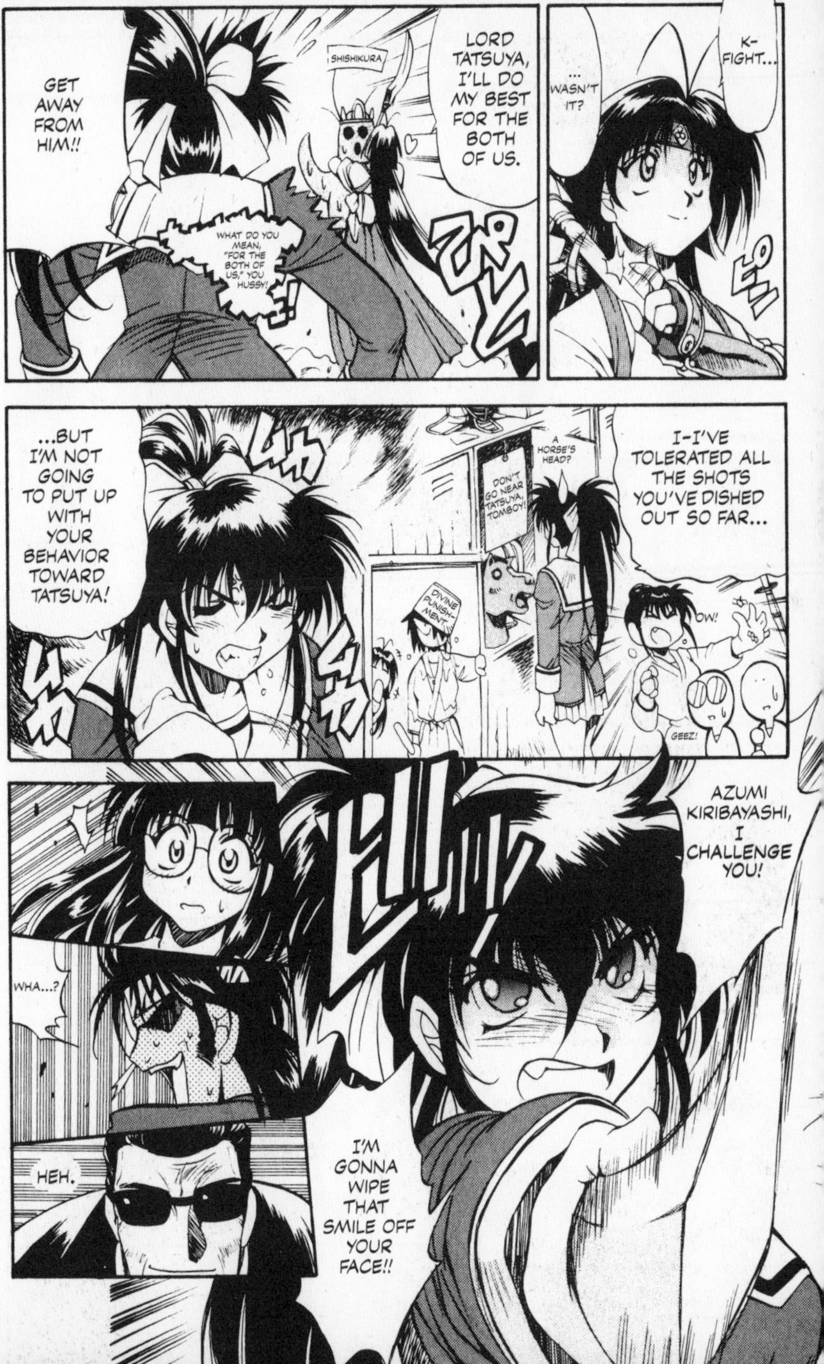
K-
FIGHT...
...
WASN'T
IT?
LORD TATSUYA, I'LL DO MY BEST FOR THE BOTH OF US.
SHISHIKURA
GET AWAY FROM HIM!!
WHAT DO YOU MEAN, "FOR THE BOTH OF US," YOU HUSSY!
I-I'VE TOLERATED ALL THE SHOTS YOU'VE DISHED OUT SO FAR...
OW!
GEEZ!
A HORSE'S HEAD?
DON'T GO NEAR TATSUYA, TOMBOY!
DIVINE PUNISHMENT
...BUT I'M NOT GOING TO PUT UP WITH YOUR BEHAVIOR TOWARD TATSUYA!
AZUMI KIRIBAYASHI, I CHALLENGE YOU!
WHA...?
I'M GONNA WIPE THAT SMILE OFF YOUR FACE!!
HEH.

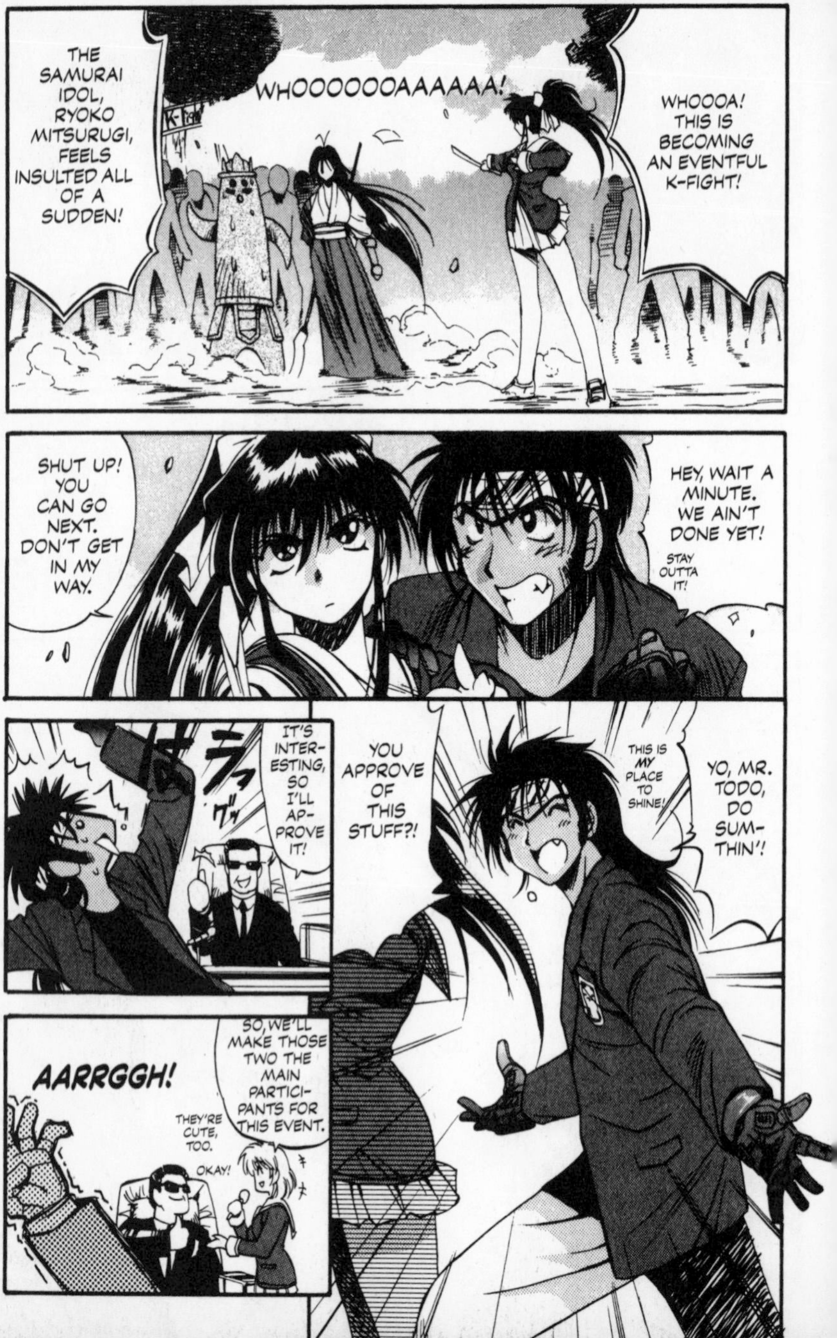
WHOOOA! THIS IS BECOMING AN EVENTFUL K-FIGHT!
WHOOOOOOAAAAAA!
THE SAMURAI IDOL, RYOKO MITSURUGI, FEELS INSULTED ALL OF A SUDDEN!
HEY, WAIT A MINUTE. WE AIN'T DONE YET!
STAY OUTTA IT!
SHUT UP! YOU CAN GO NEXT. DON'T GET IN MY WAY.
YO, MR. TODO, DO SUM-THIN'!
THIS IS *MY* PLACE TO SHINE!
YOU APPROVE OF THIS STUFF?!
IT'S INTER-ESTING, SO I'LL AP-PROVE IT!
SO, WE'LL MAKE THOSE TWO THE MAIN PARTICI-PANTS FOR THIS EVENT.
THEY'RE CUTE, TOO.
OKAY!
AARRGGH!

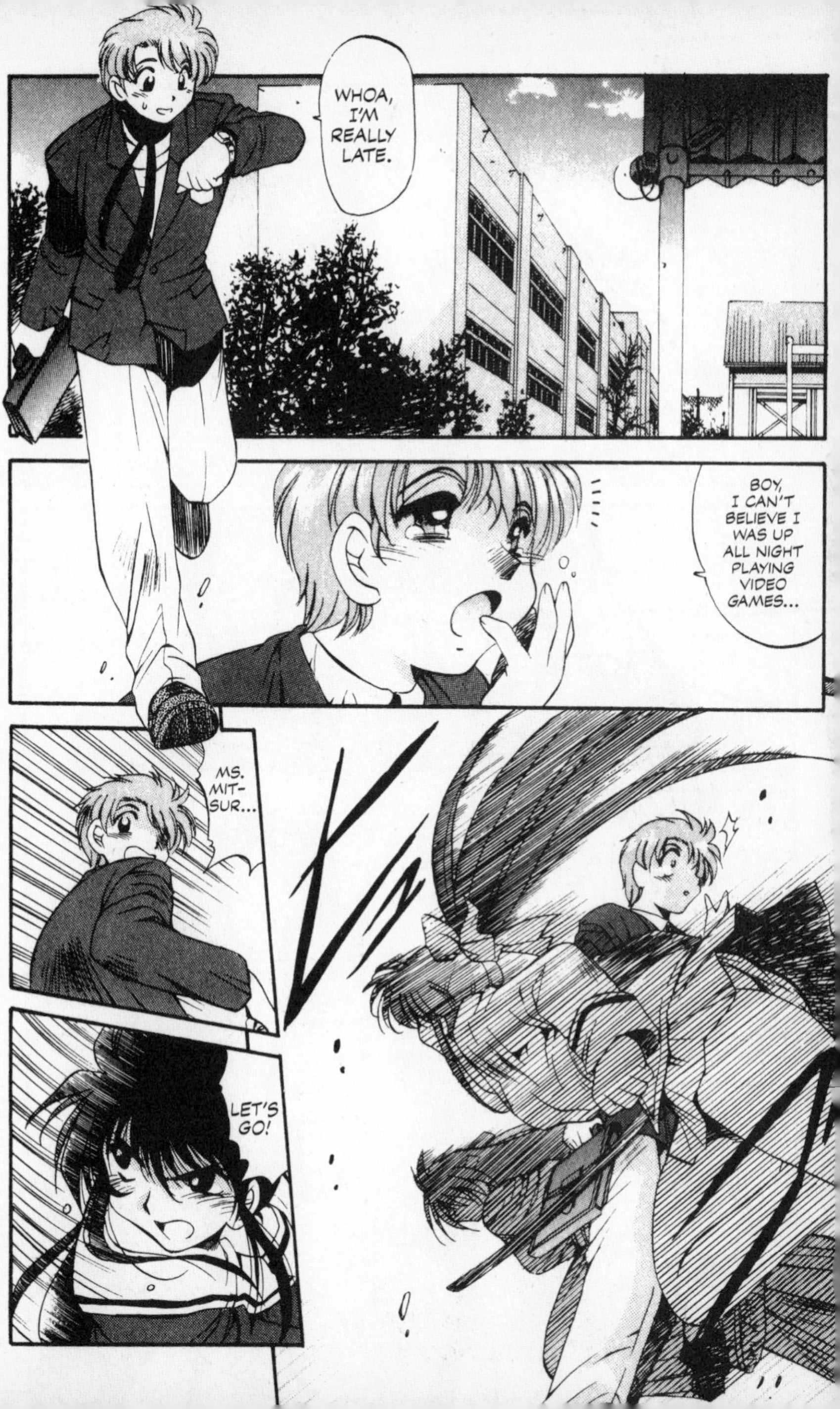
WHOA, I'M REALLY LATE.
BOY, I CAN'T BELIEVE I WAS UP ALL NIGHT PLAYING VIDEO GAMES...
MS. MITSUR...
LET'S GO!

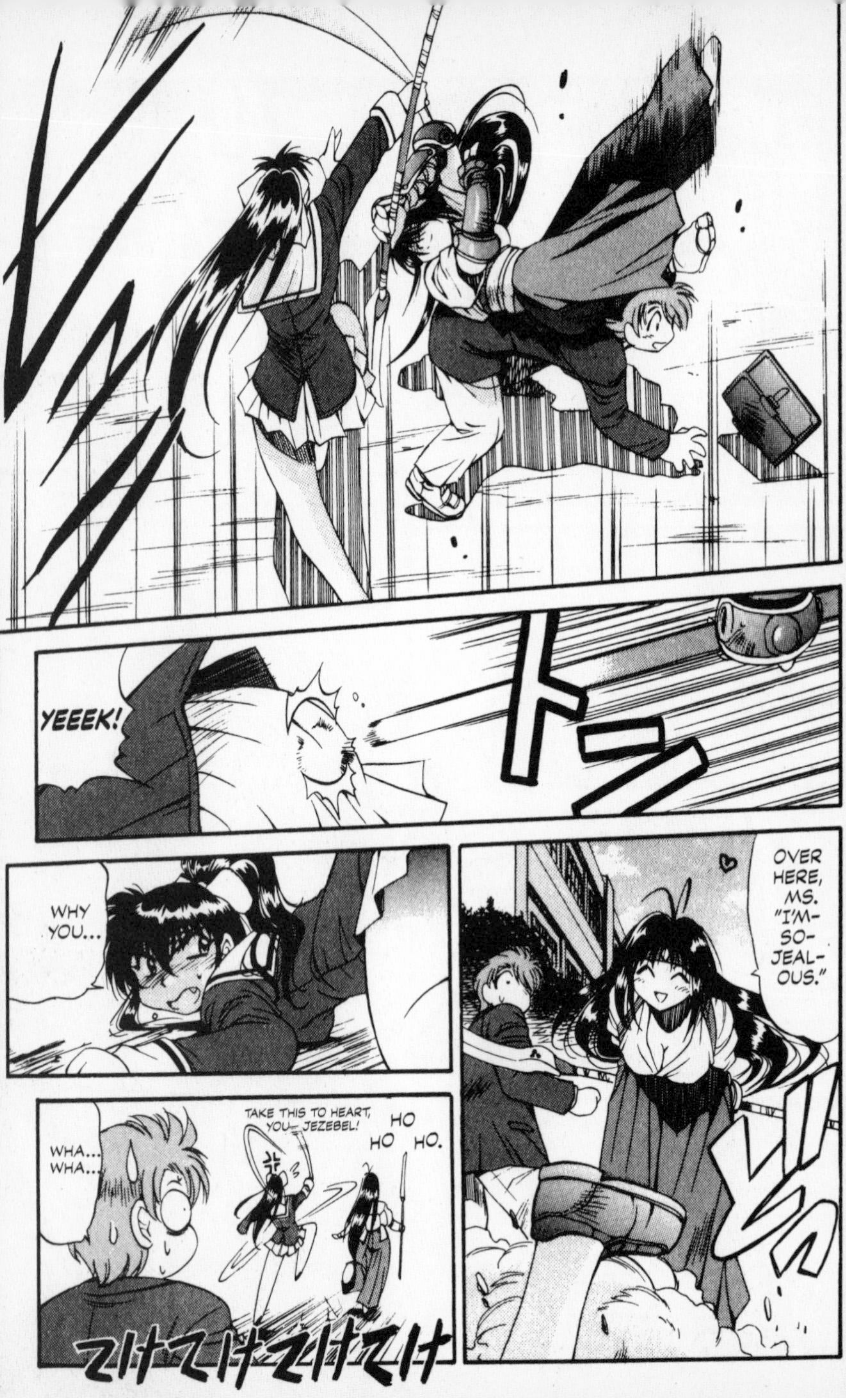
YEEEK!
OVER HERE, MS. "I'M-SO-JEALOUS."
WHY YOU...
HO HO HO.
TAKE THIS TO HEART, YOU JEZEBEL!
WHA... WHA...
てけてけてけてけ

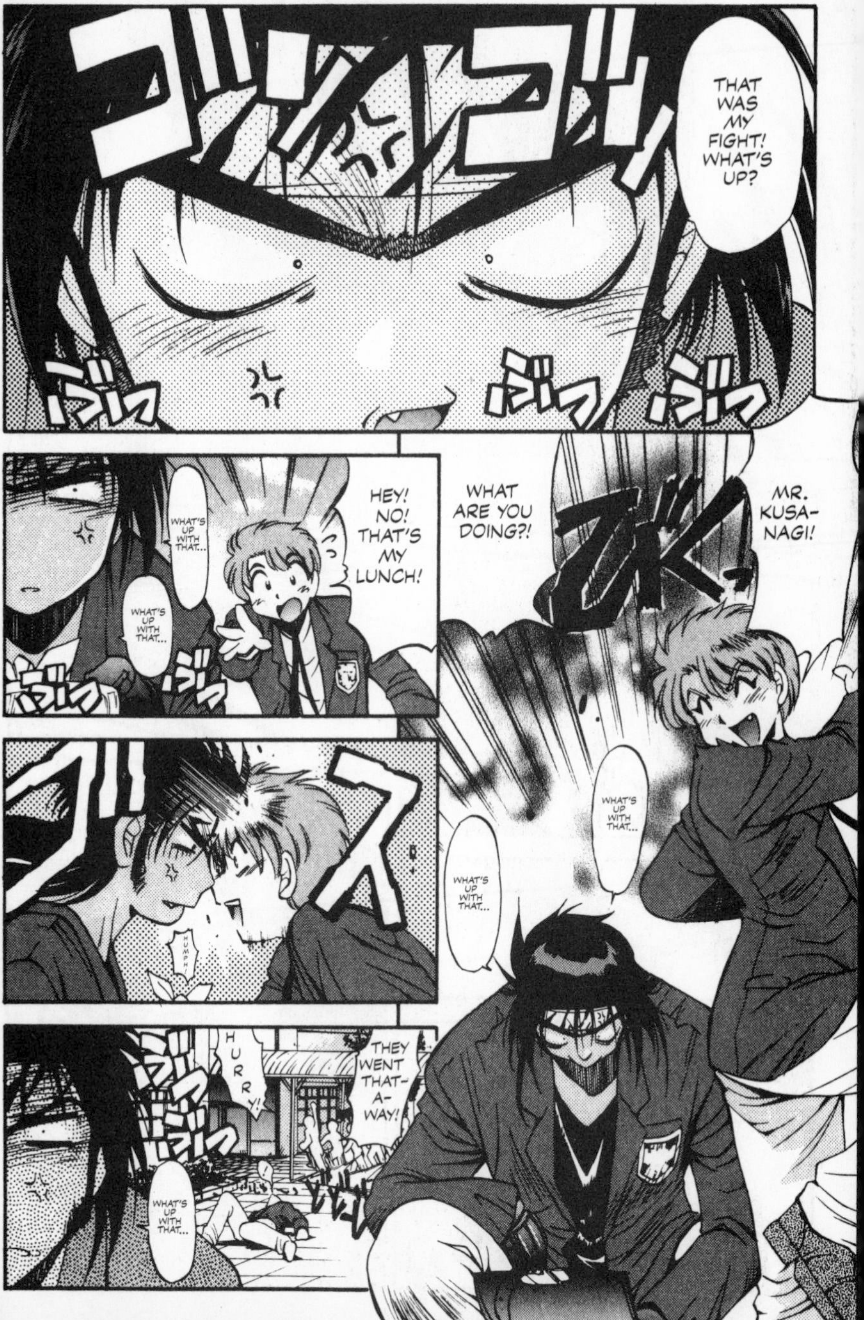
THAT WAS MY FIGHT! WHAT'S UP?
MR. KUSA-NAGI!
WHAT ARE YOU DOING?!
WHAT'S UP WITH THAT...
WHAT'S UP WITH THAT...
HEY! NO! THAT'S MY LUNCH!
WHAT'S UP WITH THAT...
WHAT'S UP WITH THAT...
HUMPH!
THEY WENT THAT-A-WAY!
HURRY!
WHAT'S UP WITH THAT...

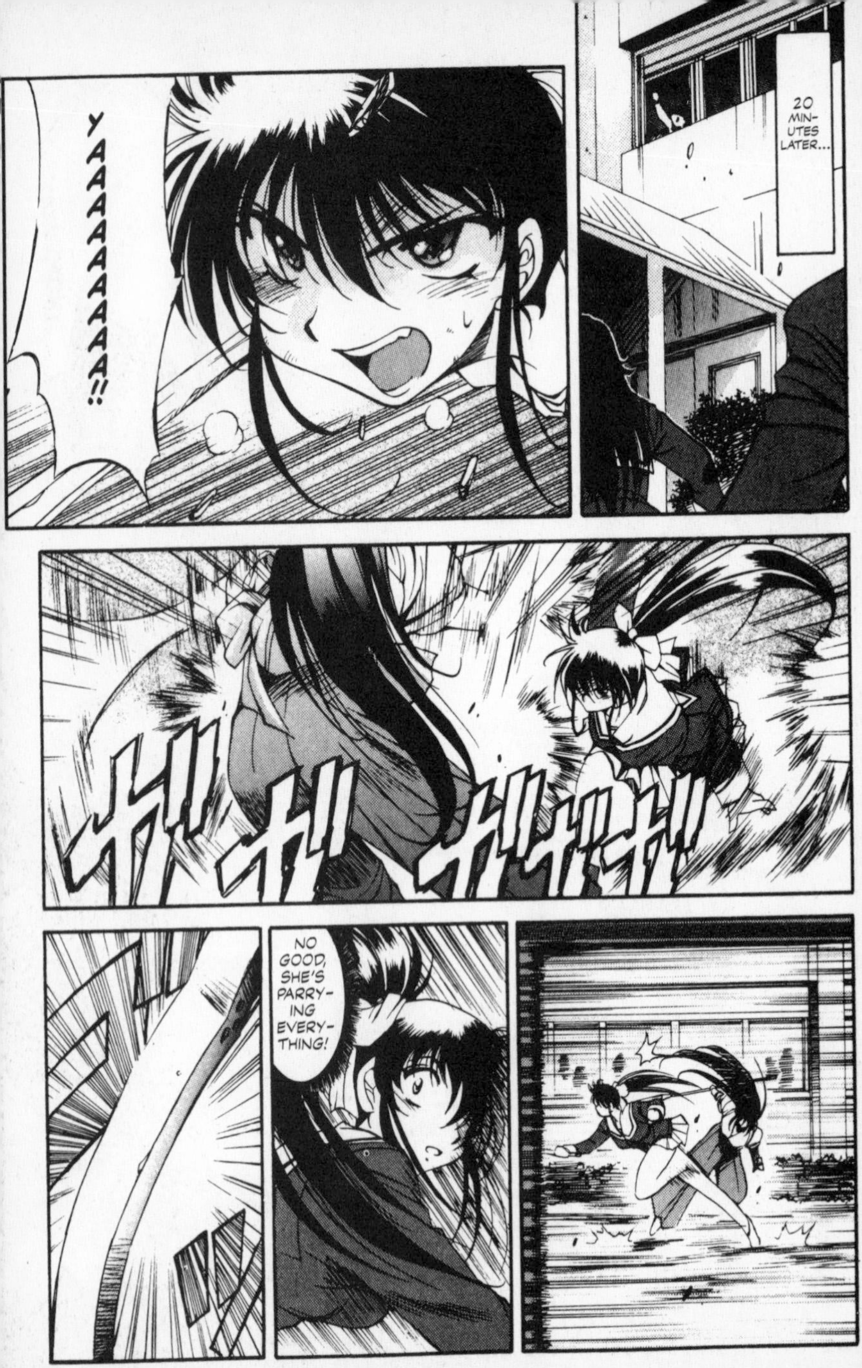
20 MINUTES LATER...
YAAAAAAAAAAA!!
NO GOOD, SHE'S PARRYING EVERYTHING!

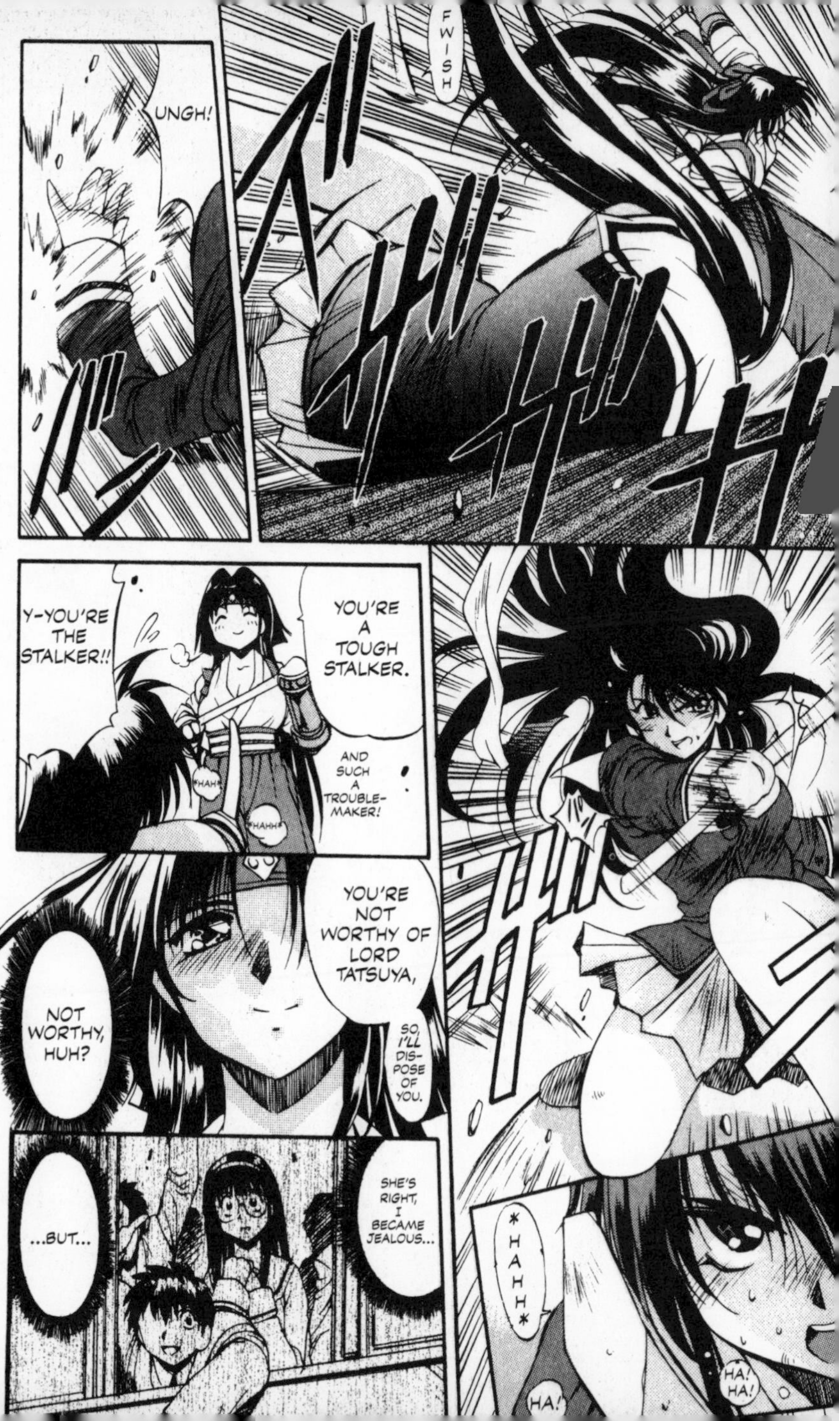
FWISH
UNGH!
HAHH
HA! HA!
HA!
YOU'RE A TOUGH STALKER.
Y-YOU'RE THE STALKER!!
AND SUCH A TROUBLE-MAKER!
HAH
HAHH
YOU'RE NOT WORTHY OF LORD TATSUYA,
SO, I'LL DISPOSE OF YOU.
NOT WORTHY, HUH?
SHE'S RIGHT, I BECAME JEALOUS...
...BUT...

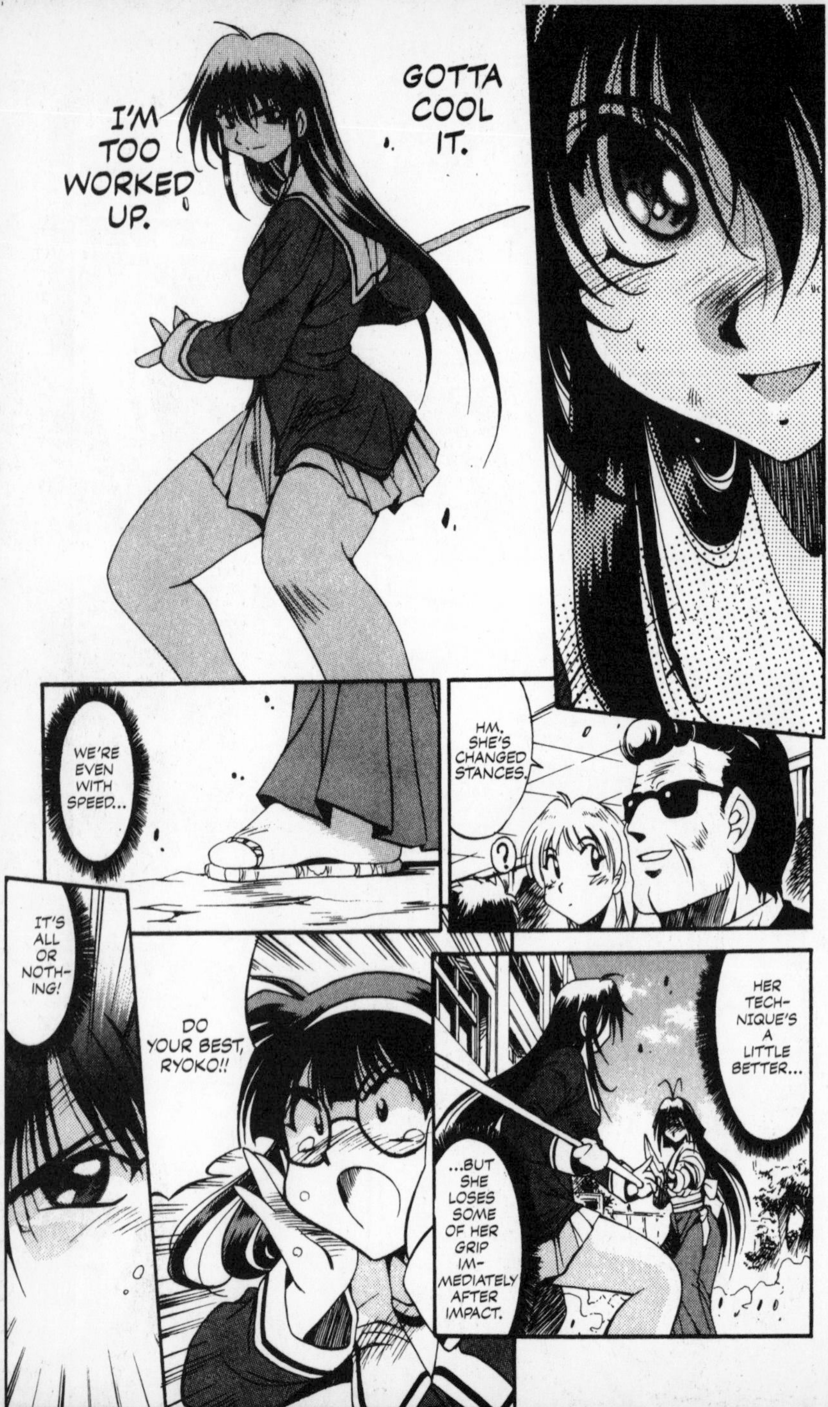
GOTTA COOL IT.
I'M TOO WORKED UP.
HM. SHE'S CHANGED STANCES.
?
WE'RE EVEN WITH SPEED...
HER TECHNIQUE'S A LITTLE BETTER...
...BUT SHE LOSES SOME OF HER GRIP IMMEDIATELY AFTER IMPACT.
DO YOUR BEST, RYOKO!!
IT'S ALL OR NOTHING!

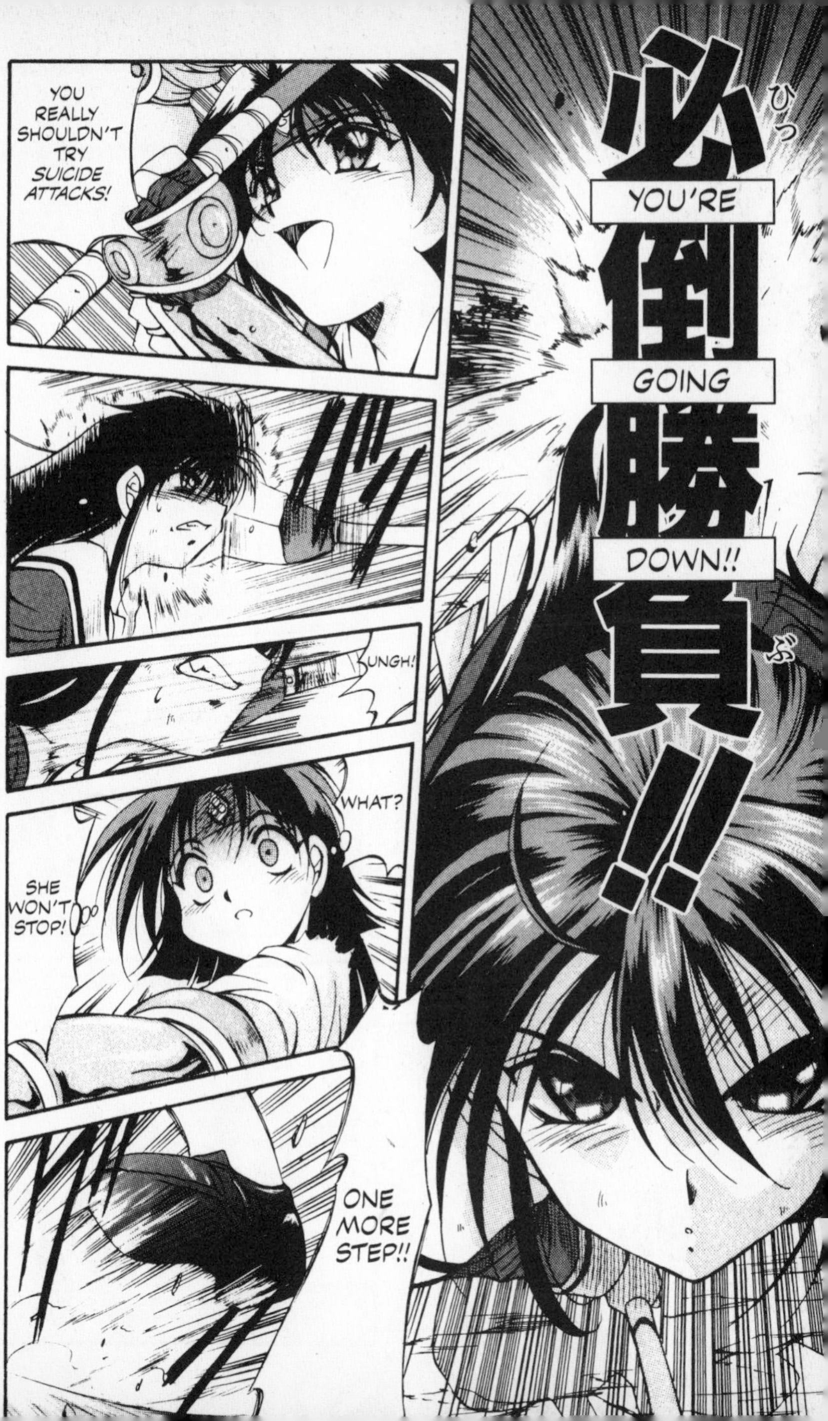
必倒勝負!!
YOU'RE GOING DOWN!!
YOU REALLY SHOULDN'T TRY SUICIDE ATTACKS!
バッ
UNGH!
WHAT?
SHE WON'T STOP!
ONE MORE STEP!!

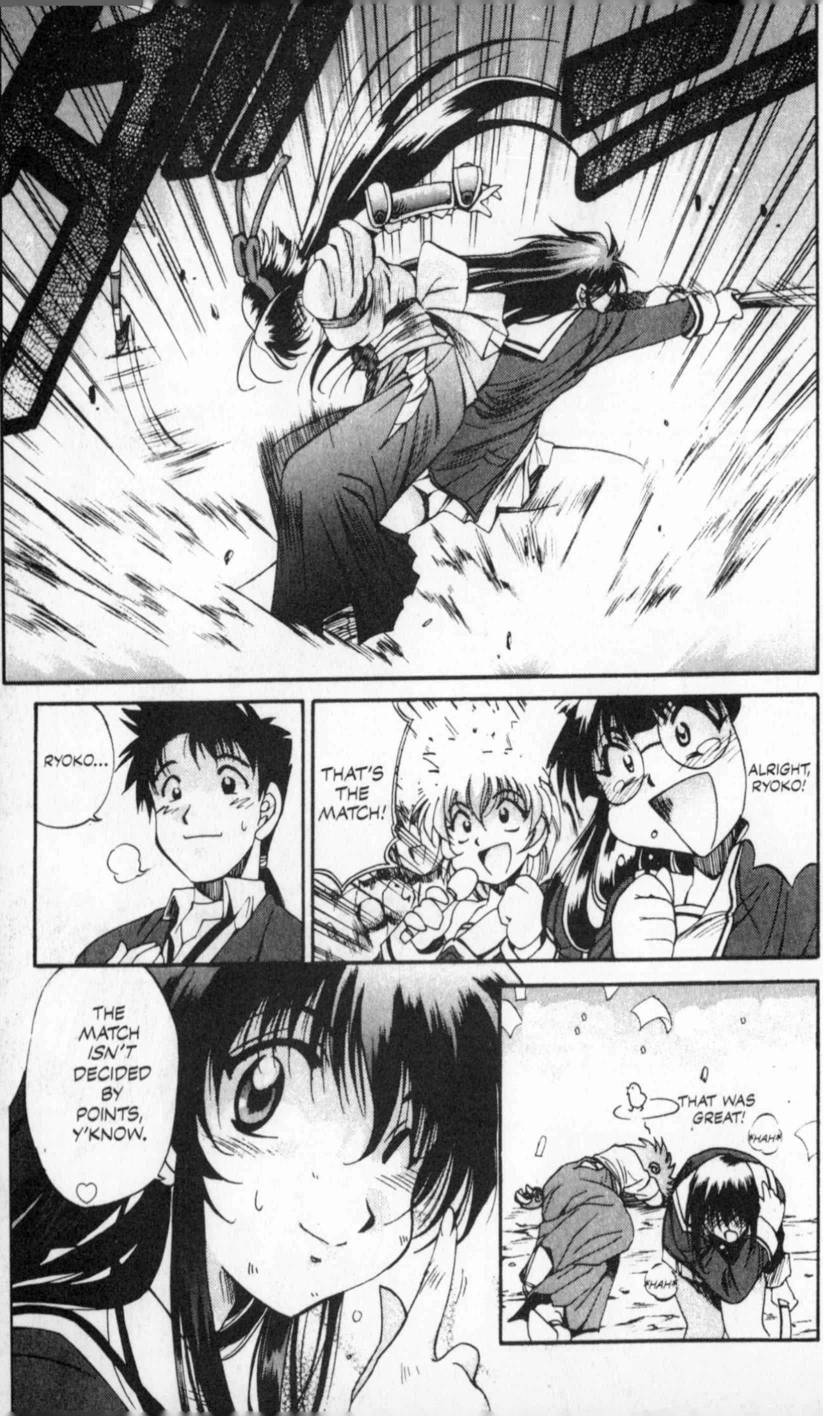
ALRIGHT, RYOKO!
THAT'S THE MATCH!
RYOKO...
THAT WAS GREAT!
HAH
HAH
THE MATCH ISN'T DECIDED BY POINTS, Y'KNOW.

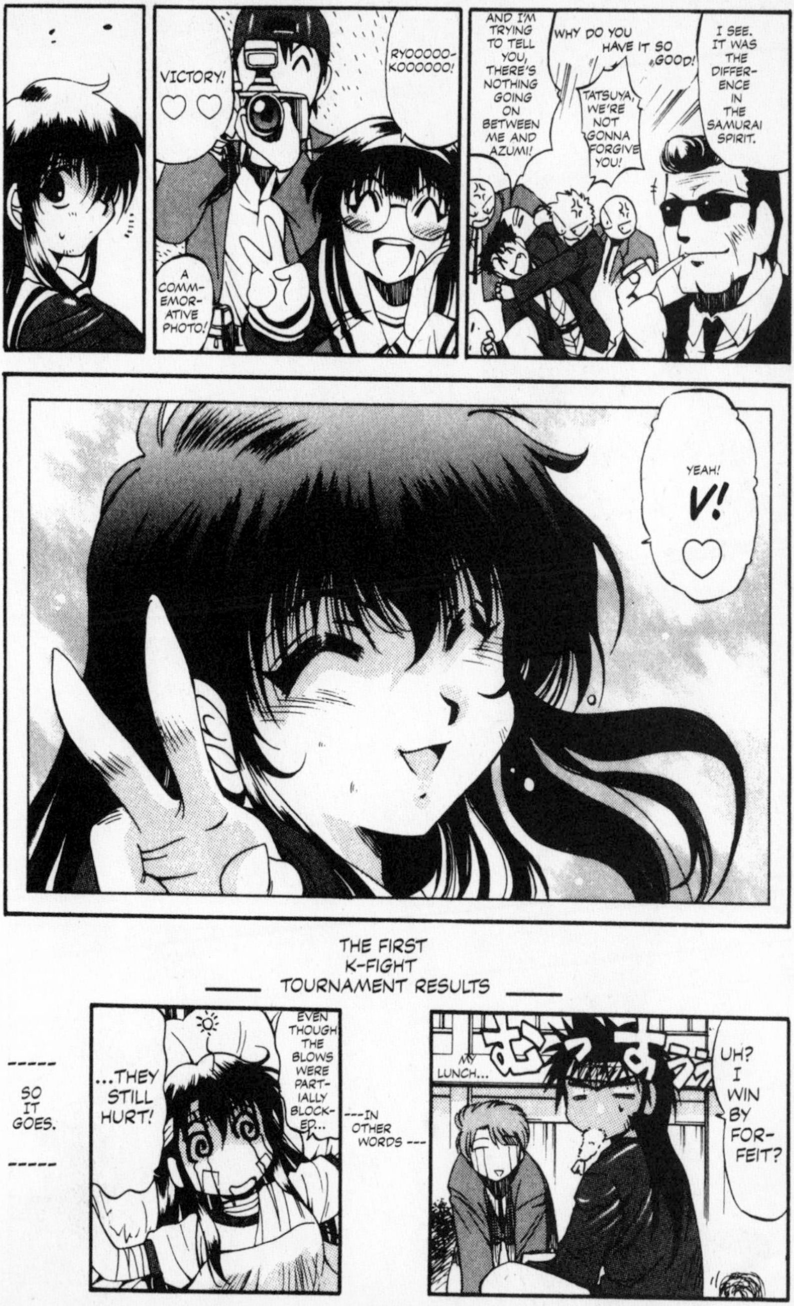
I SEE. IT WAS THE DIFFERENCE IN THE SAMURAI SPIRIT.
WHY DO YOU HAVE IT SO GOOD!
TATSUYA, WE'RE NOT GONNA FORGIVE YOU!
AND I'M TRYING TO TELL YOU, THERE'S NOTHING GOING ON BETWEEN ME AND AZUMI!
RYOOOOO-KOOOOOO!
VICTORY!
A COMMEMORATIVE PHOTO!
YEAH! V!
THE FIRST K-FIGHT
—— TOURNAMENT RESULTS ——
UH? I WIN BY FORFEIT?
MY LUNCH...
EVEN THOUGH THE BLOWS WERE PARTIALLY BLOCKED...
...THEY STILL HURT!
---IN OTHER WORDS ---

SO IT GOES.

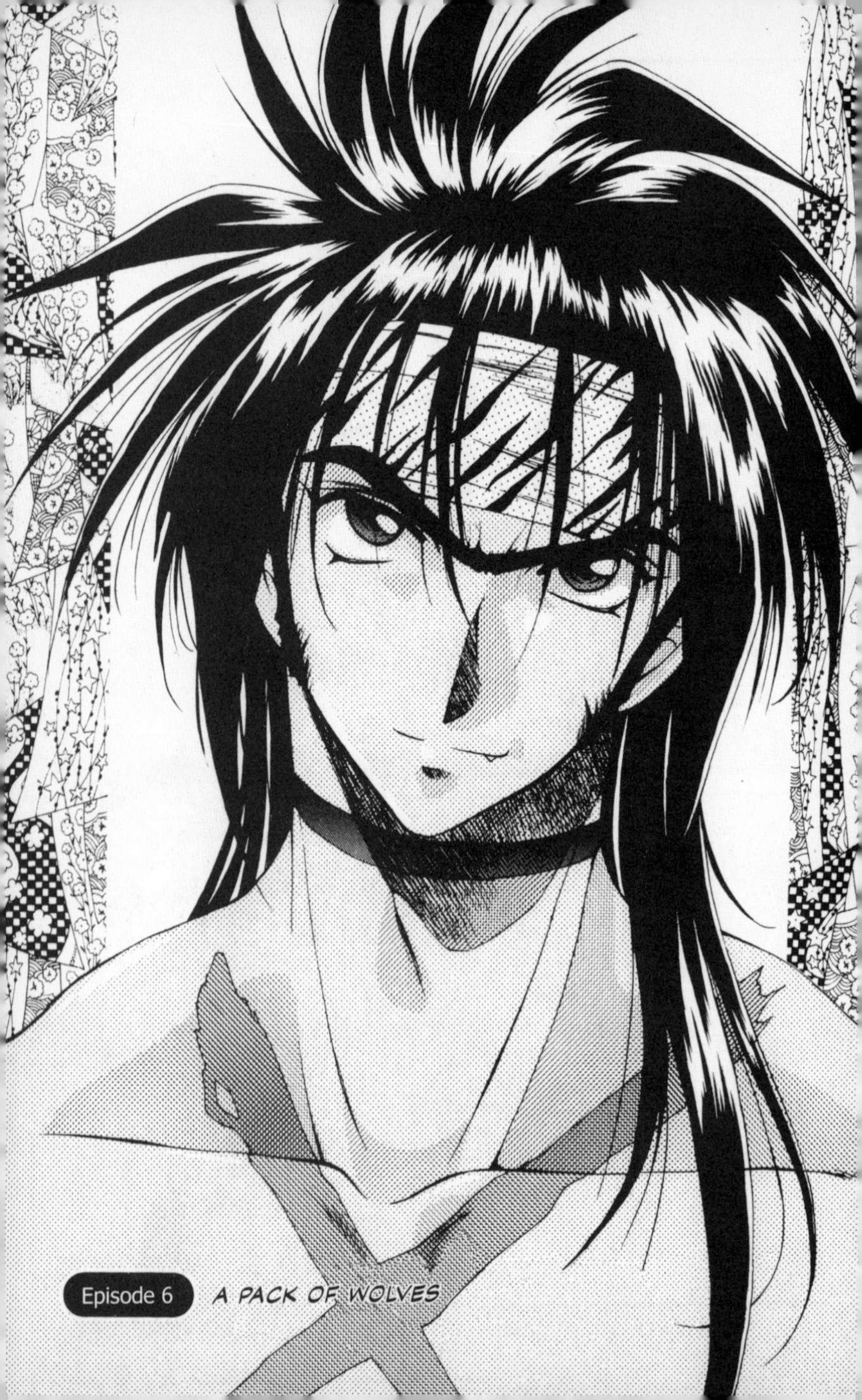

Episode 6 A PACK OF WOLVES

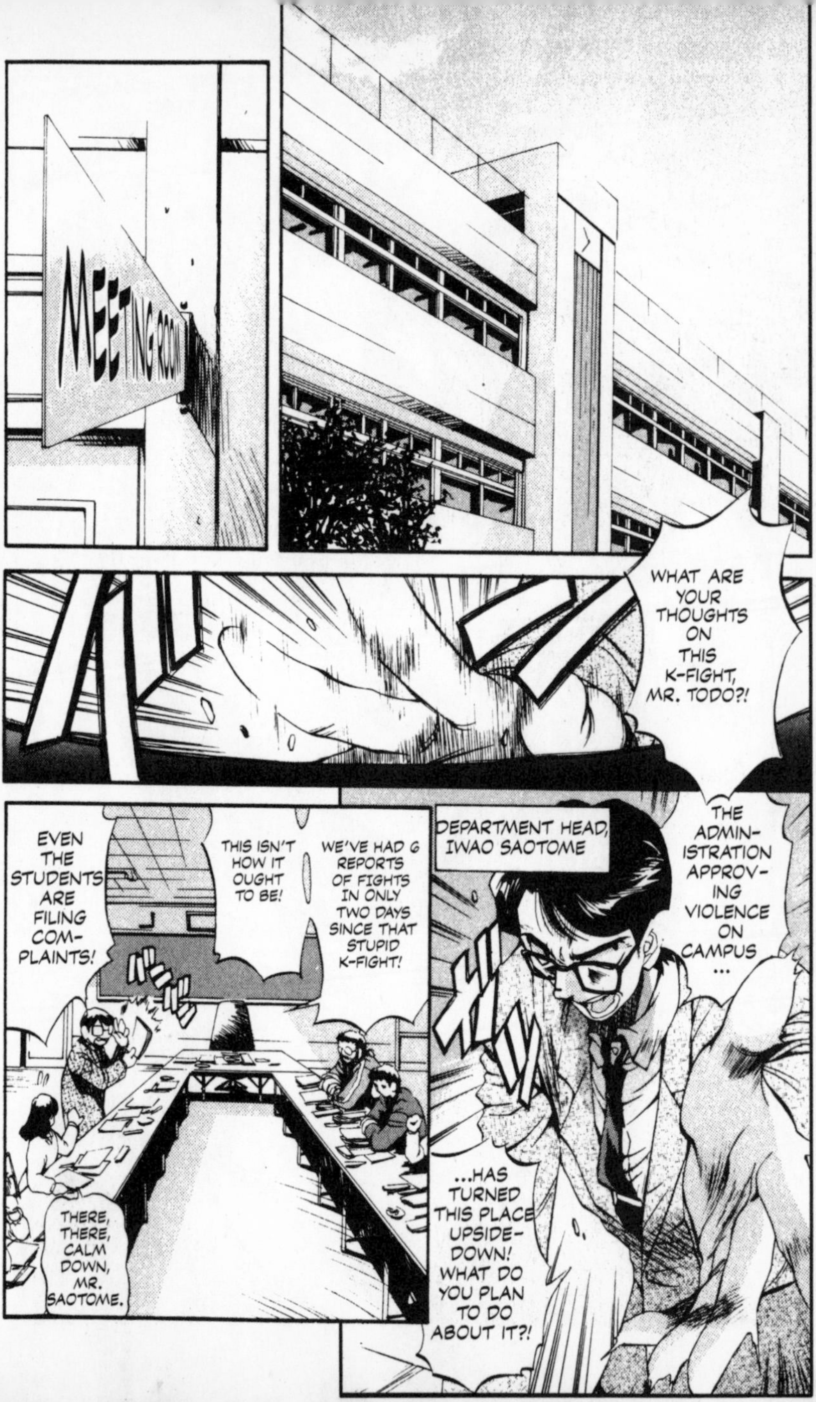
MEETING ROOM
WHAT ARE YOUR THOUGHTS ON THIS K-FIGHT, MR. TODO?!
THE ADMINISTRATION APPROVING VIOLENCE ON CAMPUS...
DEPARTMENT HEAD, IWAO SAOTOME
...HAS TURNED THIS PLACE UPSIDE-DOWN! WHAT DO YOU PLAN TO DO ABOUT IT?!
WE'VE HAD 6 REPORTS OF FIGHTS IN ONLY TWO DAYS SINCE THAT STUPID K-FIGHT!
THIS ISN'T HOW IT OUGHT TO BE!
EVEN THE STUDENTS ARE FILING COMPLAINTS!
THERE, THERE, CALM DOWN, MR. SAOTOME.

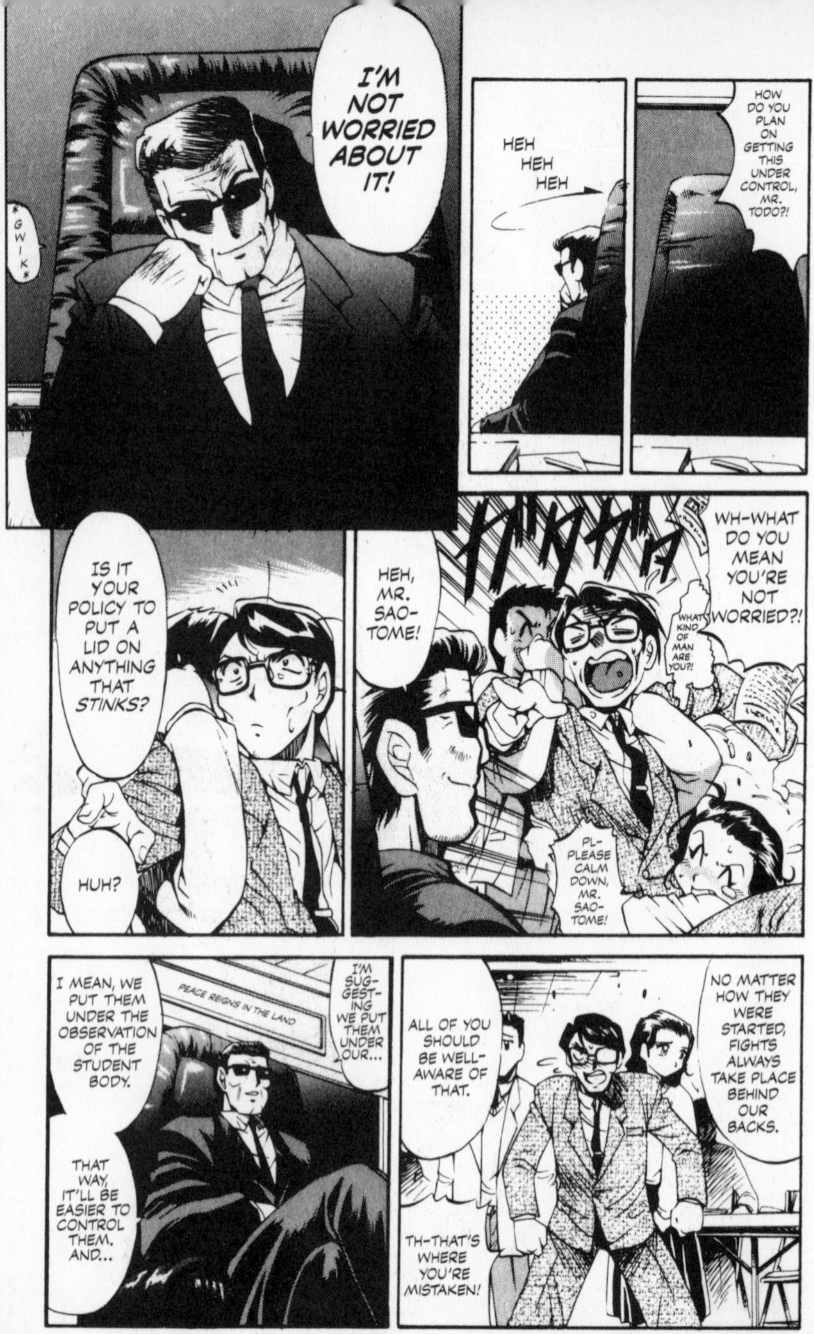
HOW DO YOU PLAN ON GETTING THIS UNDER CONTROL, MR. TODO?!
HEH HEH HEH
I'M NOT WORRIED ABOUT IT!
GWIK
WH-WHAT DO YOU MEAN YOU'RE NOT WORRIED?!
WHAT KIND OF MAN ARE YOU?!
HEH, MR. SAOTOME!
PL-PLEASE CALM DOWN, MR. SAOTOME!
IS IT YOUR POLICY TO PUT A LID ON ANYTHING THAT *STINKS?*
HUH?
NO MATTER HOW THEY WERE STARTED, FIGHTS ALWAYS TAKE PLACE BEHIND OUR BACKS.
ALL OF YOU SHOULD BE WELL-AWARE OF THAT.
TH-THAT'S WHERE YOU'RE MISTAKEN!
I'M SUGGESTING WE PUT THEM UNDER OUR...
I MEAN, WE PUT THEM UNDER THE OBSERVATION OF THE STUDENT BODY.
PEACE REIGNS IN THE LAND
THAT WAY, IT'LL BE EASIER TO CONTROL THEM. AND...

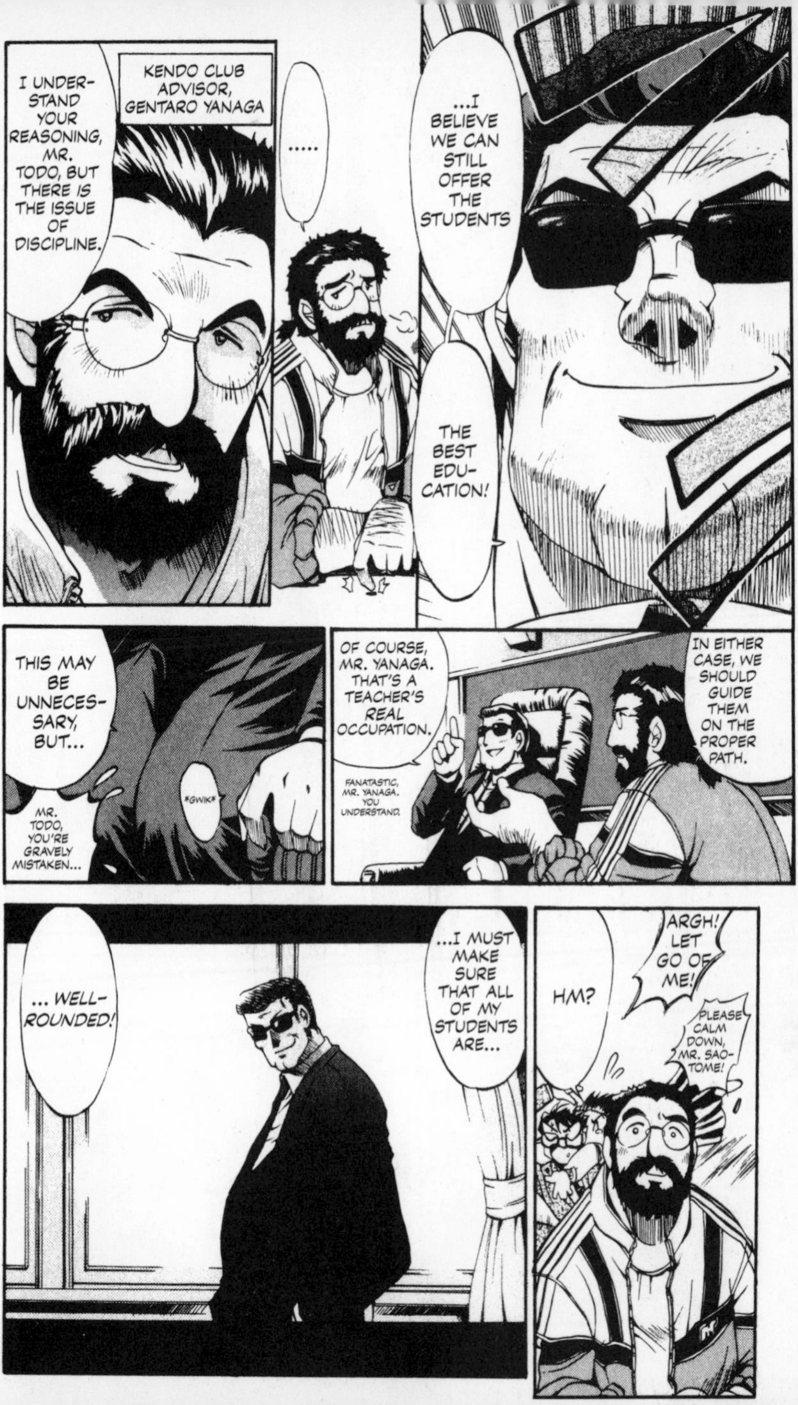
...I BELIEVE WE CAN STILL OFFER THE STUDENTS
THE BEST EDUCATION!
......
KENDO CLUB ADVISOR, GENTARO YANAGA
I UNDERSTAND YOUR REASONING, MR. TODO, BUT THERE IS THE ISSUE OF DISCIPLINE.
IN EITHER CASE, WE SHOULD GUIDE THEM ON THE PROPER PATH.
OF COURSE, MR. YANAGA. THAT'S A TEACHER'S REAL OCCUPATION.
FANATASTIC, MR. YANAGA. YOU UNDERSTAND.
THIS MAY BE UNNECESSARY, BUT...
GWIK
MR. TODO, YOU'RE GRAVELY MISTAKEN...
ARGH! LET GO OF ME!
HM?
PLEASE CALM DOWN, MR. SAOTOME!
...I MUST MAKE SURE THAT ALL OF MY STUDENTS ARE...
... WELL-ROUNDED!

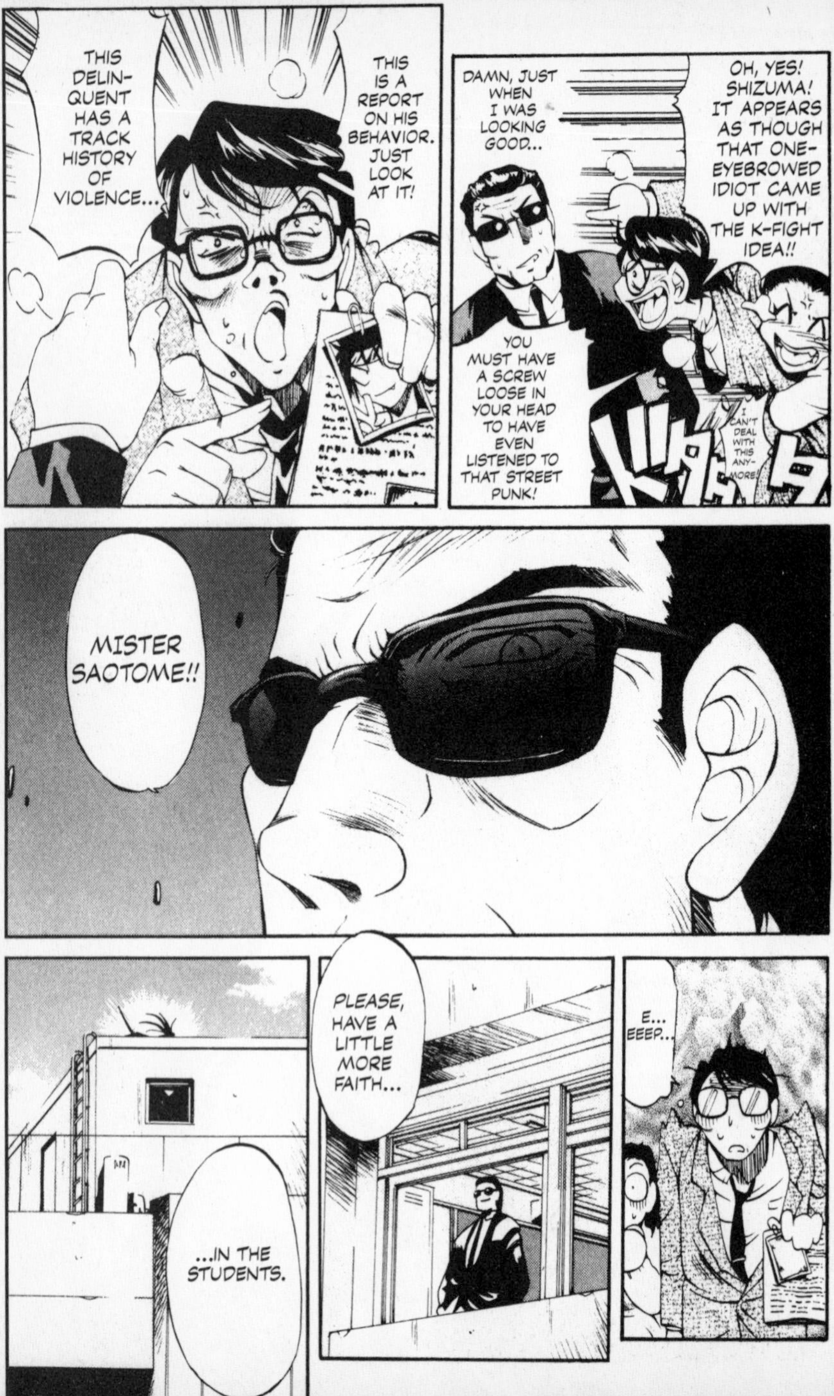
OH, YES! SHIZUMA! IT APPEARS AS THOUGH THAT ONE-EYEBROWED IDIOT CAME UP WITH THE K-FIGHT IDEA!!
DAMN, JUST WHEN I WAS LOOKING GOOD...
YOU MUST HAVE A SCREW LOOSE IN YOUR HEAD TO HAVE EVEN LISTENED TO THAT STREET PUNK!
I CAN'T DEAL WITH THIS ANY-MORE!
THIS IS A REPORT ON HIS BEHAVIOR. JUST LOOK AT IT!
THIS DELIN-QUENT HAS A TRACK HISTORY OF VIOLENCE...
MISTER SAOTOME!!
E... EEEP...
PLEASE, HAVE A LITTLE MORE FAITH...
...IN THE STUDENTS.

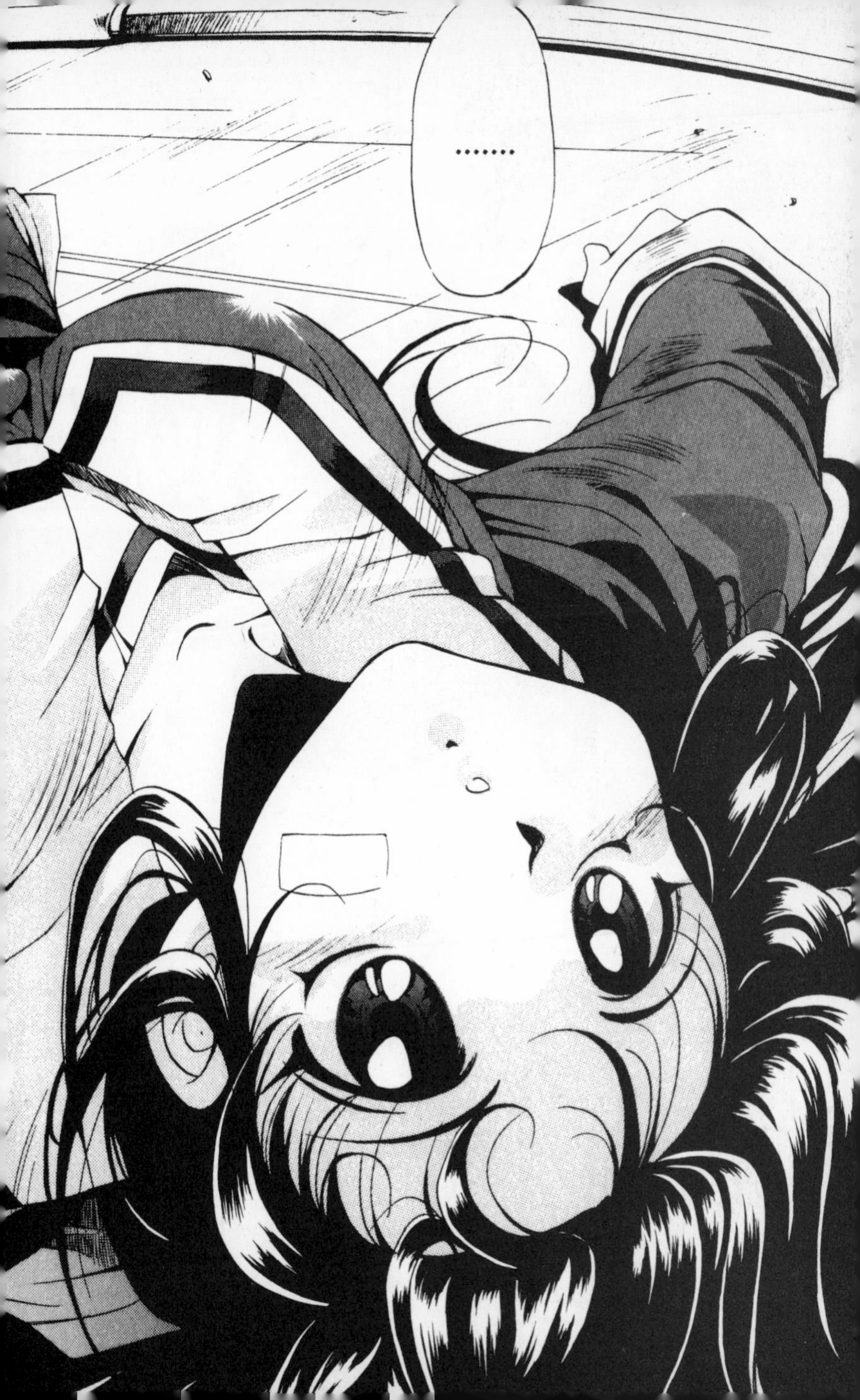
....

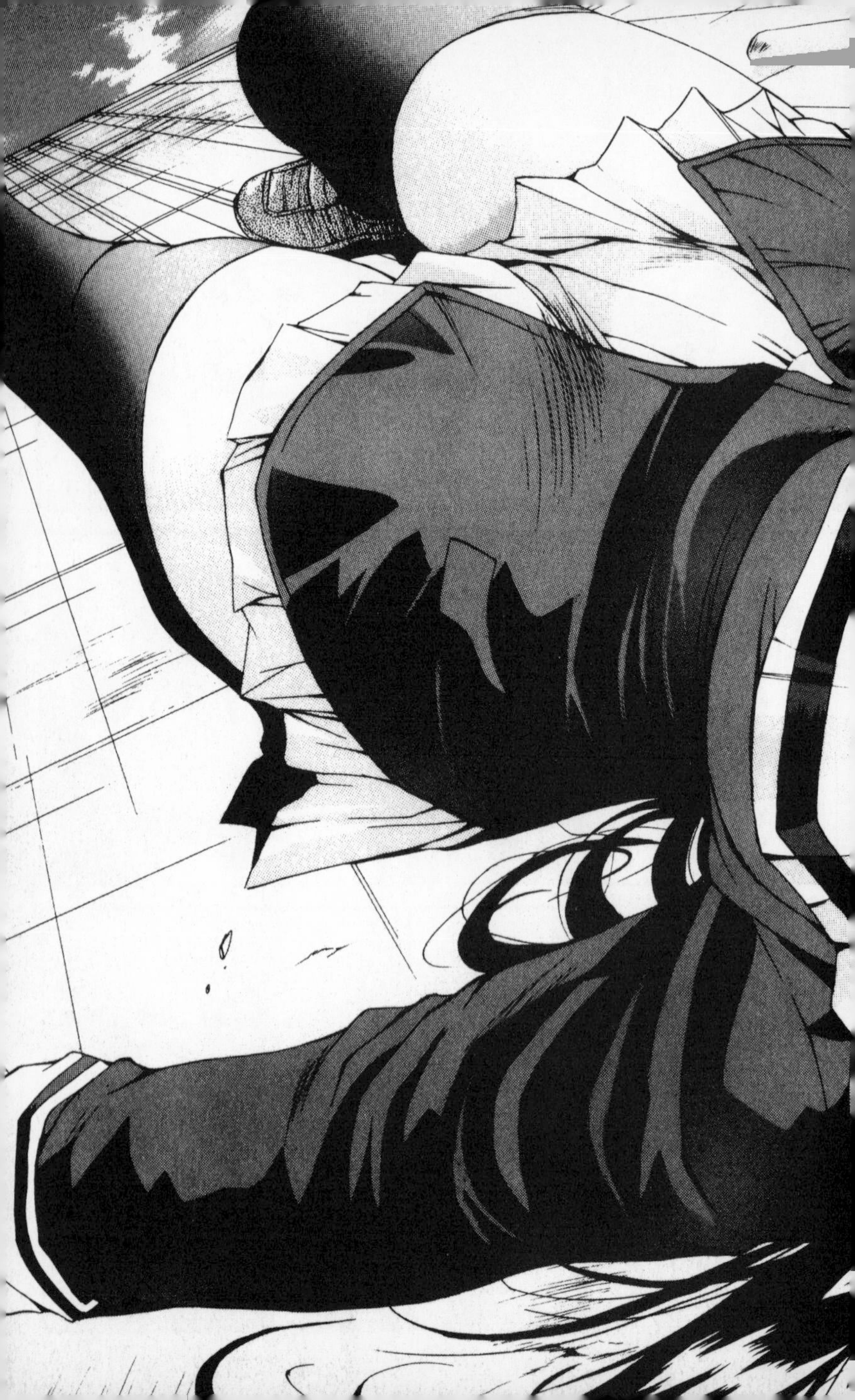

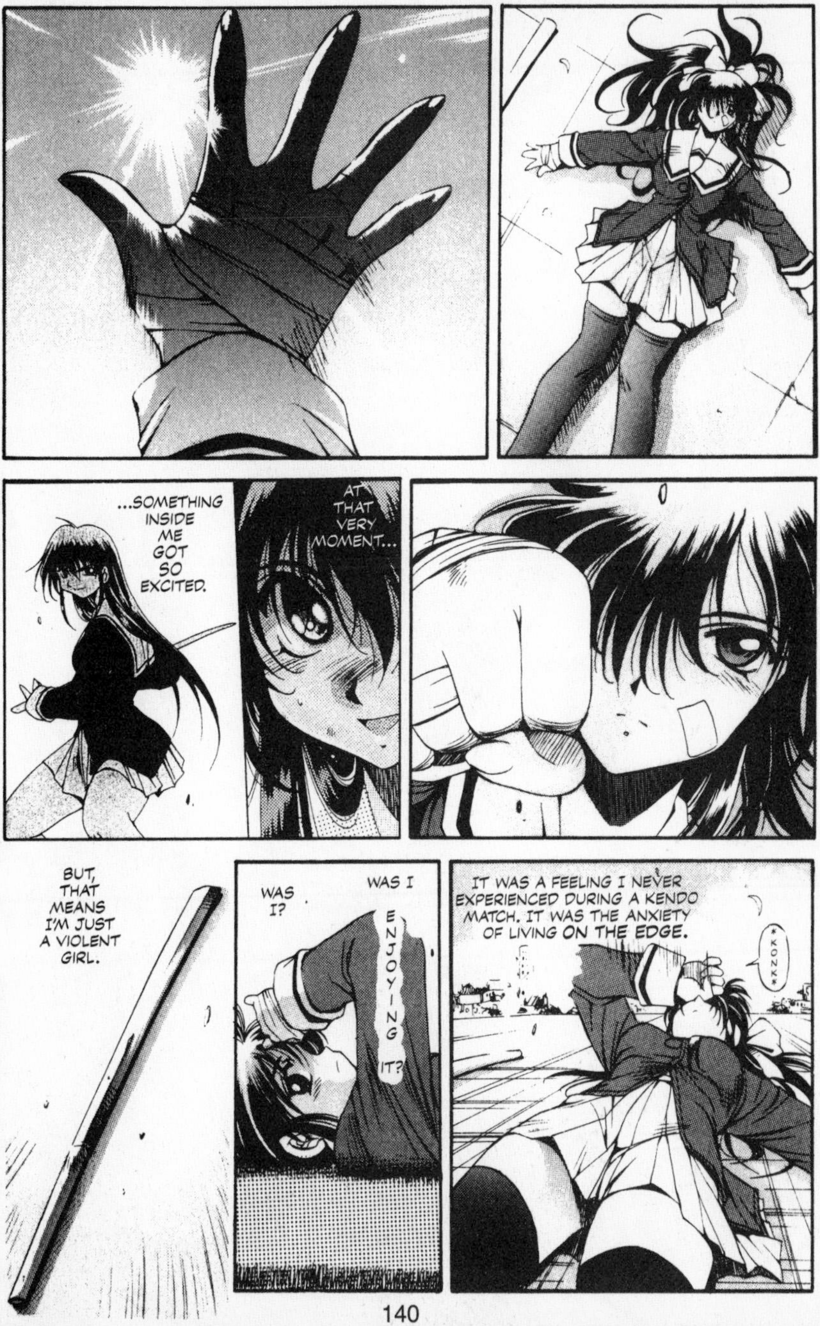
AT THAT VERY MOMENT...
...SOMETHING INSIDE ME GOT SO EXCITED.
IT WAS A FEELING I NEVER EXPERIENCED DURING A KENDO MATCH. IT WAS THE ANXIETY OF LIVING ON THE EDGE.
KONK
WAS I ENJOYING IT?
WAS I?
BUT, THAT MEANS I'M JUST A VIOLENT GIRL.

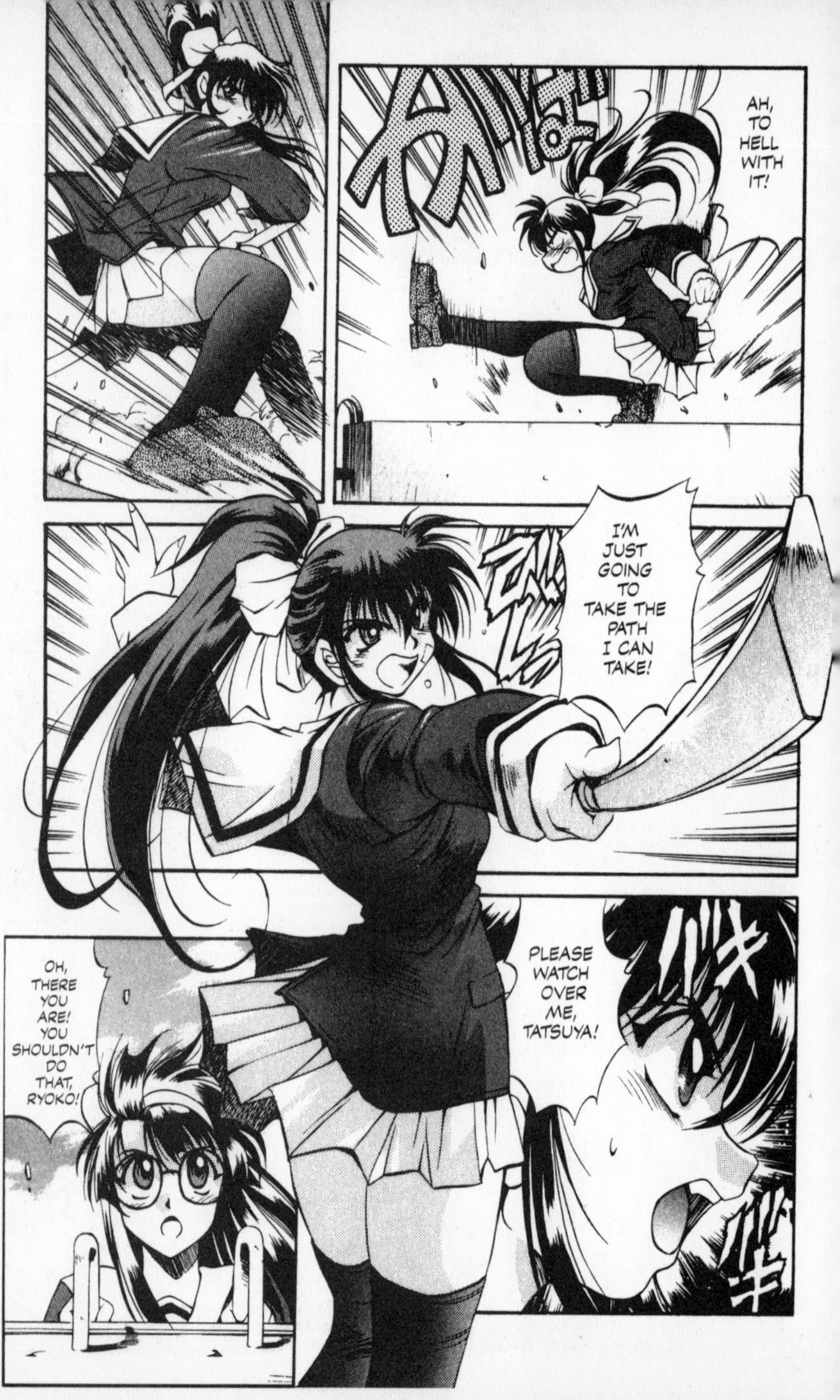
AH, TO HELL WITH IT!
I'M JUST GOING TO TAKE THE PATH I CAN TAKE!
PLEASE WATCH OVER ME, TATSUYA!
OH, THERE YOU ARE! YOU SHOULDN'T DO THAT, RYOKO!

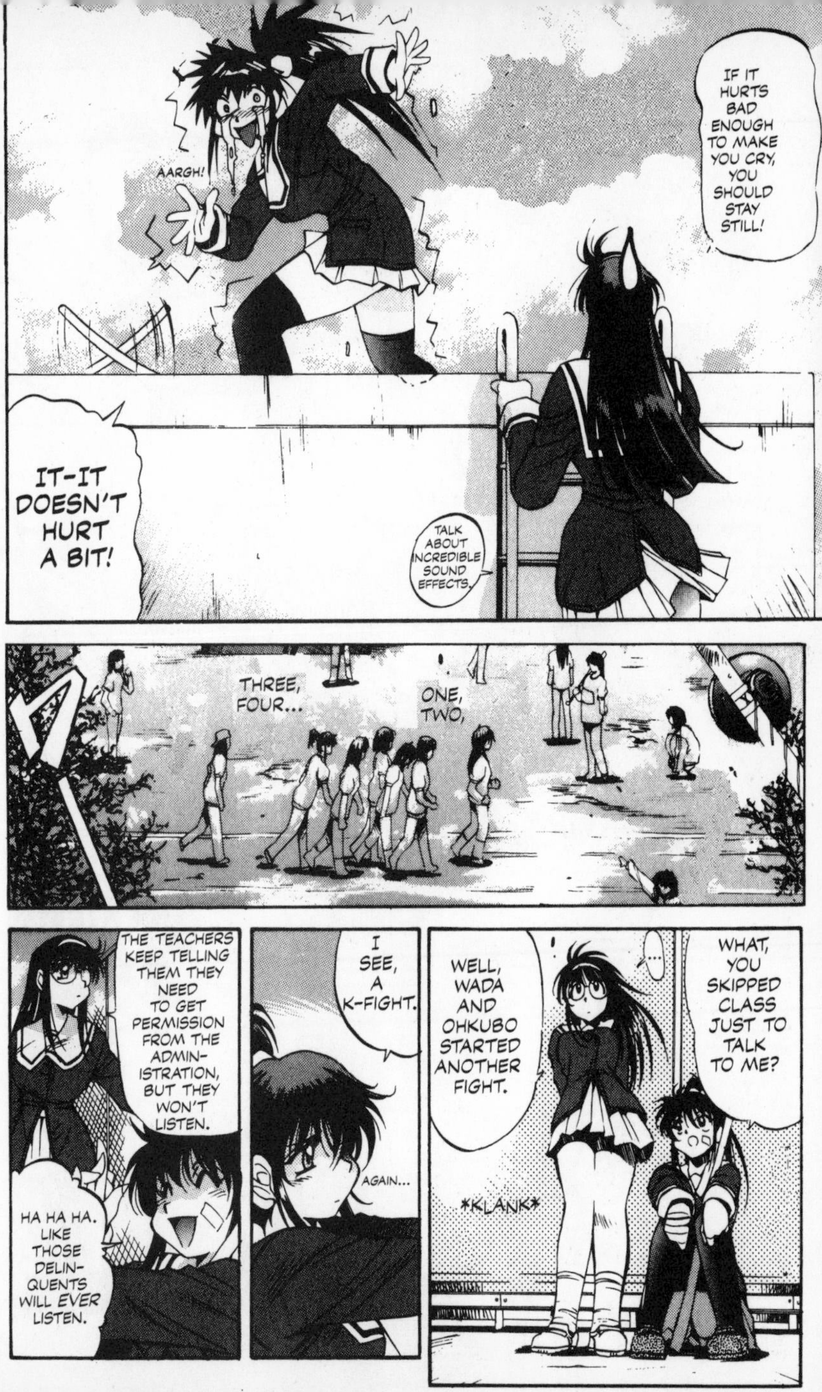
IF IT HURTS BAD ENOUGH TO MAKE YOU CRY, YOU SHOULD STAY STILL!
AARGH!
IT-IT DOESN'T HURT A BIT!
TALK ABOUT INCREDIBLE SOUND EFFECTS.
ONE, TWO,
THREE, FOUR...
WHAT, YOU SKIPPED CLASS JUST TO TALK TO ME?
...
WELL, WADA AND OHKUBO STARTED ANOTHER FIGHT.
KLANK
I SEE, A K-FIGHT.
AGAIN...
THE TEACHERS KEEP TELLING THEM THEY NEED TO GET PERMISSION FROM THE ADMIN-ISTRATION, BUT THEY WON'T LISTEN.
HA HA HA. LIKE THOSE DELIN-QUENTS WILL EVER LISTEN.

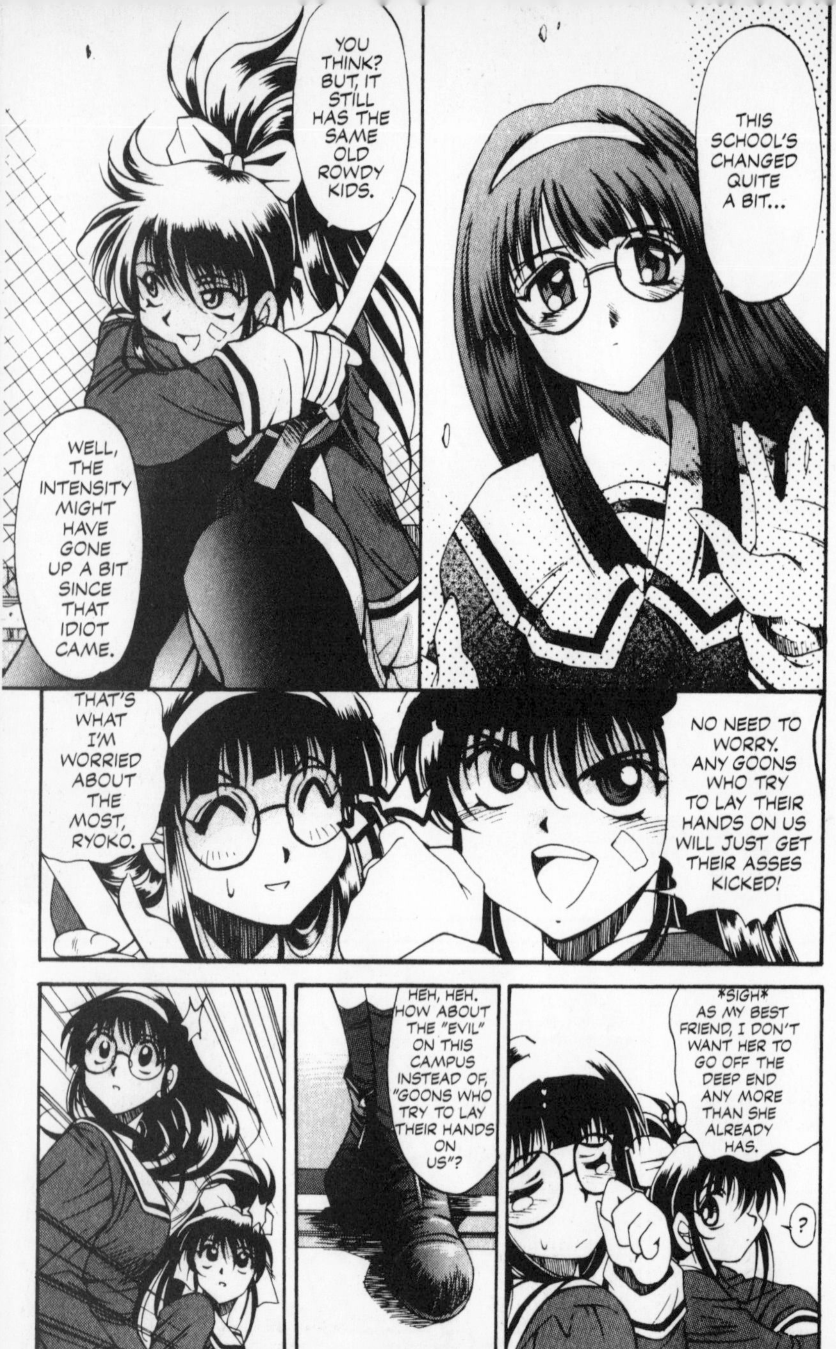
THIS SCHOOL'S CHANGED QUITE A BIT...
YOU THINK? BUT, IT STILL HAS THE SAME OLD ROWDY KIDS.
WELL, THE INTENSITY MIGHT HAVE GONE UP A BIT SINCE THAT IDIOT CAME.
NO NEED TO WORRY. ANY GOONS WHO TRY TO LAY THEIR HANDS ON US WILL JUST GET THEIR ASSES KICKED!
THAT'S WHAT I'M WORRIED ABOUT THE MOST, RYOKO.
SIGH AS MY BEST FRIEND, I DON'T WANT HER TO GO OFF THE DEEP END ANY MORE THAN SHE ALREADY HAS.
?
HEH, HEH. HOW ABOUT THE "EVIL" ON THIS CAMPUS INSTEAD OF, "GOONS WHO TRY TO LAY THEIR HANDS ON US"?

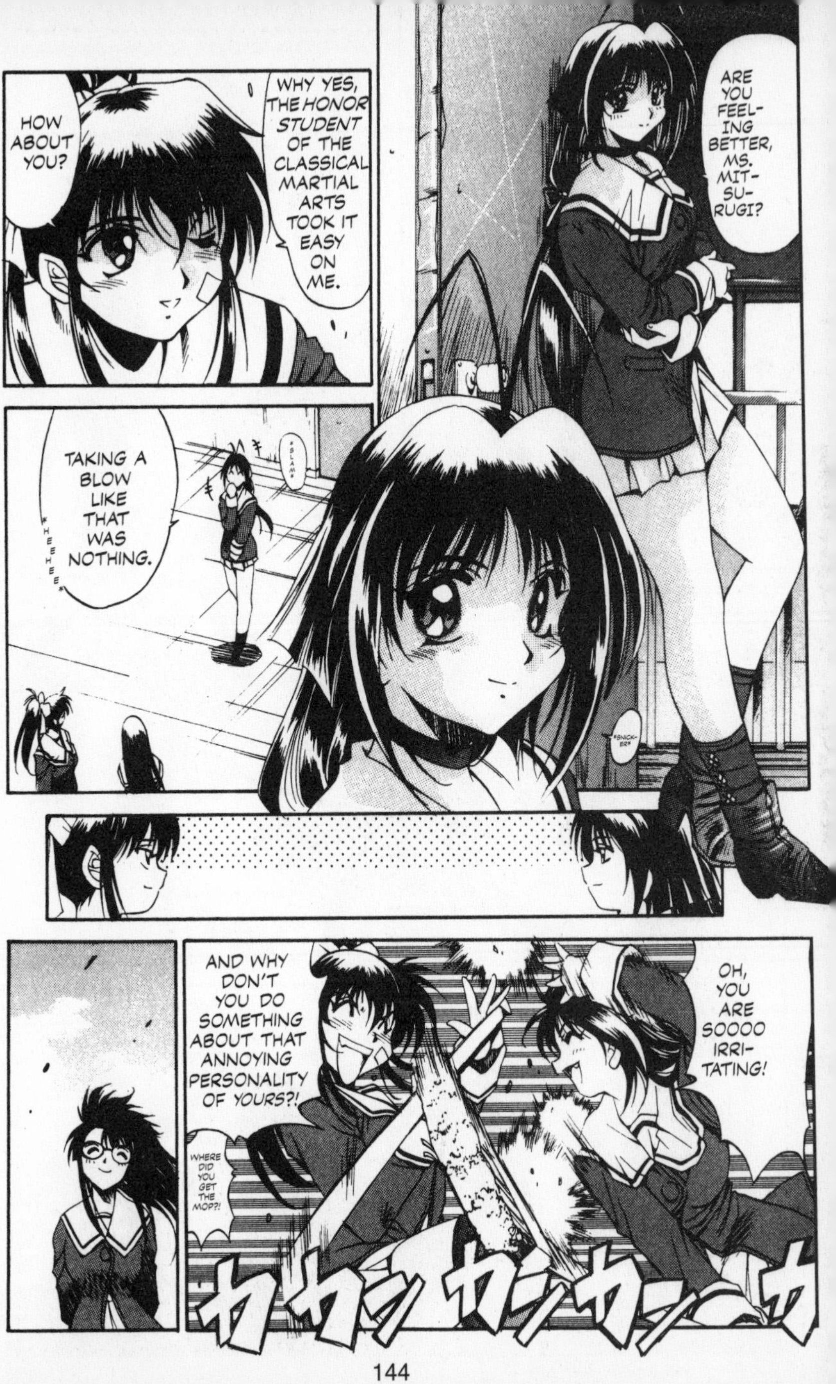
ARE YOU FEELING BETTER, MS. MITSURUGI?
SNICKER
WHY YES, THE HONOR STUDENT OF THE CLASSICAL MARTIAL ARTS TOOK IT EASY ON ME.
HOW ABOUT YOU?
SLAM
TAKING A BLOW LIKE THAT WAS NOTHING.
HEE HEE
OH, YOU ARE SOOOO IRRITATING!
AND WHY DON'T YOU DO SOMETHING ABOUT THAT ANNOYING PERSONALITY OF YOURS?!
WHERE DID YOU GET THE MOP?!

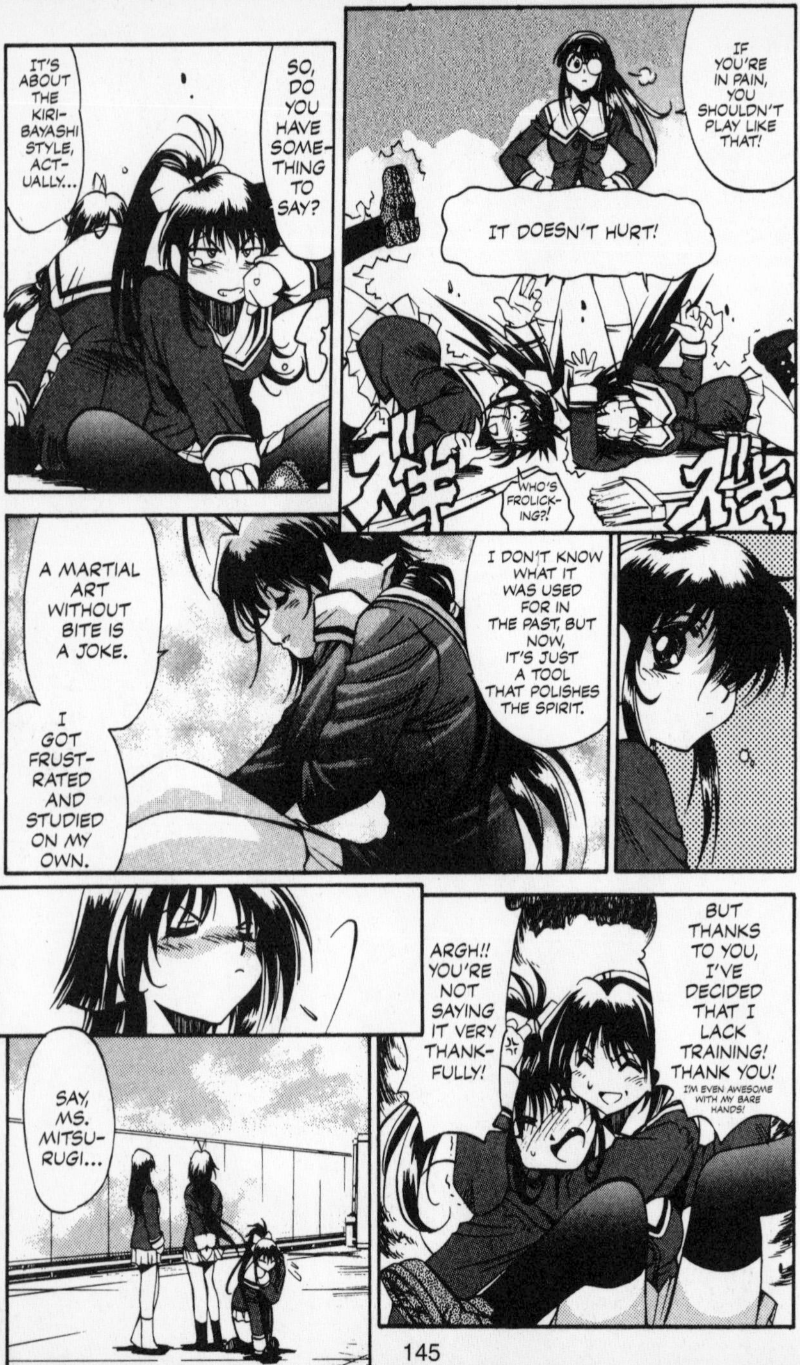
IF YOU'RE IN PAIN, YOU SHOULDN'T PLAY LIKE THAT!
IT DOESN'T HURT!
WHO'S FROLICK-ING?!
SO, DO YOU HAVE SOME-THING TO SAY?
IT'S ABOUT THE KIRI-BAYASHI STYLE, ACT-UALLY...
I DON'T KNOW WHAT IT WAS USED FOR IN THE PAST, BUT NOW, IT'S JUST A TOOL THAT POLISHES THE SPIRIT.
A MARTIAL ART WITHOUT BITE IS A JOKE.
I GOT FRUST-RATED AND STUDIED ON MY OWN.
BUT THANKS TO YOU, I'VE DECIDED THAT I LACK TRAINING! THANK YOU!
I'M EVEN AWESOME WITH MY BARE HANDS!
ARGH!! YOU'RE NOT SAYING IT VERY THANK-FULLY!
SAY, MS. MITSU-RUGI...

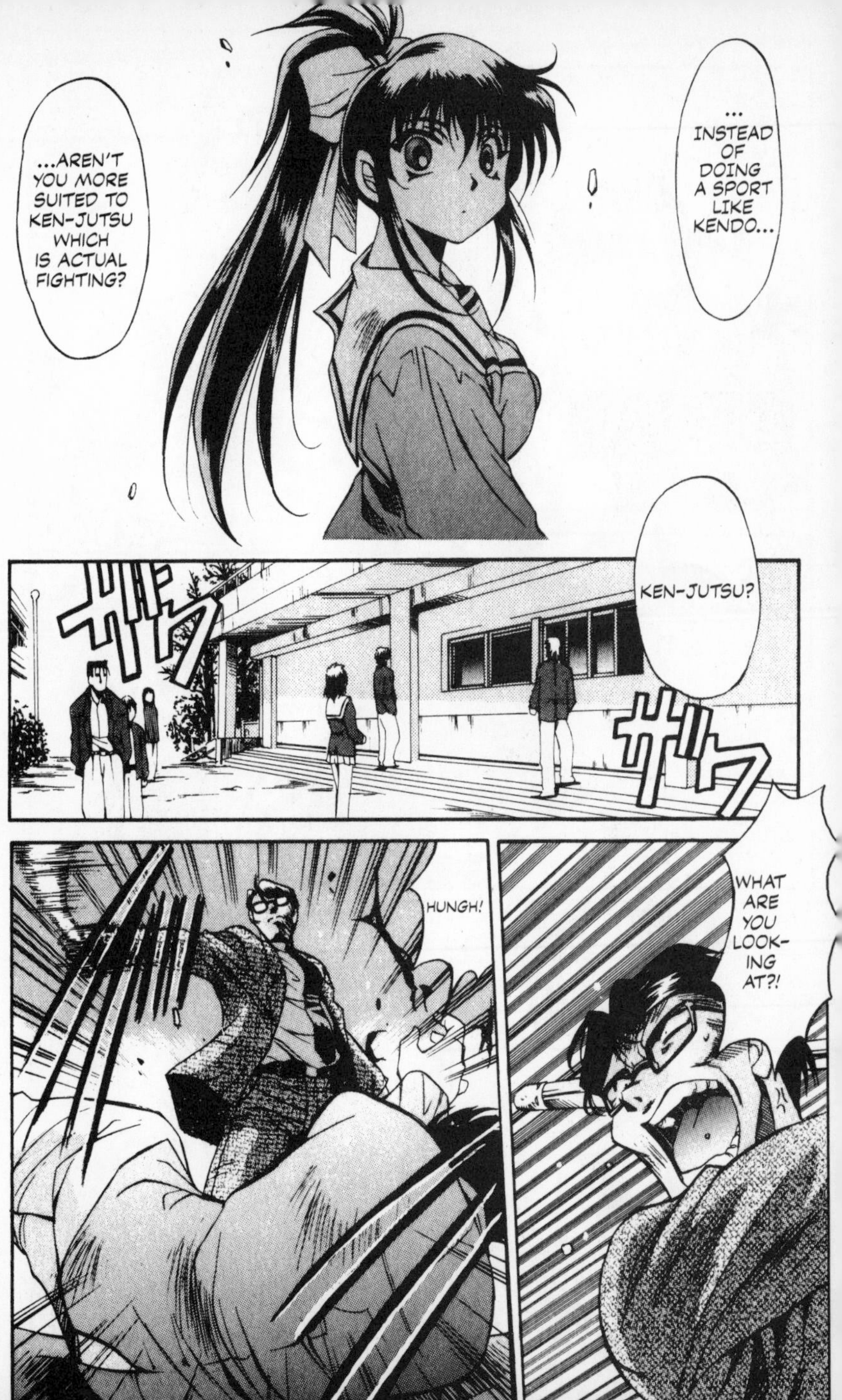
...INSTEAD OF DOING A SPORT LIKE KENDO...
...AREN'T YOU MORE SUITED TO KEN-JUTSU WHICH IS ACTUAL FIGHTING?
KEN-JUTSU?
WHAT ARE YOU LOOKING AT?!
HUNGH!

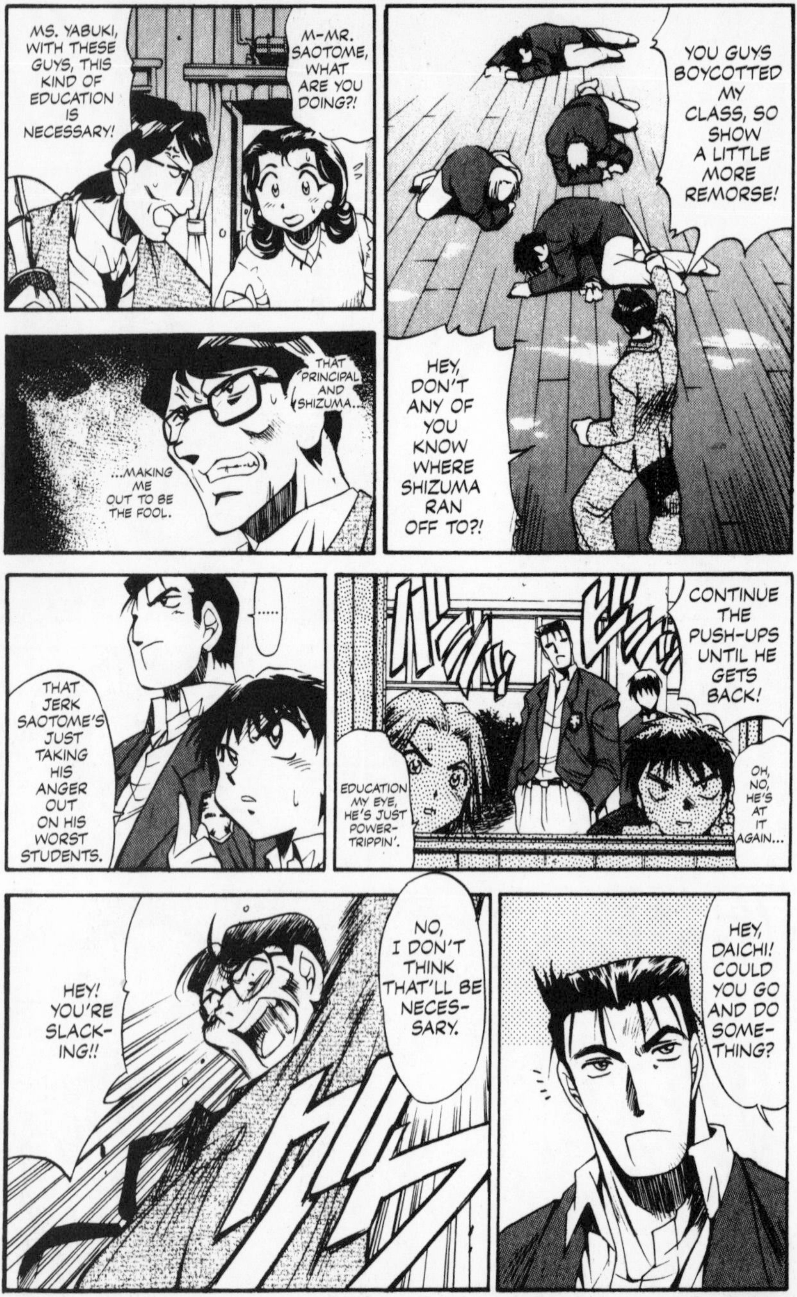
YOU GUYS BOYCOTTED MY CLASS, SO SHOW A LITTLE MORE REMORSE!
HEY, DON'T ANY OF YOU KNOW WHERE SHIZUMA RAN OFF TO?!
M-MR. SAOTOME, WHAT ARE YOU DOING?!
MS. YABUKI, WITH THESE GUYS, THIS KIND OF EDUCATION IS NECESSARY!
THAT PRINCIPAL AND SHIZUMA...
...MAKING ME OUT TO BE THE FOOL.
CONTINUE THE PUSH-UPS UNTIL HE GETS BACK!
OH, NO, HE'S AT IT AGAIN...
EDUCATION MY EYE, HE'S JUST POWER-TRIPPIN'.
......
THAT JERK SAOTOME'S JUST TAKING HIS ANGER OUT ON HIS WORST STUDENTS.
HEY, DAICHI! COULD YOU GO AND DO SOME-THING?
NO, I DON'T THINK THAT'LL BE NECES-SARY.
HEY! YOU'RE SLACK-ING!!

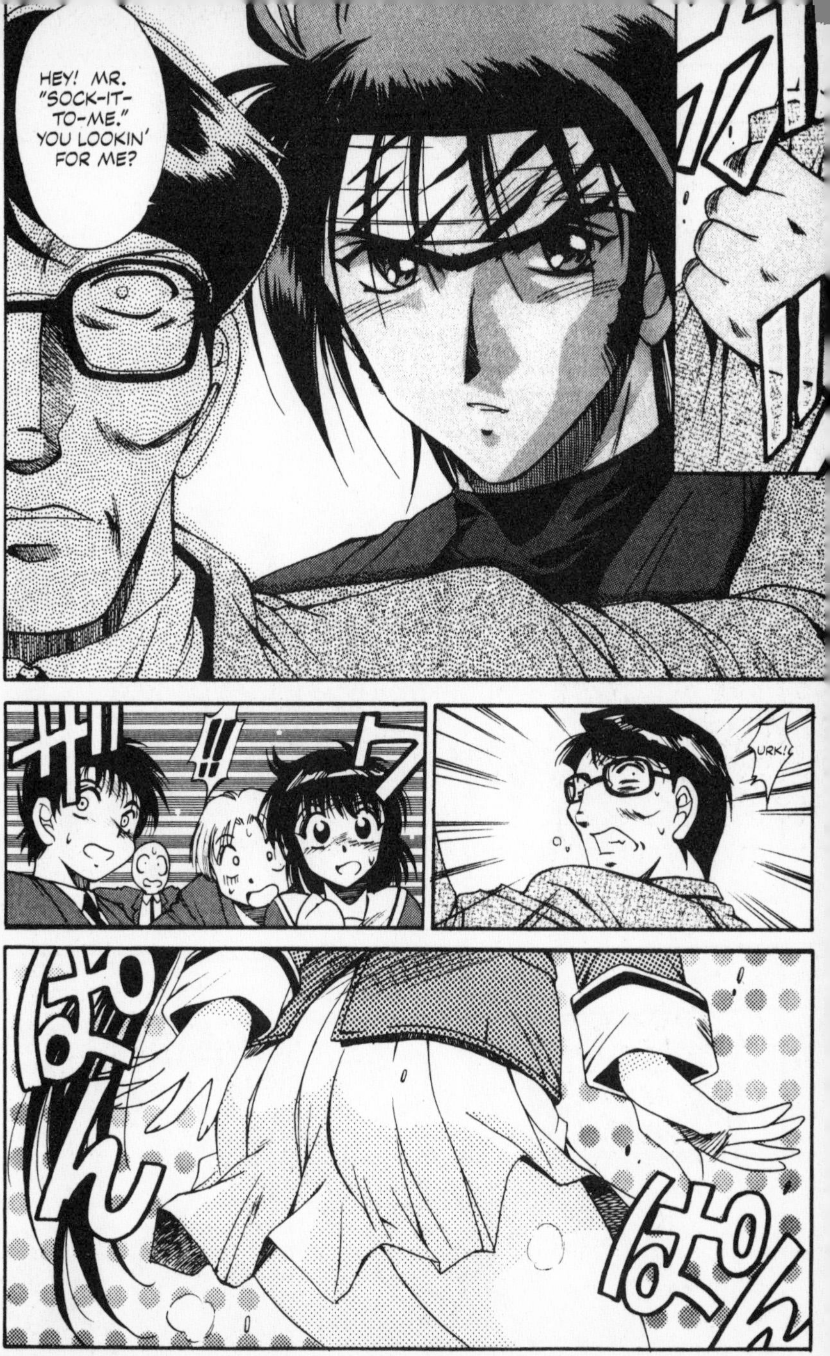
HEY! MR. "SOCK-IT-TO-ME." YOU LOOKIN' FOR ME?
URK!

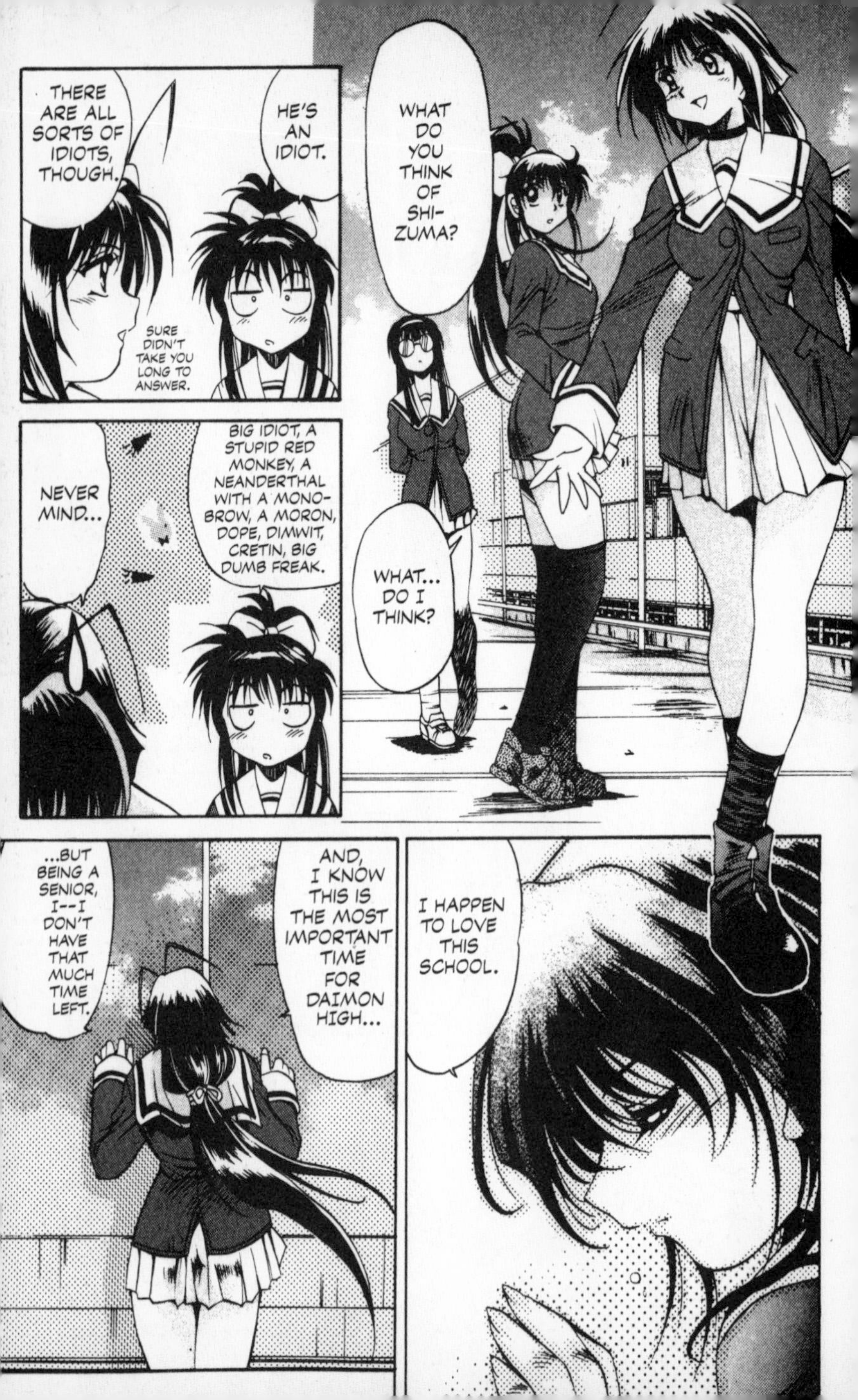

WHAT DO YOU THINK OF SHI-ZUMA?
WHAT... DO I THINK?
HE'S AN IDIOT.
THERE ARE ALL SORTS OF IDIOTS, THOUGH.
SURE DIDN'T TAKE YOU LONG TO ANSWER.
BIG IDIOT, A STUPID RED MONKEY, A NEANDERTHAL WITH A MONO-BROW, A MORON, DOPE, DIMWIT, CRETIN, BIG DUMB FREAK.
NEVER MIND...
I HAPPEN TO LOVE THIS SCHOOL.
AND, I KNOW THIS IS THE MOST IMPORTANT TIME FOR DAIMON HIGH...
...BUT BEING A SENIOR, I--I DON'T HAVE THAT MUCH TIME LEFT.

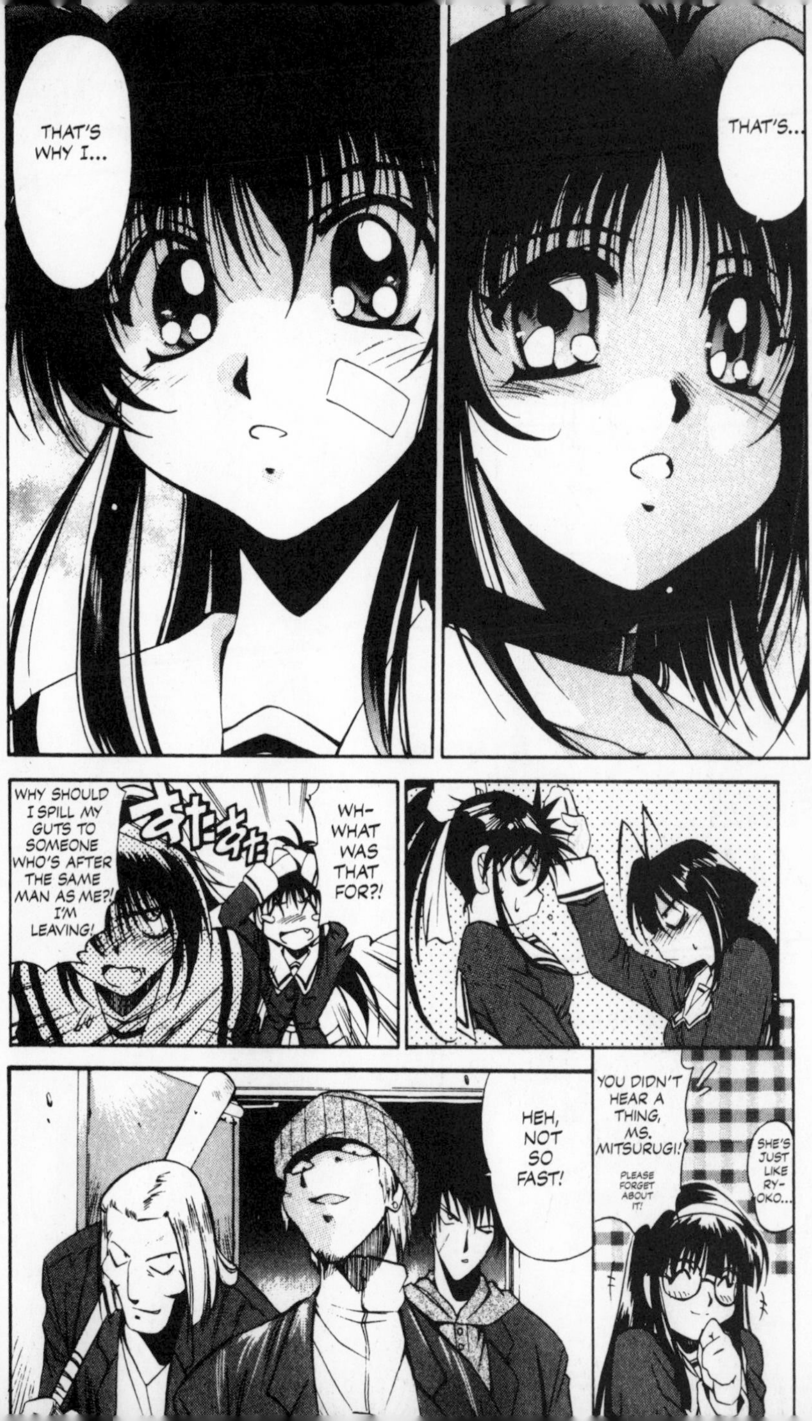
THAT'S...
THAT'S WHY I...
WH-WHAT WAS THAT FOR?!
WHY SHOULD I SPILL MY GUTS TO SOMEONE WHO'S AFTER THE SAME MAN AS ME?! I'M LEAVING!
YOU DIDN'T HEAR A THING, MS. MITSURUGI!
PLEASE FORGET ABOUT IT!
SHE'S JUST LIKE RY-OKO...
HEH, NOT SO FAST!

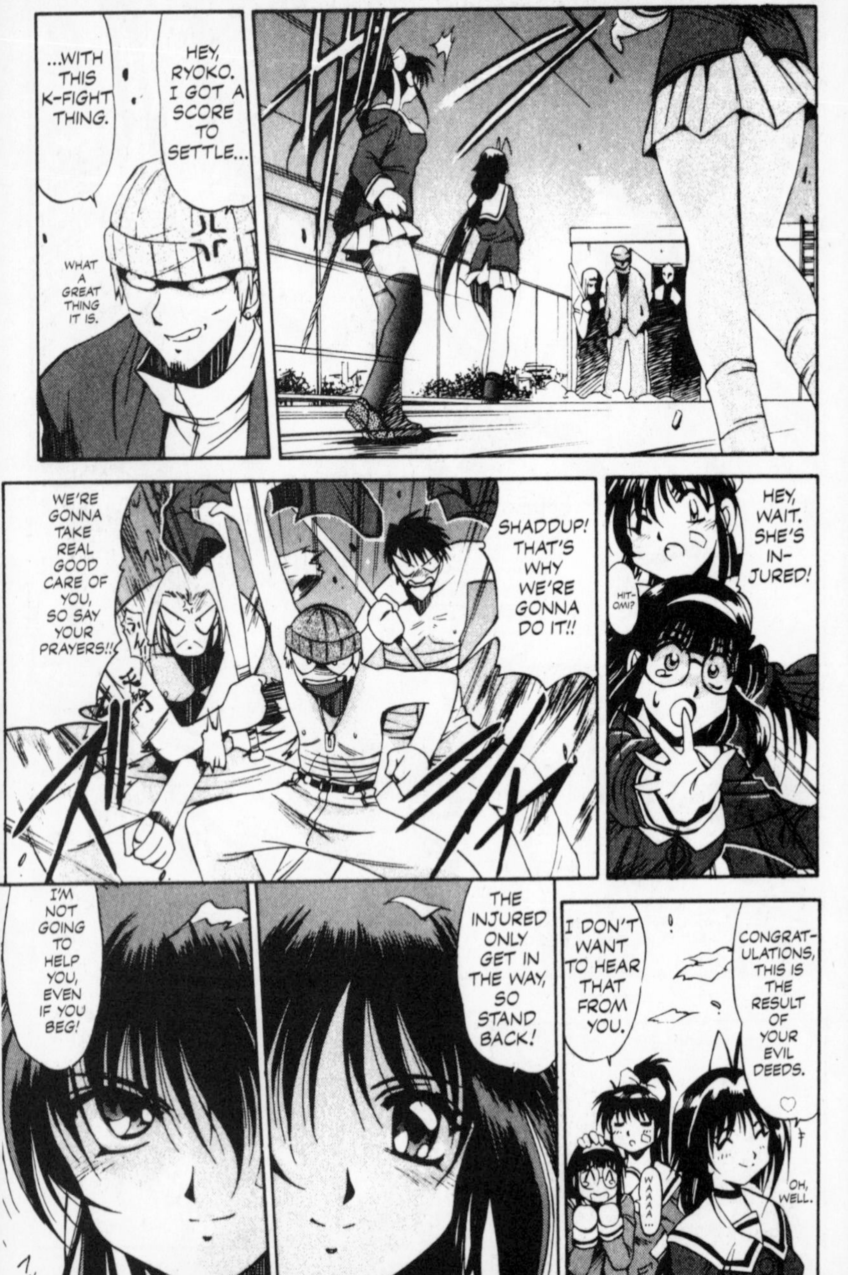

HEY, RYOKO. I GOT A SCORE TO SETTLE...
...WITH THIS K-FIGHT THING.
WHAT A GREAT THING IT IS.
HEY, WAIT. SHE'S IN-JURED!
HIT-OMI?
SHADDUP! THAT'S WHY WE'RE GONNA DO IT!!
WE'RE GONNA TAKE REAL GOOD CARE OF YOU, SO SAY YOUR PRAYERS!!
CONGRAT-ULATIONS, THIS IS THE RESULT OF YOUR EVIL DEEDS.
I DON'T WANT TO HEAR THAT FROM YOU.
WAAAA...
OH, WELL.
THE INJURED ONLY GET IN THE WAY, SO STAND BACK!
I'M NOT GOING TO HELP YOU, EVEN IF YOU BEG!

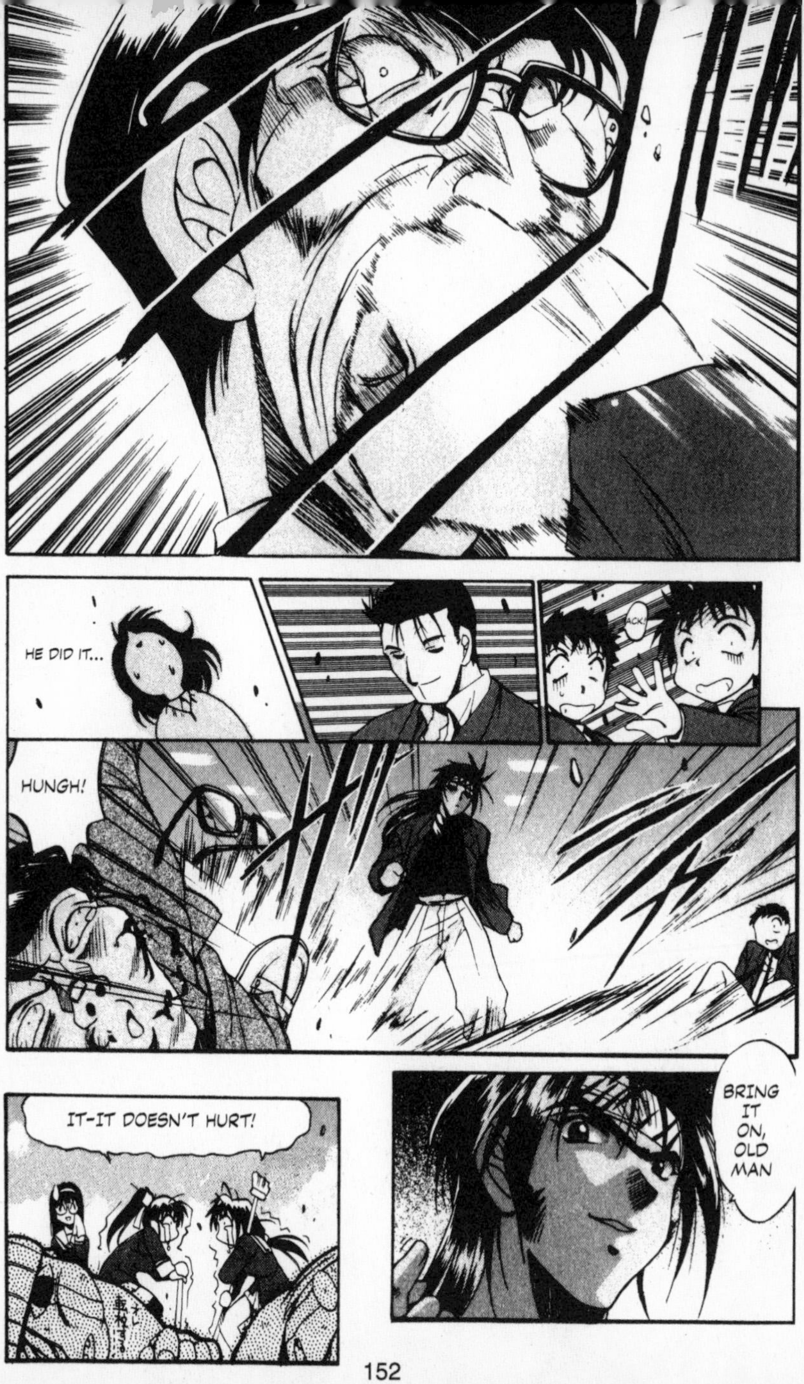
ACK!
HE DID IT...
HUNGH!
BRING IT ON, OLD MAN
IT-IT DOESN'T HURT!

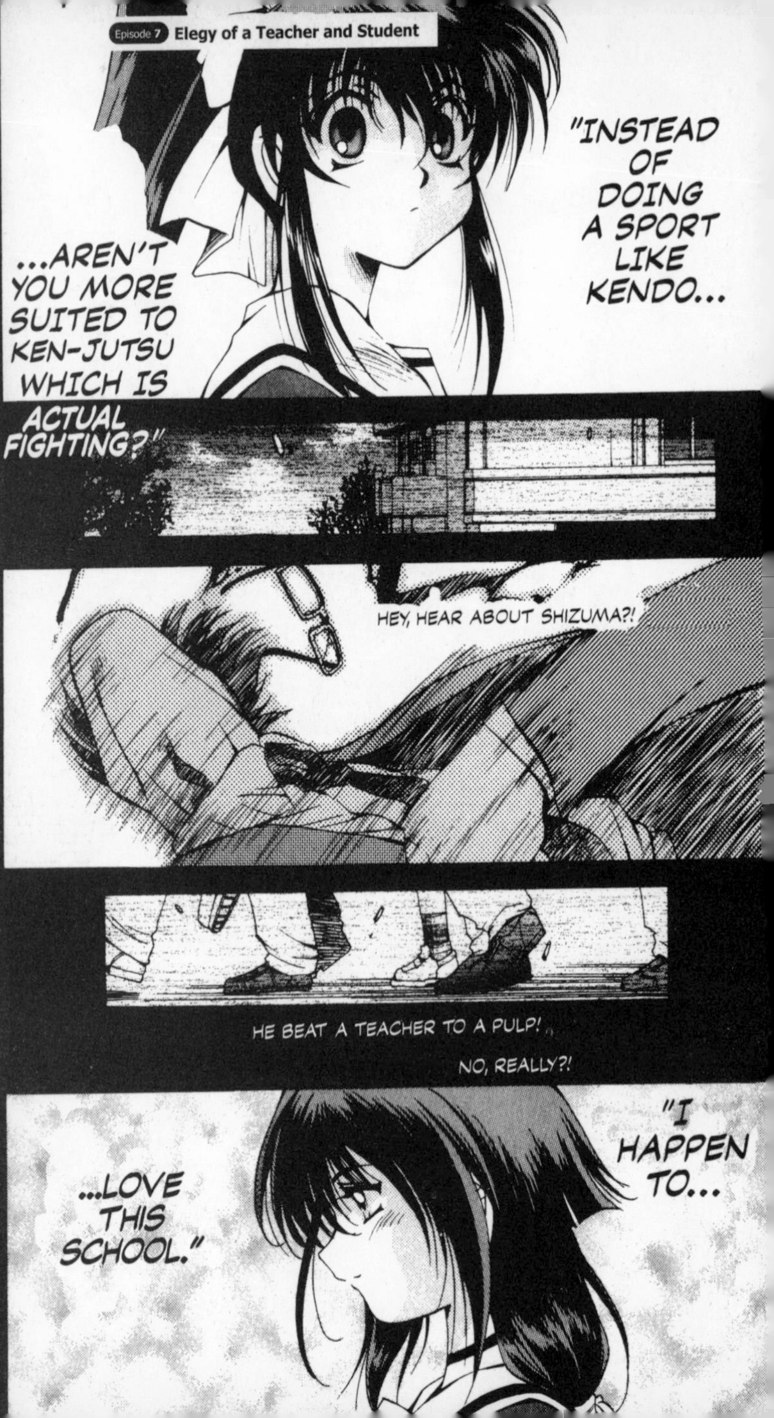
"INSTEAD OF DOING A SPORT LIKE KENDO...
...AREN'T YOU MORE SUITED TO KEN-JUTSU WHICH IS ACTUAL FIGHTING?"
HEY, HEAR ABOUT SHIZUMA?!
HE BEAT A TEACHER TO A PULP!
NO, REALLY?!
"I HAPPEN TO...
...LOVE THIS SCHOOL."

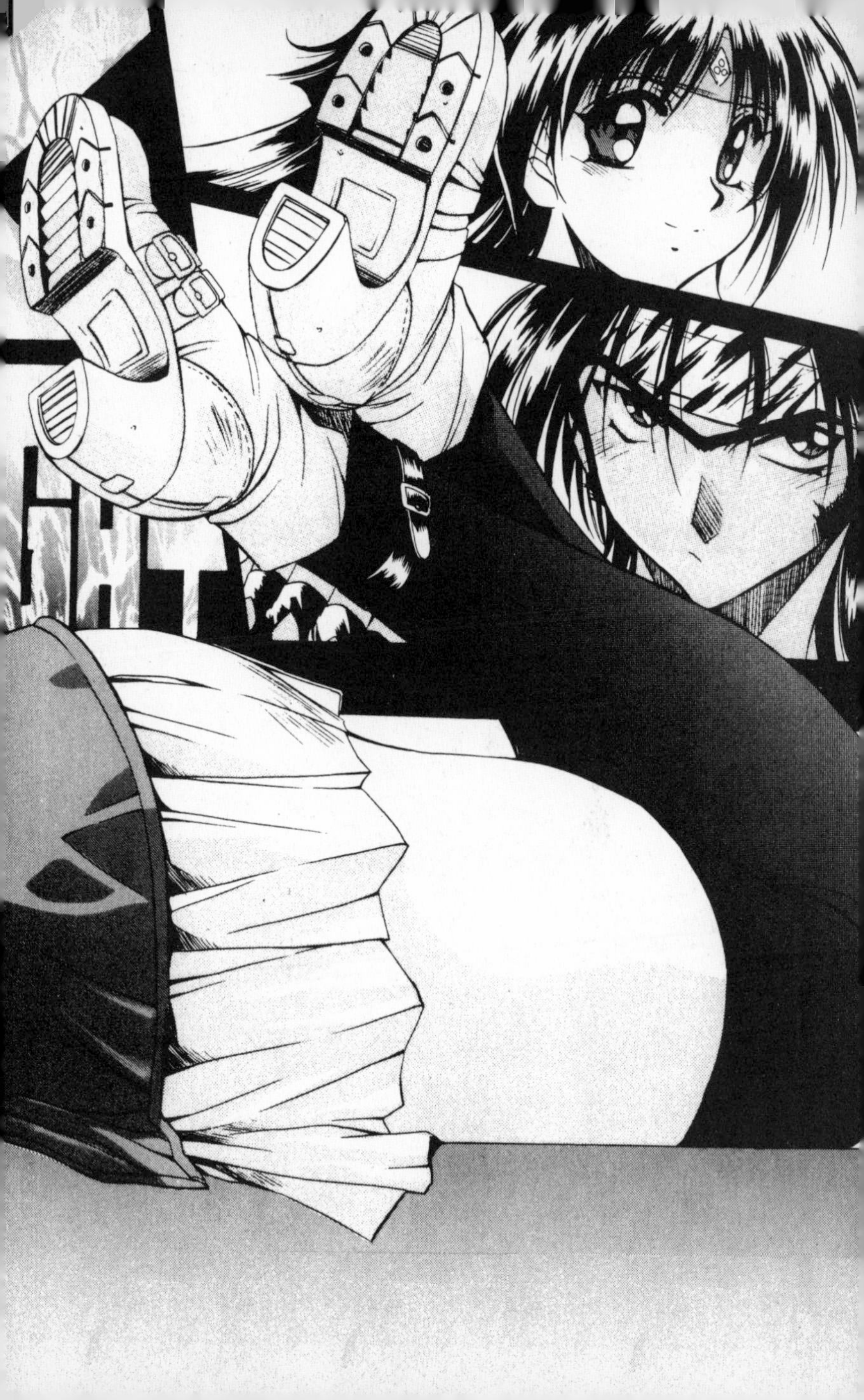

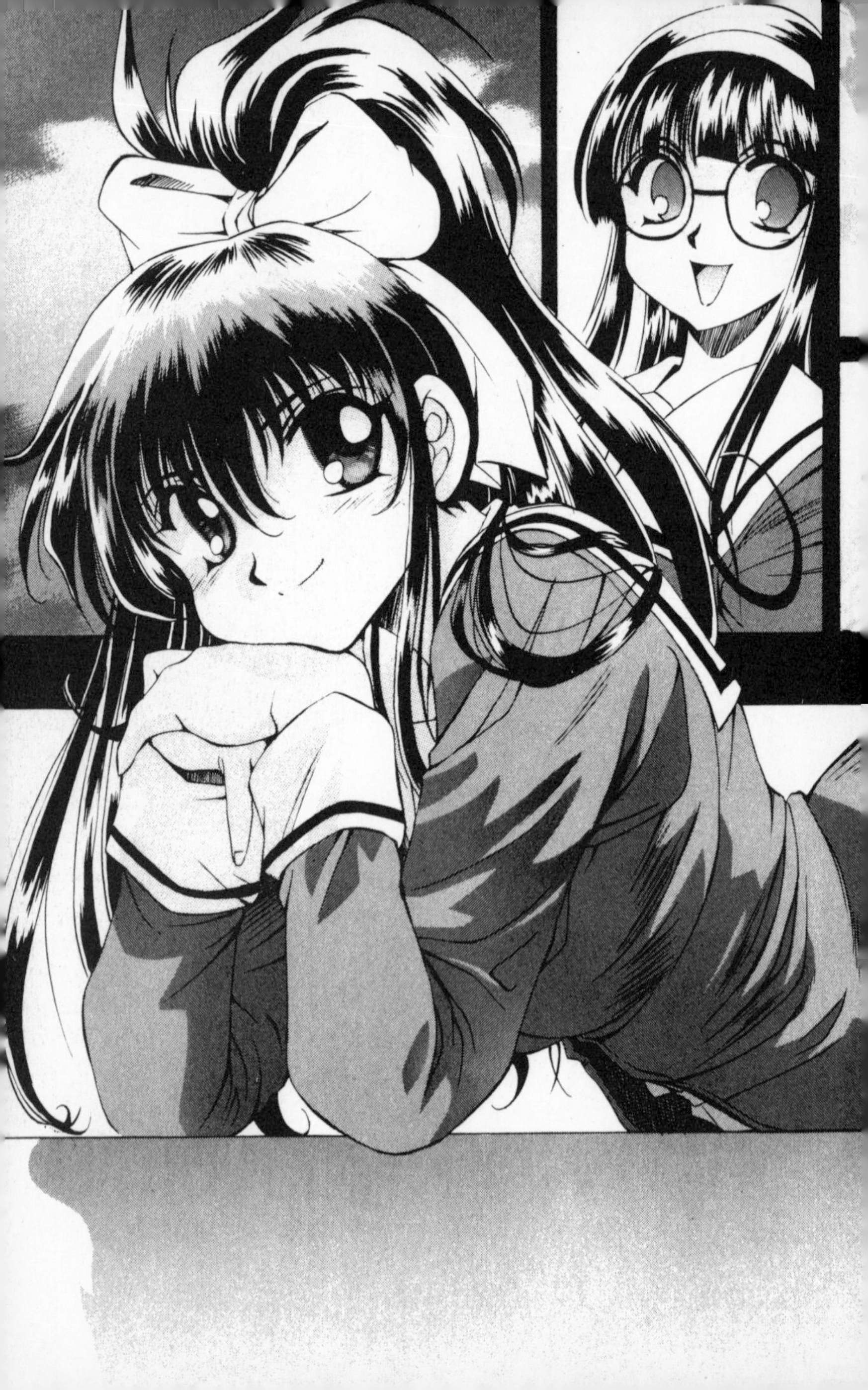

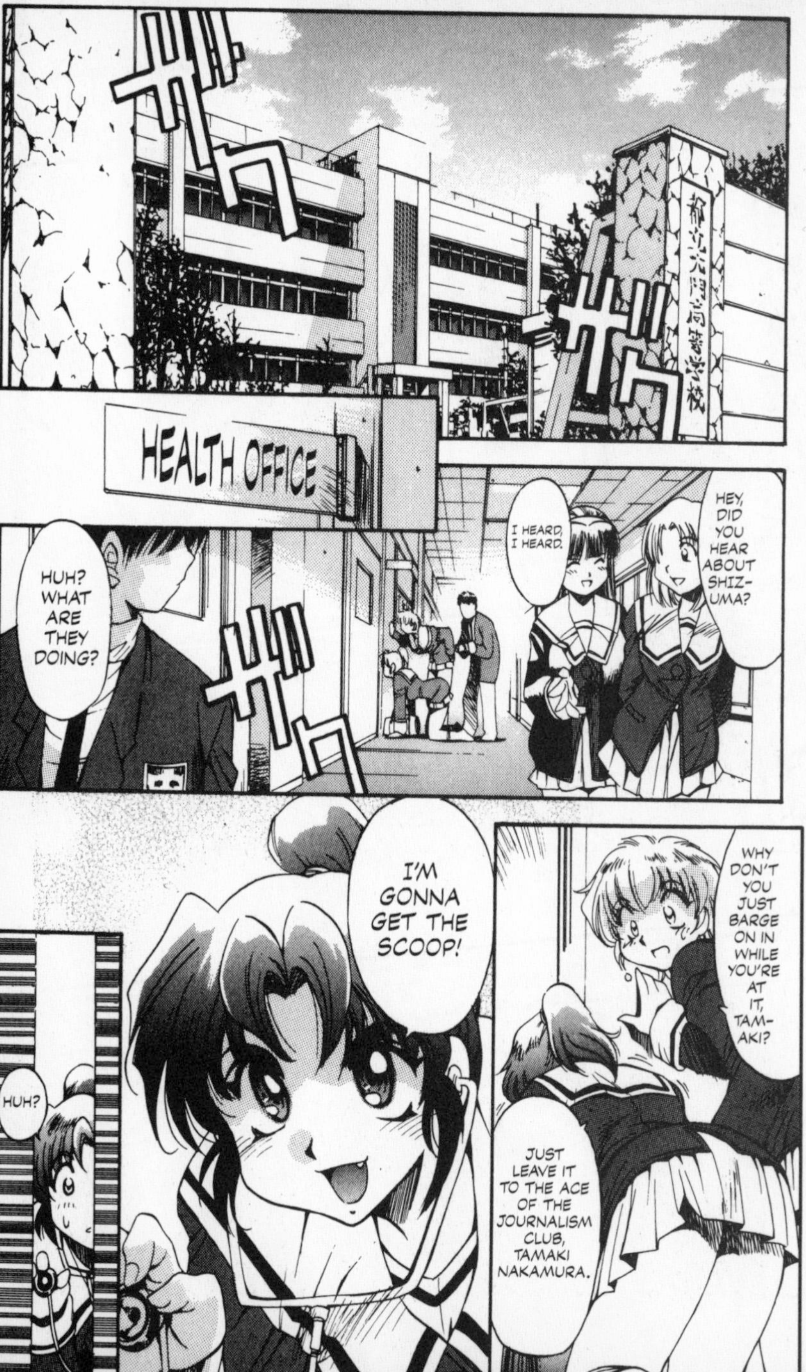
HEALTH OFFICE
HEY, DID YOU HEAR ABOUT SHIZUMA?
I HEARD, I HEARD.
HUH? WHAT ARE THEY DOING?
WHY DON'T YOU JUST BARGE ON IN WHILE YOU'RE AT IT, TAMAKI?
JUST LEAVE IT TO THE ACE OF THE JOURNALISM CLUB, TAMAKI NAKAMURA.
I'M GONNA GET THE SCOOP!
HUH?

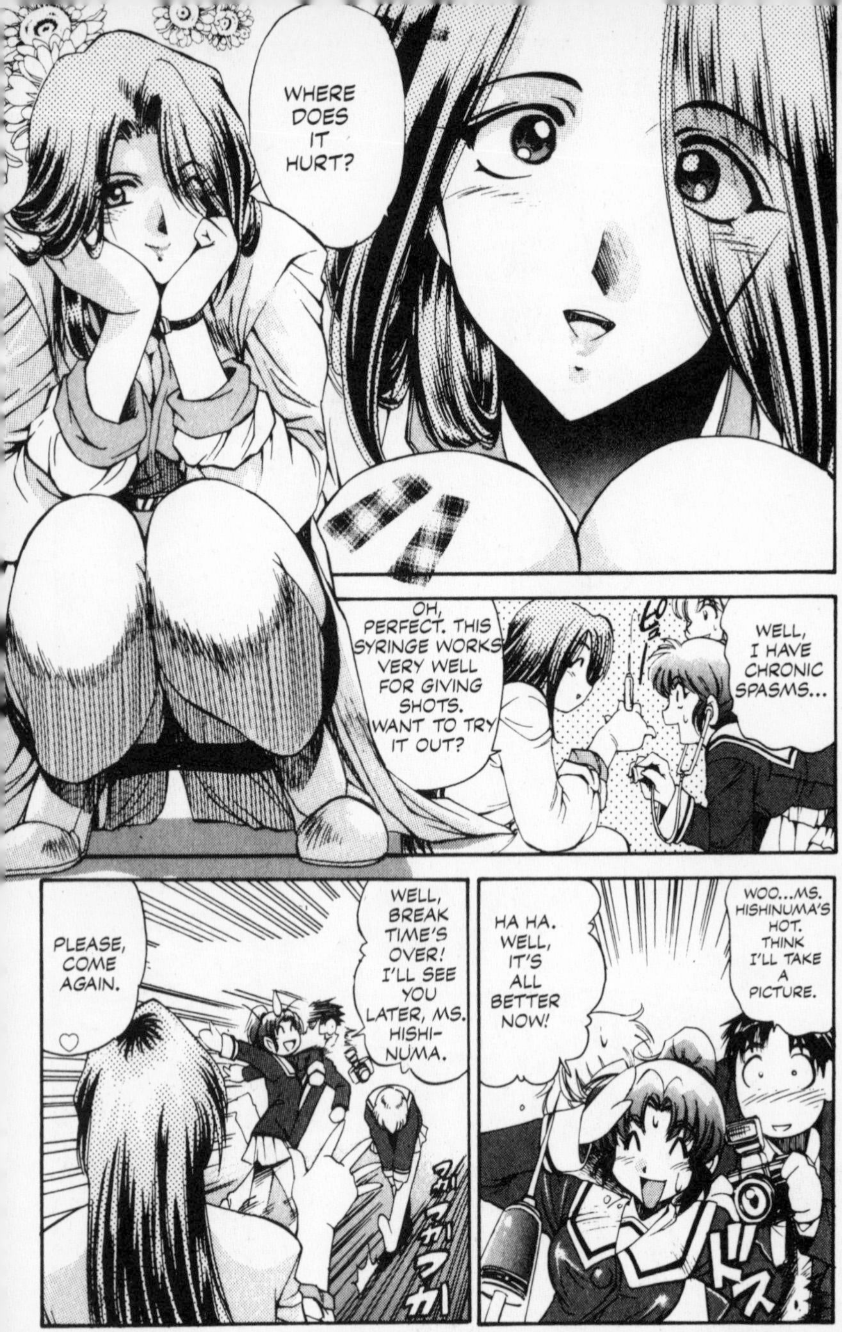
WHERE DOES IT HURT?
WELL, I HAVE CHRONIC SPASMS...
OH, PERFECT. THIS SYRINGE WORKS VERY WELL FOR GIVING SHOTS. WANT TO TRY IT OUT?
WOO...MS. HISHINUMA'S HOT. THINK I'LL TAKE A PICTURE.
HA HA. WELL, IT'S ALL BETTER NOW!
WELL, BREAK TIME'S OVER! I'LL SEE YOU LATER, MS. HISHI-NUMA.
PLEASE, COME AGAIN.

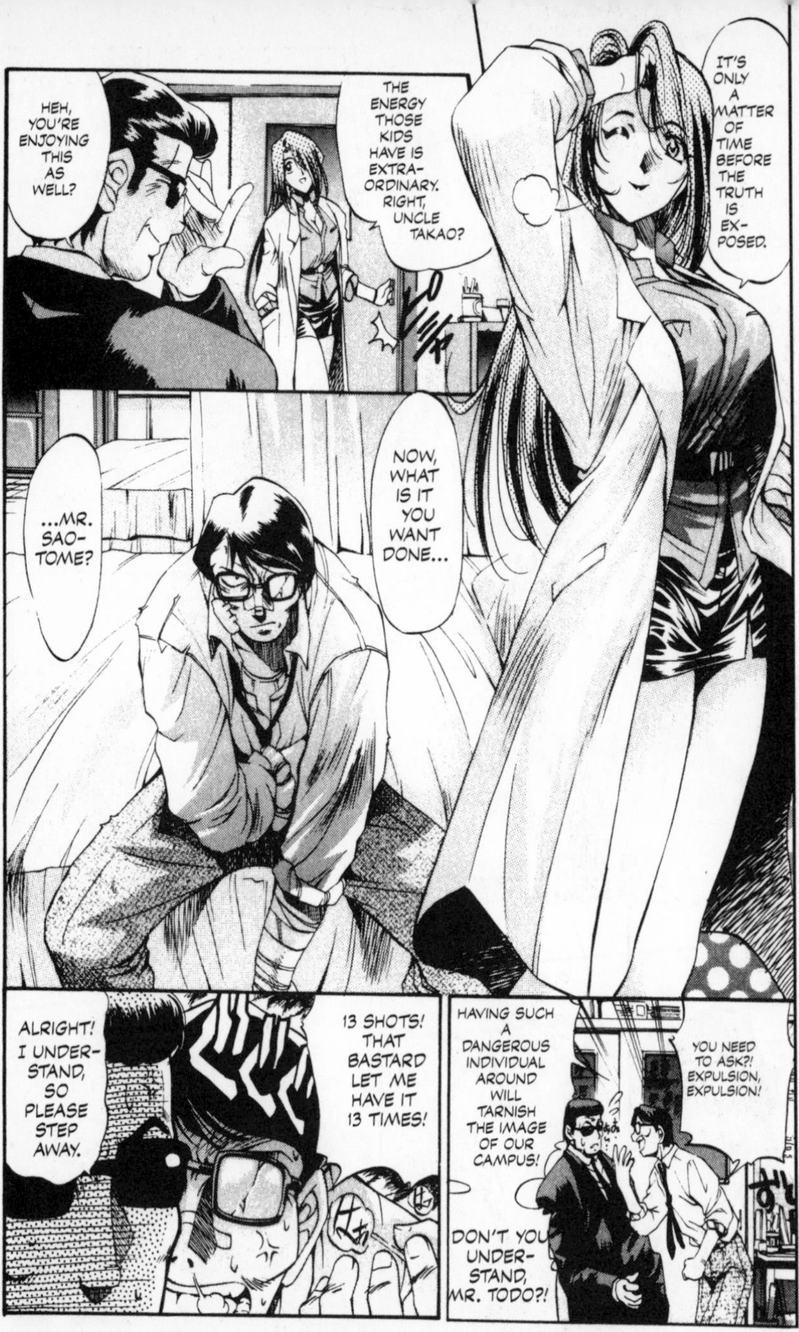
IT'S ONLY A MATTER OF TIME BEFORE THE TRUTH IS EXPOSED.
THE ENERGY THOSE KIDS HAVE IS EXTRA-ORDINARY. RIGHT, UNCLE TAKAO?
HEH, YOU'RE ENJOYING THIS AS WELL?
NOW, WHAT IS IT YOU WANT DONE...
...MR. SAO-TOME?
HAVING SUCH A DANGEROUS INDIVIDUAL AROUND WILL TARNISH THE IMAGE OF OUR CAMPUS!
YOU NEED TO ASK?! EXPULSION, EXPULSION!
DON'T YOU UNDER-STAND, MR. TODO?!
13 SHOTS! THAT BASTARD LET ME HAVE IT 13 TIMES!
ALRIGHT! I UNDER-STAND, SO PLEASE STEP AWAY.

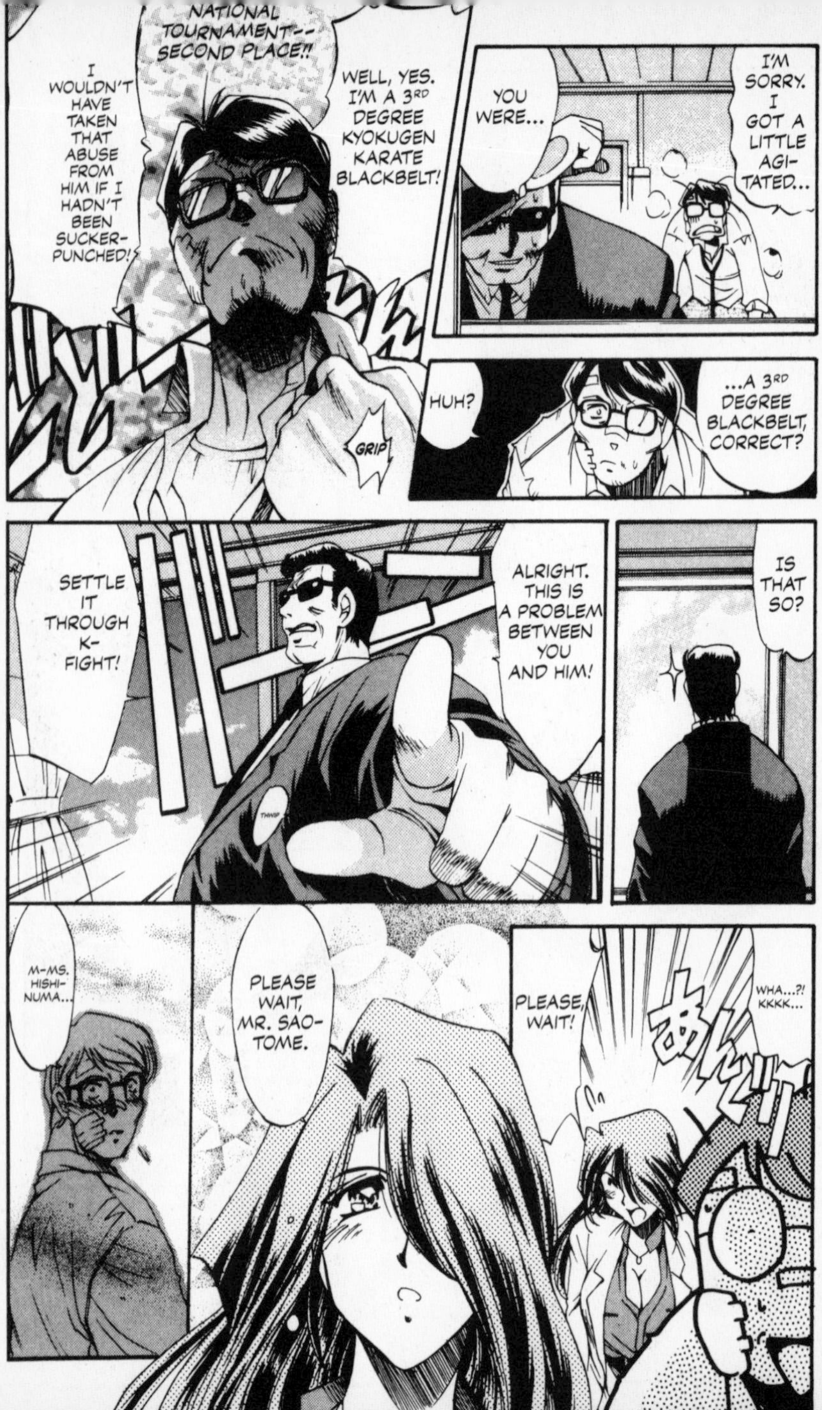
I'M SORRY. I GOT A LITTLE AGITATED...
YOU WERE...
...A 3RD DEGREE BLACKBELT, CORRECT?
HUH?
WELL, YES. I'M A 3RD DEGREE KYOKUGEN KARATE BLACKBELT!
NATIONAL TOURNAMENT-- SECOND PLACE!!
I WOULDN'T HAVE TAKEN THAT ABUSE FROM HIM IF I HADN'T BEEN SUCKER-PUNCHED!
GRIP
IS THAT SO?
ALRIGHT. THIS IS A PROBLEM BETWEEN YOU AND HIM!
SETTLE IT THROUGH K-FIGHT!
WHA...?! KKKK...
PLEASE, WAIT!
PLEASE WAIT, MR. SAOTOME.
M-MS. HISHINUMA...

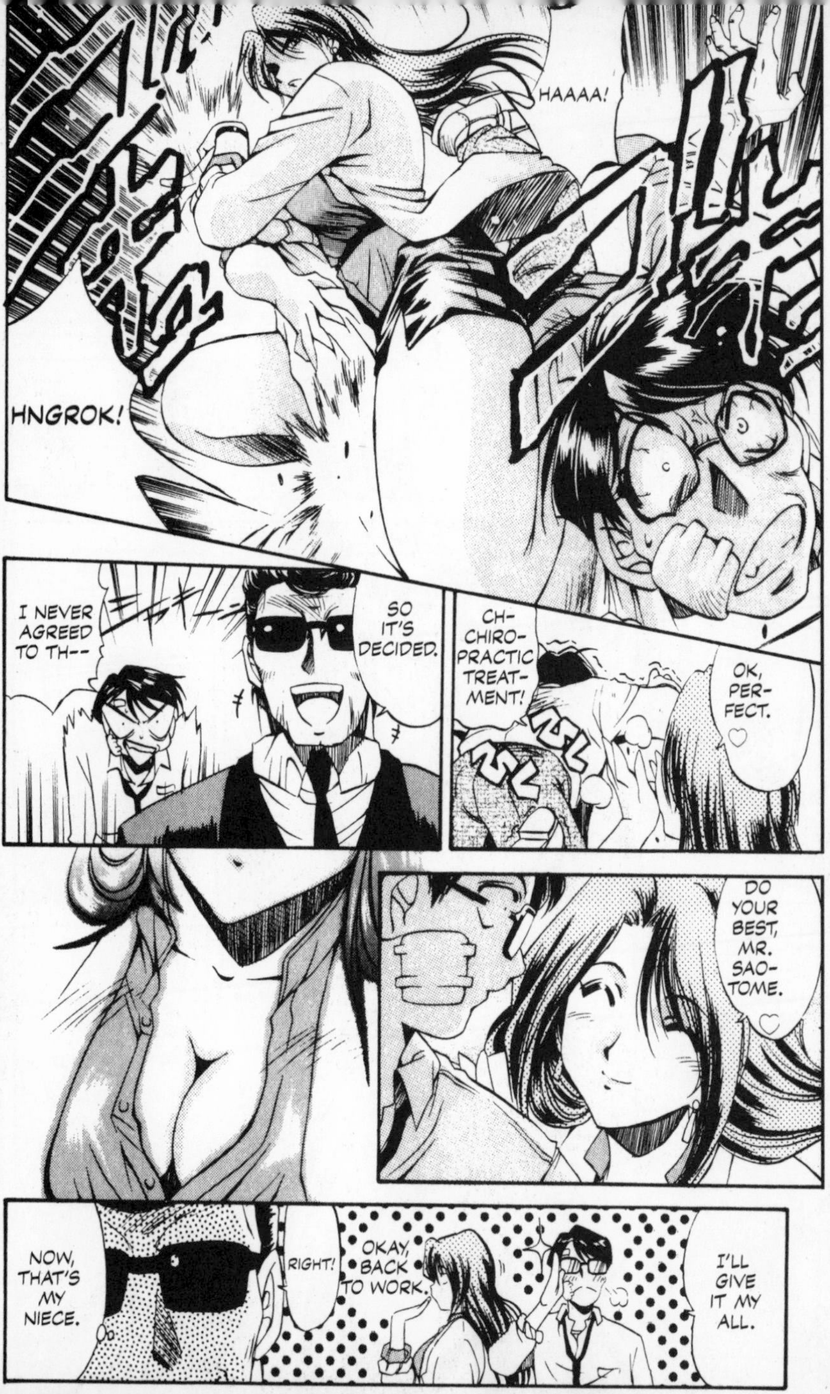
HAAAA!
HNGROK!
OK, PERFECT. ♡
CH-CHIROPRACTIC TREATMENT!
SO IT'S DECIDED.
I NEVER AGREED TO TH--
DO YOUR BEST, MR. SAOTOME. ♡
I'LL GIVE IT MY ALL.
OKAY, BACK TO WORK.
RIGHT!
NOW, THAT'S MY NIECE.

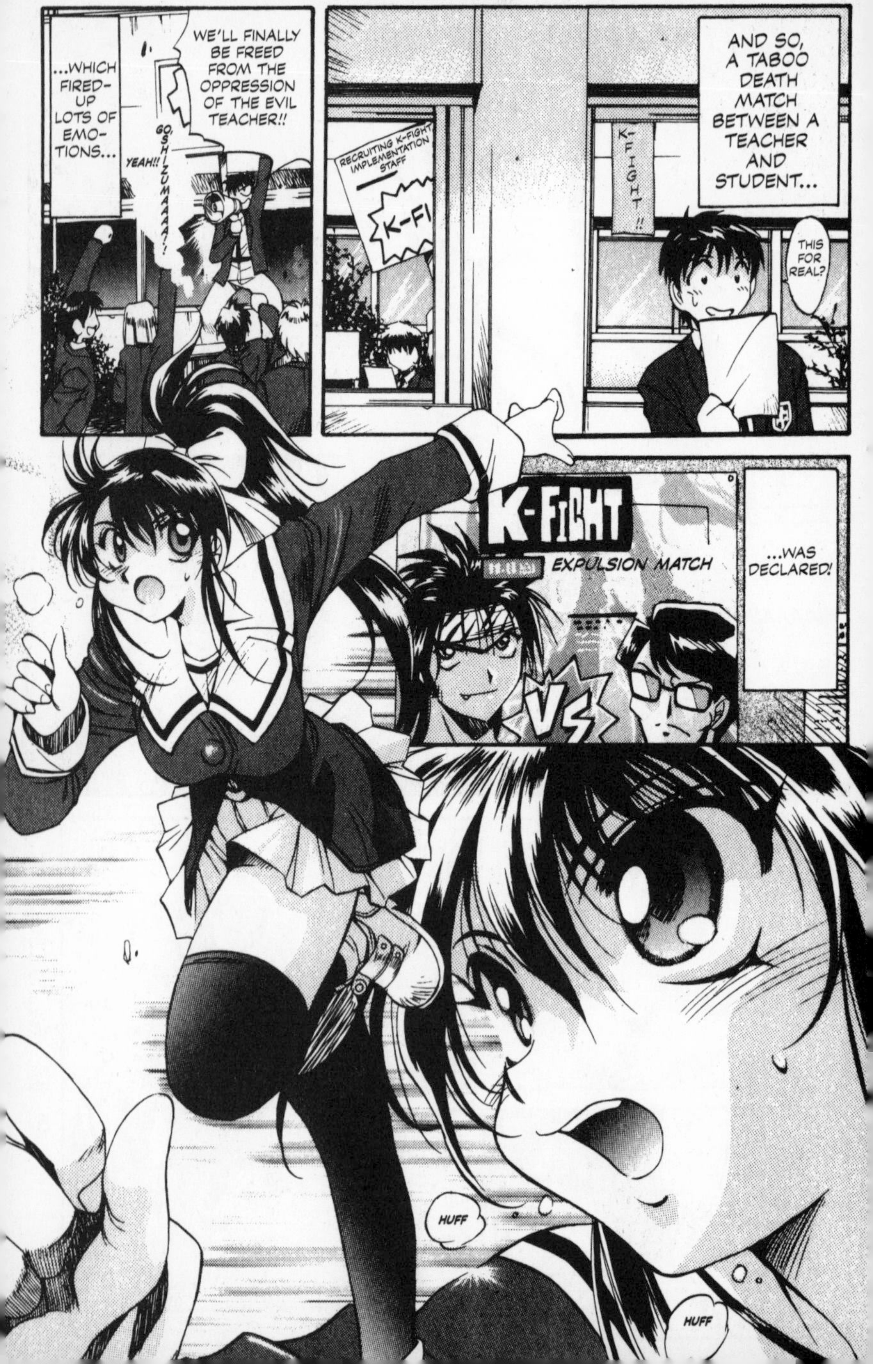
AND SO, A TABOO DEATH MATCH BETWEEN A TEACHER AND STUDENT...
K-FIGHT !!
THIS FOR REAL?
RECRUITING K-FIGHT IMPLEMENTATION STAFF
K-FI
...WHICH FIRED-UP LOTS OF EMOTIONS...
WE'LL FINALLY BE FREED FROM THE OPPRESSION OF THE EVIL TEACHER!!
GO, SHIZUMAAAA!!
YEAH!!
...WAS DECLARED!
K-FIGHT
EXPULSION MATCH
VS
HUFF
HUFF

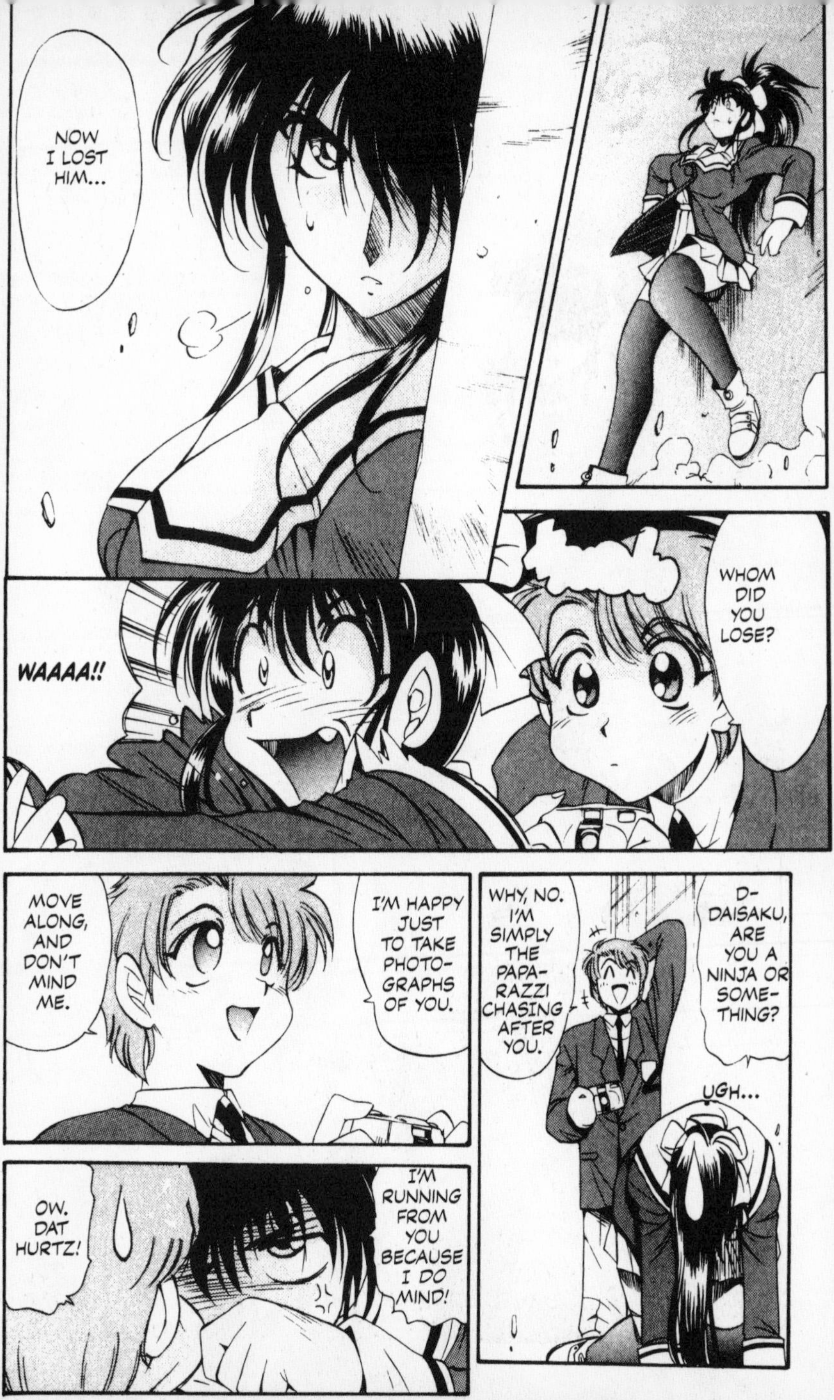
NOW I LOST HIM...
WHOM DID YOU LOSE?
WAAAA!!
D-DAISAKU, ARE YOU A NINJA OR SOME-THING?
WHY, NO. I'M SIMPLY THE PAPA-RAZZI CHASING AFTER YOU.
UGH...
I'M HAPPY JUST TO TAKE PHOTO-GRAPHS OF YOU.
MOVE ALONG, AND DON'T MIND ME.
I'M RUNNING FROM YOU BECAUSE I DO MIND!
OW. DAT HURTZ!

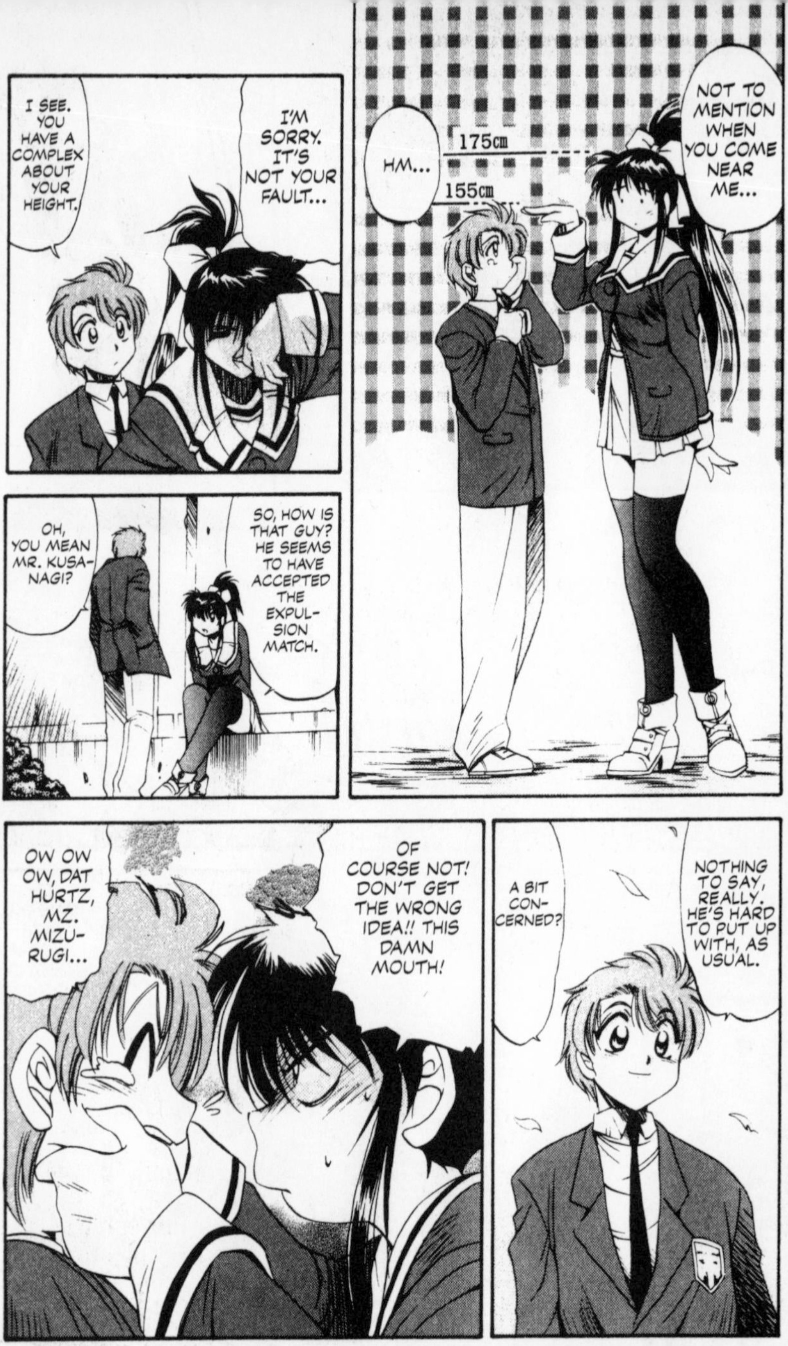
NOT TO MENTION WHEN YOU COME NEAR ME...
175cm
HM...
155cm
I'M SORRY. IT'S NOT YOUR FAULT...
I SEE. YOU HAVE A COMPLEX ABOUT YOUR HEIGHT.
SO, HOW IS THAT GUY? HE SEEMS TO HAVE ACCEPTED THE EXPULSION MATCH.
OH, YOU MEAN MR. KUSANAGI?
NOTHING TO SAY, REALLY. HE'S HARD TO PUT UP WITH, AS USUAL.
A BIT CONCERNED?
OF COURSE NOT! DON'T GET THE WRONG IDEA!! THIS DAMN MOUTH!
OW OW OW, DAT HURTZ, MZ. MIZURUGI...

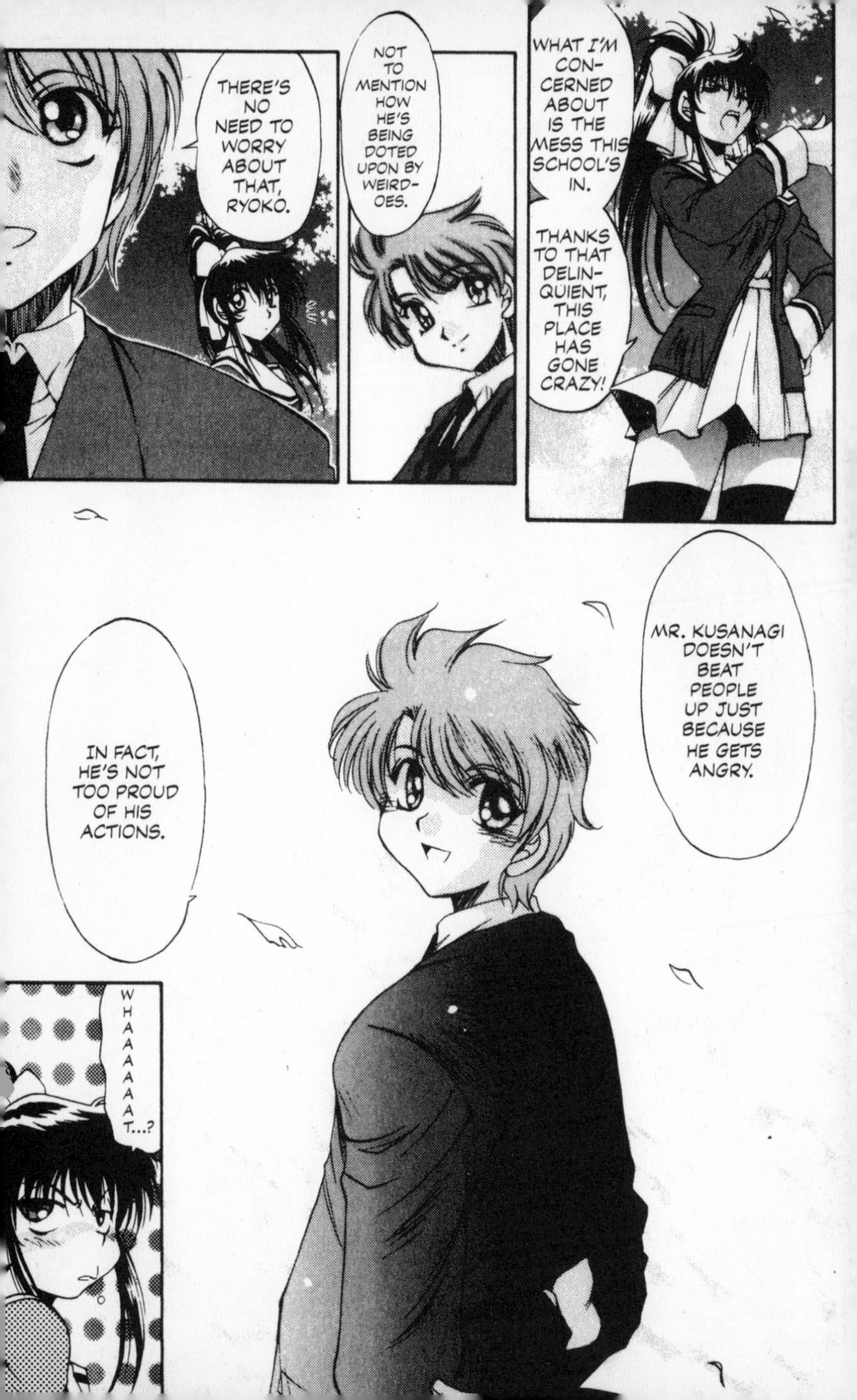
WHAT I'M CONCERNED ABOUT IS THE MESS THIS SCHOOL'S IN.
THANKS TO THAT DELINQUIENT, THIS PLACE HAS GONE CRAZY!
NOT TO MENTION HOW HE'S BEING DOTED UPON BY WEIRDOES.
THERE'S NO NEED TO WORRY ABOUT THAT, RYOKO.
MR. KUSANAGI DOESN'T BEAT PEOPLE UP JUST BECAUSE HE GETS ANGRY.
IN FACT, HE'S NOT TOO PROUD OF HIS ACTIONS.
WHAAAAAAT...?

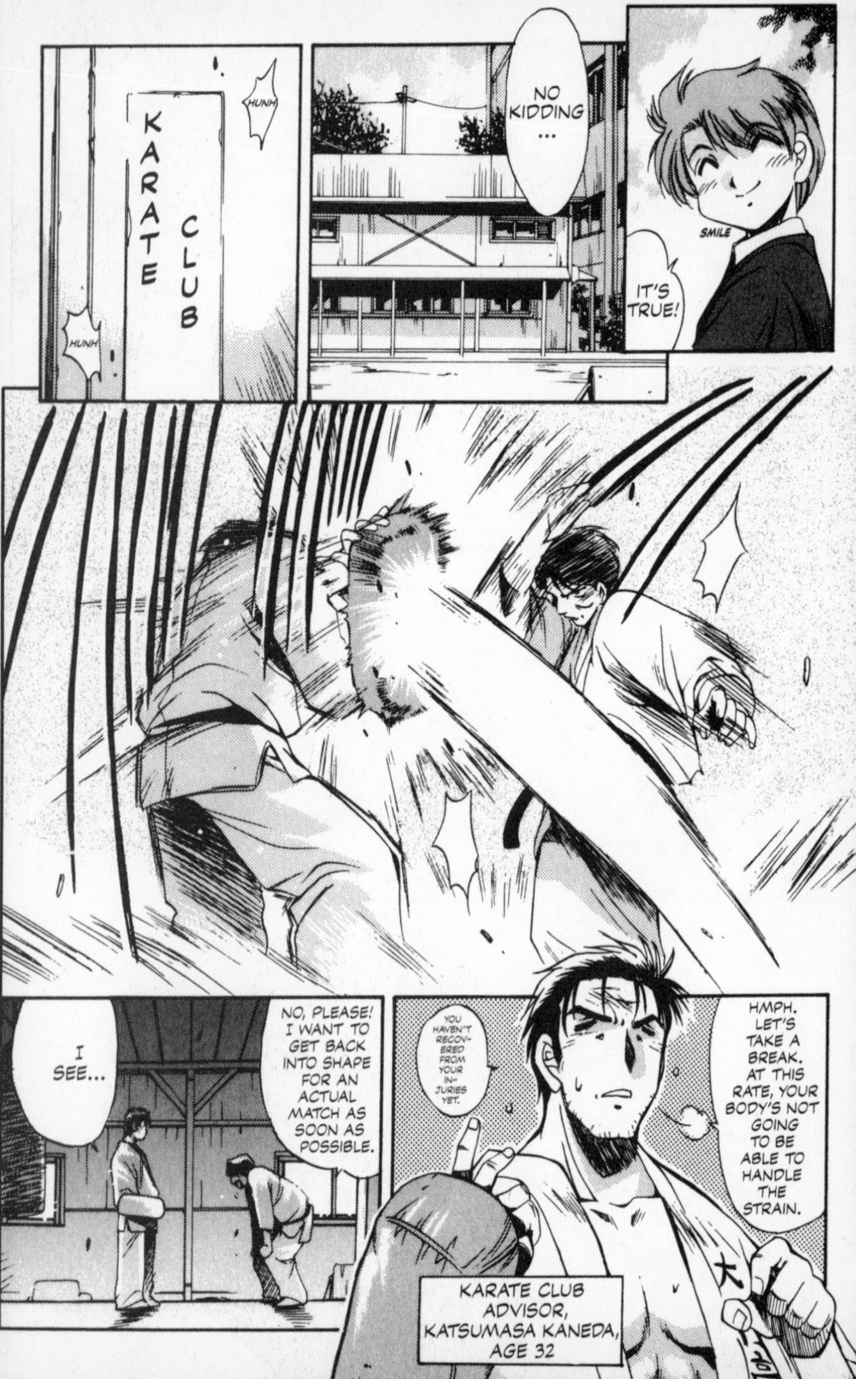
NO KIDDING ...
SMILE
IT'S TRUE!
HUNH
KARATE CLUB
HUNH
HMPH. LET'S TAKE A BREAK. AT THIS RATE, YOUR BODY'S NOT GOING TO BE ABLE TO HANDLE THE STRAIN.
YOU HAVEN'T RECOVERED FROM YOUR INJURIES YET.
KARATE CLUB ADVISOR, KATSUMASA KANEDA, AGE 32
NO, PLEASE! I WANT TO GET BACK INTO SHAPE FOR AN ACTUAL MATCH AS SOON AS POSSIBLE.
I SEE...

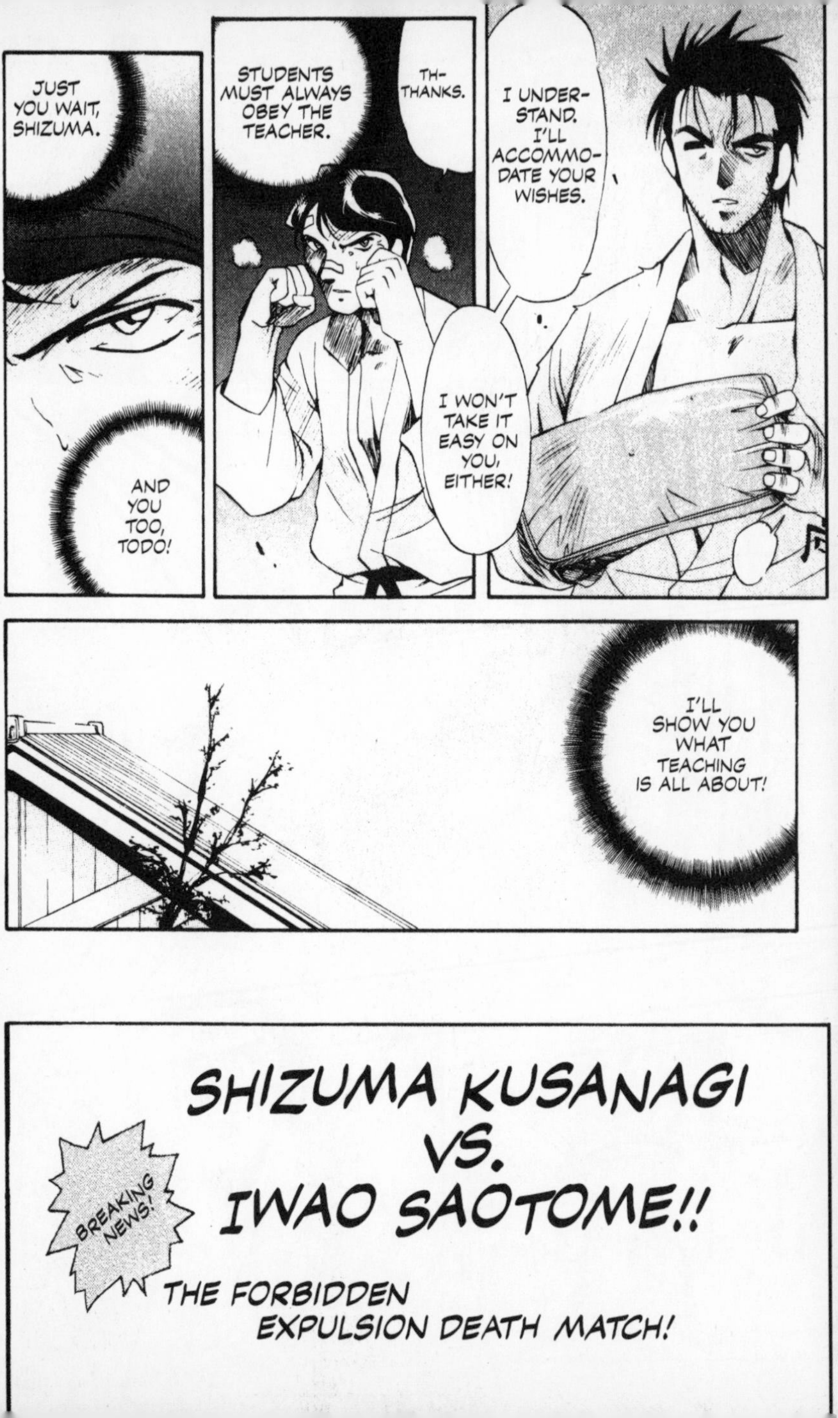
I UNDER-STAND. I'LL ACCOMMODATE YOUR WISHES.
I WON'T TAKE IT EASY ON YOU, EITHER!
TH-THANKS.
STUDENTS MUST ALWAYS OBEY THE TEACHER.
JUST YOU WAIT, SHIZUMA.
AND YOU TOO, TODO!
I'LL SHOW YOU WHAT TEACHING IS ALL ABOUT!
SHIZUMA KUSANAGI VS. IWAO SAOTOME!!
BREAKING NEWS!
THE FORBIDDEN EXPULSION DEATH MATCH!

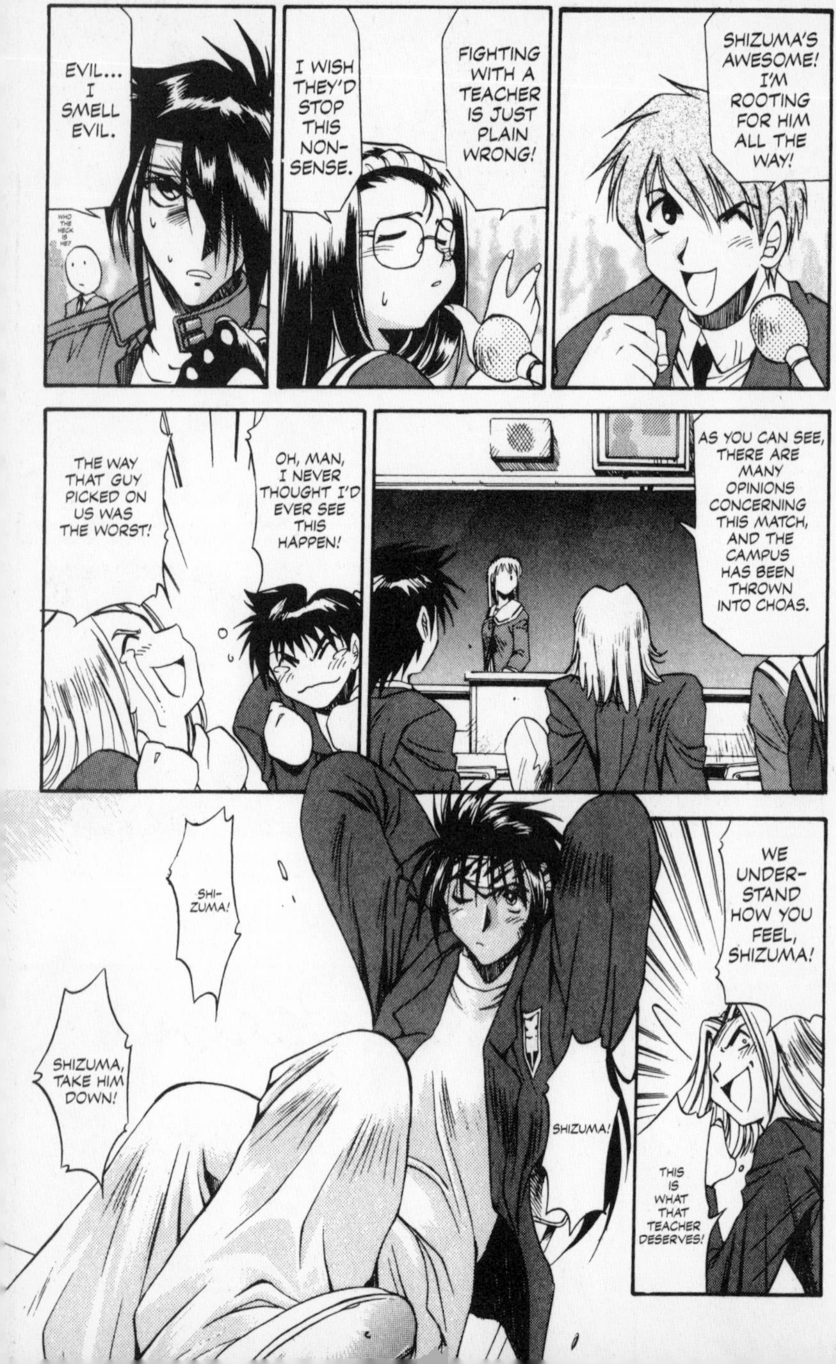
SHIZUMA'S AWESOME! I'M ROOTING FOR HIM ALL THE WAY!
FIGHTING WITH A TEACHER IS JUST PLAIN WRONG!
I WISH THEY'D STOP THIS NON-SENSE.
EVIL... I SMELL EVIL.
WHO THE HECK IS HE?
AS YOU CAN SEE, THERE ARE MANY OPINIONS CONCERNING THIS MATCH, AND THE CAMPUS HAS BEEN THROWN INTO CHOAS.
OH, MAN, I NEVER THOUGHT I'D EVER SEE THIS HAPPEN!
THE WAY THAT GUY PICKED ON US WAS THE WORST!
WE UNDER-STAND HOW YOU FEEL, SHIZUMA!
THIS IS WHAT THAT TEACHER DESERVES!
SHIZUMA!
SHI-ZUMA!
SHIZUMA, TAKE HIM DOWN!

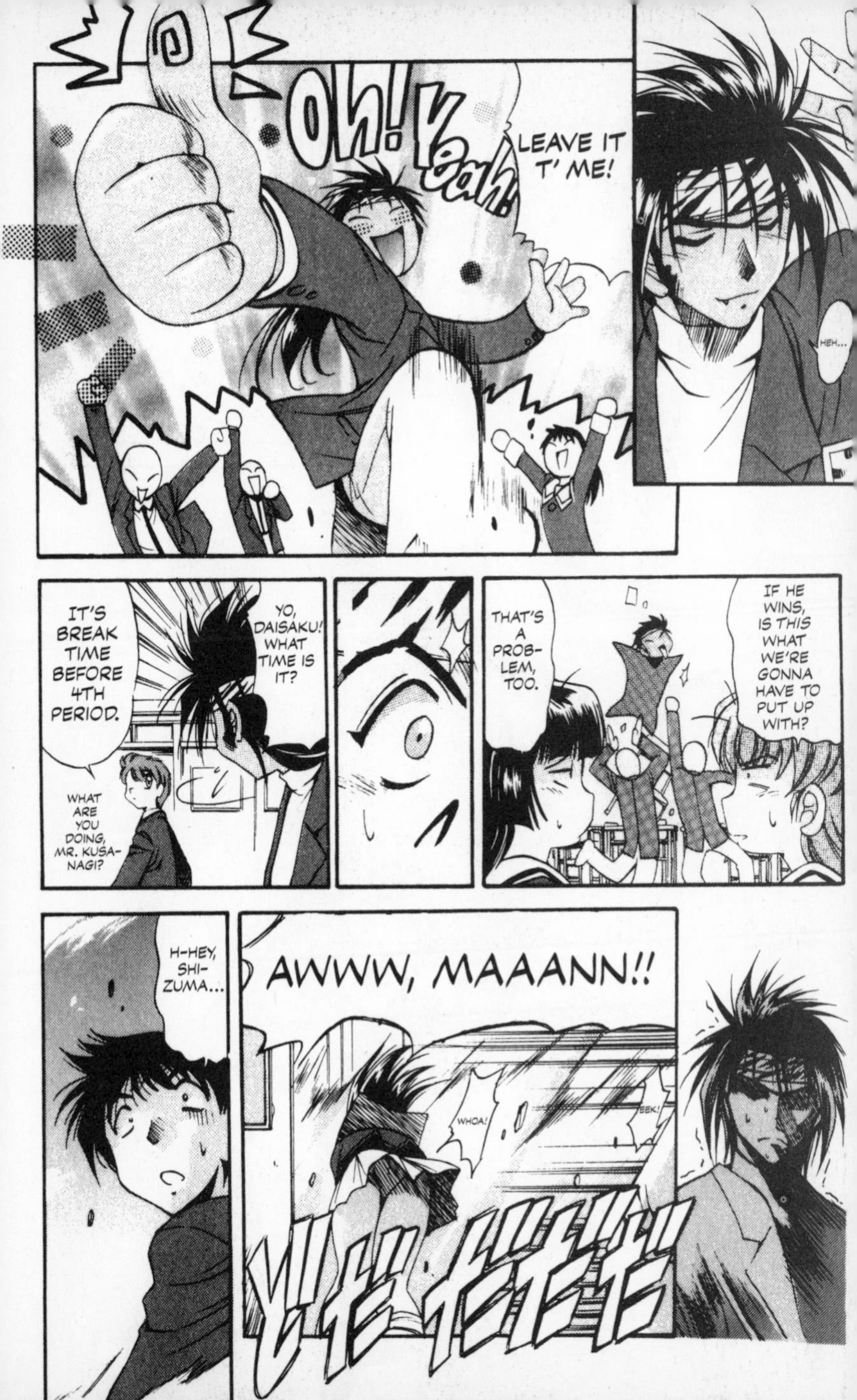
HEH...
OH! YEAH!
LEAVE IT T' ME!
IF HE WINS, IS THIS WHAT WE'RE GONNA HAVE TO PUT UP WITH?
THAT'S A PROB-LEM, TOO.
YO, DAISAKU! WHAT TIME IS IT?
IT'S BREAK TIME BEFORE 4TH PERIOD.
WHAT ARE YOU DOING, MR. KUSA-NAGI?
AWWW, MAAANN!!
EEK!
WHOA!
H-HEY, SHI-ZUMA...

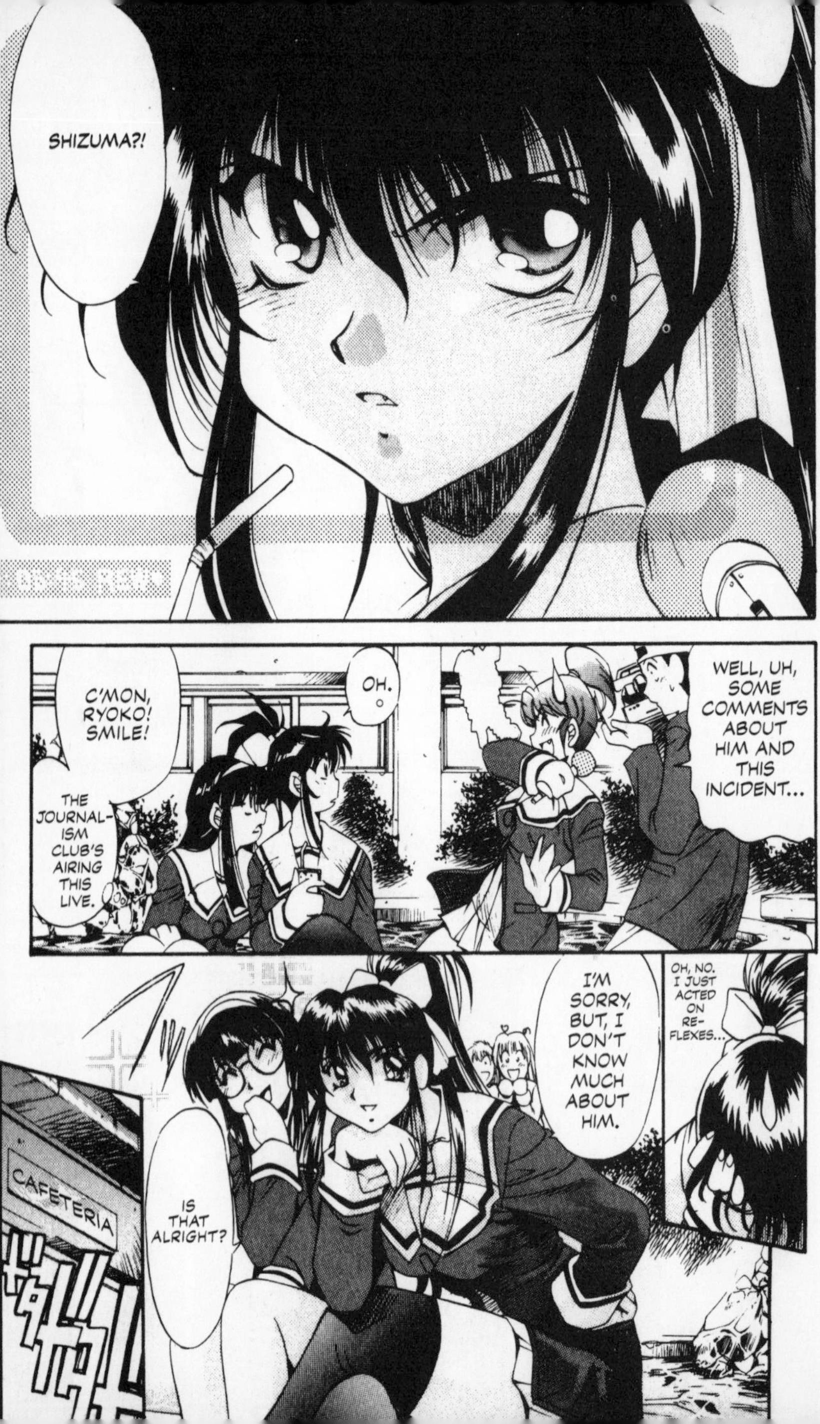
SHIZUMA?!
WELL, UH, SOME COMMENTS ABOUT HIM AND THIS INCIDENT...
OH.
C'MON, RYOKO! SMILE!
THE JOURNALISM CLUB'S AIRING THIS LIVE.
OH, NO. I JUST ACTED ON REFLEXES...
I'M SORRY, BUT, I DON'T KNOW MUCH ABOUT HIM.
IS THAT ALRIGHT?
CAFETERIA

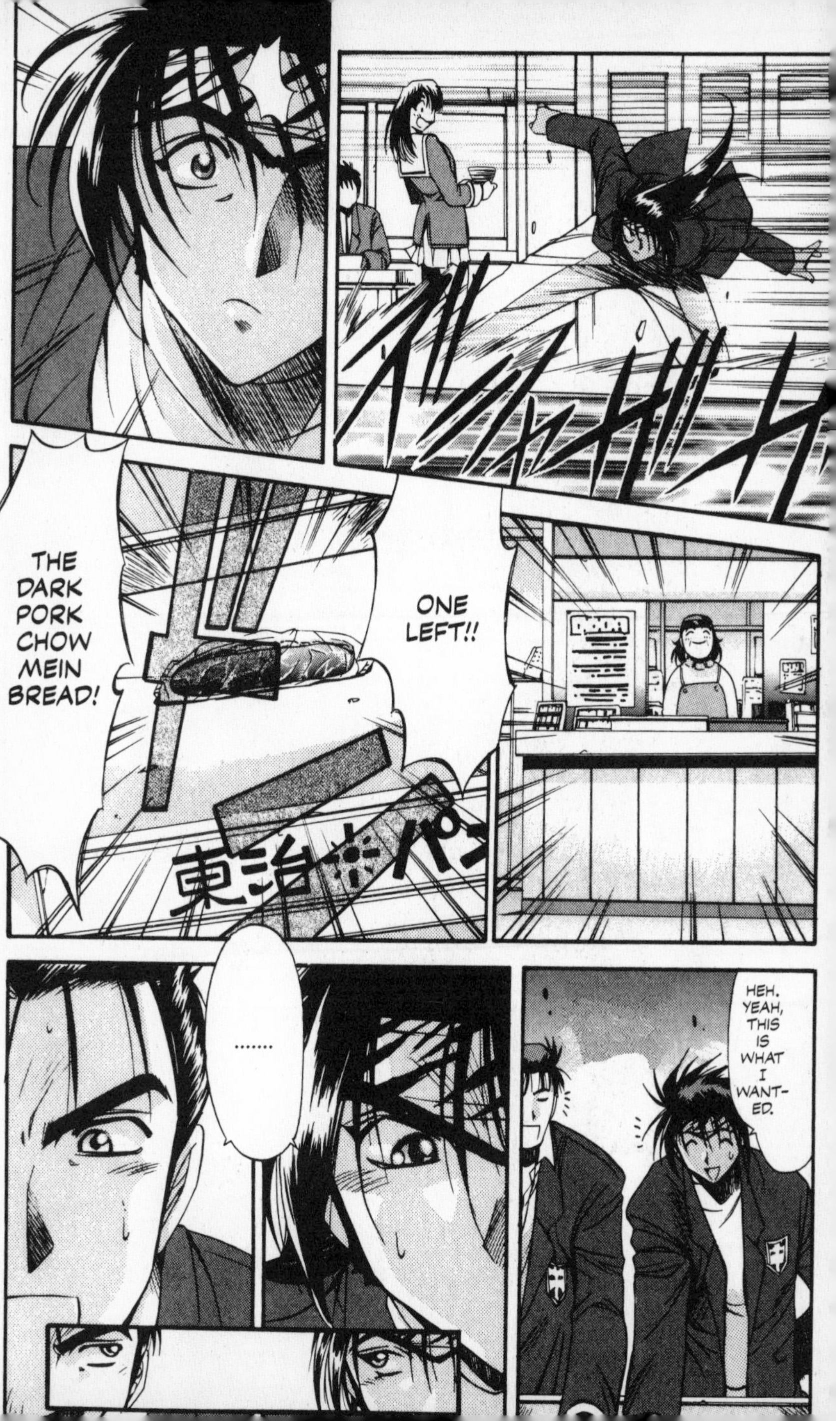
ONE LEFT!!
THE DARK PORK CHOW MEIN BREAD!
HEH. YEAH, THIS IS WHAT I WANT-ED.
....

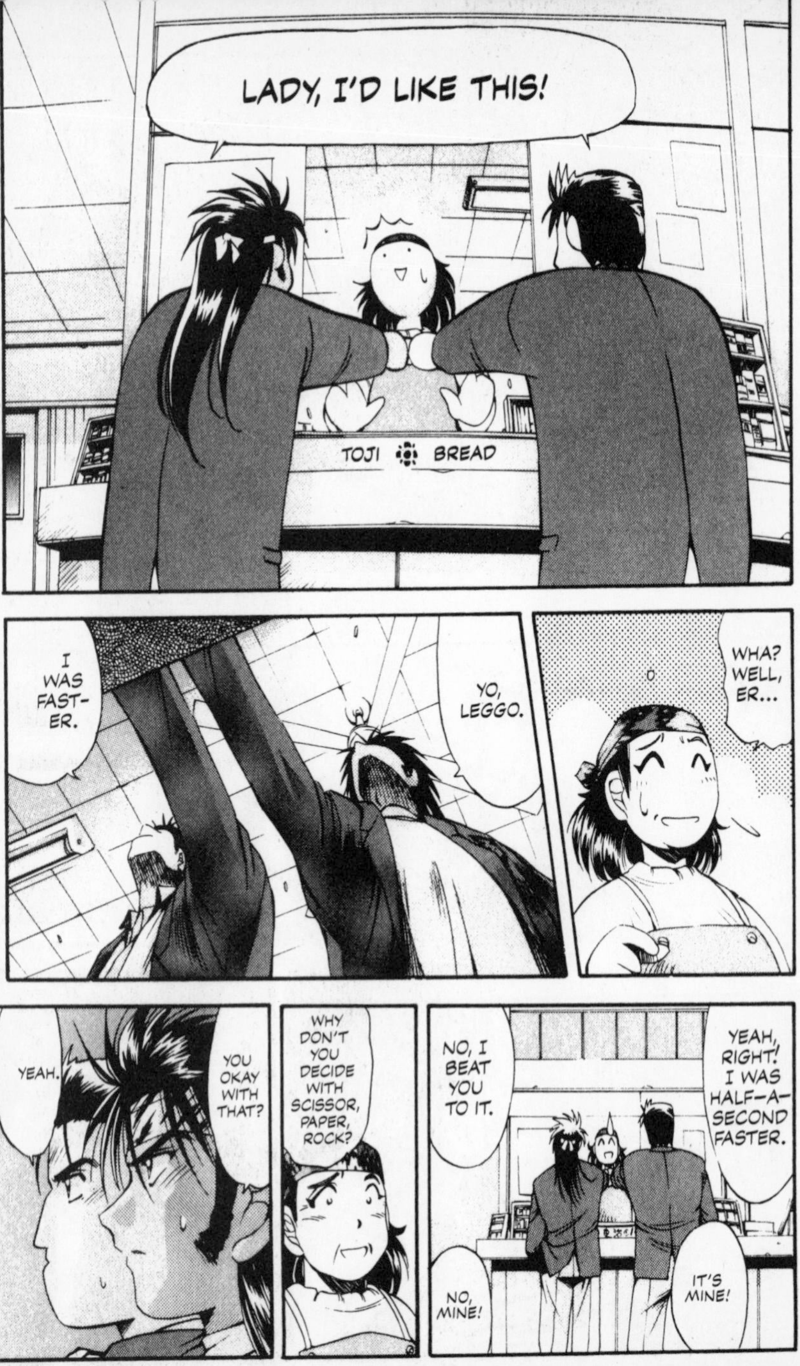
LADY, I'D LIKE THIS!
TOJI BREAD
WHA? WELL, ER...
YO, LEGGO.
I WAS FAST-ER.
YEAH, RIGHT! I WAS HALF-A-SECOND FASTER.
NO, I BEAT YOU TO IT.
IT'S MINE!
NO, MINE!
WHY DON'T YOU DECIDE WITH SCISSOR, PAPER, ROCK?
YOU OKAY WITH THAT?
YEAH.

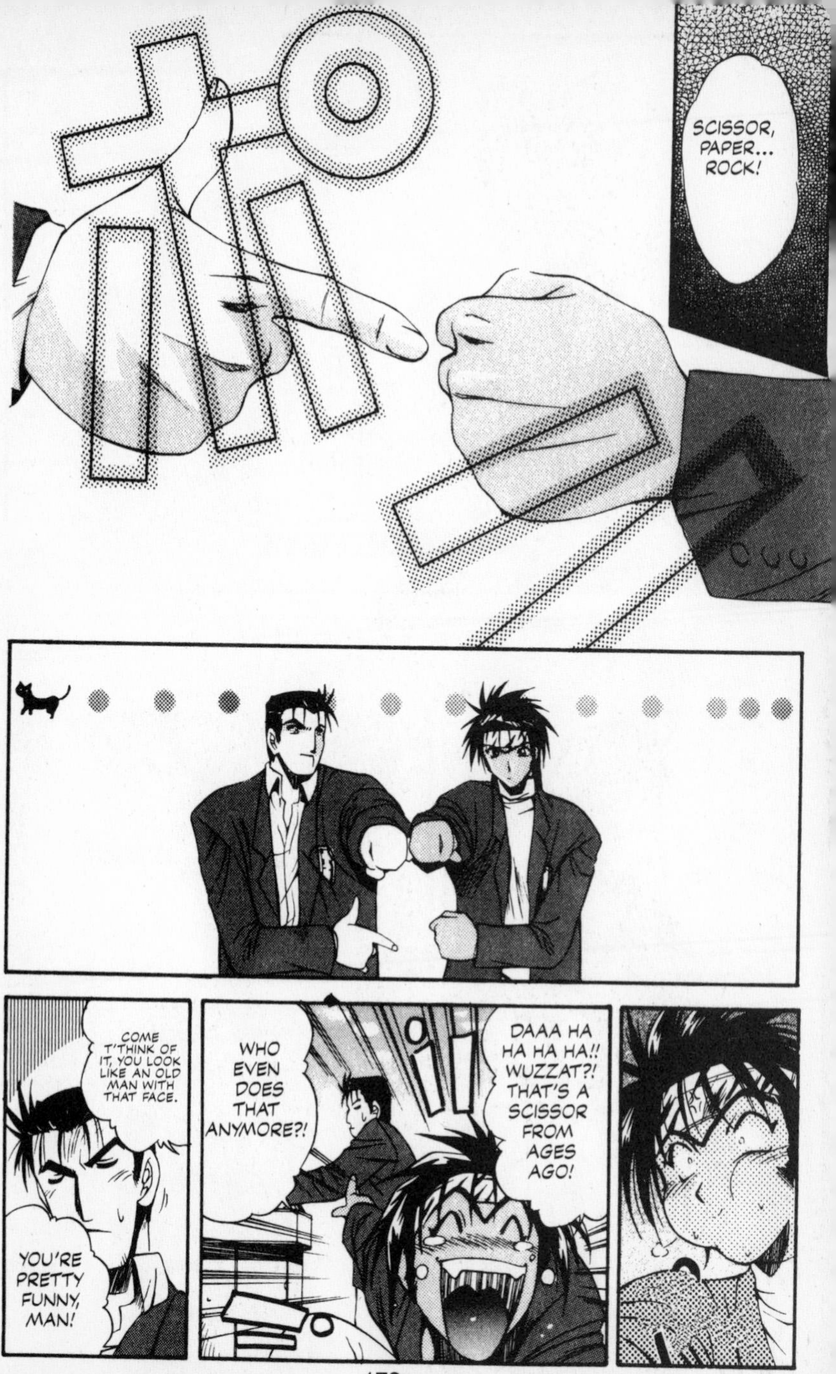
SCISSOR, PAPER... ROCK!
DAAA HA HA HA HA!! WUZZAT?! THAT'S A SCISSOR FROM AGES AGO!
WHO EVEN DOES THAT ANYMORE?!
COME T'THINK OF IT, YOU LOOK LIKE AN OLD MAN WITH THAT FACE.
YOU'RE PRETTY FUNNY, MAN!

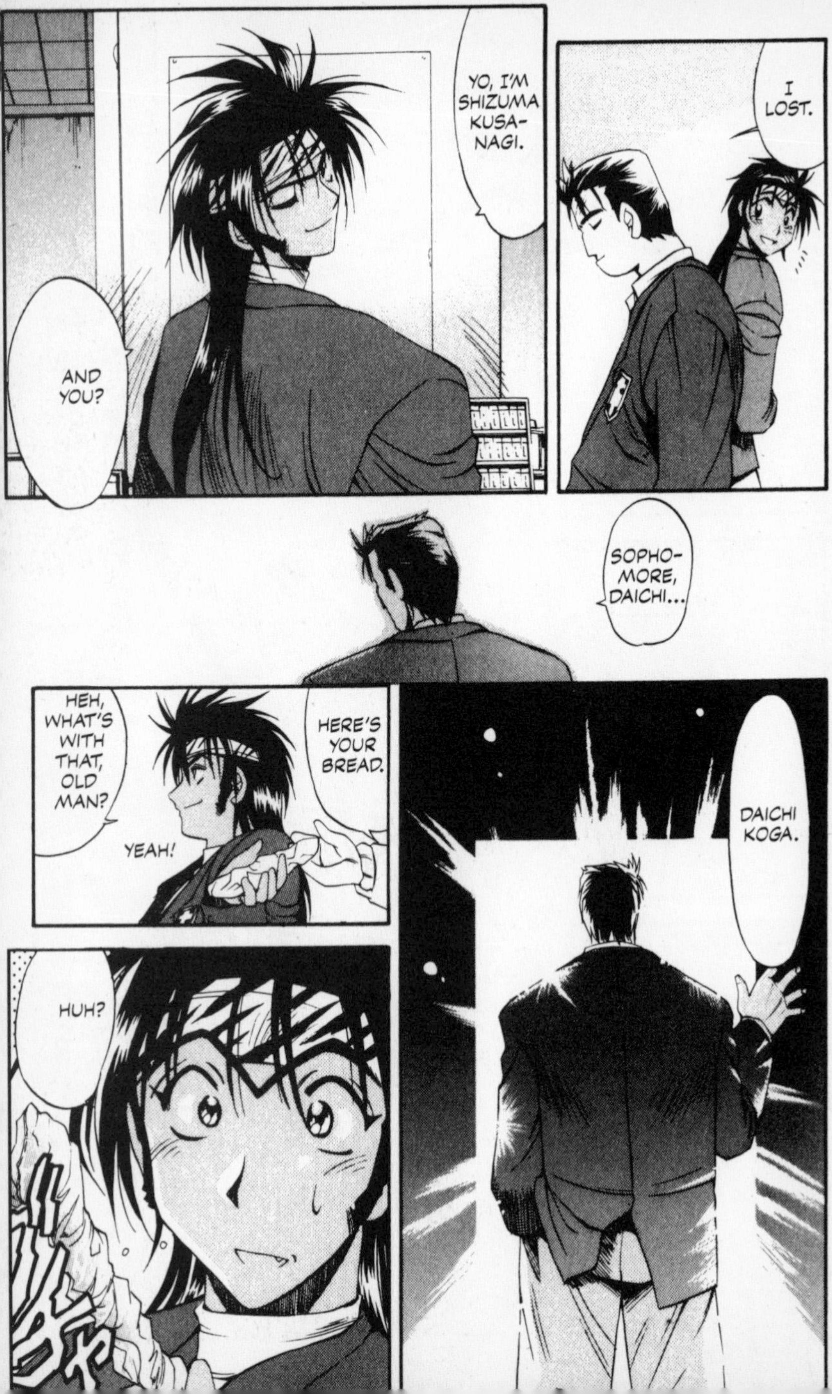
I LOST.
YO, I'M SHIZUMA KUSANAGI.
AND YOU?
SOPHO-MORE, DAICHI...
DAICHI KOGA.
HERE'S YOUR BREAD.
HEH, WHAT'S WITH THAT, OLD MAN?
YEAH!
HUH?

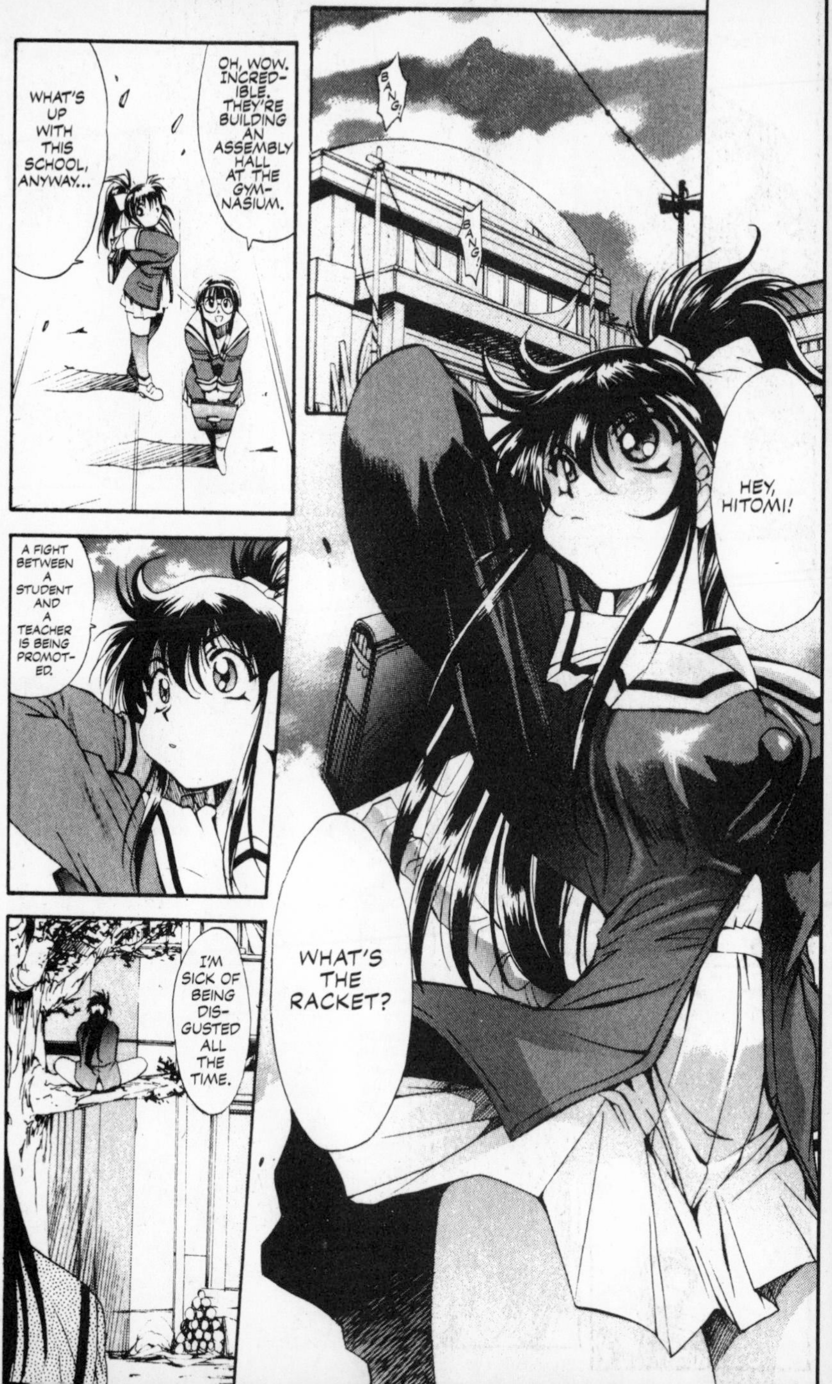
BANG!
BANG!
OH, WOW. INCREDIBLE. THEY'RE BUILDING AN ASSEMBLY HALL AT THE GYMNASIUM.
WHAT'S UP WITH THIS SCHOOL, ANYWAY...
HEY, HITOMI!
WHAT'S THE RACKET?
A FIGHT BETWEEN A STUDENT AND A TEACHER IS BEING PROMOTED.
I'M SICK OF BEING DISGUSTED ALL THE TIME.

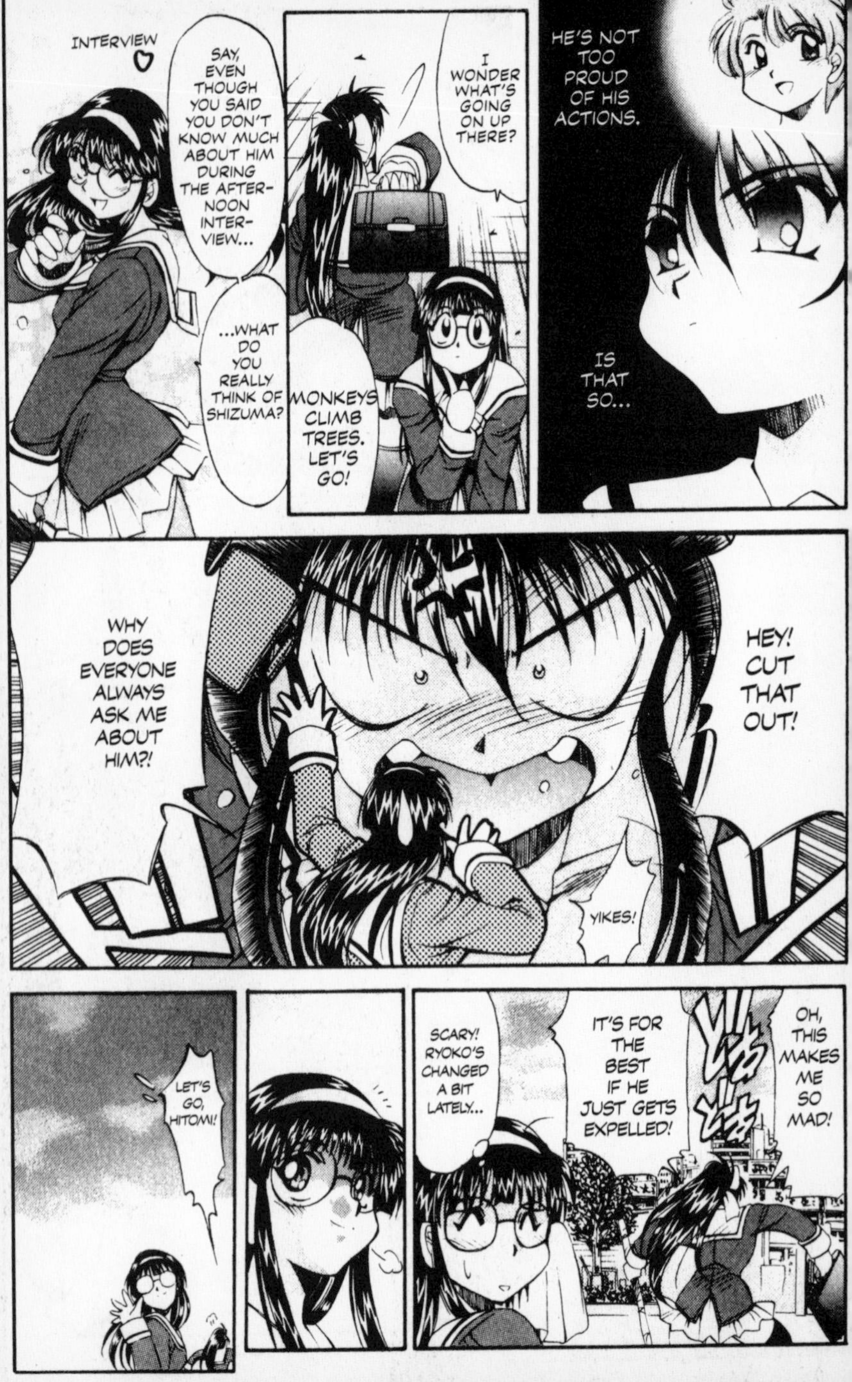
HE'S NOT TOO PROUD OF HIS ACTIONS.
IS THAT SO...
I WONDER WHAT'S GOING ON UP THERE?
MONKEYS CLIMB TREES. LET'S GO!
SAY, EVEN THOUGH YOU SAID YOU DON'T KNOW MUCH ABOUT HIM DURING THE AFTER-NOON INTER-VIEW...
INTERVIEW ♡
...WHAT DO YOU REALLY THINK OF SHIZUMA?
HEY! CUT THAT OUT!
WHY DOES EVERYONE ALWAYS ASK ME ABOUT HIM?!
YIKES!
OH, THIS MAKES ME SO MAD!
IT'S FOR THE BEST IF HE JUST GETS EXPELLED!
SCARY! RYOKO'S CHANGED A BIT LATELY...
LET'S GO, HITOMI!

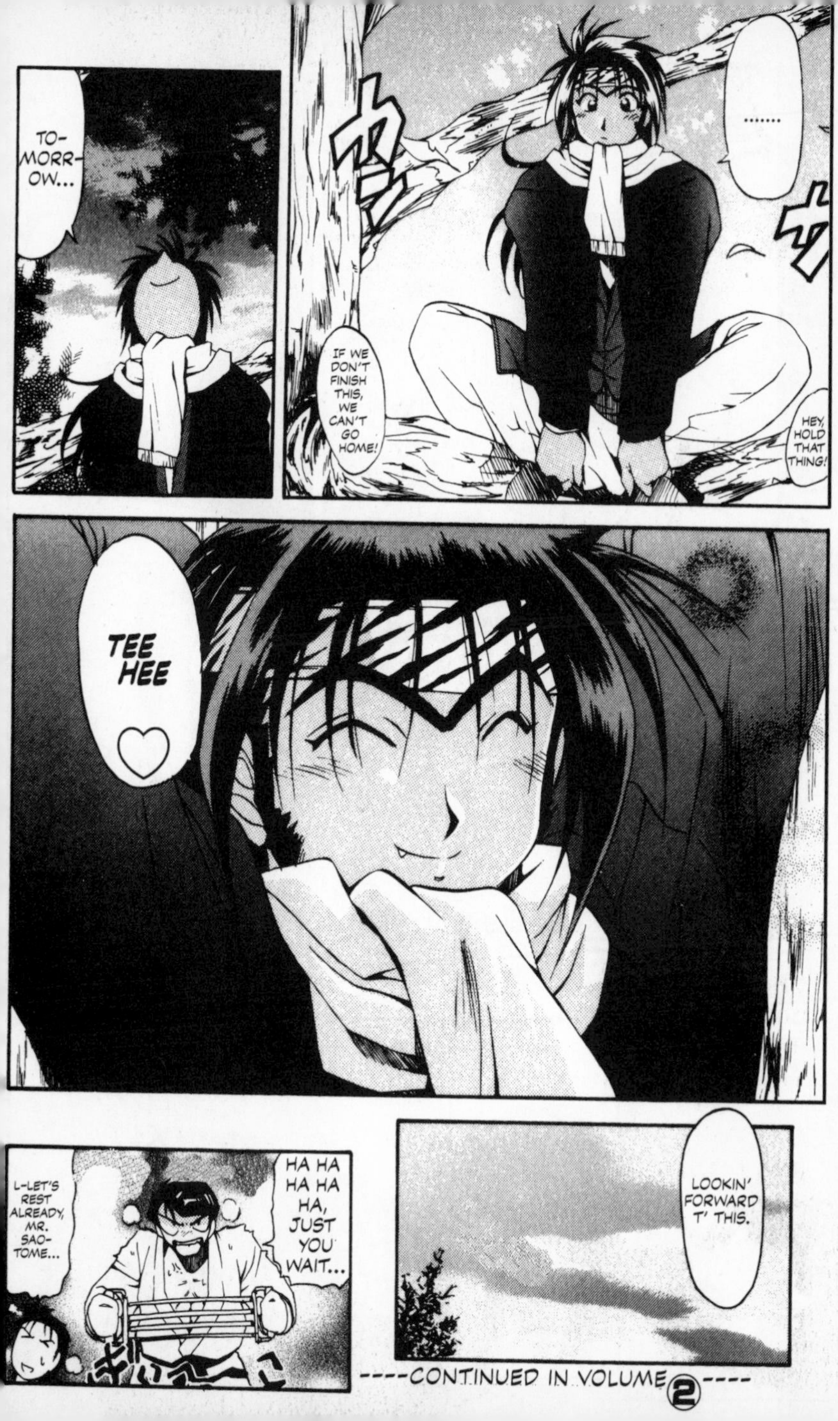
....
HEY, HOLD THAT THING!
IF WE DON'T FINISH THIS, WE CAN'T GO HOME!
TO-MORR-OW...
TEE HEE ♡
LOOKIN' FORWARD T' THIS.
HA HA HA HA HA, JUST YOU WAIT...
L-LET'S REST ALREADY, MR. SAO-TOME...

----CONTINUED IN VOLUME 2----

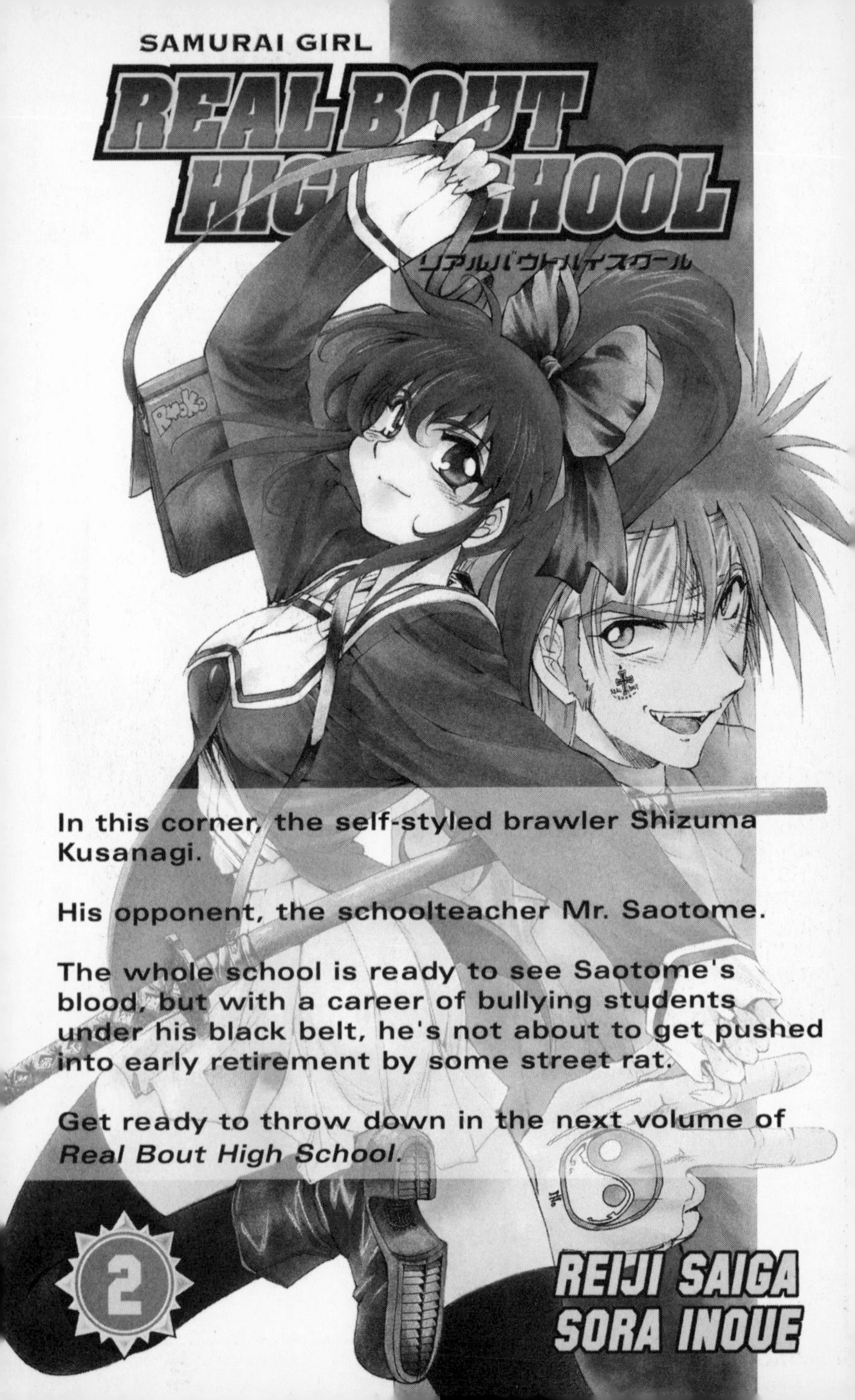
SAMURAI GIRL
REAL BOUT HIGH SCHOOL
リアルバウトハイスクール
In this corner, the self-styled brawler Shizuma Kusanagi.
His opponent, the schoolteacher Mr. Saotome.
The whole school is ready to see Saotome's blood, but with a career of bullying students under his black belt, he's not about to get pushed into early retirement by some street rat.
Get ready to throw down in the next volume of *Real Bout High School*.
2
REIJI SAIGA
SORA INOUE

ALSO AVAILABLE FROM 🐱 TOKYOPOP®

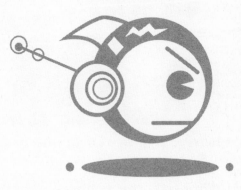

**For more
information visit
www.TOKYOPOP.com**

12.20.03T

MANGA

.HACK//LEGEND OF THE TWILIGHT
@LARGE
A.I. LOVE YOU
AI YORI AOSHI
ANGELIC LAYER
ARM OF KANNON
BABY BIRTH
BATTLE ROYALE
BATTLE VIXENS
BRAIN POWERED
BRIGADOON
B'TX
CANDIDATE FOR GODDESS, THE
CARDCAPTOR SAKURA
CARDCAPTOR SAKURA - MASTER OF THE CLOW
CHOBITS
CHRONICLES OF THE CURSED SWORD
CLAMP SCHOOL DETECTIVES
CLOVER
COMIC PARTY
CONFIDENTIAL CONFESSIONS
CORRECTOR YUI
COWBOY BEBOP
COWBOY BEBOP: SHOOTING STAR
CRESCENT MOON
CYBORG 009
D.N. ANGEL
DEMON DIARY
DEMON ORORON, THE
DEUS VITAE
DIGIMON
DIGIMON ZERO TWO
DIGIMON TAMERS
DOLL
DRAGON HUNTER
DRAGON KNIGHTS
DUKLYON: CLAMP SCHOOL DEFENDERS
ERICA SAKURAZAWA COLLECTED WORKS
EERIE QUEERIE!
FAERIES' LANDING
FAKE
FLCL
FORBIDDEN DANCE
FRUITS BASKET
G GUNDAM
GATE KEEPERS
GETBACKERS
GIRL GOT GAME
GRAVITATION
GTO
GUNDAM SEED ASTRAY
GUNDAM WING

GUNDAM WING: BATTLEFIELD OF PACIFISTS
GUNDAM WING: ENDLESS WALTZ
GUNDAM WING: THE LAST OUTPOST (G-UNIT)
HAPPY MANIA
HARLEM BEAT
I.N.V.U.
IMMORTAL RAIN
INITIAL D
ISLAND
JING: KING OF BANDITS
JULINE
KARE KANO
KILL ME, KISS ME
KINDAICHI CASE FILES, THE
KING OF HELL
KODOCHA: SANA'S STAGE
LAMENT OF THE LAMB
LES BIJOUX
LOVE HINA
LUPIN III
MAGIC KNIGHT RAYEARTH I
MAGIC KNIGHT RAYEARTH II
MAHOROMATIC: AUTOMATIC MAIDEN
MAN OF MANY FACES
MARMALADE BOY
MARS
MINK
MIRACLE GIRLS
MIYUKI-CHAN IN WONDERLAND
MODEL
ONE
PARADISE KISS
PARASYTE
PEACH GIRL
PEACH GIRL: CHANGE OF HEART
PET SHOP OF HORRORS
PITA-TEN
PLANET LADDER
PLANETES
PRIEST
PRINCESS AI
PSYCHIC ACADEMY
RAGNAROK
RAVE MASTER
REALITY CHECK
REBIRTH
REBOUND
REMOTE
RISING STARS OF MANGA
SABER MARIONETTE J
SAILOR MOON
SAINT TAIL
SAMURAI DEEPER KYO

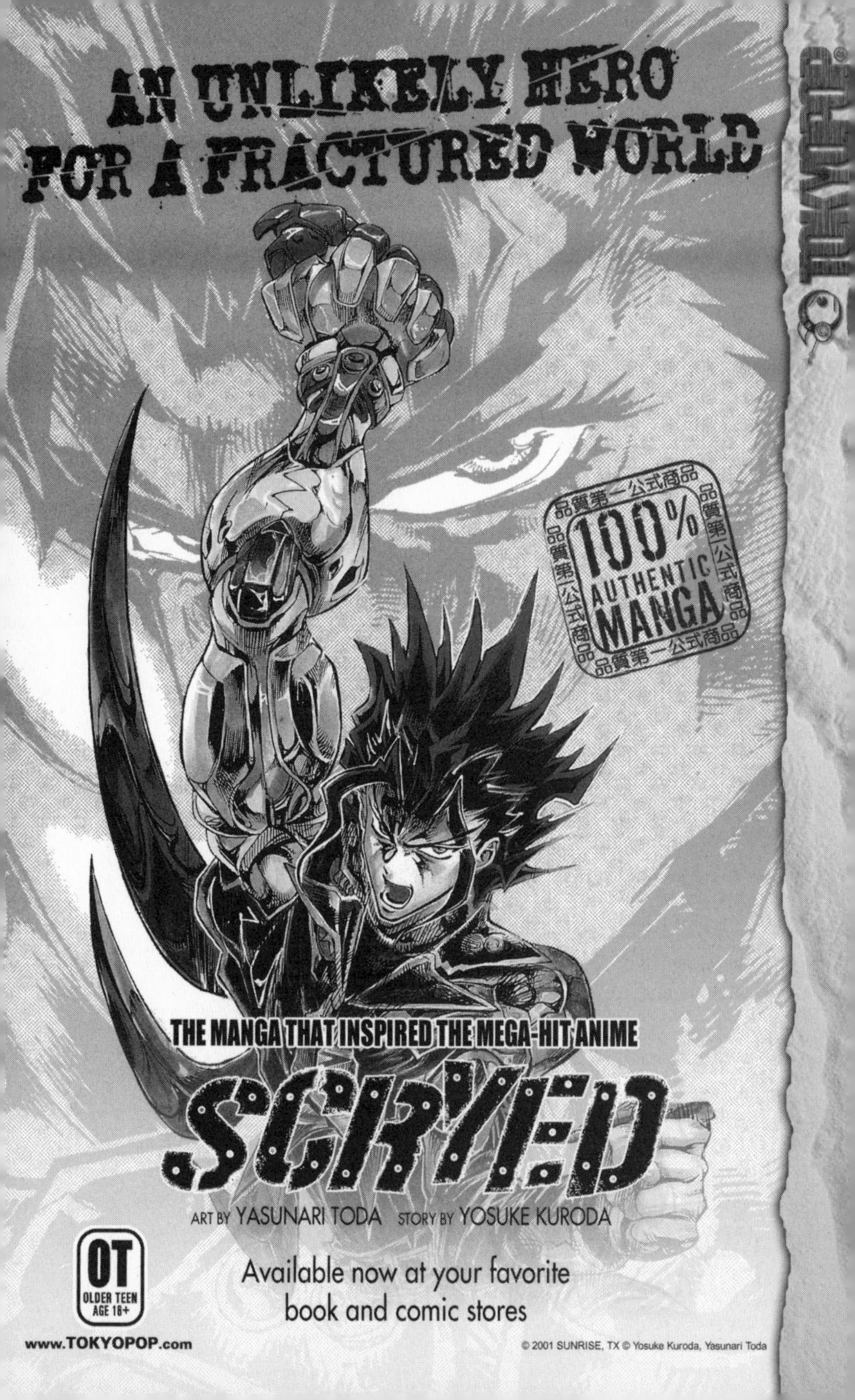

AN UNLIKELY HERO
FOR A FRACTURED WORLD
TOKYOPOP
100% AUTHENTIC MANGA
品質第一公式商品
THE MANGA THAT INSPIRED THE MEGA-HIT ANIME
SCRYED
ART BY YASUNARI TODA STORY BY YOSUKE KURODA
OT
OLDER TEEN
AGE 16+
Available now at your favorite
book and comic stores
www.TOKYOPOP.com
© 2001 SUNRISE, TX © Yosuke Kuroda, Yasunari Toda

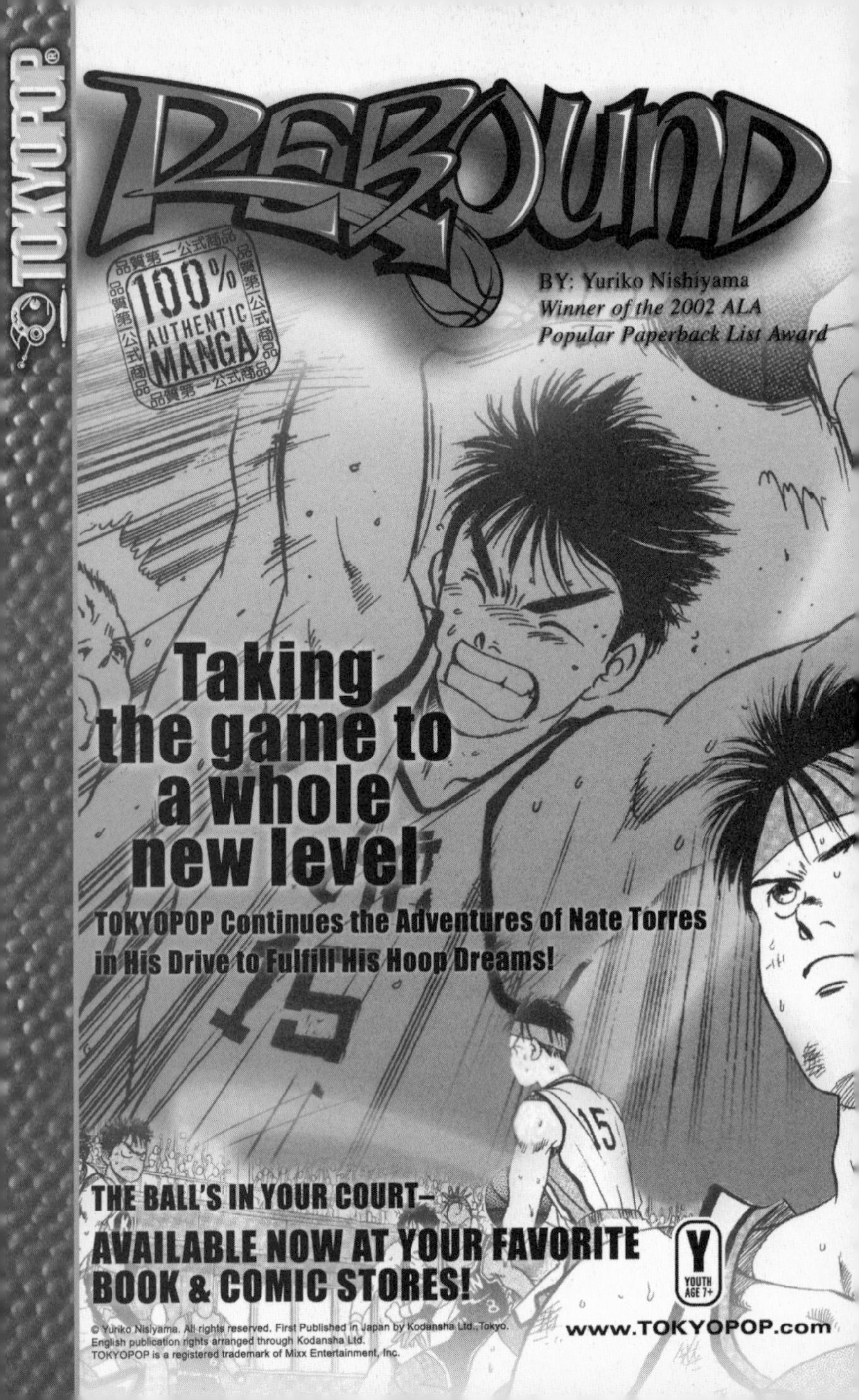
TOKYOPOP
REBOUND
品質第一公式商品
100% AUTHENTIC MANGA
BY: Yuriko Nishiyama
Winner of the 2002 ALA
Popular Paperback List Award
Taking the game to a whole new level
TOKYOPOP Continues the Adventures of Nate Torres in His Drive to Fulfill His Hoop Dreams!
THE BALL'S IN YOUR COURT–
AVAILABLE NOW AT YOUR FAVORITE BOOK & COMIC STORES!
Y YOUTH AGE 7+
© Yuriko Nisiyama. All rights reserved. First Published in Japan by Kodansha Ltd., Tokyo.
English publication rights arranged through Kodansha Ltd.
TOKYOPOP is a registered trademark of Mixx Entertainment, Inc.
www.TOKYOPOP.com

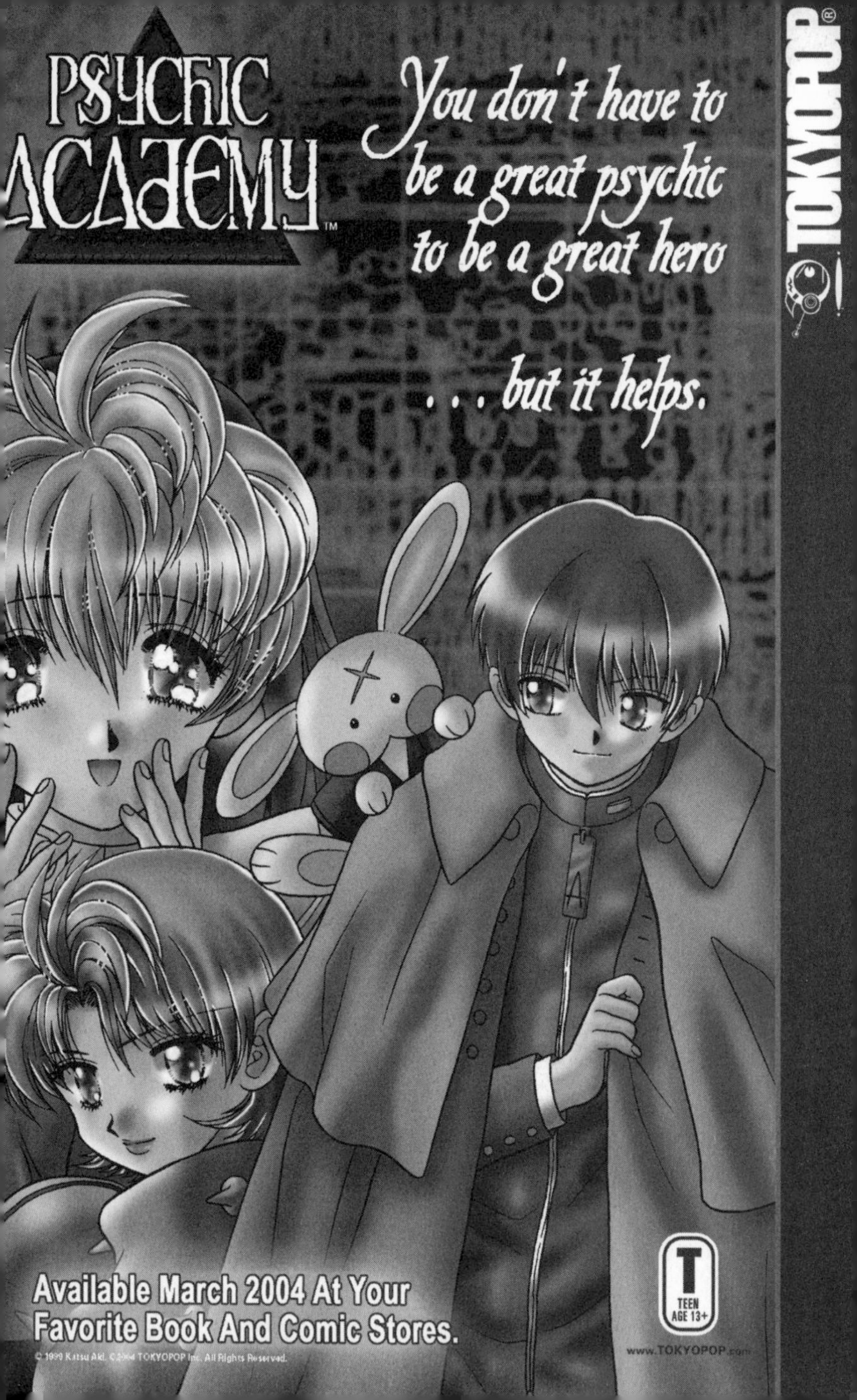
PSYCHIC ACADEMY™
You don't have to be a great psychic to be a great hero
. . . but it helps.
TOKYOPOP®
T TEEN AGE 13+
Available March 2004 At Your Favorite Book And Comic Stores.
© 1999 Katsu Aki. ©2004 TOKYOPOP Inc. All Rights Reserved.
www.TOKYOPOP.com

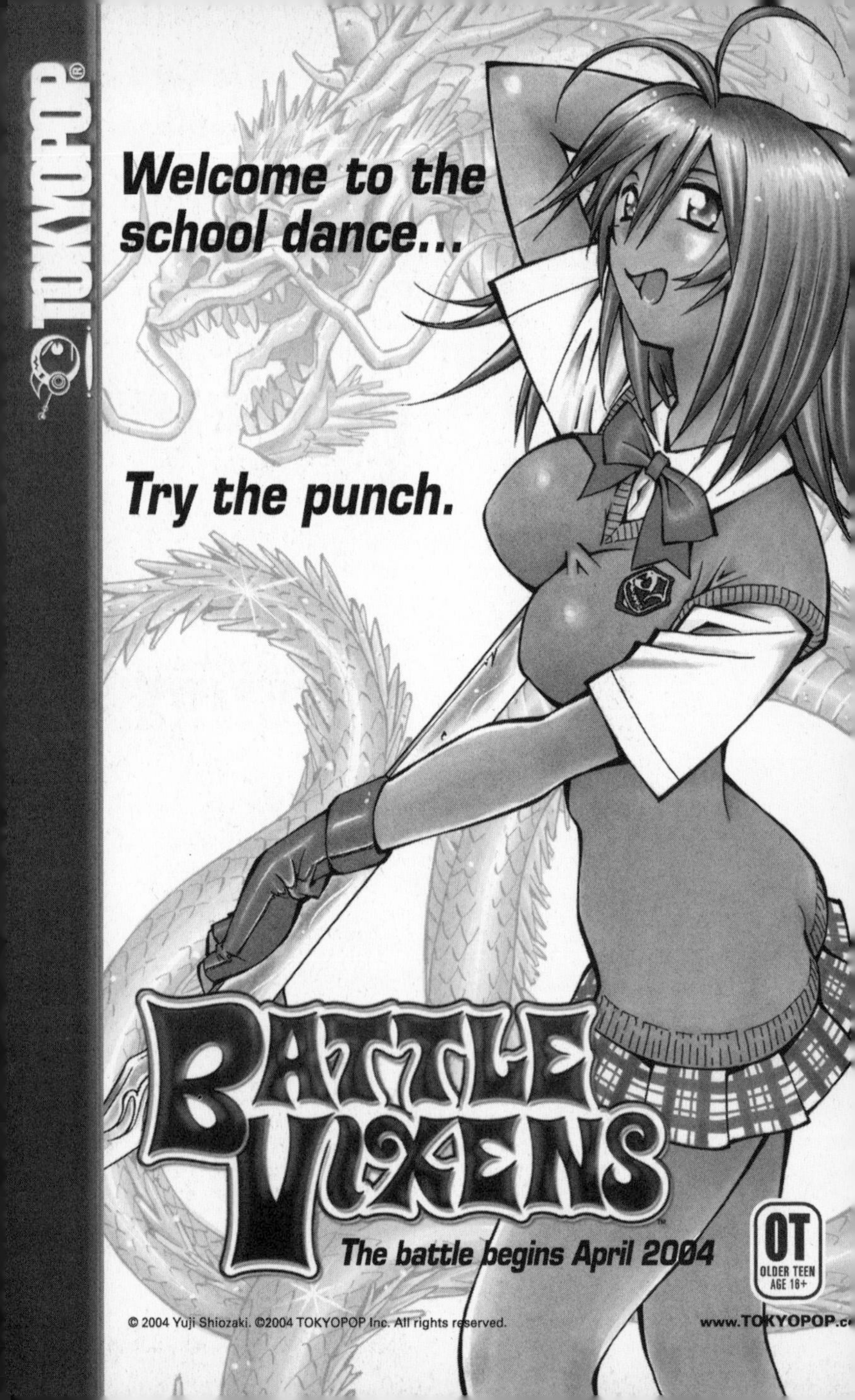
TOKYOPOP
Welcome to the school dance...
Try the punch.
BATTLE VIXENS
The battle begins April 2004
OT OLDER TEEN AGE 16+
© 2004 Yuji Shiozaki. ©2004 TOKYOPOP Inc. All rights reserved.
www.TOKYOPOP.c

P9-AOS-938

STOP!

This is the back of the book.
You wouldn't want to spoil a great ending!

This book is printed "manga-style," in the authentic Japanese right-to-left format. Since none of the artwork has been flipped or altered, readers get to experience the story just as the creator intended. You've been asking for it, so TOKYOPOP® delivered: authentic, hot-off-the-press, and far more fun!

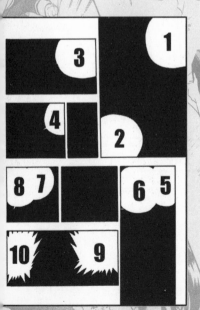

DIRECTIONS

If this is your first time reading manga-style, here's a quick guide to help you understand how it works.

It's easy... just start in the top right panel and follow the numbers. Have fun, and look for more 100% authentic manga from TOKYOPOP®!

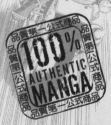